The Origin and Diversification of Language

the ORIGIN and DIVERSIFICATION of Language

P
106
.S9
1971

by
MORRIS SWADESH

edited by
JOEL SHERZER
University of Texas

Foreword
by
DELL HYMES

ALDINE · ATHERTON
Chicago/New York

Dedication

To my colleagues in the scientific study of language, especially three of them: one who has systematically studied the origin of language and was able to give me some helpful hints in my work; another who assured me that the problem intrigued him, but was afraid it might be impossible to obtain sure answers; and a third who counseled me, for my own good, to drop my study because continuing with it might cause me to lose my reputation for strict scientific judgment; and to all the ordinary people, nonspecialists, whose curiosity and questions about the origin of language have stimulated me to attempt to find reliable answers.

First published 1971 by
Aldine · Atherton, Inc.
529 South Wabash Avenue
Chicago, Illinois 60605

Library of Congress Catalog Card Number 67–27399
ISBN 202–01001–5
Printed in the United States of America

Foreword

Morris Swadesh was an original, productive, provocative linguist. He helped initiate structural linguistics in the United States and developed practical and scientific linguistics in Mexico; he worked with four or more dozen languages, devising new methods for relating and dating languages, formulating new hypotheses of linguistic relationship; and broaching a theory of the relationship and origin of all the languages of man. And while others regarded the origin of language as a point past which notions of evolution had no place, he sought the continuities in the development of language from before its full emergence to its place in human life today. This book is devoted to this last great theme.

I shall say something about the theme of the book, then about the man who wrote it. The one concerns the future of the study of language, the other its recent history; but each suggests something about the other. As need for the work broached by this book becomes obvious, one begins to ask why it was not obvious before. And a controversial career that began in a depression and spanned a hot war and a cold may offer some insight into the future.

A few years ago the appearance of this book would have been an isolated event. It appears now just when the tabu against an evolutionary perspective on languages seems about to be effectively broken. It will help secure that break and help orient the work that is to come. This book will contribute, I believe, to a major reorientation of linguistic theory in the remainder of

This introduction and the essay on "Morris Swadesh from the First Yale School to World Prehistory" that appear at the end of this book are revised and expanded from an article in *Anales de Antropología* (Hymes 1968). I am indebted to the editors of that journal for permission to use material from the article here; I am also grateful to Evangelina Arana de Swadesh, Zellig S. Harris, Alexander Lesser, Floyd G. Lounsbury, Michael Silverstein, Murphy D. Smith, and William C. Sturtevant as well as to articles by Norman McQuown (1968), Stanley Newman (1967), and Juan José Rendon (1967), for information and assistance; and to Lisa Levine for aid in preparing the manuscript.

this century. Only the renewal in modern terms of an evolutionary perspective can enable linguistic theory to connect languages and lives in a way that
satisfies the concern among linguists for relevance in their intellectual work
and that satisfies the needs of mankind.

Few indeed have the heart today to pursue studies divorced from human
problems and realities. Linguistic theory confined to the structure of
language often is justified by an appeal to the importance of language as
perhaps man's most distinctive trait. There is indeed a partial validity to
that appeal; what is already known about the complexity and richness of
any human language can refute stereotypes and prejudices that do much
harm. But a theory of the structural basis of all languages speaks only to a
natural potential. It does not speak to what has been made of language here
and now, or there and then, through selection and emergence from a universal grammar. Such a theory cannot explain why languages differ and
why they differ in the particular ways they do. The actual diversity of
character and function among varieties of language is left a mystery. A
linguistic theory is required that deals not only with structures of grammar
but also with structures of speaking, a theory in which the human functions
of language are not simply postulated as everywhere the same, but are
treated in terms of the adaptation and development of languages as a part
of sociocultural evolution.

The widespread objection to an evolutionary perspective has a history
that gives it some justification. Just as anthropologists have sometimes
denied the existence of any racial differences for fear of giving comfort to
the racially biased, so anthropologists and linguists have often felt that to
consider developmental differences among languages smacked of outmoded
views of 'primitive' languages without structure or with vocabularies so
impoverished as to have to be eked out with gesture. In reaction to the
support of colonialism and oppression, drawn from nineteenth century
evolutionary theories, American linguists and anthropologists by and large
have adopted since the First World War a humanistic, liberal, progressive,
egalitarian viewpoint. Concepts have been favored that apply equally to
all cultures and languages and that are empty of evolutionary differentiation.
Private ownership of productive resources was found among aboriginal
hunters; "religion," "law," "economics," and the like were defined as universal categories of culture, even if prefixed with "primitive"; kinship terminologies were compared and found to vary in complexity without regard to
type of subsistence or population size, linguists found morphological types
to vary independently. An evolutionary understanding of the overall course
of cultural history was not really abandoned. It was even mentioned, since
it could hardly be ignored in technology, political organization, and the
sciences. But prior theory and methods as to evolutionary stages having
been rejected, no alternative way of understanding and studying the evolutionary aspect of culture was provided.

Linguistics has shared in this parade. Linguists continued to speak for some time of "primitive languages", but insisted that it was really only languages in "primitive communities" (Whorf 1936) that was meant. One saw in them diversity only of structure, not of function. No connection of diversity intrinsic to language with sociocultural diversity was accepted. Swadesh's master, Sapir, expressed the point elegantly; "When it comes to linguistic form, Plato walks with the Macedonian swineherd, Confucius with the head-hunting savage of Assam" (1921:234). What Sapir had in mind, presumably, were the formal morphological features of nineteenth century typology, but the statement was taken to stand for whatever one might mean by linguistic form.

Vocabulary obviously differs in kind (and amount) between languages, but this has been regarded as a fact of culture more than a fact of language. Vocabulary has been called an "index of culture," suggesting its perfect adaptation to its parent culture. Functionalist harmony and equilibrium— assumptions now widely under attack in the rest of the social sciences— have continued now widely under attack in the rest of the social sciences— have continued to be assumed with a vengeance in linguistics.

Evolutionary perspectives have returned vigorously in the study of cultural and social life. In a latent sense it was never possible to do entirely without them, and some vague general evolution of culture was always assumed. Specifically, the famous case of private ownership of hunting grounds was found to be a product of acculturation and the fur-trade; concepts involving emergent levels of organization, such as "the state," were freshly studied; it was realized that proper comparison is not between kinship terminologies as such, in abstraction from general function, but between terminologies for the sphere of status and role as a whole (complexity there clearly varying with other factors). A renewed interest in ecology sharpened our under-standing of the adaptive bases of cultural change.

But linguistics has lagged. A variety of lines of study that would contribute to evolutionary theory have gone unnoticed or have lacked general per-spective to integrate them. The semantic properties of obligatory gram-matical categories (e.g., duality, shape) do not seem to be randomly distributed among "levels of sociocultural integration". Some aspects of color categories and plant terminologies are found to form developmental scales (Berlin 1970). Differential complexity in surface word-structure. may well be adaptive, complexity being a function of boundary maintenance in the case of small communities and groups, and simplicity a function of a language's use as a lingua franca. Athenian Greek and Macedonian may not differ in morphological type, but there is something to be learned from the development of Athenian Greek in response to the development of Greek systematic thought (e.g., the elaboration of derivational elements, such as *-itos*, to form nominalized terms). Classical Chinese and Assamese may go together in morphological type, but the development of the particular

Chinese traditions of lexicography and phonetics and the social role of a writing system of a particular type, as a lingua franca between regions and a barrier between classes, are a part of the history of the Chinese language (and ultimately of the Korean and Japanese languages) that is important to the understanding of the particular languages and societies and to the comparative study of the evolution of the "metalinguistic" function as well. (Any writing system embodies the emergence of self-conscious analysis.) Studies of the standardization of languages, of situations of diglossia, of linguistic acculturation, of the emergence of pidgin and creole languages, all have evolutionary implications. But such studies have remained marginal to linguistic theory; linguistics has found it possible to do without evolutionary perspective, latent or otherwise.

The present thrust of linguistic theory bodes a change from within linguistics itself. One can see in retrospect that the center of novel theoretical concern has successively moved from phonology through morphology and syntax to semantics and, incipiently, to speech acts. From this may follow attention to speech acts in their own right, to the kinds of speech acts recognized in particular speech communities and their organization as an independent, supervening, functional level of structure. It is obvious that the analysis of speech acts presupposes social analysis, since the same utterance may differ in status as an act (request, command, report) depending on the social relationships of addressor and addressee. While some kinds of speech acts and some dimensions of social relationships affecting them no doubt will be found to be universal, the number and kinds of speech acts and the social relationships on which they depend will be found to be a function of societal type and adaptation.

More elaborated is the variety of work that clusters within the nascent field of sociolinguistics. The rapid spread of interest in sociolinguistics outpaces the specification of method, theory and relevant data, and the reason is not far to seek. Many practical concerns in education, language policy, language development, and language conflict call for a basic science uniting social and linguistic analysis that unfortunately can hardly be said to exist as yet. What is increasingly clear is that the romantic image of a single, homogeneous language in a community with a single culture, however much adhered to as a premise of formal linguistics, is untenable, even harmful, as a basis for thinking about language. Linguists may have been fond of theorizing that one can say anything in any language; for the minister of education in a new nation, what can actually be said and read today in a language is a real and hard question. The diversity of languages, as they have developed and been adapted, is a patent fact of life that cries out for theoretical attention. It becomes increasingly difficult for theorists of language to persist in confounding potential equivalence with actual diversity.

The evolutionary interpretation of language poses problems to which we have hardly begun to give solutions. And one must still be concerned with avoiding the confirmation of prejudicial stereotypes. It is with respect to certain linguistic functions, not all, that evolutionary advance can be clearly seen—in the lexical resources that differentiate languages of science, part of whose task is to name everything in the world, and in the syntactic developments that make certain kinds of argument and analysis explicitly available. The differences among languages in resources for talking about language are a clear case, ranging from the folk-linguistics of a non-literate society, through the one or two language philologies of traditional India, China, Greece, Alexandria, and Rome, to the general linguistics of modern times. It is a fact that English is the primary language of science and medicine in many non-English-speaking countries, not because of a language policy but because of what is available in the language, and it is a serious conjecture that Japanese may be the last language to "make it" as a language of science. But advance here is based on the criterion of referential, informational and analytic capacity. Nothing follows as to the adequacy of languages for other functions, such as interpersonal relations, aesthetic play and poetry, or religious insight and expression. Nothing follows as to the relation between the capacity of language as a "superorganic" entity and the speaking competencies of individuals, the access each may have to the resources of a language, and the consequences that elaboration of a language along certain lines may have for other aspects of society and for personal lives.

To recognize the fact of differential adaptation, and sometimes evolutionary advance, in languages does not imply either simple optimism or indifference. The issue posed by the sociologist Georg Simmel as the "tragedy of culture"—the contrast between cultural accumulation and the shrinking of individual ability to benefit from it expressed by Sapir as the contrast between "genuine" and "spurious" culture—remains. But differences in adaptation and advance in respect to specific criteria do not disappear if ignored. To address the real problems of the place of language in social life, one must get beyond improvised paeans to the marvel of language and deal with cases wherein different varieties of language do and mean different things. One must come to grips with the different futures—extinction, obsolescence, compartmentalization, specialization of function, elaboration—that face languages in relation to each other and in relation to other means of communication. And one must come to grips with the different futures that face communities in terms of repertoires of languages and in terms of what a repertoire permits and provides.

Morris Swadesh had an unquestioning faith in the capacity of men of all kinds to be intelligent and decent, and to solve their problems if given the chance; he had an ingrained respect for what others had accomplished with their languages and ways of life. He also had faith in the scientific analysis of reality as a contribution to society. As his own discoveries in linguistic prehistory led him to recognize evolutionary differentiation, he sought to unravel its character. In this book he presents what he had found before his untimely death. It is the only book of its kind, and it is a truly anthropological book. In the evolutionary interpretation of culture, together with the ethnographic method, lies the only claim to distinctive unity that anthropology can make. It was from early writings of Swadesh that many students in one generation learned to accept and deal with the phonemic interpretation of speech. It is not too much to hope that this book will serve another generation, as it accepts and deals with the interpretation of language in terms of evolutionary adaptation and advance.

DELL HYMES

Editor's Preface

Before his untimely death in the summer of 1967, Morris Swadesh had written the first draft of a book, *The Origin and Diversification of Language*. In the spring of 1968 I was asked by Evangelina Arana Swadesh and the publisher to edit the manuscript and prepare it for publication. Before describing this task, let me indicate why it is important that it be undertaken.

Discussion of the evolution of language has been relatively tabu in the field of linguistics for a number of years. There are various reasons for this. First, the subject has been associated with the speculative and often ethnocentric evolutionary theories of past centuries. Second, even respected scholars who have done research in this area, such as Otto Jespersen, have been accused of making excessive use of the family to which their own languages belong, the Indo-European. Thus processes or developments that such scholars have claimed to be universal in language may be rather areal or typological traits particular to one group of languages. Third, past researchers have been hampered by an inadequate knowledge of the languages of the world and by poor descriptive materials.

In response to these objections, we can say this of Morris Swadesh's approach: He was always clearly aware of the dangers of speculation and realized that he was treading on ground that would attract much criticism. Nonetheless, he felt that there were a number of facts about language—both synchronic and diachronic—that seemed related to questions of origin and evolution and which required scholarly discussion. He also thought that the only way to make progress in this area was to put forth these intriguing facts and to suggest alternative plausible explanations for them. Swadesh's approach is definitely not ethnocentric. He was trained in the Boas-Sapir tradition of cultural and linguistic relativity and demonstrated through his own descriptive work that each language can and must be handled in its own terms. (See, for example, his work on Chitimacha, Eskimo, and Nootka.) His interest in the origin and evolution of language stemmed from experience with a great many languages, and he found in them data to suggest that problems of origin and evolution can be fruitfully studied. Nowhere does he state that one's own or some other language is in any sense better than any spoken by other peoples, either today or in the past. Nor are Swadesh's inferences concerning linguistic development through time based on Indo-European languages alone (as were those of his predecessors in this area), but rather on extensive knowledge of languages of various types from many parts of the world. He was unusually qualified in this respect, having personally worked with many languages of North and South America and with several in Africa, and having prepared textbooks of Russian and Chinese.

One of the major contributions of this book is simply the attention it draws to certain fascinating facts about contemporary and past languages. Whether or not we draw the same conclusions from these facts as Swadesh did, most of us will no doubt agree that they pose challenging problems for linguists and anthropologists. Some of these facts are:

1. Certain structural differences among languages spoken today seem related to certain sociocultural developments.

2. Traits found in languages scattered all over the globe seem to be due to either distant common origin (Swadesh's interpretation), human tendencies toward certain types of symbolism (a view also expressed by Swadesh in this book and related to his interpretation of the origin of language), or areal diffusion. An example is the striking cross-language similarity in the shape of kin terms and pronouns. Another is the use of phonetic symbolism to express such concepts as near and far, motion toward and motion away, big and little.

3. Everywhere languages seem to have developed in the same general ways. Consider, for example, the shift from internal inflection to external affixes and independent words; the replacement of onomatopoetic means of expression by more formal, conventional, or arbitrary devices; a particular order in the elaboration of color terms; and the derivation of words for numerals from body parts.

4. Points of possible cognancy are found among languages not usually considered to be related. Here Swadesh took the position that the door can not yet be shut on problems of language classification. Rather, as scholars acquire more data, they should constantly reformulate their proposed groupings. Swadesh's own work is an example of this approach. His view was that not only the unwritten languages of the world—the many languages of America, Africa, Australia, Oceania, and so on—are susceptible to further genetic connection, but also the more established groups: Indo-European, Semitic, Finno-Ugric, and Altaic.

There has been great interest on the part of linguists recently in universals or general properties of language, psychological or biological bases of speech, and related problems. (See the work of Chomsky, Greenberg, and Lenneberg, among others.) In this climate, it seems that a book dealing with the origin and evolution of language and its place in the evolution of culture should be most welcome. For a long time the evolutionary and relativistic approaches to language and culture were commonly considered to be in opposition to one another. Now, I think, a new synthesis of these two approaches is possible, a synthesis that recognizes the need to study each group of people and its language in their own right, but at the same time describes evolutionary developments.

Much of the discussion of the properties of language has been rather general, pointing to such traits as levels of contrast, transformational rules, and rule ordering as universal characteristics of human language. Some scholars (for example, Hockett) have compared general properties of human language with those of animal communication systems. They have tended not to be concerned with the historical development of these two systems. Swadesh, on the other hand, was interested in the details of the specific historical origin of language and its subsequent diversification. In this book he deals with such questions as the origin and growth of categories of vocabulary, the development of various types of grammatical structure, the rise of social and local dialects, and the migrations of languages along with the people who spoke them. His approach is consistently historical. He employs the techniques of historical linguistics but uses them to unravel more of the human past than is usually attempted.

It is also important to point out, as interest in linguistic anthropology and sociolinguistics continues to grow at a rapid rate, that Swadesh always studied language change in a cultural context. It is, in fact, precisely this approach that led him to the belief that particular linguistic developments occurred in response to certain sociocultural changes.

In preparing this book for publication, I have had to perform various editorial tasks.

1. Certain stylistic changes were sometimes advisable.

2. Often Swadesh had intended to provide an example to illustrate a point or support an inference. When such examples were lacking, I tried to provide them, using as sources previous published and unpublished works of his, grammars and dictionaries of various languages, and personal communications from colleagues.

3. I have made certain insertions of a mainly editorial nature: discussions of the reasons particular chapters or chapter sections appear where they do, explanations of terms or concepts, and so on. These insertions are italicized and placed in brackets.

4. Finally, I have appended a bibliography to each chapter, listing some of the sources and background materials of Swadesh's ideas and reports of other research that has been done in related areas.

The articles that are reprinted in the Appendix have been selected because they show the range of Morris Swadesh's interests within anthropology and linguistics in relation to the problems discussed in this book, and because they are relatively inaccessible; none of them has been reprinted before.

I would like to thank Ben Blount, Peter Gardner, Nicholas Hopkins, Dell Hymes, Jacob Mey, David Sapir, and Brian Stross for their encouragement and also for providing concrete examples from languages with which they have worked. I am especially grateful to Dell Hymes for several long discussions concerning the organization of the book.

JOEL SHERZER

Contents

Phonetic Symbols

			Consonants			
	Labial	*Dental, Alveolar*	*Palatal*	*Velar*	*Back-velar*	*Glottal*
STOPS						
voiceless	p	t		k	q	
voiced	b	d		g	G	
AFFRICATES						
Groove (vl.)		ts	ch			
(vd.)		dz	j			
Lateral (vl.)		ƛ				
(vd.)		λ				
FRICATIVES						
Slit (vl.)	ph, f	th, θ		x	x̣	h
(vd.)	bh, v	dh, ð		γ	$\dot{\gamma}$	
Groove (vl.)		s	sh			
(vd.)		z	zh			
Lateral (vl.)		ɬ				
RESONANTS						
Nasal	m	n	ñ	ng, ŋ		
Lateral		l				
Median	w	r	y			

Lengthened consonants are written pp, tt, etc.
' is used to mark glottalization (as in p', t', etc.) or implosion
h is used to mark aspiration (as in ph, th, etc.)
" is used to mark emphatics (as in Semitic t", s", etc.) or retroflex sounds (as in Indic t", n", etc.)
! is used to mark click sounds (p!, t!, etc.)

	Vowels		
	Front	*Central*	*Back*
High	i	ɨ	u
Mid	e	ə	o
Low		a	ɔ

Lengthened vowels are written aa, ii, etc.
Nasalized vowels are written a^n, i^n, etc.

Grammatical Terms

Affix: a morpheme that occurs only attached to a root.

  Infix: an affix attached within a root.

  Prefix: an affix attached to the beginning of a root.

  Suffix: an affix attached to the end of a root.

Agglutinative: language type in which words tend to consist of several morphemes, each with a clearly distinct phonological representation.

Alternation: the interchange of phonemes used to express modifications of meaning.

Clitic: semi-independent morpheme.

  Enclitic: preposed clitic.

  Postclitic: postposed clitic.

Imitative: onomatopoetic expression that in some way mimics the object referred to.

Inflection: variation of a root (forming a paradigm) in order to express obligatory categories like number, gender, etc.

  External inflection: inflectional paradigm formed by the addition of a prefix and/or suffix.

  Internal inflection: inflectional paradigm formed by the alternation of phonemes.

Inflective: language type characterized by the use of inflections.

Isolating: language type in which each word tends to consist of a single morpheme.

Lexeme: an entry in the dictionary or lexicon.

Morpheme: minimal unit of meaning in a language.

Phoneme: minimal functional unit of sound in a language.

Root: a relatively independent morpheme (as compared with an affix).

On the Trail of Discovery

[*In this introductory chapter, Swadesh gives the reader some notion of the intellectual tradition behind his concerns as well as the personal motivation for writing this book.*]

It was once thought that the speech of primitive tribes was something halfway between animal cries and human language, and that by studying them one could learn how this all-important medium evolved. Many such tongues have been systematically studied in recent times, however, and in each instance it was found that the language was completely formed, with an average number of speech sounds, consistently used; often with fully developed inflectional forms, comparable to those of classical and modern languages; with definite patterns of forming words and joining them into phrases and sentences; and with a vocabulary of elements expressing concrete and abstract concepts, employed in strict and figurative senses, and quite sufficient to meet old and new needs of the people who used it. Thus we cannot expect easy answers to questions concerning the origin and diversification of language. This ought not to discourage us. Many of the most important questions of science have been difficult ones, and yet with persevering search answers have been found.

The title of this book joins together two important problems. In addition to the origin of language, it poses the question of the source of the many languages known to exist and to have existed. This has long been a favorite speculation of scholars, some favoring monogenesis, others polygenesis. In other words, was language developed once only, and were all the known languages formed by the diversification of the primordial original? Or were a number of original tongues created in several places at various times? This has been considered an interesting question to pose, but one that cannot be answered definitively. This book is not intended to be sheer guesswork, but, on the contrary, a reasonable analysis of available evidence leading to relatively sure conclusions. If I take up two difficult problems, the purpose is

1

not to make my task doubly hard, but rather to clarify each question with light from the other.

The answers to the questions dealt with in this book have been described as unknown and unknowable, unverifiable speculations at best. Scholars have assumed that language developed early in the history of the human species, perhaps a million or two years ago. This is a long time back, but distances in time and space are usually not considered insurmountable obstacles to scientific inquiry. Astronomers have studied distant celestial bodies, including those beyond the range of vision or located behind other bodies that block all possibility of ever bringing them under direct human observation. What has permitted knowledge of unseen and unseeable objects is their gravitational effect on those that are directly observable. Similarly, linguists, by means of comparative and reconstructive techniques, can reconstruct earlier stages of languages for which we have no direct recorded or written evidence. Some scholars, however, have considered these techniques effective only for periods of up to about four to six thousand years, far less than the million years of life that human language has had. Hence it has been supposed that the case is hopeless. It has also been argued that no valid influences can be traced from the vocal communication of animals to human speech, because animal vocalizations are so different from human languages that it is inconceivable that speech could have evolved from them. If some scholars today try to solve these problems despite seemingly insuperable obstacles, as I do, it is because they have hit upon new approaches or new conceptions that reopen the possibility of success.

Historical Perspective: From Socrates to Jespersen

In the golden age of Greek philosophy, learned men tried to understand the nature of language and to explain its origin. There were two prevailing ideas about language: one that it is primarily conventional, the other that it is based on natural sounds that resemble the things they signify. In Plato's *Cratylus,* both ideas are brilliantly discussed by Socrates for the edification of his disciples. He gives examples of personal names, which in those days were generally meaningful, to show that men can bear names that do not describe them. Yet each man answers to his own name, and those who know him are not confused by any discrepancy between the name and the man. Then he gives examples of imitative words, including words for some animals and the designations of letters of the alphabet, which unquestionably relate to real sounds. And he refers to words that are not specifically imitative, but which are made up of sounds with a symbolic connection with the things they represent, such as *hrein,* to flow, which contains a liquid sound, *r,* because it refers to the movement of water. He further suggests that there are probably many words that started out as imitative, but whose implications may be lost to most men. In Socrates' conception, language must have been made up by wise men who alone had the intelligence to do the job; simpler people could employ language as an instrument only after it had been invented.

In later centuries the ideas of the Greek philosophers were often recalled and studied. Some men formulated new but generally less well-conceived notions or reverted to mythological explanations. In the rationalism of the eighteenth century, the German philosopher Johann Gottfried Herder wrote an essay on the origin of language which won first prize in a contest held by a Berlin journal. In it he held that man began to speak when he became mentally mature enough to do so. Even before that he made expressive sounds, like those of the lower animals. When he needed to express more than reactions of pleasure and pain, he took the sounds that in nature are connected with movements and things. In the course of time, however, the first meanings were modified until today they are no longer recognizable as imitative of sound. Herder also held that verbs were formed before nouns, and that the latter were derived from the former.

Herder's able presentation of very reasonable conceptions of the origin of language influenced thinking for a long time after him. All through the nineteenth century linguistic scholars and others continued to be interested in the origin of language. One of the last and best extensive treatments of the subject was by Otto Jespersen (1860–1943), whose analysis led him to the conclusion that there was a general trend in language toward simplification. This position directly opposed the more current view that language began with simple monosyllabic words and developed complex forms later. Jespersen pointed out historical cases of languages that had simplified their formations in the course of time. Even though there were instances to the contrary, he concluded that language developed principally in the direction of simplification. This he designated as "progress" in language development.

As for the origin of language, Jespersen's view is similar to Herder's, but with some additional suggestions. He refers to the various possible origins of words by nicknames: the bow-wow theory, reflecting the notion that the names of animals could be based on the sounds they produced; the ding-dong theory, which supposed that objects were named for the sound produced when they are struck; the pooh-pooh theory, or the notion that words could develop from exclamatory vocalizations; the yo-he-ho theory, referring to the possibility that some words began with shouts used by people working together to time their common efforts. Jespersen further suggests song as a possible origin of words, calling this the tarara-boom-de-ay theory. This was one way in which long words might have been created, and Jespersen was anxious to show that words did not always have to originate in monosyllables. Jespersen points out that these theories are not mutually exclusive, since different words might have originated in different ways. One of

Jesperson's important contributions was his exploration of the various ways in which sound imitation is evident even in modern language.

Of considerable interest for our conception of the origin of language is the interesting work of psychologists, physiologists, and biologists on involuntary and partially voluntary reactions to fear, pleasure, and the whole gamut of the emotions. One of the most interesting writers on this subject in the nineteenth century was Charles R. Darwin, who deals with it both in *The Descent of Man* and in *The Expression of the Emotions in Man and Animals*. The pooh-pooh theory of speech origin is already touched on in the second of these works. Although Darwin only occasionally deals with articulated sounds, his treatment of emotional manifestations, like blushing, the bristling of the hair or feathers, arching the back, erecting or laying back the ears, showing the teeth, pawing the ground, wagging or dropping the tail, shrugging, and spitting, suggests an approach to some aspects of our problem. One of his notions is that certain evident reactions to an emotional state started out as preparatory movements for defensive, aggressive, socializing, or other activities. Another idea is that the reaction anticipates the effect of an inferred experience. In dealing with vocal manifestations of the emotions, Darwin indicates how holding the mouth in certain positions leads to exclamations like *pooh, oh,* and *ah.*

One other origin theory has been proposed—the ta-ta theory, which has been attributed to Richard Paget. This theory suggests that some words came into being as tongue or lip gestures. That is, the movement of the vocal organs is similar to gestures of the hand. When one says "ta-ta" to bid a friend good-bye, the tongue makes two movements quite like waving the hand. Another example is a word like Latin *capio*, I take, or English *capture*, whose root begins with a *k* sound and ends in the sound *p*, made by closing the lips. It has been suggested that formation of the *k* sound at the back of the mouth, while the lips are open, is comparable to the open hand. The closing of the lips, then, is analogous to the fingers closing with the thumb as one takes hold of an object. Thus the pronunciation of the root *capio* is like the action of taking. Of course, not all words can be explained in this way; in fact, only a few. And yet the possibility that some words developed in this way is not denied by other qualities also evident in language.

Twentieth-Century Disillusionment

Jespersen straddled two centuries and carried into the twentieth the interest in language origins that characterized the eighteenth and nineteenth. Even before the end of the nineteenth century, however, and definitely in the first half of the twentieth, scholars in the field of language had developed an attitude of wariness or impatience toward all theories concerning the beginning of language. Many felt that it had been all too easy to invent ways in which language could have begun and absolutely impossible to prove which, if any, were right. Thus the subject was no longer considered proper for scholarly discussion.

Although professional scholars turned away from the problem of language origin, the public did not lose interest in the subject. In the period when few scholars devoted their attention to it, several nonspecialists felt that they could offer new and valuable insights into the problem. In consequence, even in the first half of the twentieth century a certain number of books on this subject appeared. Philosophers, psychologists, and to a certain extent linguists continued to consider the problem.

In the past fifteen years or so there has been a new interest in the problem of language origins among observers of social behavior in animals and among students of the theory of communication. A few language experts became interested in these new sources of understanding, and once again there has been a sprinkling of writings on the subject by professional linguists. These are not infrequently criticized by colleagues, who see them as straying from the paths of science.

One of the characteristics of modern science is the tendency to specialization. In linguistics, scholars may concentrate on a region, a language family, a single language, or some aspect of a language. There is also specialization in approach: communication theory, the use of computers in linguistics, automatic translation, ethnoliguistics, psycholinguistics, applied linguistics, and language teaching, as well as the older interests in descriptive and comparative study. With so many special fields, there ought to be a place also for evolutionary linguistics, or protoglottology, the study of the origin of language. It is perhaps reasonable to predict that this specialty will become established and that it will unravel many details of the origin and evolution of language, in part by the wise combination and effective application of already known techniques, and in part through new approaches that will develop as the problems are better understood.

Some Traditional Obstacles

[In this section Swadesh intended to discuss the problems involved in a study of the origin of language and to suggest that solutions are possible. In a sense, the entire book is an attempt to provide solutions. He listed three such problems and probably intended to add others. Briefly, here are the problems and Swadesh's approach to them:

1. The differences between human language and animal communication appear irreconcilable. *Although the study of animal communication is generally considered to be a valid endeavor, it is not generally believed that it will lead to understanding about the actual origin of human language. Language is thought to have arisen suddenly, and therefore it appears futile to try to imagine or reconstruct a gradual development from animal communication.*

At the same time, recent careful investigation of animal cries has shown them to be analyzable in certain ways, and one part of human speech (intuitive language) is fairly similar in significant ways to animal vocalization. Thus we have perhaps the beginning of an understanding of the nature of the gap between human and animal communication.

2. The time depth involved in the search for the origin of language seems impenetrable. *It is recognized that the older stages of languages can be inferred by the comparison of separate later languages that have developed out of the same original, but the time depth that can be penetrated in this way is limited. Some say it is no more than about five thousand years. Others hold that, with sufficient painstaking effort and in favorable circumstances, this time depth can be considerably extended. Very few, however, would expect the penetration of as much as, say, twenty or forty thousand years. Since man has been using language for presumably some hundreds of thousands of years, one cannot hope to infer anything about the first forms of language by means of the comparative method.*

Up to now there has been rather little in the way of concerted, strong efforts to reconstruct the very ancient history of languages. Until this has been seriously attempted in broad groupings in various parts of the world, it is not proper to predict exactly how far we can go. Since man has been using speech for such a very long time, we can grant that it may be impossible to go back all the way by the comparative method. By the time one has reconstructed language as far back as he can get by one method, however, it may be possible to use some other method to supply the rest of the story.

3. Though details are constantly changing, language itself is fundamentally changeless. *One of the main contributions of linguists to the scientific study of language has been the demonstration that there is no such thing as a contemporary primitive language. Even the languages reconstructed by historical linguists are no more primitive in sound patterns, grammatical structure, or vocabulary than their descendants. This fact has led many scholars to the belief that it is impossible to infer anything about the evolution of language as we know it.*

Nevertheless, languages spoken today provide certain clues to the possible lines of language development, and reconstructed ones provide even more.]

References and Suggestions for Further Reading

[*For the history of concern with the origin of language as well as discussions of theories proposed, see Brown (1958), Carroll (1953), Cassirer (1944), Diamond (1959), Gray (1939), Jespersen (1922), Lounsbury (1968), and Revesz (1956). For actual theories that have been advanced, see Brown (1958), Cassirer (1944, 1946), De Laguna (1927), Diamond (1959), Hockett (1958, 1959, 1960), Hockett and Ascher (1964), Langer (1942), Paget (1930), Revesz (1956), Sturtevant (1947), and Whitney (1875).*]

Brown, Roger
  1958. *Words and Things.* New York: Free Press, Macmillan.
Carroll, John B.
  1953. *The Study of Language.* Cambridge: Harvard University Press.
Cassirer, Ernst
  1944. *An Essay on Man.* New Haven: Yale University Press.
  1946. *Language and Myth.* New York: Harper & Row.

Darwin, Charles
  1955. *The Expression of the Emotions in Man and Animals.* New York: Philosophical
    Library.
De Laguna, Grace
  1927. *Speech: Its Function and Development.* New Haven: Yale University Press.
Diamond, A.S.
  1959. *The History and Origin of Language.* New York: Philosophical Library.
Gray, Louis H.
  1939. *Foundations of Language.* New York: Macmillan.
Hockett, Charles F.
  1958. *A Course in Modern Linguistics.* New York: Macmillan.
  1959. "Animal 'Languages' and Human Languages." In *The Evolution of Man's
    Capacity for Culture,* arr. J. N. Spuhler, pp. 32–39. Detroit: Wayne State
    University Press.
  1960. "The Origin of Speech." *Scientific American* (September), pp. 88–96.
Hockett, Charles F., and Ascher, Robert
  1964. "The Human Revolution." *Current Anthropology* 5: 135–68.
Jespersen, Otto
  1922. *Language: Its Nature, Development, and Origin.* London: Allen & Unwin.
Jowett, B., ed.
  1953. *The Dialogues of Plato,* vol. 3. Oxford: Clarendon Press.
Langer, Suzanne K.
  1942. *Philosophy in a New Key.* Cambridge: Harvard University Press.
Lounsbury, Floyd G.
  1968. "One Hundred Years of Anthropological Linguistics." In *One Hundred Years
    of Anthropology,* ed. J. O. Brew. Cambridge: Harvard University Press.
Paget, R. A. S.
  1930. *Human Speech.* New York: Harcourt, Brace.
Revesz, Geza
  1956. *The Origins and Prehistory of Language.* New York: Philosophical Library.
Sapir, Edward
  1907. "Herder's *Ursprung der Sprache.*" *Modern Philology* 5: 109–42.
Sturtevant, Edgar H.
  1947. *An Introduction to Linguistic Science.* New Haven: Yale University Press.
Whitney, William Dwight
  1875. *The Life and Growth of Language.* New York: Appleton.

Language in Space and Time

[*It may seem as though the story of the origin and diversification of language ought to begin at the beginning and go on from there, step by chronological step. The data, however, come to us the other way around. The basic approach of this book is to reconstruct earlier stages of language on the basis of languages still spoken today or attested to by written records. This chapter is thus an introduction to the techniques of historical and comparative linguistics. It discusses the nature of language distribution and linguistic change as well as the ways in which specific changes can be inferred. The basic notions presented here will be needed for an understanding of later chapters.*]

Language is an amazingly flexible instrument that can be adapted to all sorts of circumstances. It is characterized by variation in every conceivable dimension. It shows differences according to the subjective mood of the speaker, the kind of persons he is addressing in any particular moment, the nature of the occasion, and the nature of the subject matter. Adults and children do not speak exactly alike, nor do men and women, laymen and churchmen, mechanics and merchants, city dwellers and farmers, members of different sects and organizations. There may even be some special varieties of language peculiar to or especially favored by individual families. There are some special usages that vary within the lifetime of each person and reflect adaptations to a variety of personal contacts and social situations.

Norms and Norm Bundles

Despite the great amount of variation, the specific manifestations of language fall within limits imposed by the social role of communication. If each sub-group in a community or each individual talked now one way and now another, with freely varying phonetics, construction, and vocabulary, each family would be a tower of Babel and the inner thoughts of each individual would be confused. Hence, although language can and must admit variation,

8

at the same time it has to stay within such bounds as will guarantee, at least most of the time, approximate comprehension among the members of any social group.

Society can be thought of as imposing forms of behavior on its members. People in large measure accept these standards without objection. They learn behavior from those about them by adopting the models they see, hear, or otherwise experience, partly because it is man's nature to imitate and also because the individual sees in the behavior of his fellows the promise of satisfying particular desires of his own. Social control is not always kind, but neither is it always tyrannical. Much of it consists of opening paths to satisfactions; only a part is demand, discipline, or coercion.

Any form of behavior that tends to repeat itself, in the individual or in the members of a group, constitutes a *norm*. The individual acquires a norm by imitation of specific acts that have come to his attention, whether in the behavior of other individuals or in an act he himself has hit upon. The models need not necessarily be presented objectively; they may also be communicated as ideas or be the products of the individual's thinking or insight. In a way, a norm is the sum of previous acts, but these are necessarily filtered through the wish patterns of the group and its members, because anyone is more likely to follow a model if he is convinced that the result will be desirable. In matters of language, favorable results are comprehension and social approval, insofar as each person is capable of judging when these have been attained and insofar as the consequent events are of a nature to help him judge.

The individual may follow a model or a norm either consciously or unconsciously. In each attempt, his actual behavior may fall close to or far from his understanding of the model, and his understanding may be close to or far from the reality. How close he comes depends on objective and subjective circumstances. For example, the presence of food in the mouth may deflect the point of the tongue from producing a given sound; so the need to speak intelligibly may lead the speaker to move the food out of the way or shift the position of his tongue sufficiently to offset the distortion that might otherwise result. Likewise, in the choice of a remark to make in a given situation, a person may avoid or modify his expression because of the sex, age, or religion of the other persons present; or he may suffer interference from something he hears in the exact moment or that is passing through his mind, in which case he may come out with a word that does not even fit the intended expression. Because of these and other specific circumstances, performance shows a scatter around the previously existing norm. Those manifestations that fall too far out, especially if they lead to failure of communication, are often immediately disowned by the speaker, and he corrects himself. In any event, they tend to be discounted. In general, however, performance tends either to confirm or to modify the norm. Thus specific linguistic patterns may continue relatively unchanged for long periods of time, may be modified in various ways, or may be completely replaced, perhaps after a period of competition between alternate equivalent models.

Linguistic usage can be described in terms of norms and *ranges of variation* around them. Each norm represents a central type near which fall the specific instances of a usage. The range of variation is the measure of deflection in one or another direction from the average or most representative form. In some cases the norm is in flux, tending in a given direction, or vacillating between two or more main variants. Or there may be functional rivalry between two or more quite different formal patterns capable of being used for the same purpose in speech.

The simplest norm applies to a detail of phonetics, phonology, construction, or vocabulary, or their semantic correlates. Since every language is composed of a whole complex of sounds, combinatory patterns, meaningful elements, and semantic values, it is a large bundle of traits, each definable in terms of its norm. There also exist language variants corresponding to the usage of various subgroupings in a community, based on class, profession, age, sect, ideological group, or whatever. Linguistic scholars call such speech forms *dialects*, a term derived from Greek and made up of the prefix *dia-*, through or apart, and the verb *legein*, to speak. The technical term for an individual's special way of speaking is *idiolect*. In nontechnical language we can describe it as an *individual's variant*. A special way of talking in a given situation can also be called a *variant* or a *style*, the same expression that is used for an author's language in his writings—his *literary style*.

Of all the possible variations of a language, the kind that has had most to do with the history of speech in all periods of time is that determined by geography, the regional or local variant. These local variants are the ones we shall be speaking of mostly, but it is important never to lose sight of the general fact that language is by nature a variable phenomenon, held to a very approximate uniformity among the members of each social group and subgroup.

The Language Community

A *language community* may be defined as that group of people who communicate with one another by means of the same language. In the usual situation, such a community occupies a continuous territory, and each of its members is in contact with at least some other members of the same community. Some part of this contact has to be face to face and continuous, particularly in the first years of life, when the child is acquiring language. Some individuals or groups may be separated from their fellows for fairly extended periods, but even in the most primitive communities, prevailing customs provide for some shared activities—economic, ceremonial, and social—at weekly, monthly, or yearly intervals, reestablishing contact with those who might be isolated from day to day. If ties are broken for long periods, the original language may be lost. Or a separate community that continues to use the original language may be formed. Then after protracted separation for several centuries, a distinct language begins to take form as a result of simultaneous gradual linguistic change in both the old and the new communities.

The development of local, class, and other variants is a consequence of either more frequent contacts or greater group loyalties among persons who share experiences and ideas. If the community is small, geographically concentrated, and integrated, there will be little tendency to variation. With increased area and reduced contact, the tendency to form variants increases.

Within limits, subjective attitudes may augment or reduce the rate of differentiation. That is, if any class, area, or other subgrouping of the total community comes to feel that it is and ought to be distinct from others, it is likely to emphasize and add to any special characteristics that distinguish it from others. It may begin to keep apart and to dress, act, and talk differently. And yet such group consciousness is ordinarily not sufficient to bring about a complete separation. Even highly self-centered groups, if they remain in contact with the rest of the community, must maintain some economic, ceremonial, political, and social relations with the others. In consequence, they continue to speak the same language, with only a few special peculiarities. For example, the aristocracy may adopt distinctive mannerisms of pronunciation, construction, and vocabulary, but it will still be able to communicate with the peasantry, on whom, indeed, it is dependent for its privileges. The Quakers, as a religious sect, maintained the use of the archaic pronoun *thee* and some other turns of expression, but otherwise continued to speak much like their neighbors. Today, except where Quakers live in concentrated and isolated groups, they generally say *you*, like everybody else.

Intelligibility, Gradation Among Variants, and Standard Language

The function of a common language, ease of interaction, depends upon the fact of mutual intelligibility, yet this is a relative matter that at best only approaches 100 percent and at times is fairly incomplete. People generally understand other members of their own families, immediate neighbors, and close associates, but they may have some difficulty with groups that are a little further removed geographically or socially.

Frequently there are receding proportions of intelligibility as one moves further away, whether in physical or in social distance, from any starting point. This tendency is evidently related to that fact that each nucleus has most frequent contact with those next removed, but less with those a bit further on, and so on. The amount of sameness and difference reflects mostly the mobility of the people and partly their attitudes toward their neighbors, and these factors are related to the way of life of the community and of its component parts. Hunters and nomad herders move about a great deal, but are likely to cross paths with neighboring bands and to assemble at certain seasons for ceremonial and social purposes. Farmers are likely to stick close to home. Traders may travel back and forth, buying in one place and selling in another. The absence or abundance of roads reflects the mobility as well as the technology of a community. In modern countries there are not only excellent means of transport, but also various forms of communication, like publications, broadcasting, and telephone lines, which increase contact across great distances. To a considerable extent, large cities may be in closer communication with each other than any of them is with some of its neighboring rural areas, and may therefore be in considerable agreement in vocabulary and style of speech.

If one finds a particular similarity between distant places, chances are it is due to some special historical fact. For example, if the pronunciation of Boston and coastal New England shows similarities to that of southern England, this reflects circumstances in the early history of the American colonies.

The recent rapid spread of a population favors the wide extension of fairly uniform language. This is the case of English in the United States and Canada. Long settlement in an area is generally characterized by relatively sharp distinctions in speech. This may be seen in the great variation of English spoken in England and the even greater local differences in the languages spoken in Germany and Italy.

It is possible that extreme points in a sequence of speech variants, even though it is made up of easy gradations, may be very different. The speakers of adjoining variants may understand each other with reasonable ease, while the extremes are mutually unintelligible. If one finds rather different regional forms of a language in geographic contact with each other, something must have happened to bring about this unusual situation. Perhaps migrating speakers of a distant variant have come to live close by. Possibly certain regional forms have been gaining ground, as neighboring areas drop their way of speaking in favor of the new types; in the process, intermediate gradations are eliminated until notably different variants border on each other.

The linguistic variant used as the conventional or *standard* in a community in which many varieties exist need not necessarily be the variant ordinarily used by either of two individuals who are communicating. It may be the manner of speaking of some very large or especially influential portion of the total community. In a large modern nation there is usually some form of the language known as standard, regularly adopted in intervariant situations. The use of the standard variant tends to expand at the expense of the provincial forms. Modern governments generally promote the use of an official standard language by employing it in the schools, by requiring its use in official documents and transactions, and by making its use a necessary qualification for government employment. Many organizations and individuals may favor it for either idealistic or practical reasons. In general, the standard languages are more and more widely used, but there are hardly any places in which they have come even close to eliminating local variants. This is evidently due to a variety of things: the comfort of speaking in the style to which one is most accustomed; nostalgic love for the things of one's childhood, pride in one's own home region; the advantage one obtains in some situations from being able to say things to a friend that strangers are unable to understand. Dramatic examples of countries in which there is a tremendous amount of linguistic variation in addition to the recognized standard language (or languages) are India and Italy.

The motives for not dropping a local variant of a language are sometimes strong enough actually to increase its peculiarities. Thus regional pride sometimes leads people to avoid turns of speech that coincide with other localisms or with the standard variant, or even to revive old-fashioned expressions that increase local color. Group solidarity has also favored the invention of new figures of speech that help identify a person with his own group. Various forms of slang have thrived and become increasingly elaborate in this manner. The desire to hide one's conversation from outsiders has also been a strong reason for cultivating unique expressions.

The tendency for variants to develop in a language community is extremely marked. In fact, a linguistically homogeneous community is something quite exceptional. It is likely to be found only where the population is small, socially unified, and geographically limited. Just as the heterogeneous language community is much more common than the homogeneous one, the multilingual (or multivariant) individual is found more frequently than the monolingual person. Multilingualism (or multivariantism) arises in individuals who have grown up in homes or areas where more than one variant is used, who live close to a border between language zones, or who have traveled.

In more advanced or complicated societies, the types of multivariant control are likely to include passive or active use of a literary language, not necessarily identical with the standard spoken language, and perhaps various archaic forms. For instance, people who have studied literature will have some knowledge of Shakespearean English, and some may know one or more forms of Old and Middle English.

The areas in which the variants of a language are spoken naturally differ in shape and size, and they intercross in complicated ways. At any particular moment of history some variants may be on the rise while others are declining. Under these circumstances, there will be some families and localities in which only the younger generation speaks in the new way.

Language Boundaries

Not all languages are equally different from each other. Portuguese, Spanish, Catalan, Provençal, and French are fairly close to each other and represent a variant gradation. This means, for example, that speakers of Portuguese and Spanish can understand each other fairly well, and the same is true of those who speak Spanish and Catalan, Catalan and Provençal, Provençal and French. In each pair, many words are similar in form and meaning or are different only in part. The construction of words, phrases, and sentences is fairly similar. This is true if one compares the standard languages, and even more so if one takes the local forms of each language that are close together geographically.

In contrast to the similarity between Portuguese and Spanish, both of them are quite different from Basque, in inflection, word formation, sentence syntax, and vocabulary. The difference is somewhat less than it might otherwise be as a result of many centuries of contact, which has led to some assimilation in the sound systems of Spanish and Basque and to the mutual borrowing of words. Neighboring French and English are different in basic structure and vocabulary, but not so drastically so as Basque and Spanish. There is a fair amount of similarity between the English and French vocabularies because of the presence of French and other Romance words in English, of English and Germanic elements in French, and of derivatives from Greek and other languages in both.

The problem of where one language begins and the other ends is complicated for various reasons. What is essentially a single language may be given different names by different people. Nationalism plays a big role in people's conception of language identities. Thus Urdu and Hindi are considered two distinct languages by many Pakistanis and Indians, who point out that they are written with different alphabets, one based on the Arabic and the other on the old Indic tradition; that Urdu has many expressions taken from Arabic while Hindi has more from Sanskrit; and that one is associated with the Moslem religion and the other with Hinduism and Buddhism. Yet they grant that Urdu and Hindi speakers can understand each other with little difficulty. Their problems in doing so are probably less than those of two Italians, one speaking the Venetian variant and the other the Neopolitan.

People of the Spanish province of Galicia speak a variant essentially identical with Portuguese. In consequence, experts in Romance dialects often refer to Portuguese-Galician as a single language. The two areas go different ways, however, with regard to standard language, one using standard Portuguese and the other Castilian.

It is often difficult to distinguish between a case of several variants of a single language and a case of distinct but related languages. Certain cases are of course obvious. No one would hesitate to say that Spanish and English are different languages, with little mutual intelligibility, or that Chicago and St. Louis English are variants of the same language. Between the two clear extremes, however, the scale of variation is continuous. When people close their eyes to fairly marked differences or make a big point of minor variations, they probably do so for political, social, economic, or personal reasons. The scientist must try to describe objectively whatever differences exist. He may also work out generalized scales of agreement and disagreement, perhaps based on percentages of shared features. If he is concerned with the statistics of the number of languages there are in the world or in some particular region, he can decide on convenient points of division in the scale of variation. In any statistical report, the criterion of division ought to be stated. Unfortunately, this requirement has generally been disregarded. As a result, it is often difficult to evaluate information presented in language censuses.

Traits and Aggregates of Traits

Whatever problems may be encountered in determining where one language ends and another begins, a language is a sequence or network of variants. And regardless of the difficulties that arise in defining the limits of each of these, a variant is an aggregate of specific *traits:* certain sounds and sound sequences, certain meaningful elements, and certain ways of combining them into words, phrases, and sentences. A language may also be defined as the joint aggregate of the traits found in all its variants.

Usually, many of the traits of a language will be found in all of its variants; these will be coextensive with the geographic spread of the language. Other traits will be found only in some variants of a language. For the most part, the geographic extension of each trait is continuous. For example, the use of an *r* sound in a word like "barn" is characteristic of an area that extends eastwards through upstate New York and Vermont and ends along an irregular line that passes through parts of Maine, New Hampshire, and Massachusetts. East of that line people use a central vowel glide *(baain)* or omit the sound *(baan)*. Again, an area can be marked out in New England within which a shallow pan with a handle is generally called a *spider;* elsewhere it is known as a *frying pan* or a *skillet.* Likewise, there are parts of the United States where a certain animal is called a *polecat* although elsewhere it is a *skunk.*

There are some linguistic variations within one language that correspond more or less to political boundaries, like the mostly Canadian pronunciation of short *au,* almost *ou,* as against *aau* or *eeu* in words like *south;* or the British expression *lift* for what Americans and Canadians call an *elevator.* There are many other cases, however, in which the division falls within a single country or cuts across a frontier.

When scholars became aware of the interesting facts regarding the geographical distribution of linguistic traits, they adopted a technical term to describe the lines of demarcation between traits. The expression is *isogloss,* from Greek *iso,* like, and *glossa,* tongue, word, language. The usage is quite like *isotherm,* of like temperature; *isobar,* of like barometric pressure; and *isocline,* of like inclination.

To understand the nature of language variation in an extended community, it is convenient to divide the community into various subdivisions, each with a relatively homogeneous form of speech. It is then possible to compare each variant with all the others and note where the similarities and differences lie. From such studies have come our present knowledge that isoglosses tend to surround adjacent variants. Sometimes a given variant is only partly included in an isogloss, either because the usage is found only in part of the whole area of the variant or because it is weakly developed and only occasionally employed. Isoglosses may also be discontinuous, showing up in disconnected parts of the whole area. For example, the antique pronoun *vos* is used for the second person singular (along with the standard *tu*) in two noncontiguous areas within Spanish-speaking Central and South America: (1) from the state of Chiapas in Mexico southward to Panama and (2) in Argentina and parts of the countries adjoining it.

There is nothing to prevent an isogloss from going beyond the limits of a single language; the cases are numerous, involving similar sounds and sound sequences, constructions and vocabulary. Unaspirated, voiceless stop sounds *(p, t, k)* that are characteristic of the Romance language area in Europe are also found in the Flemish and Dutch dialects of Germanic, which border on the Romance areas. Yet, in the nature of things, there will be more isoglosses in common between two adjacent variants of a single language than between the adjoining portions of separate language communities. This is necessarily a rule without exception if the language boundaries are properly drawn and if the entire complex of traits is considered; that is, not just a few points drawn from phonetics, vocabulary, or any other single aspect of language. This follows from the fact that intelligibility depends on general agreement in the aggregate of individual traits, and there is no basis for counting as a single language speech variants that do not provide a reasonable degree of mutual intelligibility.

If a number of representative isoglosses are shown on a single map, the dialect areas are very likely to show up, even though perhaps with some fuzziness. Their boundaries will correspond to lines where several isoglosses coincide or at least run fairly close together. A map of variants can thus be drawn by marking boundaries wherever different isoglosses coincide, or by placing them somewhere between isoglosses where these deviate and crisscross. In making maps in this way for various countries, students of dialects have found interesting correlations with historical facts. The geographical areas of variants may turn out to correspond, for example, to the places of settlement of populations in migratory movements; to the countryside that sells products in a given market center; or to a political division, if it has existed for several generations. Students of cultural history are not surprised, then, that there are a number of isoglosses separating the northern and southern United States or northern and southern Germany. New trade, political, and social relations, if continued for sufficient time, may erase old boundaries and form new ones.

The student of language variants may use other methods than mapping isoglosses. He may determine the limits of areas by consulting observant members of the community or by making his own observations of the ease with which people understand each other. Or he may use external criteria at the outset, correcting his boundaries when he has new information. For instance, he may start by assuming that each town represents a speech variant and later join together those that are sufficiently similar. He should also check for uniformity within each town.

If the problems are simple, observations of degrees of intelligibility can be based on impressionistic judgments, either by the people themselves or by an outsider who observes the communicative process. It is also possible to set up objective tests, asking, for example, a series of questions about the content of conversations and scoring the answers; such tests have to be given to enough critically chosen individuals to guarantee a representative sample. Another approach is to set up a list of representative language traits and then count agreements and disagreements. The most important traits for judging degrees of relationship among speech forms are those most directly related to intelligibility. Thus common vocabulary counts for more than close agreement in structure and phonetics. If phonetics was the main criterion used by scholars in the past, it was only because their methods of study gave them more data on certain details of pronunciation. Nevertheless, since similarity of various kinds is a consequence of contact, it may be that phonetic similarity and common vocabulary coincide to a fair degree. The older dialect classifications may therefore be fairly good, but they need to be bolstered by additional data before they can be considered reliable.

Interlanguage Relations

The communication problems of people who speak different languages are in part similar to those of speakers of different variants of the same language, especially when the languages are closely related. Problems of intercommunication, then, can to some extent be resolved if each person speaks his own language, and if he takes the trouble to speak slowly, to avoid expressions that he suspects will be difficult to understand, to use gestures, and so on. In other situations, recourse must be had to the use of interpreters and to the employment of generally recognized languages of intercommunication. Persons who speak minority languages are often bilingual, speaking a widespread language with greater or lesser fluency. In Canada, and the United States, Indians generally speak English, which permits them to communicate with native speakers of the majority language, with foreigners who have learned it, and even with each other. Thus a Cree Indian meeting a Navajo will use English; if the Navajo does not know English, they will seek another Navajo who does to serve as interpreter.

Another solution to the problem of interlanguage communication is the *lingua franca, pidgin,* or *creole.* [*A pidgin is a simplified linguistic variant that arises to facilitate communication among individuals who have no language in common. It is in areas in which there are many such individuals that pidgins are used. When a pidgin becomes the native or first language of a group of people, it is called a creole.*] In various islands and coastal areas of the Pacific, pidgin English is used. In parts of the Indian Ocean, it is Bazaar Malay; in South Africa, Kitchen Kaffir, based on Zulu; on Curaçao, Papiamento, based on Spanish and Portuguese; in Haiti and Louisiana, two different versions of creolized French; and so forth. On Navajo reservations, a simplified version of Navajo, known as Trader Navajo, is employed. It is said that some of the traders are not even aware that they speak a broken form of the language and think it is the Indians who speak incorrectly. In few places has the use of gestures for interlanguage communication gone as far as among the Plains Indians of North America, where experts in the gesture language can discourse fluently on any subject customarily discussed among them in their ordinary language.

The Language Census

It should be apparent by now that it is no easy task to undertake a census of the languages of the world. One of the first problems to be faced is how to handle the numerous kinds of variation: geographic and social variation, intervariants and lingua francas, literary and archaic forms. The most important point is to keep the factors apart; in other words, to make each the subject of a separate chapter of any census. Of all the kinds of variation within and among languages, geographic variation is probably the most universal. Social differences in language are very important in some places and less so in others, but geographic variation is found everywhere. Further-more, as we go back in time some thousands of years, the nongeographic factors are probably everywhere far less important. Since this book emphas-izes the oldest origins of language diversity, the geographic aspect of variation must be primary. Though I would not deny the interest of any of the other aspects, it is clear that this must be our main focus.

A second vital problem is the units we are to count. In statistics that have been offered in the past, this question has been disregarded. One of the errors has been to make much of moderate differences in Europe and disregard them in aboriginal America, Africa, or Australia. There is a related tendency to give importance to minor differences where they are associated with different governments, while minimizing fairly large contrasts under other circumstances. A rational approach must separate the questions of linguistic and political identities. The political significance of a language must be considered a separate thing, with different historical causes and consequences.

The question of the units to be counted is also complicated by problems of internal variation, external contrast, and the shading of one into the other. This means we must measure as we count and set up our units in accordance with consciously chosen dimensions. Since intelligibility is the basis of linguistic community, and since vocabulary generally has more to do with intelligibility than phonetics or construction, it seems logical to devise measures of divergence based on vocabulary. Generally speaking there are two kinds of vocabulary agreement, *nuclear similarity* and *overlay*. The first can be found well represented anywhere in the world and belongs to older stages of history just as much as to modern times. The second, although it must have always existed, has reached its highest development among modern *world* languages. [*See the next chapter for a definition of world language.*] Nuclear agreement includes especially the simple words, such as those for grammatical elements, body parts, and broadly defined natural objects and activities. Overlay covers particularly manufactured articles, trade goods, advanced political, philosophical, and scientific terminology, and the like. While we must recognize the importance of both kinds of vocabulary, it is obvious that the more universal one will carry us further and must be given first importance.

In counting and statistics, it is convenient to operate with *representative samples*, that is, a portion of the entire mass of facts so selected as to reflect the essential facts. For our lexical measure of linguistic divergence we need some kind of selected word list, a list of words for which equivalents can be found in each language or language variant. [*See the Appendix for a hundred-word basic vocabulary list.*] The measure of similarity can then be based on the proportions of words on this list that agree and disagree with their equivalents in other languages and variants. A procedure of this kind may be described as *diagnostic vocabulary sampling* or *lexicostatistics*. In the past twenty years a fair amount of experimentation has been done with such word lists, and my remarks are based principally on results obtained with certain versions of this device.

With such a procedure, the percentages of agreement among language variants comprising any set may be listed in a table in the style of a mileage chart. To avoid confusing the picture with excessive detail, it is better not to include every conceivable subdivision of the speech community, but rather to select from among each grouping of variants one that will be at least 2 or 3 percent divergent from the representative of the next grouping. Sometimes, for lack of data, it may be necessary to operate with even fewer variants. It is convenient to choose an order of listing the variants that will, insofar as possible, bring into immediate sequence those that have the highest common percentages. When all the variants are compared, it becomes evident at once that some sequences are closer and some more divergent. The sequences may be grouped and described in some such way as this (the precise break points are based on considerations to be treated later):

Not to be treated separately	99 to 100 percent
Tight linkage	96 to 98 percent

Close linkage	90 to 95 percent
Loose linkage	85 to 89 percent
Open linkage	73 to 84 percent

If each of three or more variants is in tight sequence to all the others, these variants may be called a *tight bundle*. If they form a series in which the extremes shade off into a lower level of agreement, they are a *tight chain;* if the shading off is in more than one direction, they constitute a *net*.

When languages are to be grouped by intelligibility (without regard to any considerations of statehood or nationalism), it should be acceptable to consider as a single unit all variants related to each other and to no others with a diagnostic percentage of 90 or above. To avoid conflict with political conceptions we can call it a *language unit* rather than a language, at least in those cases where misunderstanding might arise. In this sense, single units are formed by Urdu and Hindi; Czech and Slovak; Serbian and Croatian; Russian, Ukrainian, and Ruthenian; all variants of German and Dutch; Danish, Norwegian, and Swedish.

When the extreme variants of a linguistic unit show a percentage of agreement below 85, this fact may be registered by describing it as an *internally divergent unit*. This would be the case with Dutch and German among the examples cited.

When at least one variant of a language unit comes as close as 73 percent or up to 84 percent (the lower limit for inclusion in the same unit) to some variant in another unit, we may consider that these variants form, or form part of, a *language cluster*. And such a cluster may be considered internally divergent if the extremes show a relationship of less than about 58 percent.

The differential qualities of a linguistic unit or cluster can be determined with the aid of the percentages of agreement for extreme and intermediate points. That is, the lowest percentage serves as a measure of its homogeneity or heterogeneity. The closer to 100 percent it comes, the more uniform it is. It is also important to note how many languages are included in the language cluster. The order of relations of variants in a language and of languages in a cluster can be shown in a comparative table, as mentioned before, or in a diagram in which the component units are shown by points connected by lines of lengths approximately proportional to the degree of divergence.

Vital Statistics of Language

[*Swadesh included this section here because he felt that in addition to "pure" linguistic information, social, political, and numerical (size of population) factors are crucial in a study of language change.*]

Very important for characterizing a language, besides its phonological, grammatical, and lexical properties in all their variability, are facts of time, place, and population, as well as the various activities in which it is used. These may be called the *external qualities*, or perhaps the *vital statistics*. Also important is the name or names by which the language is known.

Place and time are essential facts about any reality. In the case of languages, there is the important fact that they change and are therefore not completely the same from century to century, and indeed the relationship of samples from periods of, say, two thousand or more years apart may be quite un-recognizable. In addition, every language has a particular geographic area in which it is generally used. The size of the population and its territorial spread, including concentration at some points and scatter through other areas, are obviously important facts. So also are the birth rate, life span, health conditions, and mobility of the people who speak the language, and their economic and social relations with neighboring groups. Their attitudes toward their own and their neighbors' languages are still other interesting matters. All these may relate to the internal variation of the language, to the possibilities of vocabulary growth, and even to the possibilities for the con-tinuation, expansion, or contraction of the language in the future. It is particularly essential to observe the prevalence of bilingualism and multi-lingualism and the standing of the language in the opinion of the generations. Increasing bilingualism opens the way toward the elimination of a language; if the younger generations avoid the ancestral language in preference to a new one, it is possible that the old one will eventually be lost. This is the situation of many of the American Indian languages still spoken. It is also the case of most of the immigrant languages in the United States. If each of the languages of a bilingual community has a definite and respected function, one for home and ceremony, say, and the other for business and travel, there is a good chance that the local language will continue indefinitely.

The way of life, in all its manifestations, of the people making up the linguistic community is bound to have a connection with the language. In particular, the size and makeup of the vocabulary reflect the activities and customs of the speakers. The vocabulary also depends on the physical environment in which the population lives. The lexicon is sure to include expressions for all natural and elaborated products in common use and for all natural objects that have any special importance to the community. Fine distinctions will also tend to be made among concepts in proportion to their utility and sociopsychological significance in the physical and social environment.

Of particular interest to us here are what we might call *verbal customs*. These include norms of behavior as to who may or may not speak to whom, on what occasions and in what style of address; forms of address and titles, naming practices, fondness for figures of speech and literary allusions, the use of slang and special variants, and purism or the interlarding of foreign expressions in conversation. Verbal customs also have to do with the extent and manner of using intuitive vocal language and the ways of combining physical gestures with language.

A special problem is the names by which languages are known. Since many languages in the world are known by a variety of names, it is necessary to have some awareness of this matter. Let us note a few examples. The Germans call their language *Deutsch,* the French call it *allemand,* the Italians *tedesco,* and the Russians *nemetskiy.* As long as we know that all these names refer to the same language, no confusion can arise; but there are many languages, especially of lesser populations in Africa and America, that are called by a number of names in the literature, and the reader has no way of knowing exactly which language is being referred to. It also happens that the speech of towns or regions is mentioned with no indication of which are alike and which distinct. Suppose a book about English mentions people talking Kentish, Cockney, Londonese, Welsh, English, Northumbrian, Scots, Gaelic, and British. If we did not know the facts behind these names, we might suppose that nine different languages have been referred to. If we happen to know that Northumbria, Kent, and London are component parts of England, we might suppose that variants of English are involved in all cases, without suspecting that Gaelic and Welsh are completely different languages.

The main language of Mexico is known in English as Spanish. In Mexico itself it is called either *español* or *castellano,* and occasionally *mexicano* (pronounced "mehikano"); *mexicano* is also used to refer to the most important Indian language of Mexico, more frequently called *nahuatl,* and occasionally *azteca.* Not everybody outside of Mexico knows all these details. Another complication is the change of usage that may come about at any particular time. About fifty years ago, the language of Hungary was invariably called "Hungarian" in books as well as in colloquial usage. Today, serious writers tend to use "Magyar"; in speaking this name, those in the know say *Madyar* or *Modyor,* others *Meegyir.*

The name applied to a language often comes from the name of the area in which it is used, and area names may come from rivers, mountains, valleys, towns, or the name or nickname of the tribe or band or of a famous chief. Some of these names are used by the people of the area themselves; others are used by neighbors, who are not always friendly or complementary in their choice of terms. *Nez Percé* (spoken by the Nez Percé Indians in Idaho, Oregon, and Washington) comes from the French and means "pierced nose"; the tribe calls itself Numi-pu, which means simply "our people." The people of the Aztec empire called their language *nahuatl,* which means "sonorous, pleasant sounding," and used the word *nonotli* (mute, stammering) to describe other languages; or they called certain groups *chichimecatl* (lineage of dogs) or *popoloca* (barbarians); and still others were known as *chontalli* (foreigners). In consequence, there are several different languages referred to in the literature as Chichimeca, Popoloca, and Chontal, and one must be careful to distinguish among them.

Contraction, Expansion, and Multiplication

The most drastic change that can affect a language is extinction. It does not happen frequently, and yet some few hundred instances are known in recorded history, including Sumerian, Egyptian, Chaldean, Etruscan, Gothic, Pict, Cornish, Tasmanian, and scores of Australian and Amerindian languages. In very few cases has the loss of a language been accompanied by the physical elimination of an entire population, as in the case of Tasmanian. More commonly the language is replaced by some other language after at least a few generations of bilingualism. Generally there is a long period of increasing bilingualism and contracting areas of usage. Egyptian is known from inscriptions as early as 3000 B.C. and evidently enjoyed a long period of expansion. After Alexander the Great conquered Egypt, Greek gradually gained ground as Egyptian declined. In the fifth century a strong influence of Arabic came in. Egyptian, known as Coptic in its latest stage, continued to be used by parts of the population into at least the tenth century. Breton in France and Basque in southern France and northern Spain are modern examples of holdouts in the face of the expansion of Romance.

Much more frequent than the loss of languages is the extinction of language variants, as they are replaced either by other variants of the same language or by foreign languages. In fact, the history of any language may involve a long sequence of expansions and contractions of its frontiers, in competition with foreign languages, and an even more constant give and take among the boundaries of its component variants. While this goes on, there is also change in the language as a whole and in each of its variants, in part involving trends of divergence and convergence, and the creation of new variants, even while others are disappearing.

There are languages loosely called dead that never actually suffered extinction. A most notable case is Latin, which around the time of Christ was spread through many parts of Europe. Introduced as a language of administration and trade, it eventually replaced most of the local languages in present-day France, Iberia, some Alpine areas, all of Italy, some of the Mediterranean islands, and Romania. The old variants of the Latin language probably became mixed in the usage of troops, traders, and administrators, so that the number of variants was reduced and their differences were minimized. Still later, new local variants appeared and their differences deepened, but at no time was there any suspension of active use of the language. Latin never died and never went through any cataclysmic change. There is only the semblance of abrupt transformation as a result of the custom of maintaining an imitation of archaic spellings and expressions in written documents. When this practice was dropped and the common form of expression, called Romance, came to be used in writing, the contrast was more or less notable. By that time, too, localisms were sufficiently marked so that the Romance of each region had some special features. Regionalisms have strengthened in the last ten centuries, producing French, Spanish, Italian, Romanian, and other modern variants.

In the case of Greek, the ancient and modern variants of the language are both called Greek, while ancient and modern variants of Latin, except for Romanian, are called by new names. This only proves what was shown earlier, that names in themselves prove nothing. Modern French and Italian are not more different from the old language of Rome than modern colloquial Greek from the speech of two thousand years ago; nor is modern Romanian closer to ancient Roman than modern French.

What happened to Romance in the first several centuries this side of Julius Caesar was just normal change of the kind that takes place constantly in every language. What has happened since, in the deepening of local differences to the point where variants take on the status of relatively separate languages, is also a common process, the natural consequence of change itself when parts of the whole speech community become relatively separate. This process may be called the *multiplication* of languages.

The number of languages in any area or in the world as a whole is related to the effect of the two processes dealt with up to now: the multiplication and the absorption or elimination of languages. If we could be sure that human beings once all spoke alike, the two processes would constitute the sum and substance of language history. If it happened that more than one language was formed in the first instance, or that new languages were developed subsequently in any other way than by diversification, then we would have to join this fact to the explanation for the present number of languages.

The processes of multiplication and absorption are natural consequences of the use of language as the communicative cement of human society under varying conditions of contact. Multilingualism is essentially a compromise between unity and separation among linguistic variants in contact with each other, and is also a natural preliminary step to absorption.

The factors that favor multiplication and absorption are partly geographical but mainly cultural; that is, they depend on the way of life of the population. Multiplication comes from separation, absorption from contact. Distance and the presence of natural barriers are the geographical factors of separation, but they are subject to modification as man develops new techniques of travel and long-distance communication. Since man has been accumulating such techniques through the ages, the raw geographic facts have become less and less important. In fact, some barriers have been remade into roads: the oceans, once the most formidable separation, have become the means of linking parts of the world. By means of the seas Canada and the United States have maintained contact with England; and in the same way Greenland has maintained contact with Denmark, the Latin American countries with Spain and Portugal, French Canada with France, and so on. This explains why people in the several American language areas continue to talk reasonably like their ancestors in the corresponding parts of Europe after three and four centuries of separation.

Geographical contiguity and transport mean little except in relation to the patterns of travel and communication that are followed by human groups. These are related to economic practices to a considerable degree. Within some limits, hunting favors mobility over large areas. Commerce can be an even more telling influence. Military conquest and political unification are further factors. There are also contrary influences that engender resistance to linguistic as well as political absorption or economic control.

It is interesting to study linguistic maps and to observe where the large and small language areas are found. For example, the linguistic map of Amerindian languages at the time of first European contact shows large linguistic areas throughout the Great Plains and elsewhere in northern North America. These are the parts where hunting was the mainstay of life. Along the Atlantic and Pacific coasts there are various extensions where the language areas are quite small. The prevailing factor here is evidently fishing in the rivers and along the coast. Another circumstance may be outside pressure, since other bands, attracted by this food source, may have tended to crowd in. At the same time we find some larger language areas at several points in these regions, particularly in the southeast and around the Hudson River. These are the areas of the large Muskogean and Iroquois confederacies, which practiced agriculture and joined together for defense against outside raids. In the southwest and in certain parts of Mexico, we find very small areas where farming is also practiced. Here, apparently, an early development of agriculture permitted subsistence on relatively small amounts of land. The pressure of militant hunting bands perhaps explains the reduced areas. As we carry this sort of observation into Mexico and South America, the patterns repeat themselves in similar fashion, with differences connected with the state of things in each region.

We know that two to three thousand years ago there were more languages than there are today in the parts of the world that history tells about (city-states, for the most part, dependent on the agriculture of the surrounding countryside). Perhaps in more isolated parts of the world, where hunting was still dominant, the number of languages may have been smaller. Ten thousand or so years ago, before the development of agriculture, languages must have been fewer. Fifty thousand years back, when the New World was still uninhabited, the population was sparce in all parts, and hunting techniques were primitive, it is reasonable to infer that the number of languages was still smaller.

Analysis of various historical cases permits some generalizations about the factors that determine which language is likely to expand and which to contract in any given situation. In general, a large or fast-growing population will have a strong advantage. If the large population is both mobile and integrated—that is, if the people travel about without breaking ties with their own group—its influence will be especially strong. Material and cultural superiority, as well as military and political domination, play a role, but do not by themselves guarantee that one language will replace another. The actual effect will be in some way the product of the several factors. There is often a first consequence that opens the way to later events. In particular, the language of a mobile group introduced into an area where a number of local languages exist is likely to become the lingua franca, used when the various groups meet outsiders or each other. Once a language has become a lingua franca, it is a relatively easy step to eventual replacement of the various local languages, one after the other.

Change, Divergence, and Convergence

[At this point there is a major shift of interest or focus. Up to now, Swadesh has discussed the notion of linguistic variation, the characteristics of language communities, and the relationship between a language and its speakers. He begins here to describe the actual nature of linguistic change and to talk of the possibility of reconstructing the details of particular developments.]

The linguistic divergence found in various parts of a language community is a consequence of the changing models of usage. When people are out of touch, either literally or psychologically, they drift apart in their manners of speaking, as well as in other ways. If they are in contact part of the time or if they have relations with the same third parties, the drifting apart will be slowed. When people of different backgrounds are thrown together, they may begin to mold themselves along similar lines. Thus change may be either divergent or convergent.

Some of the facts of linguistic change are, as it were, visible to the naked eye. Any older person can remember some expressions formerly popular that have dropped out of general use. And there may be speech traits that are on the increase among the younger generations, while others are being lost even among the older people. Thus we can observe change taking place. We do not always know which new expressions are only a passing fad and which have come to stay, but there is no question that new forms are being introduced. This can be stated as a general rule: Linguistic change is always going on.

No drastic change ever takes place in a short time, however. The oldest generation and the youngest may think each other's speech peculiar, but they understand each other. Except when children have not been reared by their parents, the only serious linguistic problem that arises among the generations comes as a result of the rapid adoption of a new language. In such a case, it is possible that old people speak one language, their children two, and their grandchildren only one, different from that of the grandparents but identical with one of the languages of the parents. Though this does not happen frequently, it has occurred, for example, among some Amerindian families that have suddenly come into contact with English under conditions that make for drastically rapid replacement, and on occasion among immigrants in the big cities. It is more usual for language replacement to stretch out over several generations or to be completed only after centuries of bilingualism.

The rate of replacement for a new variant of the same language may conceivably be faster than that for an entirely different language. It frequently happens that a person, especially if he is young at the time, changes his variant on moving to a new area or on finding himself in close contact with one or more people from a different area. Whether he accepts the new model or not must depend on various factors, including especially admiration for either the new form of speech or the individuals who use it.

The change that takes place in language in the course of one person's lifetime is generally fairly limited. It may at best cover one or a few details of pronunciation or construction; there may be a few new words, and it is likely that there will be some new expressions and new meanings given to old ones. But in general there will be only minor differences applied to a small percentage of the total inventory of material used in the language. When new languages or new variants are introduced, chances are they will affect only a small portion of a population in any one generation, unless the community speaking the old language has been greatly reduced or widely dispersed, so that small numbers of individuals are actually involved at any one place and time.

Because of its normally gradual rate, linguistic change is best seen over a long lapse of time. We are able to do this in the present epoch because the history of the past centuries and millennia has been preserved in written form, and older versions of our language and others are available for our study. We are thus able to know that the boundaries of languages and their variants have changed over the centuries, that some old tongues have dropped out of use, and that none of those that have survived have remained unchanged. As a result of a careful study of the facts, we can generalize about the possible directions and limits of change and devise techniques of inferring older forms of language, so that we may gain insights into languages as they existed even before the time when they were first written. An astronomer, understanding the laws of physics, is able to draw inferences about things far off or hidden from his direct observation on the basis of things closer at hand or more directly observable. In similar fashion the student of linguistics infers things of long ago from evidence closer at hand. It is important in this enterprise to make use of all possible resources and piece together many bits of evidence, including some that by themselves may be somewhat vague in their implications, as long as there is a reasonable chance of narrowing the possibilities and coming closer to the actual facts.

VOCABULARY GROWTH AND LEXICAL CHANGES

Since human cultures have always tended to acquire more and more artifacts and concepts, one of the main directions of change in lexicon has been expansion. In English, for example, dictionaries for the epoch of *Beowulf* list some thousands of meaningful items, or *lexemes*, as against hundreds of thousands today. A similar growth is found in other great world languages. Among classic and local languages, the rate may be much slower, but the tendency to increase is also found to some extent. [*See the next chapter for definitions of the terms "world," "classic," and "local language."*]

Even while the vocabulary is growing, some elements are falling out of use. Lexicon growth is thus actually the difference between the acquisition of new items and the loss of old ones. There must be times when gain and loss is proceeding at an approximately equal rate so that the size of the vocabulary remains more or less stable. It is even possible for a vocabulary to contract, if elements are going out of use faster than new ones are coming in. Still, no language will ever lose all its meaningful elements, except by going out of use, nor will the number ever fall below some limit that corresponds approximately to the lowest level to which human culture may fall in a community made up of people of the mental plane our species has by now attained. An exceptional case might be a language that survives only in a few elements that live on in the memory of a few individuals, or in certain activities, ceremonies, games, etc., after the language as such has gone out of use.

Though size of vocabulary is related to richness of culture, this relation need not be strict in a mechanical sense, because of a certain property that may be called *lexical profusion* or *synonymy*. For some artifacts or concepts a language may be, as it were, content to have a single name, even when the thing exists in a number of sizes, shapes, varieties, or associations. In other cases, there is a variety of expressions for the same thing or for minor variations on the same theme. Unquestionably some languages are more prone than others to lexical profusion. This is often related to literary traditions or to concepts of what is elegant or clever in conversation.

There is another interesting variable to be noted among languages, one that may be called *lexical economy*. This refers to the extent to which a relatively few elements are employed in a variety of combinations to express different related ideas. Both profusion and economy can be illustrated in English: *child, colt, calf,* and *chick* refer to the young of the human, equine, bovine, and gallinaceous species, but no corresponding words exist for elephants, giraffes, monkeys, and ants. A king's male offspring is a prince, but a hunter's son is only a hunter's son. Insofar as a language uses combinations, it can get along with a small inventory of elements, a fact that accounts for differences in the sizes of the lexicons of languages employed by cultures of similar development. A language with few elements is easier on the memory and especially convenient for those who have to learn it as a second language. This principle has been employed to great advantage in pidgin languages, whose vocabularies consist of a couple of hundred components, more or less. Indian sign language is similarly constituted, with something like a hundred basic signs, used in various combinations to express thousands of concepts.

The process of vocabulary gain and loss naturally begins with individuals or styles and spreads to variants or to the entire community. If it does not go beyond the individual, it has no effect on the history of the language. New items may remain in one or a few local variants of a language for a long time without pervading the whole area. Possibly the community may split before the innovation has spread through it, in which case the new item may show up in one of the derived separate languages and be absent in the others. This is one of the facts that make diverged languages different from one another.

Innovations and changes as a rule come bit by bit. A new expression is often used in a limited way or in specific situations before it gains wider application. The loss of old items is likely to begin with one or another reduction in their sphere of application. Not infrequently, the use of an old element hangs on in some special sense or in some special combination. To cite an example, *yule,* the old word for Christmas, is now archaic and used mainly in the compound *yuletide* and the phrase *yule log.* When new terms take the place of old ones, they are likely to begin as occasional synonymous alternate expressions, and for quite a long while there may be a division and vacillation of usage before a final stability is reached with the establishment of one and the loss of the other, or a clear division of the field of application between them.

As for the source of new items, there are several possibilities. The forms may come from another language or variant, or from the same one. New lexemes may come from inflectional forms or from combinatory groupings of elements. The status of lexeme is attained when the formation acquires a special meaning different from its original one and possibly also a new inflection. For example, *tailings,* referring to the refuse left as a result of certain processes, comes from the participle *to tail,* to follow behind; as a participle, *tailing* has no plural, but in the new meaning it is used mostly in the plural. *Tenderfoot* comes from the phrase *tender foot,* used with a shift of accent. The plural of *tender foot* is *tender feet,* but that of the derived lexeme is *tenderfoots.*

Even a simple root may be made into a new lexeme by a shift of inflection or, if its new meaning is radically different from the old, in such a way as to be no longer associated with it. *Sack* as a noun and a verb must be regarded as two separate lexemes, not only because *to sack* has a different inflection but because the meaning need not have anything to do with sacks, as when one speaks of being sacked from his job. When we speak of a *tomcat* or a *turkey tom,* we are employing a reduced form of a proper name in a totally different way. The primordial meaning of *Thomas,* originally from Aramaic *te'ooma,* twin, is unknown to most speakers of English, and even its function as a name also lies far behind when we use *tom* to mean male.

When a derived form is used as a lexeme, it becomes separated to a degree from its origin. It may come to be pronounced differently and eventually even cease to be recognized as related. Only the spelling, not the pronunciation, recalls the origin of *breakfast*, the meal with which one breaks the night's fast, or that of the second half of *shepherd*. Not even the spellings of *lord* and *woman* suggest that the first comes from *loaf-ward*, keeper of the bread, and the second from *wife-man*, a female person. Examples like these, in which the origin is known from older records of a language, teach us that all tongues may contain what look like unanalyzable roots but which may be old combinations of separate parts.

A fair number of words, when traced back to early forms, turn out to be of sound imitative origin. If we think of a stovepipe or the piping to trim a garment, there is little to suggest any imitative origin, but these words can be traced to *pipe*, a musical instrument, and eventually to Latin *pipare*, to make a piping or peeping sound. Unquestionably, sound imitation represents one of the important sources of new lexical material. Vocables first formed as exclamatives and imitatives come to be used as nouns and verbs referring to the emotions and sounds so represented. Through a series of transfers of meaning, accompanied at times by inflective changes and formative additions, the intuitive origin may be totally obscured.

CHANGING SOUNDS AND STRUCTURE

[*See the Grammatical Terms for definitions of the terms employed in this section.*]

Just as new vocabulary may be borrowed from neighboring languages, formed from already existing items in the same language, and created by means of imitation, phonetic and grammatical structure may be added to or reshaped by the same three means. When new words are taken from neighboring languages, it is quite usual to adapt their sounds to those of the borrowing tongue. Occasionally some or all of the foreign sounds are imitated more or less closely. Thus, new phonemes come into the language. When this happens, the new sounds have to be fitted into the general scheme of the native ones, often calling for some modification of phonetic detail. Sometimes, presumably under the influence of considerable bilingualism, native sounds are assimilated to those of neighboring languages. There never seems to be much phonetic assimilation going on at any one time, and yet in the long run the influence is apparently considerable. Thus in various parts of the world we find that languages that have been neighbors for many centuries tend to be very similar in phonetic pattern. A striking example is the northwest coast of North America, where most of the American Indian languages have a glottalized series of sounds and a proliferation of sounds pronounced in the back of the mouth, in addition to other similarities. In part under the influence of neighbors and in part independently, the phonetics of any language may undergo changes. These are generally very slow or partial, affecting only one or another small detail at any one time.

Only when the end result of a series of changes is compared with the original may one get the impression of drastic transformation. Changes in pronunciation may begin with some features of accent or rhythm, which tend to strengthen or weaken certain sounds. There is also a fairly frequent tendency for neighboring sounds to affect each other, usually in the direction of increasing similarity, only occasionally in the opposite direction of strengthened contrast.

Another interesting and important tendency in phonetic change is toward the parallel development of sound patterns. That is, the modification that affects any given sound tends to affect other similar sounds in approximately the same fashion. For example, at a certain period in the prehistory of the Germanic languages, *p* at the beginning of words was transformed into *f*; at that time *t* became *th*, and *k* became *h*. In each case a voiceless stop became a voiceless spirant.

Among the changes that may come about within the phonemic system of a language, whether from external or internal influences, are the loss of phonemes by the merging of two or more into one; the creation of new phonemes by the splitting of old ones; the introduction of phonemes from foreign sources or, occasionally, from intuitive language; the modification of minor phonemic sequences by phonetic simplification; and the development of new phonemic sequences as a result of phonetic changes or from new combinations of elements.

Changes in inflection and grammatical structure likewise involve additions, reductions, and transformations, either under foreign influence or spontaneously. The most usual spontaneous changes include the development of fixed sequences out of variable ones, the pulling together of phrase forms into single words, and the replacement of functions (for example, affixes may take over the function of internal modifications in a word, and independent words may take over the function of affixes). Old functions may be abandoned as the elements expressing them are reduced to the vanishing point, or they may be rescued by being rephrased in looser expressions. There are known cases of internal inflection dropping out of use, of affixes becoming fossilized as parts of the stem, and of agglutinated formations developing out of phrase structure. The precise direction of change often follows the patterns of assimilation to prevailing structural types in the area.

RATES OF CHANGE

One general rule applies to all forms of linguistic change: It goes on slowly. Insofar as change is influenced by contact with neighbors, it is obvious that something can happen only when there are languages close by that present different patterns. Vocabulary expansion in response to culture growth will occur only when cultural development is under way and will affect mainly the part of the lexicon that reflects the new products and ideas. We can therefore modify our first general proposition, and say that, while linguistic change is always slow, its rate of change varies with social, economic, political, and geographic factors; furthermore, some portions of language change less slowly than others.

There is one aspect of language in which change has been found to move along at an approximately constant rate: that portion of the lexicon which has least to do with cultural advance, and which has been called *basic vocabulary*. A number of studies made in the last twenty years have shown that it is possible to set up a diagnostic word list that reflects the passage of time reasonably well. With one such list, already referred to in connection with the measure of variant similarity, the retention of vocabulary after one thousand years has been found to average 86 percent, with not too much fluctuation above and below this figure. After two thousand years, 86 percent of the previous balance of 86 percent gives 74 percent, and so on. [*See the Appendix for a hundred-word basic vocabulary list and a chronological table.*] Cases of retention much greater than the normal have turned out to be extremely few, and to be confined to the rather special condition of communities that consciously and energetically strive to maintain a revered ancient norm, preserved in a traditional literature. Cases of retention much lower than the norm are equally scarce, and have been found to exist only in some pidgin or other semiartificial languages.

When language variants are in the process of formation, the rate of diversification depends on the extent to which they are out of contact with each other. If two variants are changing at a rate corresponding to the thousand-year retention figure already mentioned, their correspondence at the end of any period cannot fall lower than the combined effect of that change in both lines. This is easily calculated as 86 percent of 86 percent for every thousand years, for an overall change of 74 percent, provided there is no other factor than chance that makes one variant change in the same way as the other. To the extent that the two variants continue in contact, however, they will tend to make the same changes and to retain the same old vocabulary elements. In consequence, instead of dropping to 74 percent of common vacabulary after a thousand years, the agreement between them may be anywhere from 74 percent to nearly 100 percent.

By means of the diagnostic word list, it is possible to estimate the least amount of time that two variants or related languages have been diverging. If they share 74 percent of the items in the diagnostic list, we infer that they began to diverge not less than a thousand years ago. If they share more or less than this proportion, we estimate the minimum separation time from the precise percentage according to the table of equivalences that has been calculated at the rate of 74 percent per thousand years.

Since language diversification mostly begins among variants still in contact and rarely with a sudden and complete break, the calculated time estimates have to be considered minimum periods. When we have data for a number of interrelated speech forms, some more and some less divergent from each other, we may be sure that the lowest reported percentage comes closest to reflecting the beginning of diversification.

RELATIVE CHRONOLOGY AND THE NOTION OF THE FAMILY TREE

Even before the discovery of lexicostatistic time estimation, as described in the last section, linguists learned to use relative time scales in certain favorable situations. This was possible, for example, when two phonetic changes were interdependent. An excellent example is the development of old *kwe* into *cha* in Sanskrit, while *kwo* became *ka*. Two sets of phonologic changes are involved: (1) the consonant *kw* probably first became *k* before all vowels, and the *k* became *ch* before a front vowel; and (2) the vowels *e* and *o* fell together and ended up as *a*. It is obvious that the splitting of the consonant must have taken place before the fusion of the vowels, since, if they had fallen together first, there would have been no basis for the consonantal split.

Anywhere that a relative chronology can be established, whether in phonetics, structure, vocabulary, or semantics, this information may be useful in increasing the accuracy of inferences about details of linguistic prehistory. There are rather few actual cases in which such sequences can be clearly proved, however.

One aspect in which it is very convenient to obtain relative chronology is the order in which language variants appear. At one time it was a favorite procedure of linguists to set up sequences of *language splits* that were represented as *family trees*. Nowadays linguistic genealogists are generally too sophisticated to believe that languages always divide by abrupt splits. They therefore accept the model of gradual dialect formation, but claim that in the long run, when intermediate variants have been lost, it is the same as if there had been a sharp split. This is logically correct in one kind of situation: when all variants except two are lost, or when all but a few are lost and the groups that speak them are geographically and socially separated from each other in such a way that they remain equidivergent linguistically. In other situations, however, linguistic divergence is better represented as a *chain, mesh,* or *net* (rather than a tree). Figure 1.1 contrasts the family tree and the net models, using the Indo-European family of languages as an example.

Phonologic Regularity

Since language changes take place slowly or by small bits, it is often possible to recognize where a change has occurred by the presence in two languages or variants of forms that are partly similar and partly different. For instance, if in German we find words like *Nase,* nose; *Auge,* eye; *Ohr,* ear; *Mund,* mouth; *Kinn,* chin; and *Nacken,* neck, it is evident that here is a language close to English. Even if we did not have history to tell us so, we would suspect that these were once identical or close variants of the same language.

FAMILY TREE

NET MODEL

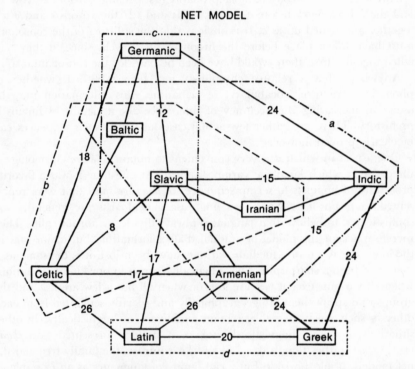

Numbers indicate minimal centuries of divergence, given by glottochronological counts.

Letters indicate some ancient isoglosses:
  a: *k > sh*
  b: *dh > d*
  c: case endings with *m*
  d: feminine nouns with masculine suffixes

Figure 1.1. The Family Tree vs. the Net Model of Indo-European Languages

The evidence is not only in vocabulary but also in construction patterns and inflections; a particularly striking common feature is the formation of the past tense by vowel change, as in *singen-sang-gesungen* and *denken-dachte* in German, corresponding to *sing-sang-sung* and *think-thought* in English.

There are other cases of languages with similar vocabulary and structural features in which the agreement shows up less clearly or in a smaller number of details. Consider the following agreements between Russian and English:

menyá	me	*polniy*	full
dva	two	*sértse*	heart
tryi	three	*mésyats*	month
shesty	six	*vodá*	water
sem	seven	*zhóltiy*	yellow
dérevo	tree	*beráty*	carry, bear

or these between English and Arabic:

ard"	earth	*"ayn*	eye
k"arn	horn	*huu; hii*	he, she
thalaatha	three	*k"atâ"*	cut
sitta	six	*yi-d"rub*	thrash
sabâ"a	seven	*yi-duur*	turn, twist

With such similarities, one thinks of the possibility of common origin. Since they are few and the resemblance is sometimes small, one may infer that the relationship must go back a very long time. Or one may hesitate to draw any inference of relationship, fearing that the similarity might be only illusory in some cases and accidental in others. What is needed here is some test of common origin that will separate the substance of agreement from the will-o'-the-wisp of chance. Fortunately, there exists not one device but a whole system of verification. Its most spectacular feature is the principle of phonologic regularity, but this procedure is weak and of limited value if it is used alone, without the verification of the additional criteria. Let us begin with a simple test.

Phonemic change tends to be regular. That is, when a change occurs in a given phoneme in given phonetic surroundings, the result will normally be the same for all words that contain that phoneme under the same conditions. This implies that for almost any specific change, there are more than one and sometimes a considerable number of instances. Hence, wherever we find a number of sets of words in which the sounds correspond in two languages, we can be reasonably sure that the correspondence is caused by the ancient identity of the words. Each of the pairs of Russian and English words listed above displays certain phonetic correspondences, such as: *m* to *m* in *menyá*, me, and *mesyats*, month; *d* to *t* in *dva*, two, *dérevo*, tree, and *vodá*, water; *t* to *th* in *tryi*, three; *r* to *r* in *tryi*, three, *dérevo*, tree, *sértse*, heart, *beráty*, bear, and so forth. By searching further in the two languages, we find still other examples: *m* to *m* also in *maty*, mother, *málenkiy*, small, *molokó*, milk, *myod*, mead, and others; *d* to *t* also in *do*, to, up to, and *desyaty*, ten; *t* to *th* also in *tísach*, thousand, *ti*, thou, *to*, that, and *tónkiy*, thin; and so on. It is evident that the agreements between English and Russian are phonologically consistent and are confirmed by a fair number of parallel instances for each phonetic equation. The comparison of English with Arabic is not so easily confirmed, from which fact we infer that any relationship of common origin in this case must date much further back in time.

When we use the diagnostic list to obtain an estimate of divergence time, the comparison of English with Russian gives us about five thousand years as the minimum time of divergence. The same test for English and Arabic is hard to make because of uncertainty of the specific comparisons, but in any event, if the two languages have a common origin at all, it must lie much further back than five thousand years ago.

False Identities and Hidden Realities

The successful tracing of old linguistic unities depends on the accurate recognition of common elements that go back to the common period. The enterprise is full of hazards, some of which deceive us into thinking that items are *cognate* (descendants of the same common form) when they are not, others of which prevent us from recognizing them as cognate when they really are. Any successful study of the prehistory of language, if it is to go beyond the most simple and obvious inferences, must be based on effective means of reducing the errors from both classes of pitfalls.

Some of the most similar words in two languages are those that one has borrowed from the other or that both have borrowed from a third language in relatively recent times. Scientific words of Latin and Greek origin prove nothing about the common origin of the languages in which they are found. The same is true of the Russian word *stepy*, which has come into English with the French spelling *steppe*, and the English word *dock*, which in Russian is *dok*. One of the first precautions, then, is to eliminate from comparisons aimed at establishing old linguistic communities all identities caused by recent borrowing. Needless to say, one must not be blindly drastic, sweeping out elements that might really date back to an old common period. That this warning is necessary is evident from the suggestion of some historical linguists that marked similarity of words in two or more languages, or any similarity of words in languages not known to be related, must be due to borrowing. All such rules are obviously exaggerated. Continuing the Russian–English example, we have cognates that are quite similar in form and others that are quite distinct. An example of the former is *nos*, nose; of the latter, *sertse*, heart. The safest identification of words as recent borrowings is made on the basis of good information on the earliest use of the word in each language: when it is first known to have been used, by what author, and in what context. Sometimes the fact of borrowing is definitely indicated by the first known usages. If the word is registered in one language long before it is found in the other, this is reasonable evidence of borrowing by the second. In many cases the form of the word betrays its original affiliation. For example, if a word contains affixes or roots that are at home in one of the languages but not in the other, or if it is an item of common use in one tongue but literary or technical in the other, or if the phonetic form is in keeping with normal patterns in one but not in the other, then it is reasonable to assume that the second language borrowed it from the first.

Borrowings made long before the first record of the language will have had time to become adapted phonetically, morphologically, and in usage, thus making detection of borrowing more difficult. To some extent one can use certain guiding principles, such as the fact that basic vocabulary is less apt to be borrowed than cultural vocabulary. In the last analysis, however, reserve should be maintained when the evidence is not completely clear. Individual items may have to be counted as more or less indeterminate until additional evidence can be found.

Items common to two languages as a result of borrowing in an old period may show phonologic correspondences not unlike those due to common origin, or there may be differences by which loan words from different periods may be distinguishable. Thus words like *baggage* and *village* were probably borrowed by English from French earlier than words like *garage* and *mirage*, since they have more completely assimilated English pronunciation patterns.

The second great pitfall for the linguist seeking phonologic correspondence is chance. Adequate knowledge of phonology helps minimize this danger, especially in relatively complicated forms—those made up of three, four, or more phonemes. Still, many roots in many languages consist of only one or two fixed phonemes, so that inevitably the chance factor will leave doubts in relation to many legitimate comparisons.

The illusion of relationship may also present itself as the result of coinciding sound imitations. That is, the effort of separate communities to imitate a like natural sound may lead to like sound imitatives, which eventually find their way into their general vocabularies. The scholar must be wary of such coincidences, but should not go to the extreme of ruling out every comparison that might originally have involved sound imitation. Forms that were at one time imitatives behave like elements of the formal language once they find their way into it. An example is the French word *pigeon*, pigeon, which is descended by regular processes of derivation from Vulgar Latin *pipio*, a young bird, although the latter first appeared as an imitative or onomatopoetic form. The question, then, is not the ultimate origin of a word but whether it was or was not a part of the formal language in the presumed common period of the languages that are being studied.

The historical linguist needs to make himself as familiar as possible with the structure of each language with which he is dealing, and he must take particular pains to recognize archaic structure. For instance, once one understands that in English *be-* in words like *believe, begin, berate* is an old particle, one is in a position to recognize the cognancy of English *between* and German *zwischen*. Often old facts of structure become evident only in the process of comparison.

Old phonemic alternation is a great disguiser of old identities. A relatively simple instance is involved in the interchange of vowels, still preserved in a few roots in Germanic but lost in many of them. English *horn* looks more like Latin *cornus* than like Greek *keras*, but actually it is equally related to both. The old form that produced the English must have been **krn-*, which gave the Latin *korn-* and the Greek *kern-*. (An asterisk preceding a form is commonly used to indicate that the form has been reconstructed.) The consonants were the same in all three, and the vowel differs according to a principle of interchange that was evidently applicable to all roots at some early period. For some old stages of language, there is evidence that consonant alternations also occurred. This makes it more difficult to recognize cognates, but any serious scholar must be prepared to meet such complications as they arise.

There is generally less difficulty in tracing the development of sounds that have been transformed than in tracing those that have disappeared for one reason or another. In the latter case, the linguist can identify cognate elements only by the other sounds in the same form which have escaped elimination. The shorter the conserved portion, the more difficult the comparison. If different portions of a form have been preserved in two languages under comparison, it may be possible to piece together the original. Occasionally when phonemes are lost as such, they leave some phonetic trace, such as the lengthening of a neighboring sound, the conservation of something that might otherwise be lost, or some different phonetic development than might otherwise occur. All such clues must be thoroughly investigated.

The problems of identification created by the loss of phonemes in an element are often complicated by the fact that some other element has become permanently attached precisely at the point where the loss took place. For example, English *head* agrees only in the first consonant with Greek *kephala* (the basis of our technical term for head measurement, *cephalic index*). Knowing that the Old English form was *heafod*, with a labial consonant also in the second consonantal position, helps us to recognize that the words might be cognate; without this information, one might hesitate to connect them. A further comparison with Latin *caput* (whence our *capital* and, through French, *captain* and, with loss of final syllable, *chief* and *chef*) makes things even clearer. This example demonstrates the need to pursue as much evidence as possible.

The historic transformation of phonemes is such that a single one may be converted into two or more according to the accentual conditions or the phonetic surroundings. In this case, the linguist tries to ascertain what conditions produced each development and thereby obtain added data about the early forms. At times he can only suspect such a splitting without being able to pin it down. Lost morphologic alternations give a similar problem: two compared languages may show divergent phonemes, without any apparent cause, in words otherwise fully comparable.

When two phonemes have become fused into one by phonetic changes, the separation of old forms depends on the additional use of other related languages that provide the necessary clues, either because their forms have not undergone fusion or because they fused in altogether different ways.

The problems of cognate identification are, of course, also complicated by semantic change, which, as we have seen, is extremely frequent. It is thus a commonplace rule of comparative linguistics that the meanings of cognate forms need not be identical. When the phonology of compared words fits the established patterns, we recognize them as of probable common origin; for example, Latin *tumor* (tumor) and English *thumb*, assuming that the original reference was to the pad of flesh; Latin *currere* (to run) and *horse*, an animal that runs fast; Latin *arcus* (bow) and English *arrow*; Russian *pod* (under), Greek *podo-* (foot), and English *foot*; Sanskrit *kr* (to work, make, or do) and Latin *colare* (to plow).

If any one line of evidence is insufficient to give assurance of the correctness of a comparison, the only way out is to bring together additional facts that may narrow the possibilities. Fortunately, the ramifications of linguistic prehistory are great and open up a large field of evidence bearing on any detail. All the various uses of an element in a language may be examined for clues as to its earlier forms and meaning. These elements should be traced back into the past as far as the material permits. Again the occurrence of the form in different variants of the language and in closely related languages is likely to add important additional clues.

After exhausting all the information close at hand, we still have recourse to multiple comparisons. For example, if we are comparing an English form with a Sanskrit form, we help to clarify our problem greatly by also bringing in parallels not only from other Germanic languages, but also from Celtic, Slavic, Latin, Greek, Armenian, and so forth. If we suspect further relationships of Indo-European languages with other groups, these also may be used. Finally, we need not confine ourselves to cognate occurrences: the form the element has taken in languages that have borrowed it, particularly if the borrowing took place long ago, may help to complete the picture with data that may well increase the accuracy of the comparison.

When we have exhausted all possible evidence in any detail of comparative linguistics, we may end up with a very strong case, a reasonable one, or a still shaky one. We have yet one more task: to estimate the strength of the detail and use it accordingly. In a large collection of highly probable cognates, it is possible that one or another false one, accidentally combining characteristics that appear to be related but are not, may have crept in.

Possibly new evidence will someday betray the ringer. The wise scholar will therefore not insist that every last one of his apparently strong comparisons is absolutely safe. Instead he will seek insurance in numbers. His confidence will be in a total body of comparisons, based on the notion that, even if some of the cognate sets should be false, the languages are still related. Nor should any linguist pooh-pooh the weak-appearing cognates. If there is a reasonable chance that even a few sets in a collection may be sound, the possible clues they give should be respected. Surely future research will clarify, either positively or negatively, many notions that now appear doubtful.

Extralinguistic Evidence

If it is essential to make full use of all directly linguistic evidence, it is equally important to relate it to geological, archeological, and all other pertinent facts.

Geological and geographic information indicates where human life was feasible in various epochs, the prevalent physical environment, and the type of adjustment that human groups would have to make to it. At the same time, the comparative vocabulary of a linguistic group will contain clues as to the environment and culture of the people who spoke the language in the common period. The time dimension helps to relate the clues of vocabulary with those of geography and geology.

Archeology reveals the existence of human life and many of its details in certain sites at certain times. Dating methods now available permit the determination of the time period with considerable exactness. When time estimates of archeology and comparative linguistics are in harmony with each other, and when the lexically suggested old culture fits with the archeological artifacts, the possibility is opened up that a given site corresponds to a given group, or possibly to another closely related one.

Whether the data of geology or of archeology are being considered, the task of narrowing the clues to a definite focus depends on bringing all evidence together. Information from recorded history takes us back into time, and we must follow it as far as possible. A chain of reconstruction should begin as far back in time as history will permit. The location of all languages in a set gives a geographic pattern suggesting where they may have been located in a still earlier period. Thus the great linguistic diversity of the English of the British Isles compared with the much more homogeneous English of such large and discontinuous areas as the United States and Australia suggests a European origin for this language.

The archeologist compares the artifacts found in various prehistoric sites with each other and, whenever possible, with present-day and historical cultures. He also tries to find sequences of cultural similarity that can be inferred to represent successive periods of the same people. In a series of levels at a given site, gradual variation is inferred to mark a single culture in its natural development. If two successive levels are found to be very different, an immigration is understood to have taken place. The associated skeletal remains also can reflect the arrival of new populations.

Linguistic prehistory and other sciences of the past have many possible forms of operation, but the most effective is the use of all of them together. To know the past is not a simple task. But since it is the nature of human beings to desire to know, there can be no doubt that scholars will continue to work ever harder in this great undertaking.

References and Suggestions for Further Reading

[*For a general introduction to the methods and techniques of historical and comparative linguistics, see Bloomfield (1933), Hockett (1958), Lehmann (1962), and Sapir (1921). Hoenigswald (1960) is a more technical formulation. Swadesh's definition of the language community is essentially that of Bloomfield (1933). For a recent reformulation, see Hymes (1967). For the relationship between a language and its community of speakers as well as a description of speech usage, see Hymes (1967, 1968).*

Garvin (1964) reviews the concept of a standard language. A linguistic method for determining the degree of mutual intelligibility between dialects is presented in Voegelin and Harris (1951). For cultural factors involved in intelligibility, see Wolff (1964). The influence of social groupings on linguistic change is discussed in Weinreich, Labov, and Herzog (1968) as part of a presentation of a general theory of linguistic change. For bilingualism and languages in contact generally, see Macnamara (1967) and Weinreich (1953).

Bloomfield (1933) contains a good introduction to dialect geography. Hall (1966) discusses the structure and history of pidgins and creoles, as well as some aspects of their cultural background.

For the notion of basic vocabulary and its use in determining the time distance between dialects and languages, see Gudschinsky (1964) and Swadesh (1964a). For a general review of lexicostatistics and glottochronology, see Hymes (1960).

For some case studies of language extinction, see Swadesh (1948). For comparison of the family tree model of linguistic diversification with other models, see Bloomfield (1933), Southworth (1964) and Swadesh (1959). For use of linguistic information in reconstructing prehistory, see Sapir (1949) and Swadesh (1964b).]

Bloomfield, Leonard
1933.   *Language.* New York: Holt.
Fishman, Joshua A.
1968.   *Readings in the Sociology of Language.* The Hague: Mouton.
Garvin, Paul
1964.   "The Standard Language Problem: Concepts and Methods." In *Language in Culture and Society,* ed. Dell Hymes. New York: Harper & Row.
Gudschinsky, Sarah
1964.   "The ABC's of Lexicostatistics (Glottochronology)." In *Language in Culture and Society,* ed. Hymes.
Hall, Robert A., Jr.
1966.   *Pidgin and Creole Languages.* Ithaca: Cornell University Press.
Hockett, Charles, F.
1958.   *A Course in Modern Linguistics.* New York: Macmillan.
Hoenigswald, Henry
1960.   *Language Change and Linguistic Reconstruction.* Chicago: University of Chicago Press.

Hymes, Dell
  1960.   "Lexocostatistics So Far." *Current Anthropology* 1, No. 1:3–44.
  1967.   "Models of the Interaction of Language and Social Setting." In "Problems of Bilingualism," ed. John Macnamara. *Journal of Social Issues* 23, no. 2: 8–28.
  1968.   "The Ethnography of Speaking." In *Readings*, ed. Fishman.
Hymes, Dell, ed.
  1964.   *Language in Culture and Society*. New York: Harper & Row.
Lehmann, Winfred P.
  1962.   *Historical Linguistics: An Introduction*. New York: Holt.
Lehmann, W. P., and Malkiel, Yakov, eds.
  1968.   *Directions for Historical Linguistics*. Austin: University of Texas Press.
Mandelbaum, David G., ed.
  1949.   *Selected Writings of Edward Sapir*. Berkeley: University of California Press.
Sapir, Edward
  1921.   *Language*. New York: Harcourt, Brace.
  1949.   "Time Perspective in Aboriginal American Culture: A Study in Method." In *Selected Writings of Edward Sapir*, ed. Mandelbaum.
Southworth, Franklin C.
  1964.   "Family-Tree Diagrams." *Language* 40:557–65.
Swadesh, Morris
  1948.   "Sociologic Notes on Obsolescent Languages." *International Journal of American Linguistics* 14:226–235.
  1959.   "The Mesh Principle in Comparative Linguistics." *Anthropological Linguistics* 1, no. 2:7–14.
  1964a. "Diffusional Cumulation and Archaic Residue as Historical Explanations." In *Language in Culture and Society*, ed. Hymes.
  1964b. "Linguistics as an Instrument of Prehistory." In *Language in Culture and Society*, ed. Hymes.
Voegelin, C. F., and Harris, Z. S.
  1951.   "Methods for Determining Intelligibility Among Dialects of Natural Languages." *Proceedings of the American Philosophical Society* 45:322–29.
Weinreich, Uriel
  1953.   *Languages in Contact*. New York: Linguistic Circle of New York.
Weinreich, Uriel; Labov, William; and Herzog, Marvin
  1968.   "Empirical Foundations for a Theory of Language Change." In *Directions for Cultural Linguistics*, ed. Lehmann and Malkiel.
Wolff, Hans
  1964.   "Intelligibility and Inter-Ethnic Attitudes." In *Language in Culture and Society*, ed. Hymes.

TWO

Modern World Languages

[*Modern linguists have stressed the equality or equivalence of various languages (from the point of view of what the languages are capable of expressing) in order to counter earlier notions that some languages were inferior to or more primitive than others. It is true, however, that in certain ways languages spoken today do vary according to the type of culture or society in which they are used. Swadesh indicates mainly variations in size of vocabulary, but he also suggests some differences in lexical and grammatical structures. I might point out here that Swadesh is not arguing that contemporary languages are not cognitively equivalent. He is simply noticing that when one considers other functions of language in addition to the cognitive function—that is, all the many purposes for which a language is used by its speakers—certain differences become apparent. These differences are related to such factors as the number of people who speak the language, the social and technical complexity of the society, and the presence of a writing system.*

Thus, this chapter opens by pointing out that among languages spoken today there are representatives of the last three stages of language development: the local, *the* classic, *and the* world. *I have selected this terminology from several sets of alternatives with which Swadesh was apparently working. He had evidently not yet settled on any particular one. For "local," he also used the terms* folk *and* tribal; *for "classic,"* urban; *and for "world,"* metropolitan *and* superurban. *For the much earlier stages of language, he talks of the* eoglottic, paleoglottic, *and* neoglottic, *words formed by analogy with the archeological terms* eolithic, paleolithic, *and* neolithic. *The analogy is purely terminological, however; it is not meant to imply that the archeological and linguistic periods correspond chronologically.*

Swadesh goes on to demonstrate the characteristics (both sociocultural and linguistic) of world languages by discussing generally those language families that have given rise to such languages. The discussion of each of these language families includes such topics as the cultural and political histories of the peoples involved, including the migrations of the speakers of the descendant languages; the present geographic distribution of the languages of the family and the number of speakers; the type of writing

43

system employed; and the basic structural changes that the descendant languages have undergone (that is, a structural sketch comparing the contemporary languages with their ancestors or protolanguages). The focus on sociocultural factors, especially the presence of writing systems, reflects Swadesh's belief that these factors are related intimately to the rise of world languages. Swadesh considered a writing system to be essential to the development of language to the world stage. The reader will probably feel, as I do, that Swadesh intended to develop the grammatical-structural-historical sketches more fully. Even as they now stand, however, they provide the basis for the conclusions stated at the end of the chapter: that there are certain structural trends that can be identified as languages move from the local through the classic to the world stage.]

Stages of Language

Two thousand years ago there were about 250 million people in the whole world. Today there are over 300 million who speak English alone, and the entire world population is ten times greater. Man's way of life during the same period has changed enormously in some respects, but certain details are very much the same. As for language, it is in part what it was before and in part very different. Then there were no superhighways, vacuum cleaners, or bicycles, and there were no languages of 500,000 words. There were men versed in all the wisdom of their people, and who knew their language completely. Today there are outstanding experts in given fields who are quite ignorant of some others and who do not know the meaning of some of the words employed by others. A modern world language is the sum total of the usage of millions of people. Nobody, or practically nobody, possesses the language in its totality. In fact, it is a characteristic of our time that the wisest men make use of dictionaries, encyclopedias, manuals, and tables of reference to piece out their knowledge of the world and their own language. In the years still to come, dependence on extrahuman equipment in language use will surely be far greater. In the distant past, say ten thousand years ago, languages could have been quite different than they were in the recent past; a hundred thousand or a million years ago the differences must have been much more profound. Ten million years before our time, the forerunners of man communicated as do other species of animals. In that period they did not have language at all, but only a form of communicative behavior that would someday develop into language. Just when it reached this stage is one of the problems with which this book is concerned, but it seems evident from the changing nature of language that what we need is a sliding concept, a parameter, as the mathematicians say, and not a rigid measure.

For the last ten thousand years of human history, we may do well to recognize three main levels or stages of language: *world*, referring to the large complicated societies of recent times, like English, French, German, Russian, Arabic, Chinese, and Japanese; *classic*, referring to the classic stage of the city-states and the early empires: Latin, Greek, Egyptian, Hebrew, Persian, Sanskrit, and, in the New World, Nahuatl, Maya, and Quechua; and *local*, referring to the relatively dispersed societies of earlier times, before they developed permanent centers of government and trade. In our times it is possible to find representatives of the two earlier stages, classic and local, in peripheral isolated areas, but they have generally come under the influence of some of the large metropolitan cultures; there are inevitable reflexes of this situation in the way people speak the classic or local languages, and in the fact that in the marginal areas there are usually some individuals who also employ a world language, alternating between one and the other according to circumstances. There is thus interdependence between the classic or local and world languages.

When we go much further back in time, knowledge of the early characteristics of human speech is harder to come by. It seems probable that language developed along the same general lines as other aspects of human culture: very slowly at first and gradually faster and faster. In the area of toolmaking, a matter that can be followed through time on the basis of archeological finds, it has been noted that man first learned to split stones in order to obtain a sharp cutting edge; later to shape and sharpen his tools by taking off flakes from the first rough form; and finally to grind and polish stones into the desired shape. These three broad stages are given the names *eolithic*, or dawn stone age; *paleolithic*, or old stone age; and *neolithic*, or new stone age. From the last of these stages, man comes into the age of metal, and eventually into the scientific age. In the earliest stage, the hominids also used other tools, made of wood, bone, leaves, vines, and so on; but the eolith was, as it were, his most powerful tool. In the paleolithic era he was able to hunt much more effectively; he learned to fashion clothing, to do simple weaving, and to paint; in the neolithic era he acquired agriculture and pottery.

The eolithic period goes back at least 1.75 million years ago, and is associated with the old finds of *Australopithecus*, or southern ape, in eastern Africa. This kind of toolmaking continues for hundreds of thousands of years before the first flaking techniques appear, ushering in the paleolithic period. About 1.25 million years were required. The accelerated but still slow progress through the paleolithic period lasts a few hundred thousand years. Then comes the neolithic period, beginning, in some parts of the world, about ten thousand years ago. In just a few thousand years, we pass into the age of metals and then into modern industrial society.

If we assume that the development of language followed a similar course in man's history, we may suppose three successive stages, *eoglottic*, *paleoglottic*, and *neoglottic* (dawn tongue, old tongue, and new tongue), preceding the recent stages of local, classic, and world language. The periods of time must have been, as in the case of toolmaking, long for the first, shorter for the second, and relatively short for the most recent.

The greatest transformation in this development belongs to the last few centuries. During this period some populations have advanced tremendously, others have stayed where they were or decreased, and perhaps a thousand languages have gone out of use. Between the sixteenth century and the present, English broke out of its island limits and became the almost exclusive language of enormous areas, including most of North America and Australia and important areas in Africa, Asia, and the Pacific islands; Spanish, Portuguese, and French reached out to the Americas, and also to Africa and Asia; Dutch followed a similar trend for a while, but ended up with a more limited expansion; Russian spread through Asia; Chinese expanded in Asia and Oceania; and other languages grew in more limited degrees. One of the outstanding developments has been the establishment of certain languages as media of international trade, scientific interchange, and general communication over large portions of the world. These include particularly English, German, French, Spanish, Italian, Russian, Arabic, Chinese, and Japanese. Certain regional languages have also spread, such as Swahili in eastern and southern Africa, Hausa in western and central Africa, Malay in southeast Asia and nearby Oceania, and Tagalog in the Philippines.

Some of this outward pushing has been in the form of *creolized* versions of the respective languages. [*See the discussion of pidgin and creole languages in Chapter 1.*] Thus there arose the creolized French of Louisiana, Haiti, and some Caribbean islands; West African Portuguese and Spanish; Bazaar Malay in parts of the Indian Ocean; Pidgin English along the Asian coast and among the Pacific islands; and Taki-Taki in Surinam.

History rarely moves in a straight line, and neither does language in the period we are discussing. Dutch was once the main European tongue in what is now New York State. Into the sixteenth century, Quechua was used in South America as the native language of some millions of people, as the government language of the Incas, and, in a pidginized form, as a general trade language. After the Spanish conquest Quechua continued to serve as a lingua franca among Indians, and also became the medium for transacting the official business of the Spanish colonial government in South America and for spreading the Christian gospel. Something similar occurred in Mexico, where for a while Nahuatl, the language of the Aztecs, was adopted by the Spaniards as the best general medium of communication, and in eastern South America, where Tupi-Guarani was used. Eventually Spanish and Portuguese were generalized in these areas. Quechua and Nahuatl today are mostly regional, local languages, the first spoken by about 6 million people, the second by .75 million; Guarani is recognized as an official language, alongside Spanish, of one small country, Paraguay. On the other hand, certain classic languages have come forward as the official languages of new states, and have in some cases rapidly gained in importance and influence. An example is the rapid spread of Swahili in eastern Africa.

In this period of quick and violent change, few languages have escaped untouched; but the outstanding phenomenon has been the shaping of giant media of communication, attuned to the complex culture of our times.

Communication as Never Before

This is an age of great governments, of giant economic enterprises, laboratories, universities, libraries, printing plants, newspapers, telephone and telegraph networks, radio and television stations. There are coordinating societies and agencies that interlock many large component organizations. Each such institution is an organism that requires communication, both inward and outward, and some of them are specially formed to function as means of keeping people or organizations informed or in contact with each other. Some operate in a single language, while others operate in various languages or are specially designed to carry out the job of translation between or among languages. To do all the work required in so many institutions, a large number of people are specially trained in a variety of trades and professions. All this is a long way from the days of the local stage of language, when everyone was both speaker and messenger, and knew how to make and use a signal drum, mark a trail, and make gestures instead of speaking words when the situation called for it. If a person knew two or more languages, it was not because of any special course of study he had taken, but because of some accidental circumstance.

Not only were there no professional communications specialists, but in general there was very little division of labor except between the sexes. A man hunted and manufactured his weapons and tools. A woman looked after the children, prepared the food, and contrived or made her utensils. Some men and women had special abilities in certain activities, and were recognized for them; but rarely did any group have knowledge about things completely unknown to the rest of the band. Hence, the vocabulary of one was the vocabulary of all. By contrast, skills and knowledge today are endlessly divided. Even though everyone goes to school to learn many things, one never becomes familiar with everything. In his lifetime a person may change his trade or profession more than once, may acquire hobbies and interests, and may read constantly in books and periodicals that aim to stimulate his desire to learn; yet no one ever acquires the world's whole store of knowledge. And with this fact goes the parceling of language. In the supercommunities of the modern world, some people have smaller and some larger vocabularies, but no one knows all the words of his language. As a rule, each person understands many more expressions than he actually uses, but even passive knowledge rarely even remotely approaches 100 percent.

Reference works of many kinds are a hallmark of modern life. These include large and small dictionaries, encyclopedias, atlases, gazeteers, directories, manuals, guides, factbooks, instruction books, and notebooks.

Even top engineers use manuals of facts and formulas, and fine cooks keep fat cookbooks on a handy shelf to help recall old recipes or find new ones. The manufacture of filing equipment is a large industry, and the principal libraries are colossal. There are information agencies, research corporations, and great universities, dedicated to the assembling and dissemination of knowledge. Electronic computers are kept in service not only to calculate, but also to arrange and rearrange information so that it may be found quickly on need. Many experts all over the modern world are working on what are called information-retrieval systems, to make it possible to locate complicated facts with a minimum loss of time. Such equipment and procedures help modern science tackle complicated research in difficult fields.

There are obviously many advantages in modern specialization. It even simplifies getting born. In the first million and a half years of man's evolution when he developed from the near-human to the fully human state, the size of the brain increased with the growth of intelligence and the ability to accumulate knowledge. Moreover, as the brain grew, so did its container, the skull. From the invention of writing down to the present, however, and every day more and more, man has used facilities outside the brain for storing the knowledge he has accumulated through exercising his intelligence. Human mothers, unlike other mammals, sometimes have difficulty in giving birth because of the size of the baby's head. Better not to think how things would be if brain size had continued to grow in proportion to the sum of human knowledge!

The Course of Events

For convenience I have divided language development into various stages. The last three stages I call the local, classic, and world, covering approximately the last ten thousand years (since the first appearance of agriculture). There is considerable evidence that there were already a number of different languages in the world by the beginning of these last three stages of language. As man's awareness grew and as his own inventions made his world even more complicated, each language increased its vocabulary. How this took place is one of the key problems of this book, to be traced in part in the present chapter. Another and more difficult question is whether and to what extent the growth of vocabulary may have led to changes in phonetics and in structure.

In broad terms, the introduction of agriculture led to a settled life and eventually to the city-states and early empires of classic times, the period of what we are calling the classic stage of language development. As we begin to move into the modern period, the world stage, we find important theaters of cultural development in China, India, the Near East, and the Mediterranean. Trade and efforts at conquest keep these areas in touch with each other, and there is a great deal of interchange of products and ideas. Navigation becomes more and more important. The full-time search for knowledge becomes an important profession as universities arise and proliferate, supported by governments and religious organizations. With the industrial revolution, all these activities are heightened. Navigation becomes the means to carry products to new markets and to bring in raw materials for processing. New lands are sought and discovered. Each of them leads to the further growth of industry, adds to knowledge, and nourishes the thirst for more. Eventually even primitive areas beyond the old horizons of civilizations assume roles in the broadened cultural drama of increasing knowledge.

In Europe the universities have largely grown out of the old Roman tradition, which in its turn had built upon the Greek. The language of learning at first was Latin, and it was considered important to know Greek and Hebrew also. Only in the last few centuries did Latin cease to be the language of the classroom and of scholarly writing, and only in the present century has it become admissible to grant higher degrees to persons who have not studied Latin. Little wonder, then, that Western science has got into the habit of deriving its technical terms from Greek and Latin. In the old days every scholar could compose expressions in the classic languages. Today many of them search the dictionaries for the classic roots they need or consult with colleagues in departments of ancient languages.

For a long time three languages had the role of providing scholarly terms in Africa and Asia. These were Arabic, Sanskrit, and Chinese, each with its area of influence, with considerable overlapping. Eventually, there was a fusion of scholarly traditions. Arabic mathematical terms early came into the European tradition. Later some Sanskrit terms entered the technical vocabularies of grammar and philosophy, and even a few Chinese terms are coming into use. In most of the sciences, the Latin and Greek usage of the West has spread to the East, as well as to America, Africa, and Australia; this gives a considerable degree of internationality to the technical vocabularies.

But by no means have all the new vocabulary elements of modern languages been drawn from classic languages. Many have come from the far corners of the world, particular names of plants and animal species, of fruits and vegetables, and of typical artifacts, foods, and customs. *Skunk* comes from Algonkian of North America, *chocolate* and *tomato* from Nahuatl of Mexico, *condor* from Quechua, *kayak* from Eskimo, *kimono* from Japanese, *okapi* from Congolese, and *taboo* from Tongan in the Philippines. In the process of borrowing, the form of the word may be modified, and even the meaning may change. *Quinine*, for instance, is spelled and pronounced with *qu* because it comes to us through Spanish, in which these letters are used for a simple *k* sound before front vowels, but the original Quechua was *kina*, and its meaning was "bark." *Jaguar*, in Tupi, is used for any beast of prey, and the word *punch* for a beverage of mixed fruit juices comes from the

Hindi word for "five." Another source of new words has been proper names, especially of places and of men. *Tangerine* comes from the city of Tangiers; *china* from the country of the same name; and *cravat* from Croat, a native of Croatia. Three terms used in electricity come from the names of Watt, Volta, and Ohm, an English, an Italian, and a German scientist, respectively; a *pullman*, a railroad car with beds, comes from the name of the manufacturer.

A great many new words are formed out of the established elements of the language, by rearrangement into new combinations or by the acquisition of new meanings. Often an expression peculiar to a limited region comes into general use elsewhere. Or a slang or colloquial innovation may become established. Professional writers and advertising men may originate new words, or help to popularize words formerly used only by some limited segment of the population. Scholars and inventors, who in an earlier day would invariably have adopted classic expressions, today frequently take the names for their discoveries from the common language. In this respect there has been an important change in the recent period. Beginning around the tenth century, the idea of general education began to be entertained, and movements were begun to develop literature in the regional languages. Notions of nationalism began to develop, with cultural and political consequences. In some countries national academies were established to encourage literature in the language of the people and to promote scholarship in order to increase national prestige. One of the issues in the Protestant religious movement was the translation of the Bible and other church literature into the common languages. All this made for the development of modern vocabularies, both by adapting the classic terms to the phonetics of each tongue and by giving currency to native expressions. Part of the general movement was the compilation and publication of dictionaries.

As a result of the rise of national languages, many new expressions became available. Scholars made it a point to learn the languages of their neighbors, and diplomats, instead of transacting their business in Latin, had to acquire the languages of other nations. It became a sign of culture to be able to interlard, in speech and in writing, expressions from languages other than one's own. Under these circumstances, the basis was laid for the liberal borrowing of expressions by one language from another.

In various parts of Europe and Asia, common trends in vocabulary growth developed among related languages, spoken by people located side by side or otherwise in close contact. Thus the vocabularies of various Germanic languages in northern Europe grew in the same general direction, as did the Slavic languages in the east, and the Romance languages in the south and west. In India and in China, the regional languages were similarly related to each other. A new expression formed in one language of a close-knit family can easily pass into others, either as an easily understood loan word or by a new parallel formation out of cognate elements.

Some of these language families could make use of an older classic language, similar to all of them, as a source of new expressions. Thus when new expressions were taken by the Romance languages from classic Latin, by the Slavic languages from Old Church Slavic, and by the modern Indic languages from Sanskrit, the new forms generally bore some resemblance to words already in use. This meant that even the common people could learn them quite easily, a fact that has played a role in vocabulary growth.

Before we leave the question of word sources, it is necessary to mention two wholly recent means of forming compounds, of which one was impossible in the preliterate ages and the other undocumented before recent times. Both techniques are based on abbreviation; one uses the initial letters of the spelled form, the other uses key syllables. They are applied principally to names, both of people and of organizations, but also to things and substances. One of the most familiar letter words is *TNT*, which is used much more frequently than *trinitrotoluene*, on which it is based; other examples are *DDT, TV, TB, M.D.*, and *Ph.D.* Sometimes, if the letter group contains vowels adequately distributed, they are read phonetically (NATO); and the names of organizations are often purposely chosen to permit such readings of their abbreviations (Volunteers in Service to America, which conveniently becomes VISTA). The technique of forming a compound from key syllables of its component words is used more frequently in Russian than in English. *Kolhoz* is abbreviated from *kolektivicheskoe hozyaystvo*, collective economy; *Comintern* and *Politburo* work so well in English, as well as in Russian, that no translation is necessary.

The increasing ease with which information can be diffused in the modern period is only partly related to efficiency of travel; it also owes a great deal to technical devices for dealing with linguistic material. Printing with movable metal type was the first great opening wedge. Based on Chinese block printing, this technique was wonderfully adaptable to alphabetic systems of writing, since only a comparatively few signs are required. It has tremendous advantages over the old procedure of copying documents by hand. Before printing was invented, a man took weeks or months to copy a single book; with the development of the printing press, even in its first primitive form, a few men working together could make thousands of copies in the same time or less. Little wonder, then, that printing spread so quickly. Introduced around 1430, it was in use everywhere in Europe within about thirty years, and from there it spread through the world.

The factors of change affected each language in a different degree. When we discount the profusion of synonyms for stylistic reasons, the size of vocabularies is a fair index of how far languages have developed. Another touchstone is the extent to which they are used in higher education and all forms of advanced research. By these measures, perhaps the only true giants of our time are English, Russian, French, German, Italian, and Japanese.

The scientists and technicians using these languages often consult publications in other tongues, but are able to take all their notes and discuss their problems in their own. On a second level of development is a language used in many fields, but not in all, at least not up to the present. Among such languages are Chinese, Spanish, Arabic, and Hungarian. Some languages are moving rapidly to raise their level of usage; others accept a lesser level on a more or less permanent basis, taking it for granted, for example, that their more important discoveries ought to be published in some more widespread language. In order to obtain a clear review of the present trends, it will be worthwhile to survey a number of the major languages of our time.

[*At this point there is a shift of focus, from a general presentation of the notion of stages in language to a discussion of the various world languages spoken today.*]

English and Its Sisters

When the children of Rome's best families were studying grammar, geometry, and astronomy with Greek schoolmasters, there lived, in a large territory beyond the Alps, a number of unlettered tribes collectively called Teutons. Tacitus described them as hard-working and brave. As the empire expanded, Rome fought the Teutons, then made pacts with them and hired them as soldiers. By the time the empire weakened, the Teutons were skilled and well armed, and some of the tribes struck southward, becoming dominant at various times in parts of Spain, Italy, and some eastern regions. Eventually the Teuton kings lost their power and their people were absorbed in the general population. The westernmost Teutons, known as the Franks, gave their name to France, but ended up speaking the Romance language of that area. In its own area, however, Teutonic speech continued.

Scholars today call the Teutonic language group Germanic. Around the time of Christ there may have been three main regional variations: eastern, western, and northern. The first, generally known as Gothic, continued to be spoken by one last group in Crimea until about the seventeenth century, then disappeared. The western type eventually gave rise to a series of new variations, which are by now fairly noticeable. There are very marked differences in pronunciation as one goes, say, from Holland and northern Germany to Switzerland or Austria, but the basic vocabularies remain moderately close. In the sixth to eighth centuries, some northern bands settled in England. In the course of time their speech drifted apart from that of their brothers in the old country, perhaps more in vocabulary than in pronunciation. The north Germanic variants continued to be spoken in Denmark, Norway, and Sweden, and the community members retained sufficient contact with each other so that their speech is still fairly similar in all parts of the area. Migrants settled in Iceland in the ninth century, and Icelandic is today the most divergent form of Norse. Curiously, the language of this small group has remained quite close to the written form of the old language as it is preserved in its old literature. Another migration carried "Northmen" to France, where they gave their name to Normandy and became its rulers; but they soon gave up their Germanic speech for French.

The Germanic colonists in England fought the Celts there to win the right to stay and later had to defend themselves against Norse raiders. In the eleventh century they were defeated by the French-speaking Normans, and they remained under Norman rule for about two centuries. Later they built up their maritime power and were one of the leading nations in the exploration and conquest of the New World. Still later they gained a foothold in India. When in later centuries England lost its control of the United Colonies, it had already given them its language. England also settled Australia and New Zealand and won control over various territories in Asia and Africa. Eventually various territories had to be granted their independence, but by then the English language had become well entrenched in each of them, and it is likely they will continue to use it. In some areas, especially east Asia, Oceania, and Australia, English became known to people of many native languages in a pidginized form that is still much used.

From the time of the earliest knowledge of Germanic speech, some of the localisms became more pronounced while others diminished or disappeared. In the course of time certain forms came to be used more and more in writing, and became the bases for standardized languages. In the early centuries, every duchy or city-state had its local form of speech, but eventually a few came to be generally accepted. When Luther translated the Bible into German in the sixteenth century, he chose the language of the Saxon court as a convenient norm, but added vocabulary elements from other areas when necessary. The language of the Luther Bible became the basis of standard German. In the Netherlands another type was adopted, in England a third, in Denmark, a fourth. Later Swedish was added. And finally, when Norway separated from Denmark, an effort was made to replace the imperial language, the *Riksmål*, by something based on local speech, known as *Landsmål*. Counting Icelandic, then, there are seven official Germanic languages today. Of these, Norwegian and Danish are almost the same, and Swedish is not very different from them. German and Dutch are rather different in pronunciation, but the vocabularies are only moderately distinct. English is about equally distinct from Scandinavian and German; in the pronunciation of the common words, it is perhaps closest to Scandinavian and furthest from standard German. In the colloquial speech forms there is least variation in the Scandinavian countries, a fair amount in the country speech of England, and a great deal as one goes from west to east or from north to south in the Dutch- and German-speaking areas. And yet, even in this last area, the differences generally appear gradually. English shows less variation overseas than in the home country. In India, one of the largest English-speaking populations has a pronunciation all its own, influenced by Hindi-Urdu and other languages, and a vocabulary with many special items. Similar but far less localism is found in other countries, including the Philippines, Malaysia, and the West Indies, as well as Australia, South Africa, Canada, and the United States.

In number of speakers, two Germanic languages, English and German, are among the world leaders, 300 million and 100 million respectively. Dutch is spoken by 17 million, the Scandinavian tongues by a total of 20 million.

English and German are among the languages with the largest vocabularies, especially English, because of unusual profusion of near synonyms. The comparatively small vocabularies in the other languages are related to the fact that they are used in smaller areas, with consequently fewer differences in regional products, customs, and usage. In the earliest period of Germanic speech, it already contained loan words from Celtic, Latin, and Greek. As time went on, the borrowings from book Latin and Greek began to increase, and they were added in roughly the same way in all the Germanic areas. When the Angles, Saxons, and Jutes went to England, they took new words from the Celtic languages there. With the Norse raids and subsequent settlement, Scandinavian forms came in, and the Normans brought in abundant French. Then came a large sprinkling of terms from all over the world, including especially France and Italy, in addition to the other Germanic languages.

The alphabets of the Germanic languages were based on the Latin one, with the addition of the small letters. The angular Gothic version of the letters was used in Germany up to the present century, but it is now definitely on the wane. The rounded type of letter has been the main form in England from the beginning of printed texts. There have been problems regarding spelling. The tendency was to keep close to classical spellings of Greek and Latin derivatives even when the pronunciation was different. In England there were Anglo-Saxon and French-based traditions, at variance with each other in many details. William Caxton, who introduced printing there, felt that each word should have one and only one spelled form, chosen from among those current at the time. Consistency for each individual word was obtained, but consistency among different words was disregarded. To make matters worse, sweeping changes in the pronunciation of the vowel sounds took place after the fixing of orthography. As a result, English today has the most difficult spelling of any written language in the world. In the other Germanic countries, greater efforts were made to bring spelling back into harmony with the spoken sounds. One cannot always tell from the sound of a German word how to spell it, but at least one always knows how to pronounce the written or printed word. In English, one can neither spell from the sound nor sound from the spelling. In the English-speaking countries a child needs more time to learn to read than in other countries with comparable schools.

In the historically known period, the Germanic languages have undergone considerable changes in structure. One that applies to all of them has to do with the role of vowel and accent alternations. Old Germanic used replacement of the vowels to express tense in a long list of verbs. The process is still operative, but the number of elements to which it applies has been reduced, especially in English. The *-ed* ending of verbs like *work, walk, talk,* and so on is now felt to be the "regular" past-tense formation, while the vowel alternation of *eat-ate, come-came, see-saw,* and so on is felt to be irregular. Furthermore, the borrowing of so many new verbs to which the old process was not extended has meant that verbs in which vowels are interchanged now form a small proportion of the total number. Again, vowel changes were used to differentiate derived nouns from their verbs, a process still reflected in words like *wrath,* originally related to *writhe,* and *song,* which came from *sing.* This type of variation has lost ground, but a new one has developed in connection with classic Latin borrowings, as in *divide* and *division,* pronounced with different sounds even though the same letter is employed in the orthography. An extension of vowel alternation came in during the early Germanic period as a result of the presence of a palatal suffix in the plural of some nouns and the causative of some verbs; thus *men* from old *manniz,* and *to fell* from *falyan.* A new feature due to borrowing is the great increase in derivative suffixes from Latin and Greek: *-al, -ary, -ive, -ist, -ism, -ine, -tude, -tion, -ment, -ery* (Latin *-aria*), *-ize* and others. Most of these require accent shifts and with them sometimes modification of the vowels. The "classical" suffixes have also been extended to roots of Germanic origin, leading to such words as *fishery* and *hatchery.*

In old Germanic, the verb indicated person by means of endings in the present tense. Except for the irregular verb *to be* and the third person singular, this process has been lost in English. An old distinction between singular and plural of the past has disappeared except in *was-were* and *has-have.* Substantives formerly showed case by means of their endings. Apart from the possessive, this no longer applies in English, Dutch, and Scandinavian, except in the pronouns (*he-him*). Gender distinctions in the noun have been lost in English; two genders are still used in Scandinavian, and all three— masculine, feminine, and neuter—are retained in German.

Nouns formerly could be used without any form of demonstrative, and if a demonstrative was used it could precede or follow the noun, according to emphasis. Today all the Germanic languages require the presence of a form of demonstrative, known as the definite article, in many constructions. Interestingly, it precedes the noun in English, Dutch, and German, but follows it in Scandinavian.

The Romance Languages

A few centuries before Christ, according to the earliest records, a number of languages were spoken in Italy. The one associated with the most advanced culture was Etruscan. There were also Ligurian, Celtic, and Venetic in the north; in the south there were Oscan, Umbrian, and Latin-Faliscan, three closely related languages. Greek-speaking colonies were located along the coast.

Rome, which acquired the art of writing and many other cultural traits from the Etruscans, prospered as a trading center on the Tiber, and around 300 B.C. began to extend its power in Italy and throughout the Mediterranean area. Later it spread northward through much of Europe. The influence of Rome spread at first through trade, then through military and political dominance. Later the Christian religion was added, and continued as a force in Europe after the empire collapsed in the fifth century. Thus Latin continued to spread and became the principal language of France, the Iberian peninsula, Italy, and Dalmatia, but regionalisms began to take form. Religious and lay scholars tried to maintain the archaic form of the language, while popular speech went its own way. In time people came to distinguish between the Latin of the scholar and the Romanic or Romance of the common people. Charlemagne urged the use of popular Romance for education and religion so that the people could understand with ease. In the course of time, the local forms of Romance came to differ notably from each other. Eventually the forms that attained literary and political importance included French, Provençal, Catalan, Galician and Portuguese, Italian, and Romanian. At the present time the leading Romance languages are Spanish, with 145 million speakers, mostly in Spain and the New World; Portuguese, with 85 million in Portugal and Brazil; French, with 65 million; Italian, with 55 million; and Romanian, with 20 million.

In the process of spreading territorially, Latin evidently became for a while more uniform than it had been earlier, probably as a result of the acquisition of a city vocabulary by legionnaires from rural areas and vice versa. Some expressions fell out of use or were restricted to a special meaning. An example of this process is reflected in the use today of modern forms of *caballus*—French *cheval*, Spanish *caballo*, Italian *cavallo*—for "horse," in place of the classic *equus*; the feminine form of the latter, *equa*, is conserved in Spanish *yegua*, mare. There is also evidence for a certain amount of evening out of pronunciation and structure. This kind of partial uniformity is evident in Spanish and Portuguese as they spread through the New World in a later period, just as it also happened in English and other languages that have spread to new areas. It is the opposite of regional differentiation. Its cause is the throwing together of once separated populations as they become organized into military units, ships' crews, political, religious, or commercial missions, and the like, and as they find it necessary in their activities to make themselves understood by people from other parts. Once there were sizable Latin-speaking populations stabilized in the various regions, the process of local differentiation set in once again, until modern urban mobility gave rise to a new movement toward uniformity.

In the early centuries of the Roman Empire it would have been impossible to predict which Romance regionalisms would become the basis for the eventual standard languages. In fact, the wheel of historical chance moved round and round, pointing first in one direction, then in another, before finally coming to rest where it did. In Spain, for example, the Galician kings were once dominant, and the language of their region was correspondingly favored and extended in use. Later it was Catalonia that was dominant, and only around the fifteenth century did the language settle and stay with Castile. The domination of the whole southern region by the Arabs between the eighth and the thirteenth centuries was a large factor, both because it prevented a southern type of Spanish from gaining ascendency and because it was the acid test of the northern rulers. The prince who showed strength against the Moors gained in influence, and it was the victory of Alfonso VIII of Castile that led to the development of Madrid as the center of Spanish political life and culture. Similar influences in each of the other countries determined the emergence of its dominant speech form.

Latin had several centuries of adhesive development before any serious local differentiation took place. Even today, speakers of different Romance languages can understand each other to a fair degree without special training. Romanian stands somewhat apart from the rest because of reduced contacts. Apart from early political separation, there is the geographic fact that non-Romance languages, like Albanian and Serbian, are located between Romania and the others.

The anciently established tradition of writing in Latin has played a role in linguistic history. At least learned men were in constant contact with the classic language, and from them archaic expressions passed into general usage. Although variations developed in the adaptation of written Latin to the particular needs of each language, the variant forms remained roughly similar, and this facilitated interchange among languages. Even new words that came into some of the languages from overseas contacts could easily pass from one language to the next.

Despite these favorable factors, regional variation did eventually take place. Some of the regional variations subsequently found their way into the standard language. When Romance languages spread to the New World, numerous new words were taken from the local populations. Many new terms remained largely local, used mostly in the regions of their adoption, while others reached the homeland and continued to spread from there. The extension of Romance to the New World did not necessarily create new languages. With all their localisms, American Spanish and Brazilian Portuguese continued in full contact with their respective language communities and traditions in the Old World; and Canadian French is still today close to continental French. Nor is it to be expected that the future will change this situation, because international contacts are even easier today than they were in past centuries.

Before any serious diversification in the Romance languages had taken place, the old structure of Latin had undergone considerable modification. One notable change was the simplification of the nominal inflection. In Romanian, the six old cases were reduced to three: general, dative, and vocative. In the western languages, the case distinctions were completely lost. The new general case is based on the old accusative. Some of the functions of the declensional endings were taken over by prepositions. The pronouns and demonstratives, however, retained some of the cases of the old system.

The three genders of Latin were everywhere reduced to two, masculine and feminine, with most neuters becoming masculine. The distinction between singular and plural has also been retained, but the endings were simplified. In French and the Iberian languages, the ending -s for the plural was extended to all substantives, while in Italian and Romanian certain final vowels mark the difference.

The old verbal categories are retained fairly well, but the manner of expressing them has changed in part. This came about through the use of phrases containing auxiliary verbs to form expressions approximately equivalent to certain of the tenses. Eventually the auxiliary adhered to the stem as though it were an ending and the new suffixed formations took over the function of the old-style tenses. Endings to distinguish person and number of the subject have held up quite well, except in spoken French, in which most of the verb inflections indicating the grammatical persons sound alike. In compensation for this, French requires the use of independent pronouns with the verb.

The article, though nonexistent in classical Latin, is required in the modern Romance languages. In Romanian it comes at the end of the noun phrase; in the western Romance languages, at the beginning. Thus Romanian *poporul* is equivalent to French *le peuple* and Italian *il popolo*, the people. In similar fashion, Romanian postpones the possessive pronoun, as in *poporul meu*, equivalent to French *mon peuple* and Italian *il mio popolo*, my people. It is evident that both of the two orders are derived from Latin, since in classic times the demonstratives and possessives could optionally precede or follow the noun. It happened that Romanian usage became fixed on one of the possibilities while the other languages chose the other.

In various ways the modern languages are less flexible in the order of components than classical Latin was. Formerly any adjective could either precede or follow the noun. Today there are a certain number of adjectives that convey different meanings if they precede the noun than they do if they follow it. In French, for instance, *un homme grand* means "a tall man" while *un grand homme* means "a great man."

Slavic

Much less is known about the early history of Slavic than about Romance or

Germanic languages, but it is clear that the Slavic is a linguistic family of somewhat similar divergence. From the sixth century there are reports of western, eastern, and southern Slav tribes, all speaking the same language. This probably means that the local differences were small. In the ninth century Cyril and Methodius were sent as missionaries to Moravia, present-day Czechoslovakia. Their translation of the Bible was evidently understood by all the Slavs. It was written in an alphabet called Cyrillic, based principally on the Greek but with some characters modeled after Latin and Hebrew. Later Latin-based alphabets were introduced for Croatian, Czech, and Polish, under the influence of the Roman Catholic church or its Lutheran Protestant offshoot.

From about the thirteenth century on, the Slavic regional forms were sufficiently diverse to establish and maintain separate literatures. At the same time, they were sufficiently similar so that contact among the various groups was easy to maintain. Greek borrowings constantly entered the speech and writings of the groups allied to the Orthodox church, while Latinisms came in through the Roman church and through the universities. Furthermore, the eastern Slavs were in contact with various Turkish languages; the western Slavs were likewise in touch with Germans; and the southern ones were in contact with Italians. At a certain stage there were influences from French and English. Invasions from the east at various times overran parts of Slavic territory, and the Russians later expanded eastward. All these movements left their imprints on the Slavic vocabularies.

Possibly because of the circumstances under which the concepts of nationality developed among them, Slavic peoples maintained separate literary traditions to a greater degree than the Germanic groups have done, with the exception of the Scandinavian branch. Although they are considered separate languages in Czechoslavakia, Czech and Slovak are nearly alike, and both use the Roman alphabet. Similarly, Bulgarian and Macedonian, using Cyrillic, though considered distinct, are quite similar. Serb and Croatian (spoken in Yugoslavia) are more disparate in their respective alphabets, Cyrillic and Roman, than in anything else. For purposes of advanced science and technology, some of the Slavic languages are little used, others more so, and Russian most of all. Learning to read another Slavic language is no difficult task for any Slav, and there are adequate educational facilities for the purpose.

In linguistic literature the Slavic languages are grouped in three geographic subdivisions: eastern, including Ukrainian, Belorussian, and Russian; western, with Polish and Czechoslovak; and southern, with Serbo-Croatian, Bulgarian, and Macedonian. The classification can be supported by some phonologic isoglosses, but in vocabulary the languages shade into each other in network or chain fashion.

Structurally, from its earliest known forms Slavic has had and has largely kept a fairly extensive noun inflection and a moderately inflected verb. Only

Bulgarian and Macedonian have lost the nominal cases and have adopted prepositions to carry the function of the old instrumental and dative cases. The Slavic verb distinguishes between perfective and imperfective, or durative and momentaneous, and between simple and repetitive aspects, expressed by verbal prefixes and suffixes. Present and future are indicated by imperfective and perfective aspects of the same set of forms, with the same personal endings. Compound nouns are built on a plan similar to that of Greek and Latin.

Other Indo-European Languages

The three groups of languages we have taken up, Germanic, Romance, and Slavic, are distantly related to each other in the superfamily, or *phylum*, called Indo-European. This relationship goes back to a period when they were all one language, with, of course, regional variations. With the relationship go many similarities of vocabulary and structure. Thus, in tracing their development in the recent period, we have in each case started with a certain general type of noun and verb inflection, fairly well retained at its older level, but generally simplified in Germanic and Romance. Several other Indo-European languages remain to be taken up at this point.

Latvian and Lithuanian belong to the Baltic division of Indo-European, resembling Germanic in some features of phonetics and vocabulary, but otherwise closer to Slavic. They have preserved the use of final -*s* in the nominative singular of masculine nouns and so are strongly reminiscent of classical Latin and Greek; this can be strikingly shown with an example like Lithuanian *plonas*, thin, corresponding to Latin *planus*, flat. The Baltic languages are generally conservative in their inflection, and conserve old tonal accents that correspond in general with the classic Greek differentiation of acute and circumflex. About a million people speak Latvian and three million Lithuanian. In the thirteenth century the Lithuanian tribes were consolidated to fight off the Livonian and Teutonic knights, and in the subsequent two centuries Lithuania became a political power dominating a large area. It developed in close association with Poland and adopted Roman Catholic Christianity. Other relations brought it into contact with German, Russian, and neighboring languages of the Finno-Ugric family, especially Estonian. The Latvian and Lithuanian alphabets are Latin-based. The languages are employed for all purposes up to the most advanced aspects of science and technology, which depend to some extent on foreign sources, formerly German and French, now principally Russian.

Greek, which today has ten million speakers, has one of the longest continuous literate traditions in the world. After some early beginnings of writing, the most notable being the type called Linear B, of Cyprus, an adaptation of Phoenician writing was introduced. The continuous literary tradition begins in the fifth century B.C. At first writing was done in several local variants of Greek, but a unified form, the *koine*, which means "common," developed and spread, beginning around the first century B.C. The political power of Greece spread over a large part of the world under Alexander in the fourth century, but later it was in turn dominated by Rome. Still, the Romans held Greek civilization in high esteem and sought to be educated by Greeks, either in Athens itself or in Rome. Early Greek culture was enriched by knowledge of other lands as a result of navigation and commerce, and was strengthened by political control in the Alexandrian empire. This brought many foreign words into use. Even after Greece came under the political hegemony of Rome, it still continued to be active commercially. Eventually Greece regained an independent and dominating position as the center of the Orthodox Christian churches. It was at the same time a crossroad for East and West, receiving influences from both sides. Greece lagged behind western Europe in the industrial revolution, but there was never any serious problem about acquiring new vocabulary. The general bases for word borrowing had been laid in earliest times. Then the structural similarity between Greek and Latin permitted easy transfer of any expression from one to the other.

Written Greek has clung to the tradition of the ancient language down to the present. Although there have been many changes in pronunciation, for the most part the words are still spelled as they were before. This leads to no greater problem than some of those we know in English spelling. In fact, the difficulties are fewer, since at least one can infer the modern pronunciation from the ancient spelled form, even though one cannot always spell correctly from the sound. There is a problem in vocabulary, since some of the archaic words have fallen out of popular use, and the meanings associated with words have often changed. As a result, a compromise revision of Greek has developed in newspapers and in other publications intended for mass consumption. The main variation has been in the avoidance, to some degree, of expressions that will not be generally understood.

The Indic languages number a dozen, each spoken by at least a million people, for a total of more than 400 million, roughly a tenth of the world population. Of these, 165 million are classed as speakers of Hindi and 20 million as speakers of Urdu. Hindi is the leading language of India; Urdu is the official language of Pakistan. Since they are mutually intelligible, we can sum the two figures. Thus Hindi-Urdu, with 185 million speakers, is the third-ranking language in the world, preceded only by Mandarin and English and followed by Spanish and Russian. Other important Indic languages are Bengali with 85 million speakers, Marathi with 35 million, Punjabi with 37 million, and Gujarati with 22 million. Oriya, Rajastani, Nepali, Sinhalese, and Assamese follow, in that order. In modern advanced usage, only Hindi-Urdu comes close to matching the major languages in the world stage and perhaps has some likelihood of being rounded out fully in the future. Up to the present, while India has top scientists in practically all fields, they consult publications and often write in foreign languages, especially English. As for literature, history, and philosophy, most of the Indic languages have rich traditions.

There is an old writing tradition in Indic that comes down from the ancient Sanskrit, with a literature dating to about 1200 B.C. In dramatic compositions written about the time of Christ, the common people are represented as speaking in variant forms of language, known as *prakrits*; this term means "early-made, original, natural," and contrasts with *Sanskrit*, which means "together-made, elaborated, perfected." Thus it is evident both that there were speech variants in very early times and that Sanskrit was regarded as something special. So it has remained through all these centuries, and it is still considered a necessary part of the education of scholars and religious persons. It also serves these people as a lingua franca, in the way that Latin formerly did in Europe, and has been the source of technical terms, like Latin and Greek in the West.

The writing used for the Indic languages *(devanagari)* is a variant of an earlier system, based on Semitic. It is a consonantal writing, but with additions to show the vowels. Forms of writing derived from it are used in the non-Indic languages of southeast Asia, including the Dravidian languages, Burmese and Thai.

Early Sanskrit already shows loan words from Dravidian. The oldest writings are of legendary history, philosophy, and religion. Later there are also literary and grammatical works, the latter intended to teach the proper use of the language. In the second half of the sixth century, Buddha, "the Awakened," began his preaching, which formed the basis of one of the chief religions of Asia. Buddhism gave rise to a continuing religious and moral literature, much of it in Sanskrit, and to a movement of missionaries between India and many other countries. Together with trade and warfare, this gave rise to much cultural and lexical interchange.

India attracted many conquerors and would-be conquerors, beginning with the Indic tribes themselves. Then came Alexander, as far as north India, in the fourth century. Later came Moslems, Mongols, Persians, and finally Europeans. In response to the invasions and in between them, native states developed, with their rulers, capitals, and cultural drives. Sanskrit continued to be the main native written language in most parts of India until the sixteenth century, when the local languages began to be used extensively in written form for literature and for political and business affairs. In north-central India two separate traditions developed, one with Hindu leanings, the other with Moslem. This separation accounts for the Indic and Arabic scripts used by Hindus and Moslems, and for the fact that Hindus preferred Sanskrit and Moslems Arabic as the source for new terms. Under British rule, English was the language of commerce and industry, and also was used in the schools. After partitioned independence, Pakistan continued to accept English as the principal language of advanced education but some Indian political leaders conceived plans for eventually replacing it by Hindi. This idea has met considerable resistance in the southern, Dravidian-speaking parts of India. At the present time, it is impossible to predict whether the change-over will be achieved.

Grammatically, Hindi shows considerably less inflection than Sanskrit. The substantive distinguishes only two genders, masculine and feminine. It has a plural, but has lost the ancient dual. As for cases, though there are substitute devices, based on the employment of postpositions, which are sometimes called "cases," there are only two actual variations of the stem, which may be described as *direct* and *oblique*. There is some verbal inflection formed by the variation of endings, but distinctions of tense, moods, and voice are indicated more often by the use of auxiliaries than by inflection.

The Iranian division of Indo-European includes several languages, of which Persian (Farsi) is the most important, with fifteen million speakers; others include Afghan or Pashto, with about fourteen million, and Kurd, with five million. There was an ancient language in this group, called Old Persian, used in the Avesta and other Zoroastrian writings and in the monuments of the Persian kings. It was represented in a cuneiform writing, based on the Assyrian. After the seventh century, Moslem religion and culture dominated the area known today as Iran. The modern literary tradition began in the ninth century in an Arabic-based alphabet. Omar Khayyam wrote in it in the eleventh century. In recent centuries Iran has come under the domination of European countries. Most of its technical literature is written in Western languages, especially English and French.

In adjoining parts of Soviet Armenia and Turkey there are some four million speakers of another Indo-European language, Armenian. Written in an independent alphabet specially designed for it around the fifth century, it has a long-standing literature on both religious and lay subjects. It is the language of higher education and scholarship in matters of history and philology, but usually not in advanced technology and the natural sciences. The vocabulary has Semitic, Persian, and Greek elements, which have been in use for many centuries.

In the small Balkan country of Albania and in neighboring Yugoslavia, there are about three million speakers of an independent Indo-European language, Albanian. It is written in a Latin alphabet. The vocabulary has many Latin borrowings, and some from Turkish, Arabic, and other languages.

The Celts in ancient times played an important role in European history, but their languages were largely eliminated by Romance and Germanic tongues. The members of this division of the Indo-European phylum that are still used today include Breton (in France) and Welsh and Gaelic (in the British Isles). Gaelic is the official language of the Irish Republic, and with the winning of Irish independence in 1921 the government attempted to reestablish it in general use, but by that time English had come to be used by most of the population, and it still is.

Semitic Languages

The Semitic language of Akkad, known as Akkadian or Assyrian, was one of the first languages to be written. This writing began about 3000 B.C. and continued for many centuries. It employed the wedge-shaped or cuneiform type of script, learned from the Sumerians. Assyrian contains a great number of Sumerian words.

The next Semitic languages known to be written were Phoenician and Hebrew. The Phoenicians taught the Greeks to write and established cities as far west as Spain, but eventually they disappeared. Hebrew was the language of the Old Testament, whose earliest manuscript dates from the third century B.C., though parts of it evidently were composed as early as the tenth century. Hebrew continued to be a language of religion and scholarship among the Jews until the recent present, when it was artifically restored to the status of a national language in Israel, and is spoken today by more than a million people. Although foreign languages, especially English, are widely used by scholars and technicians in Israel, there are efforts to make Hebrew adequate to all modern needs. Much scholarly study has gone into this task. The tendency has been to use Hebrew compounds in preference to loan words, but still the latter are not excluded.

Apart from the religious and scholarly tradition, Hebrew went out of use before the time of Christ. It was replaced in Palestine by Aramaic. To the south other Semitic languages were spoken, and out of these there came the beginning of the Arabic literary tradition around the third century after Christ. Besides vocabulary that had come into Semitic in the distant past, Arabic received Greek and Latin expressions by way of Aramaic, and Persian ones from the east. The first Arabic literature was apparently courtly poetry. In the seventh century Mohammed began to preach and formed the theocratic state that was to grow and grow in the following centuries, spreading the Arabic language through several countries as the general medium of communication, and to many others as a vehicle of religion and scholarship. Arabic-speaking countries today include Saudi Arabia, Iraq, Syria, Egypt, Libya, Morocco, Tunisia, and Sudan. The combined Arabic-speaking population is around ninety million, including communities in many non-Arabic countries where the Arabic language and traditions are generally maintained. The language is also studied by non-Arabs for its religious and cultural values.

After long being a cultural leader, the Arabic world lagged behind and came under the domination of European power. Lately it has come full force into the modern epoch. At present the Arabic countries make considerable use of modern technical and scientific publications in French and English, but are coming more and more to express the same ideas in Arabic. New loan words are much used. The standard for literary Arabic in other matters is based on the Koran. Spoken Arabic departs from this standard in pronunciation and usage. Although written first, classical Arabic is much more recent than classical Hebrew. Still, it has some features that seem to be even more archaic. It has a somewhat richer sound system, which is partly simplified in contemporary speech. Also, three nominal cases are written in the literary language, but no distinction is made among them nowadays in speaking.

The Arabic writing system has the same origin as that of Phoenician and Hebrew. All three were based on a Semitic adaptation of the underlying principle of the Egyptian consonantal script. The basic signs omit the vowels, but there is an auxiliary system of diacritics used for teaching purposes and in dictionaries. Since the vocalic marks are omitted in most publications, a problem arises with recent borrowings. Those who meet a word for the first time in print must supply a vowel, with nothing to indicate which vowel it should be. One way out is the use of certain consonants to show the length of certain vowels. Writers sometimes use these signs as approximate indications of the vowel desired; that is, they use a consonant that indicates a certain long vowel if that is the vowel they wish to suggest, even though the vowel may be short in the source language.

The reason that ancient Semitic and Egyptian could comfortably employ a purely consonantal writing system is that the vowels of any native element vary regularly in accordance with the grammatical form, which can be inferred from the context. The root is in principle identifiable by its consonants, normally two or three. By the manipulation of the vowels and the addition of prefixes, suffixes, and infixes, one expresses different tenses, voices, aspects, and participles; the subject is also expressed in this way. Thus from the Arabic root *ktb*, write, we have *katabnaa*, we have written; *ma ktubu*, we write; *kaatibun*, writer; and *kitaabun*, book. Where English uses nouns, Semitic languages use some participial formation. This is essentially like some of our expressions, such as *song, singer,* and *singing,* which are derivatives of *to sing.* The Semitic system works smoothly with Semitic elements and with borrowed verbs that happen to fit or have been made to fit one of the native verbal patterns. Most words likely to be borrowed in modern times, however, are nouns. Theoretically, either the new word could be molded to the Arabic pattern or exceptions to the pattern could be permitted. In actual practice, the latter direction is being taken, and there are thus more and more exceptions or irregularities.

Amharic, the official language of Ethiopia, is a Semitic language spoken by seven million people. It has a long tradition as a literary language, going back to the fourth century, when Ethiopia was Christianized by the Copts. The alphabet is based on the Coptic, which in turn was based on the Greek. The old form of the language, known as Ge'ez, contributed to the formation of Amharic and is still studied as an ancient language; the modern writing system, having been adopted in recent centuries, is closer to the colloquial usage.

Chinese

The written history of China dates back to the sixteenth century B.C. It begins with city-states and dukedoms, but these fairly soon became consolidated into larger and larger units. During this long stretch of time there were many shifts of power and periods of outside domination. Many smaller tribes were absorbed, and there was much give and take among the great Manchu and Mongol tribes. Under Chinese domination, these groups became so consolidated that they in turn were able to impose their power on parts of China. In one period of over a century, China was ruled by a Mongol dynasty, the Yuan, founded by the khan Kublai; and the last dynasty before the republic, which continued for three centuries, was of Manchu origin. Throughout its history China has developed its arts and crafts, expanded its industry and commerce, and advanced its culture. The Chinese language itself came to be studied systematically and works were published about its phonetics and structure. The economy was able early to support a large population, and in recent times the Chinese population has continued to grow at a fast rate.

There must have been local variation in Chinese during all of its long history, but evidently there has been a tendency for the more divergent forms to disappear. At any rate, the present Chinese languages are enough alike so that their present differences must have developed in the last thousand or fifteen hundred years. There are five Chinese languages today, with a total of over 600 million speakers. One of these languages, known as Mandarin and used as the standard language, is the native tongue of 500 million people—more than speak any other language in the world. Other Chinese languages are Cantonese, with 55 million speakers; Wu, also with 55 million; Min, with 50 million; and Hakka, with 20 million.

The first example of Chinese writing dates from before 1800 B.C. It is found on charred bones, evidently used in a procedure for divining the future. The symbols incised on a bone represented a question, and the answer evidently depended on the way the bone cracked when it was thrown into a fire. Then there are inscriptions in bronze; writing on parchment and paper came later. About 100 B.C. the system was thoroughly revised and rationalized by Li Si, who devised a style for writing on small seals. Formed with smooth lines and curves, this form of character is still used for ornamental purposes. For general use it has been replaced by a new type, vaguely reminiscent of cuneiform, because the lines are generally thicker at one end than at the other. This is a consequence of writing with a brush and forming the characters with sets of strokes, some curved but most of them straight. When people today use ball-point pens in writing Chinese, the lines are naturally even, but they are otherwise modeled after the brush strokes. As in other early forms of writing, the signs were originally based on pictures, much simplified and conventionalized, so they could be made rapidly and would fit into a small space. The pictograms are more recognizable in the seal style than in the brush style, but with imagination one can recognize what they are supposed to represent after it is pointed out.

A Chinese character represents a monosyllabic root word. This corresponds to the essential linguistic structure of the language, since, barring a few partial exceptions, there are no affixes or internal phonological changes, and each unit has only one syllable. Elements may be joined to make compound words, phrases, and sentences, but always without serious complications. The founders of the graphic system, beginning with ideograms, perfected it by rounding out a sufficient number of characters to represent all root elements. As time went on, additions were made and variant forms were employed for some of the old ones, until there were between thirty and forty thousand known signs: about ten thousand in current use and the rest needed for reprinting classic works. To be reasonably literate, it is said, one needs to know about four thousand signs. It takes considerably longer to learn to read and write in Chinese than in languages with phonetic alphabets or syllabaries, but obviously it can be done; the Chinese, after all, have been doing it for hundreds of generations. Today schooling is required for everyone, both in mainland China and on Taiwan. Chinese scholars and planners have often weighed the question of shifting to alphabetic writing, and a number of appropriate systems have been devised. These have so far proved useful mainly for providing pronunciations in dictionaries and to some extent in beginners' textbooks but attempts to introduce them for mass use have met with popular opposition. It is possible that an alphabet may someday be adopted, but it is not likely to replace the old writing in the very near future. One of the basic facts behind the persistence of ideographic writing is that in principle it is a complete system, adequate in itself for almost all the purposes of a national orthography. It even has some advantages of its own. For one thing, it can be and is used for different languages of the Chinese family, and has been used for others. People who know the signs can read another language that uses them in its written form, even though they do not understand it when it is spoken.

Chinese characters may be simple or may be composed of two or more component signs, written side by side or one above the other. Those composed of more than two signs are frequently doubly compounded, with each of its two portions coinciding with a known compound character. The components of compound forms are reduced in size and squeezed together to fit the space corresponding to a single character.

Most single characters are pictograms representing an object—a man, a tree, a hand, a foot, the sun. Each is read as a definite word, not to be replaced by synonyms. Some of the simple signs are related to each other. Thus *tah*, big, is basically the same sign as *ren'*, man, but shows him with his arms outstretched; and the sign for *peen*, root, is "tree" with an addition at the bottom. The compound signs are of two quite different types, which may be described as *composed pictograms* and *combined pictogram-phonetics*. In the first of these, two or more pictograms are put together to represent an idea. Thus the signs for sun and moon side by side give the character *ming'*, bright; two trees make *lin'*, forest; "woman" and "child" together represent "good." The pictogram-phonetic characters add a sign, usually on the left or above, which gives a clue to the meaning, and has been called the *signific*. Another sign that gives a hint of the sound is called the *phonetic*. Thus the signific for "water, liquid," in combination with the phonetic *lin'*, forest, represents *lin'*, drop of liquid; that is, a word that refers to liquid but sounds like the word for "forest." The degree of phonetic similarity involved in these signs is sometimes complete, but often only approximate. Careful studies of the old language indicate that the sounds of the underlying word and the one indicated by the compound were generally more similar in earlier times than they are now, and that some of the present disparity between them is due to changes in the language since the system was worked out.

The fact that the device of the semantic clue was available to the originators of the ideograms seems to have led to the graphic differentiation of words that sound the same but have two or more meanings. Thus uncolored silk is called *pai'*, which also means "white, clear," in the same way that our "white goods" means sheets, pillowcases, and the like. The character for "uncoloured silk" is composed of the signific for "cloth" plus *pai'*, white, used as a phonetic. This kind of semantic specification has evidently been built up all during the history of Chinese writing and is one of the causes of the great number of characters that have accumulated. It was often resorted to for foreign words, which could be written with the character for a similar-sounding native word with a differentiating signific. Whether words were native or borrowed, it was possible to distinguish in writing what was not different in speech. This eventually made for a rather large amount of artificiality in the written language. The spoken language solved the problem by creating compound words, like *hiaau-hai'-tsi*, small-infant-child, to make the concept perfectly clear. In recent times there has been a movement toward making the written language less abstract and more readable; this is called *pai' hwah*, clear language. Following colloquial usage, it calls for the use of compounds instead of glossed phonetic signs.

In the last several decades the Chinese have advanced their industry and science along modern lines. To meet the new vocabulary needs, various devices have been used: switching to a foreign language, using a borrowed word, and creating a new Chinese compound. All three have been used in print as well as in speaking. One simply shows the foreign item in its own alphabet, uses a series of native words whose pronunciation more or less coincides with that of the successive syllables of the foreign expression, or writes it in Chinese. Thus *penicillin* can be written as in English; rendered as *pan-ni-ci-lin'*, which means literally "dish-nun-west-forest" but creates no problem of interpretation for the Chinese, just as we do not ordinarily think

1. Many signs remain similar to their pictographic origins; for example:

ren'	muh	peen	niou'	rih	yueh	chu'
man	tree	root	cattle	sun	moon	bamboo

tjian'	men'	xan	xoou	juoo	che	kjoou
field	door	hill	hand	fire	wagon	mouth

2. Some ideas are suggested indirectly:

kung	chung	shangh	siah	tah	tanh
work	center	above	beneath	big	dawn
(tool)				(man with arms extended)	(sun over the horizon)

erh	ming'	ching	chiuh	tsuoh	lin'	feih
two	bright	clear, crystal	a speech	to sit	forest	to bark
	(sun and moon)	(three suns)	(large number of words)	(men on a bench)	(trees)	(mouth and dog)

3. In certain cases, a sign for an idea is combined with another to suggest the sound:

ren'
man

chioou
new

xueei
water

lin'
forest

chjou (enemy)
(the word refers to
a man and sounds
like "new")

lin' (drop)
(the word is related
to water and sounds
like "forest")

Figure 2.1. The Chinese Writing System

of French *potage* as a compound referring to the age of a pot) ; or rendered as a new Chinese compound : *chhing-mei-suh*, blue-germ-essence.

The simple structure of Chinese, based on unanalyzable and essentially unvarying elements, evidently already existed two thousand years ago. The principal change since that time is the increasing importance of compound words. Educated Chinese with knowledge of Western languages introduce words with Latin and Greek affixes, which can be regarded as a step toward introducing synthetic word formation. (Synthetic word formations are those making use of inflections.)

Chinese does not use inflection to mark such categories as gender and number. The language does, of course, have expressions that make distinctions of physical sex and between one and more than one, when such distinctions are important to the context in which they are used. The one inflection-like feature of Chinese is the distinction of physical form with regard to numerals and demonstratives. The distinctions are made by means of certain particles that indicate long, flat, and round objects, containers, pairs, sets, and others; there is also a generalized particle used for humans, animals, and unspecified objects and concepts. This usage continues in force, but there may be a certain tendency to increase the use of the generalizing particle at the expense of the specific ones.

Japanese and Korean

Japanese is spoken by about 95 million people. Besides the official language of the empire, there is a cluster of local variants in the Ryuku Islands which amounts to a distinct sister language; the population speaking it numbers under a million. Korean is spoken by 37 million people; it has no sister tongues. Japanese and Korean are isolated linguistic entities, not closely related to any other language groups. Some scholars have held them to be very distantly related to each other and to the Ural-Altaic language complex — Tungusic, Mongolian, and Turkic.

In the third century A.D. the Japanese emperor Sujin fought the Ainu to consolidate control of Hondo, the main island of the archipelago. In consequence of his success and subsequent developments, most of the early Ainu were eventually absorbed into the Japanese-speaking population. In the fourth to sixth centuries the Japanese sent expeditions to Korea and eventually came to dominate this mainland country, in which Chinese culture had been transplanted. From Korea and through trade with mainland China, the Japanese came to know Chinese writing and literature, and also became acquainted with Buddhism, which had spread from India. Until the ninth century Japanese scholars read and wrote only Chinese, pronouncing it according to two different traditions, one called *go-on,* Wu sound, based on the Wu language of southeast China, and the other *kan-on,* Han sound, or China language, based on northern Chinese. In the tenth century a third tradition became established, according to which Chinese writing was read off in Japanese. Since the order of the words is different in the two languages, the reader had to hop about among the characters. To simplify this process a system of *kari-ten*, or "return points," was invented: the text was marked with little signs to indicate where to go next. The reader had also to supply the inflectional endings and relational particles required by Japanese.

By the ninth century a system had been devised to represent Japanese syllables by means of selected Chinese characters, simplified for easier writing, without regard to the meaning of the corresponding words in Chinese. This system is the *hira-kana* (even Chinese); a further simplified and modified version is the *kata-kana* (half Chinese). A mixed writing system came to be generally used. It employs the Chinese signs *kan-ji*, for some of the root elements and shows the inflectional endings and relationals in the syllabary. When unfamiliar signs occur, they are sometimes glossed by small characters written alongside them. It is of course perfectly feasible to write Japanese with only the syllabic signs, but this is not considered to be as elegant as the combined writing.

The Japanese vocabulary acquired some scattered terms from Ainu and Korean in early times. Then it took over Chinese expressions wholesale, much as the European languages adopted Latin and Greek words. Finally, beginning in the sixteenth century, it began to absorb words from European languages, beginning with Portuguese but later borrowing most from English. Along with the words borrowed from European languages, Latin and Greek technical terms were also adopted.

Japanese phonetics is relatively simple. In the fourteenth century it consisted of eleven consonants and five vowels. A few new phonetic distinctions have developed in more recent times. When Chinese words were adopted in early centuries, their sounds had to be considerably modified to fit Japanese phonetics. Japanese forms compounds or phraselike terms with the same ease as English. And yet, again like English, it has been extremely receptive to foreign words. The Japanese use dictionaries and encyclopedias as extensively as the English-speaking peoples.

Korea is first mentioned historically in Chinese sources as early as the twelfth century B.C. Commercial and cultural relations with China were actively maintained through the centuries. In the seventh century A.D. the country was united under one king. From the sixteenth century on, Korea was invaded by Japan three times and was under its influence even when it was not under its actual rule.

Chinese was the first language of scholarship in Korea, as Latin was in Europe. Under the Buddhist influence, Sanskrit was also studied, but it never replaced Chinese. In the fifteenth century Price See Chong set up a royal academy and assisted in the formation of a writing system on a phonetic basis. Reminiscent of Sanskrit and the analytic concept of Chinese philology, it divides the syllable into parts—initial consonant, vowel, and final consonant, if any. It was made extremely logical and simple because from the first it was intended for popular use, and schools in which it was used were established in the villages. Scholars continued to use Chinese characters, the *han-muu* (Han-sound), interspersing them in texts the way the Japanese do. Literacy today is practically universal. Native texts are used exclusively through high school and the first year of college. After that, texts in Western languages were employed.

Korea has experienced industrial and cultural developments similar to those of its closest contacts, China and Japan. Philosophical and technical vocabularies are rich with both native compounds and borrowed forms. Learned and specialized words are frequently created out of Korean elements but based on Chinese compounds. There is a ten-volume dictionary of old and new terms. In this and other works, borrowed words are specially marked for the information of the users.

Other Languages

Magyar, or Hungarian, spoken by 12 million people, and Finnish, spoken by five million, are the most important and most advanced languages of the Finno-Ugric family. There has been a considerable development of learning, technology, and science in both Hungary and Finland, and both countries have correspondingly developed vocabularies that have been expanded, in the European mode, by Latin and Greek elements and loan words from other European languages. Their alphabets are of Latin origin.

Malay-Indonesian, essentially one language with only local variation, is spoken by 17 million people. It is used principally in Malaysia, Singapore, and Indonesia. It is one of hundreds of languages that make up the Malayo-Polynesian linguistic phylum. Other important languages of the group are Javanese, spoken by 45 million people in Indonesia; Tagalog, by 6 million in the Philippines; Madurese, by 7 million in Indonesia; Malagasy, by 5 million in Madagascar; Ilocano, by 3 million in the Philippines; Balinese, by 2 million in Indonesia; and Bikol, by 2 million in the Philippines. Malay-Indonesian has probably advanced farthest toward the world stage. It is today written mainly in a Latin-based alphabet, though formerly an Arabic writing system was employed.

The Dravidian language family of India, centered chiefly in the south, is spoken by at least 120 million people. It includes Telugu, spoken by 42 million; Tamil, spoken by 37 million; Kannada, by 17 million; Malayalam, by 15 million; and Bihil and Gondi, each spoken by 1 million. They employ Indic (*devanagari*) writing systems and show considerable Sanskrit influence. Their literatures go back to the early centuries of the present era. English is used among them as the principal medium of advanced technology.

Osmanli Turkish has 27 million speakers. Other important languages of the Turkish family are Uzbek, with 7 million speakers; Azerbaidjani, with 7 million; Kazakh and Tatar, each with 5 million; Uigar, with 4 million; and Tadzhik and Turkoman, with one million each. In the past the writing system was an Arabic type; today it is mainly Latin or Cyrillic.

Important languages of the Tibeto-Burman family include Burmese, spoken by 18 million, and Tibetan, spoken by 7 million. Both are written in variants of the Indic system. Burma in particular is attempting to bring its own language into use for higher education. The Tibeto-Burman family is distinctly related to Chinese and Thai in the Sino-Tibetan phylum. Thai has 24 million speakers; it is written in an Indic alphabet. Vietnamese is an isolated language whose classification has not yet been clearly determined. It is spoken by 31 million people. At one time the Vietnamese used a Chinese writing system, but, they went over to Roman when the country was governed by France. The language has many Chinese loan words.

There are several African languages spoken by large numbers of people, including Hausa and Galla, with 9 and 6 million speakers, belonging respectively to the Chad and Cushitic families, classed as part of the Hamito-Semitic phylum; Swahili, Ruanda, Zulu, and Xosa of the Bantu family, with 11, 5, 4, and 2 million speakers; and Fula, with 6 million, Ibo and Yoruba, each with 5 million; and Malinke, with 4 million, classed as distinctly related to Bantu and to each other. None of these has advanced to the world stage, but several have the status of official languages of states and regions, and there are advocates of their development into all-purpose languages.

Georgian, a Caucasian language of about 3 million speakers, with a long literary tradition in an independent alphabet, is the official language of one of the component republics of the Soviet Union. It is probably used more extensively for modern purposes than some others that are spoken by far greater numbers of people.

[*At this point there is once again a shift in focus. Having discussed briefly the contemporary world languages, Swadesh now concludes the chapter by characterizing the current world scene, especially those developments (both linguistic and sociocultural) that have given rise to the world stage of language.*]

The Current Status of Non-world Languages

Though this is the age of world languages, the remnants of the past linger on. There are isolated areas of the world in which local languages still are used largely in the old ways, but in most places these have come under the influence of more advanced languages. They have usually become interpenetrated by at least one outside language, and have therefore been essentially changed. If the local tongue is used by a limited population, and the younger generation is gradually giving it up, it is to be expected that it will eventually disappear. In the period that remains to it, it may conserve its old character, or it may be so reduced in vocabulary and usage that we may properly describe it as "impoverished." Where efforts are made to maintain the use of local languages and to develop their literature, we may describe them as "enriched." A language of the most advanced development (a world language) is often not uniformly developed in all the communities that employ it. Parts of it may have characteristics of the local or classic stage. There are some communities in which a portion of the population is using the language in a pidginized form, or as a pidgin in the process of enrichment.

In some instances the status of a language has been changed as a result of or with the help of conscious planning. The results of such projects are not always the ones anticipated, either because their engineers have not understood the processes of language change sufficiently or because they have had insufficient means to carry them out. Still there can be no doubt that some things can be and have been achieved with language by conscious design.

Since Leibniz' preoccupation with a scientifically constructed language in the seventeenth century, various invented languages have been proposed, either as replacements of natural language or as instruments of international communication; in the latter case, they have been called "auxiliary languages." When such a device is first invented, it is a mere design, an instrument for communication without a community that employs it. If people are persuaded to use it, it comes into being to the extent to which it is used and with the status that this use permits.

Summary: The Formation of the World Language

The case histories of world languages sketched in this chapter give some indication of the types of linguistic and sociocultural processes involved in their development. Let us review first the sociocultural processes that underlie the development of the world stage of language:

1. Man becomes increasingly capable of forming larger and more efficient economic units than those of the past, of producing abundantly, and of exploring new fields of knowledge.
2. The communities speaking a single language generally experience considerable growth in territory and population.
3. The number of languages in the world decreases.
4. As some communities enlarge themselves at the expense of others, or extend their influence over neighbouring areas, regional, national, and standard languages are formed.
5. Pidgin and creole languages also develop and are widely adopted, mainly as a transitional stage.

6. When the influence of a language is expanding, the mobility of the population typically leads to a uniformity of speech, temporary or permanent, depending on whether the mobility is maintained and on the degree of intercommunication.

7. The new conditions of intercommunication in the world favor the continued extension of uniformity in a speech community and the diffusion of certain favorably situated languages.

8. All world languages employ writing as an essential device. They also develop many other additional procedures of information storage and manipulation.

9. Individual persons and parts of the total community participate in varying degrees in the use of the world language.

Undoubtedly, in the stage of development we are discussing, changes in the sociocultural characteristics of language communities are more obvious than real qualitative changes in the language. Yet the study of language change is our principal task. For our purposes it is of only incidental importance to trace specific changes in individual words, constructions, or sounds in each particular language. There are, however, a number of points that can be treated in general terms so as to shed some light on the trends of qualitative linguistic direction. These are vocabulary, grammatical structure, and sounds.

It should be fairly obvious that modern world languages have far larger lexicons than the earliest classic languages. This can be verified by comparing dictionaries of English, French, Japanese, or any other modern colossus with such giants of the past as Latin, Greek, Sanskrit, and ancient Chinese. In making such comparisons, we recognize that no dictionary is 100 per cent complete, and that the techniques of lexicography are better today than they were in the past. But even if we assume that modern lexicons may be 95 per cent complete and that ancient ones, even in favorable cases, were only 75 per cent complete, there can still be no doubt that today's vocabularies are larger.

Another interesting measure is the relative proportions of various types of words. Proper names, of persons, places, organizations, and all others, run into astronomical figures today. In ancient times the number was also large, and our records of those times are far from complete; yet there can be no doubt that the number of names has grown enormously. Then again, the proportion of nouns to verbs shows nouns very strongly in the ascendancy. The actual proportion varies from language to language, depending on such structural facts as the ease with which nouns can be formed out of verbs and vice versa, but the general rule holds in all of them.

The extent to which vocabularies have been made uniform, especially through borrowing from the same sources, is very notable in the modern period.

In the area of grammatical structure, it should be obvious by now that no single type of structure is required to permit a language to enter the world stage. It can be isolating, agglutinative, externally inflective, or internally reflective; that is, it can make use of any of a number of word-forming processes. And yet there are certain trends that become evident if one views the whole assemblage of cases. Here are some points:

1. Internal inflections formed by consonantal and vowel alternations have been lost or reduced in number. New instances of internal inflection are few and limited in scope. The old ones are generally confined to traditional elements of the language; rarely are they applied to new loan words.

2. There are more instances in which inflective categories formed by affixation are reduced in number than cases in which new categories of this type have been added. Relational particles and auxiliary words sometimes fill the function of old inflective endings.

3. The average size of morphemes (minimal meaningful elements), in terms of the number of phonemes or syllables, is generally greater today, as a result of either the fossilization of old compounds or the borrowing of unanalyzable words from other languages. Although phonetic reductions have taken place, thus shortening some old elements, they have not generally been sufficient to offset the other two processes.

4. In the classic languages, there is a general uniformity of the length of morphemes. For example, ancient Semitic mainly employed roots of two or three consonants; modern Arabic, Amharic, and Hebrew still have such roots, but they have added both shorter and longer forms in their loan words. The same general trend away from a uniform length of morphemes is seen in the other world languages.

In the matter of phonetic systems, various directions of development can be noted. Old phonemes have sometimes coincided with each other, reducing the number of phonemes, and sometimes phonemes have split into two or more distinct entities. The latter development has sometimes been induced by the introduction of loan words with foreign phonemes. An analysis of different areas of expansion, such as the number of articulating types as against the number of articulating positions, might possibly show overall trends, but we would probably obtain clearer results by extending our analysis over a longer segment of time than that involved in the recent stage.

All these generalizations may appear to be obvious and trivial. They may seem obvious because some of the structural differences are only consequences of vocabulary growth, which in turn is based on cultural change. And yet if cultural influences in the recent period have led to such partly uniform trends, then a clear understanding of the development of culture in the past may shed light on early prehistoric linguistic structure.

References and Suggestions for Further Reading

[*Important factors in Swadesh's distinction of three recent stages in language (local, classic, and world) are the various functions for which a language is used. For the notion of functions of language, see Garvin and Mathiot (1968) and Hymes (1968). Hymes (1961) discusses functions of speech in an evolutionary perspective. Swadesh's discussion of linguistic complexity parallels to a degree Redfield's discussion (1956) of nonlinguistic culture. I have chosen not to use Redfield's terms "folk" and "urban," however, so as not to confuse the two approaches. Gumperz (1968) distinguishes types of linguistic community according to the level or nature of sociocultural complexity. Swadesh devised the terms "eoglottic," "paleoglottic," and "neoglottic" by analogy with the archeological terms "eolithic," "paleolithic," and "neolithic." See Kroeber (1948) for the significance of the archeological terms.*

For vocabulary growth and sources of new words, see Bloomfield (1933), Hockett (1958) and Sapir (1921). The figures in this chapter on the number of speakers of languages are from Muller (1964). Other surveys of the languages of the world are Meillet and Cohen (1952), and the "Languages of the World" series in the journal Anthropological Linguistics. *For writing systems see Chadwick (1963), Diringer (1948), and Gelb (1963).*

The Faber and Faber "Great Languages" series provides general surveys of a number of languages, usually including structural characteristics, cultural and linguistic history, and writing system. The other works on individual languages cited here tend to deal with these same areas. For English, see Baugh (1935), Bloomfield and Newmark (1964), and Jespersen (1948). For German, see Priebsch and Collinson (1946). For the Romance languages in general, see Elcock (1960). For Latin, see Palmer (1935). For French, see Ewert (1943). For Spanish, see Entwistle and Morison (1964). For Greek, see Atkinson (1933). For Sanskrit and the Indic languages, see Burrow (1955). For Chinese, see Forrest (1965). For Japanese, see Miller (1967). For African languages, see Greenberg (1966). Swadesh's discussion of linguistic trends leading to the formation of the world stage of language is in the framework of language typology. For language typology, see Greenberg (1968), Lehmann (1962), and Sapir (1921).]

Atkinson, B. F. C.
   1933.   *The Greek Language.* London: Faber & Faber.
Baugh, Albert C.
   1935.   *A History of the English Language.* New York: Appleton-Century.
Bloomfield, Leonard
   1933.   *Language.* New York: Holt.
Bloomfield, Morton, and Newmark, Leonard
   1964.   *A Linguistic Introduction to the History of English.* New York: Knopf.
Burrow, T.
   1955.   *The Sanskrit Language.* London: Faber & Faber.
Chadwick, John
   1963.   *The Decipherment of Linear B.* New York: Vintage.
Diringer, David
   1948.   *The Alphabet: A Key to the History of Mankind.* New York: Philosophical Library.
Elcock, W. D.
   1960.   *The Romance Languages.* London: Faber & Faber.
Entwistle, William J.
   1936.   *The Spanish Language, Together with Portuguese, Catalan, Basque.* London: Faber & Faber.
Entwistle, William J., and Morison, W. A.
   1964.   *Russian and the Slavonic Languages.* London: Faber & Faber.

Ewert, A.
  1943. *The French Language.* London: Faber & Faber.
Fishman, Joshua A., ed.
  1968. *Readings in the Sociology of Language.* The Hague: Mouton.
Forrest, R. A. D.
  1965. *The Chinese Language.* London: Faber & Faber.
Garvin, Paul L., and Mathiot, Madeleine
  1968. "The Urbanization of the Guarani Language: A Problem in Language
          and Culture." In *Readings in the Sociology of Language*, ed. Fishman.
Gelb, I. J.
  1963. *A Study of Writing.* Chicago: University of Chicago Press.
Greenberg, Joseph
  1966. *The Languages of Africa.* The Hague: Mouton.
  1968. *Anthropological Linguistics: An Introduction.* New York: Random House.
Gumperz, John J.
  1968. "Types of Linguistic Communities." In *Readings in the Sociology of Language*,
          ed. Fishman.
Hockett, Charles F.
  1958. *A Course in Modern Linguistics.* New York: Macmillan.
Hymes, Dell H.
  1961. "Functions of Speech: An Evolutionary Approach." In *Anthropology and
          Education*, ed. Frederick C. Gruber. Philadelphia: University of Pennsyl-
          vania Press.
  1968. "The Ethnography of Speaking." In *Readings in the Sociology of Language*,
          ed. Fishman.
Jespersen, Otto
  1948. *Growth and Structure of the English Language*, 9th ed. New York: Macmillan
          (Doubleday Anchor, 1955).
Kroeber, A. L.
  1948. *Anthropology.* New York: Harcourt, Brace.
Lehmann, Winfred P.
  1962. *Historical Linguistics: An Introduction.* New York: Holt.
Meillet, Antoine, and Cohen, Marcel
  1952. *Les Langues du Monde.* Paris: H. Champion.
Miller, Roy Andrew
  1967. *The Japanese Language.* Chicago: University of Chicago Press.
Muller, Siegried H.
  1964. *The World's Living Languages.* New York: Ungar.
Palmer, L. R.
  1955. *The Latin Language.* London: Faber & Faber.
Priebsch, Robert, and Collinson, W. E.
  1966. *The German Language*, 6th ed. London: Faber & Faber.
Redfield, Robert
  1956. *Peasant Society and Culture.* Chicago: University of Chicago Press.
Sapir, Edward
  1921. *Language.* New York: Harcourt, Brace.

THREE

The Genesis of Classic Languages

[*We go further back in time now, in an attempt to discover the characteristic features of the local stage of language and to trace the development from local to classic. Swadesh uses the comparative-historical linguistic method to reconstruct these aspects of the development of five language families and the characteristics of their common languages or protolanguages.*

It was Swadesh's belief that although there is much structural or typological diversity in languages spoken today, as one pushes back in time one finds more uniformity. Thus certain traits seem characteristic of all five of the protolanguages he discusses. These traits are summarized at the end of the chapter.]

The time span between the first dukedoms of England and the great English-speaking nations of today is over a thousand years. The period of the development of modern Russia from the time of the first local nobles is about as long. Over two thousand years separate the young city-state of Rome from modern, industrial Italy and France. The rise of modern China took more time; of Japan, less. Those who come late into the stream of movement generally take less time to get up speed, because they ride a wave that has already gained momentum. If the first urban civilizations, with writing and with a development of language that met complicated needs, appeared for the first time five thousand years ago, one wonders how much time had elapsed before then since man began to move out of his more primitive stage and into the new crafts and activities that eventually carried him to civilization. To guide our estimate, we can start with the archeological evidence that agriculture existed in a simple state in the Middle East about twelve thousand years ago. This means that it took man at least seven thousand years to advance from the tribal or local to the urban or classic

79

stage of development. Preliminary developments perhaps include the planned use of naturally occurring patches of food plants; the first domestication of animals; the devising of baskets and pottery as food containers; and the improvement of tools and weapons. For those who joined the advance after the way was improved, things went faster.

If we could choose our materials for study, we would certainly want to compare languages in the classic stage with their antecedent forms some thousands of years earlier; but history began with writing, and writing developed in the classic stage. To get behind the classic, we have to make use of comparison and reconstruction, which normally, in current scientific practice, provide a blurred but helpful picture of things as much as five thousand years before writing was developed. Some scholars have worked to extend our knowledge to considerably earlier periods, and someday rich materials will be accumulated by their patient effort. Even five thousand years is a long way into the past, sufficient to give some indications of what language was like in the local stage. In addition, we can piece out our conception by making a broad study of languages still spoken or recorded in earlier centuries by peoples that continued longer in an earlier way of life.

Of course, there are cautions to be observed when one tries to combine various kinds of evidence. For one thing, we must realize that the presence of high culture in one part of the world could have indirectly influenced distant languages by effects diffused from one to the next. For another, in the important matter of inferred evidence, we must be realistic and severely critical of all our conclusions so as not to persuade ourselves that some theory that appeals to our imagination is therefore correct. The reconstruction of the past requires a combination of imagination and scientific accuracy.

The Art of Unraveling

[*It is the task of this chapter to gain insight into the characteristics of earlier stages of language by reconstructing it backward. Before looking at the details of particular protolanguages, however, it is necessary first to consider the art of reconstruction or unraveling in general. Swadesh does this here, paying special attention to the question of etymology. In this way he enables the reader to have some understanding of the ways in which he arrived at the inferences presented in the following sections.*]

In making scientific inferences it is necessary to observe well everything that comes within direct range of perception and to find additional ways of bringing things under observation. To find the key to interrelationships, we have to go even deeper than direct observation. We must not only see isolated objects and events but discover how they are connected. It is like undoing a complicated puzzle or working one's way through a maze: it requires patience, perseverance, and the willingness to try first one way, then another.

The evidence of the past is to be found in the living languages of the present. If a language has been written, the oldest known form is the one that has the most to show about the still earlier past. Whenever two or more languages have diverged from the same original or from related variants, one can infer past forms from those in the diverged languages that show signs of having come from the same earlier form. The procedure is a sort of triangulation: you sight back from two or more known points to determine the common point in the past. And yet we know that language does not always move in a straight line. The method is therefore not simple sighting, but reconstruction; in other words, trying to determine logically, in view of what we know about language development, what conditions in the past could have produced the later developments. We must then test out each of the possibilities to eliminate all those that definitely do not fit the evidence and narrow the remaining interpretations in our attempt to reconstruct as best we can what actually happened. Often there are similarities among different possible theories; the wise scientist does not put alternative ideas completely out of mind, but is always ready to switch to another of the more likely ones or to make new combinations as additional evidence and insights throw fresh light on his work.

One of the first problems in linguistic reconstruction is to decide which languages can fruitfully be compared for projective triangulation. For this it is convenient to choose languages with enough similarity in phonetics, structure, and vocabulary to suggest they had a common history not too far in the past. It is then fairly easy to find specific structural features and particular roots and affixes that give clear clues of having come from the same earlier form. When enough apparently cognate forms have been found and listed, it is possible to compare one with the other to see whether the similarities and differences present the kind of consistency that confirms common origin. This almost invariably means that some of the items first listed as possible cognates have to be set aside, because they are not consistent with the lines of sound change indicated by the bulk of the material. Nothing should be rejected carelessly, however; it often happens that cases that at first seem inconsistent are examples of a further detail of development that has not yet been understood.

The first discovered cognates are usually those that show phonetic and semantic similarities of a fairly obvious sort. Even with them certain cautions need to be observed. The first is that borrowed words should not be confused with those that date from the common period of the languages in question; note, however, that very old loans made during the period of local variation, before full separation or before serious differentiation had developed, can be just as useful as complete cognates in reconstruction, since they may show the same characteristics of change. Here are some examples that might come up in the comparison of Spanish and English:

	SPANISH	ENGLISH
1.	*cuerno*	*horn*
2.	*corazón*	*heart*
3.	*colina*	*hill*
4.	*cutis* (skin)	*hide*
5.	*cámara*	*camera*
6.	*yelmo*	*helmet, helm*
7.	*queso*	*cheese*
8.	*cucurucú*	*cock-a-doodle-doo*

In the first four examples, there is a consistent correspondence of the Spanish k sound (spelled c) with English h. The second consonants are identical in the two languages in the first three examples (r in the first two, l in the third), and both are dental stops in the fourth (t, d). The meanings of the words are identical or similar in all four cases. The consonantal agreement is sufficiently consistent to suggest that the forms in question are *cognate* (descendants of a single common form) and that the vocalic differences are due to either sound change or old alternations, still to be studied. Similarly, the diverse endings of the words may be due to additions of different suffixes. When we come to the fifth example, we find that both languages have k sounds and that the words are very similar. It is interesting, too, that English *camera* refers to a manufactured instrument. A little checking will reveal that one of the first people to use the *cámera oscura* (dark chamber) to see light images was Leonardo da Vinci, in the fifteenth century. Therefore, the reference of the words being compared is to something that could not date back even remotely close to the common period of the languages under comparison. Even before looking up the background of the case, the historian would already have suspected that the similarity of the words is due to borrowing, either by one of the languages from the other or by both from a common source. The correspondence $k = k$, because it is inconsistent with the equation $k = h$ posited on the basis of the first four examples, is a clue that this case is different; the kind of meaning expressed, since it belongs to the category of manmade goods, is a further sign. Examples 6 and 7 are once again inconsistent with the $k = h$ equation, and the words again refer to manufactured products. In these cases, however, there is less phonetic similarity than in example 5. We must suspect that these are old borrowings, yet not old enough to show identical phonology with actual cognates, like examples 1 to 4. It happens that *yelmo* stems from a term taken from Germanic, perhaps in the fifth century, when Spain was dominated by the Goths; and *cheese* is the modern version of old English *cese*, which goes back to Latin *caseus*, borrowed by the Germanic tribes perhaps in the first century. Example 8 illustrates similarities in sound-imitative words. Linguists realize that such agreements may have little reference to common origin and may resemble each other because they are attempts to imitate the same sound. Nonetheless they can be very old and can reflect history in interesting ways. The first syllable in the English version coincides with the independent work *cock*, which, despite its similarity to *coq*, has been traced as far back as Old English *cocc*, which was itself a sound-imitative word.

As we can see from these examples, each word and each detail in the chain of evidence that leads us back in time needs separate examination with as much information as can be brought to bear upon it. In reconstructing the history of individual words, one must evaluate all apparent cognates. Historical phonology is built up out of the sum of individual word comparisons, and these should be checked by learning as much as possible about their earlier use in each of the compared languages. The basic operational rule of scientific evidence is to use information that is as complete as possible. For reconstruction of the past, an additional guiding principle is to give special attention to the oldest available data. For this reason, although it was convenient to compare English with Spanish, the serious scholar would prefer (instead of modern English) Old English or its sister tongues, Old Norse, Old Saxon, Old High German, or Gothic; and (instead of Spanish) Latin. However, the modern information occasionally adds something to what we know from the older period, so we use it as an additional source when this is helpful.

Often the interrelationships of forms within a language give clues about the older period, and not infrequently the most irregular manifestations turn out to be fossil traces of what was once more regular or general. One of the most interesting examples of this in English is the formation of tenses by vowel change, as in *eat* = *ate* and *come* = *came*, a process that applies to only a few verbs today, but which reflects the typical state of affairs some thousands of years ago.

[*Having presented a general survey of the techniques of reconstruction, both here and in Chapter 1, Swadesh is now in a position to apply these techniques to a number of language families in order to reconstruct their ancestors. He does this in the sections that follow.*]

Indo-European Languages

One of the language groups most favorable for the study of past linguistic development is the Indo-European. It includes three languages for which there are fairly abundant recorded data from the second millennium B.C. (Hittite, Greek, and Sanskrit) and a few more (Persian, Latin, Oscan, and Umbrian) from the first millennium B.C. Data on other Indo-European languages begin in the early centuries of the Christian era or later. Still, in most cases there are clusters of closely related languages that can be traced back to a common period around the time of Christ, so that inferences may be drawn about the languages of that period. In sum, then, we have multiple triangulation points from which to reconstruct a very early common period, which, from linguistic and archeological evidence, may go back at least seven thousand years before the present. To obtain our picture of the language in that period, we use in principle all available evidence; but for the purposes of this book it will be convenient to refer mainly to three of the older languages about which we have particularly good information— Sanskrit, Greek, and Latin—and one a bit more recent, Gothic, a language that adds a great deal of light and at the same time is fairly close to English.

These four tongues show marked differences in their phonetic structures, but also a certain degree of similarity. Furthermore, by comparing words in the various languages and using the techniques described in the preceding section, it is possible to reconstruct the old sound system. For example, Gothic *ber-ars*, to bear, matches Latin *fer-re*, Greek *pher-ein*, and Sanskrit *bhar-a-ti*. All have *r* at the end of the root and a labial stop at the beginning, though the latter is different in each one. Two of these labials are aspirate, Sanskrit *bh* and Greek *ph*; and two are not, Gothic *b* and Latin *f*. Two are voiced, the Sanskrit and the Gothic; and two are voiceless, the Greek and the Latin. If we try to infer what the original sound was, we have to reason that aspiration is a feature more likely to be lost where it once existed than to be added where it did not; we therefore infer that the original sound was an aspirate. As for the question of a voiced versus an unvoiced aspirate, the matter is more complicated, particularly if one considers the development in the two remaining languages, Gothic and Latin, including the fact that the sound comes out as medially voiced in Latin. A balancing out of the evidence would perhaps favor the inference that the original in the common period was voiced; that is, *bh*. There is also the possibility that it might have been voiceless in its initial position and voiced between vowels, or that it was voiced in some of the local variants but voiceless in others. Still, one does not expect to pin down every last detail at this stage of reconstruction, and it may be best to leave the matter in abeyance until new evidence can be found. For now, we shall write *bh*. We can also say, without going into all the reasons, that the vowel of the root in the common period of Indo-European must have been *e*, making the root **bher*; in other forms of the verb the vowel was articulated nearer the back of the mouth and is usually cited as *o*, although there is some suggestion that it might have been *a* in some local variants of common Indo-European. There were also forms with the vowel lengthened or omitted. The absence of a vowel can be shown in English, if we recognize that *bring* must have been built up out of **ber*, to bear, by the addition of another vowel and two consonants.

Many sets of cognate words can be found in the various Indo-European languages, and from them it is possible to reconstruct the form of roots and affixes in the common period.

By reconstructing a good number of old forms, while bearing in mind the nature of languages and the laws of change, we eventually can make out a complete phonetic system for the old common language or *protolanguage* and can reconstruct the phonetic changes that took place in each line of divergence from it. We can express the facts for old common Indo-European and each of the four languages we are discussing in Figure 3.1, which omits only some of the more complicated details of development.

Table 3.1.   Indo-European Phoneme Trends

| | Phonemes | | | | | | | |
	Labial	*Dental*	*Apical*	*Velar*	*Back Velar*	*Labio-velar*	*Back Labio velar*	*Glottal*
Common Indo-European	p	t	s	k	q	kw	qw?	
	b?	d	z (M. S.)	g	G	gw	Gw?	
	bh	dh		gh	h" (M. S.)	ghw	h"w (M. S.)	h
	m	n						
		l	r	i (= y)	e	u (= w)	o	
Sanskrit	p	t, t"	s, s", h	k	k, ch	k, ch		
		d, d"	y, i	g, j	g, j	g, j		
	bh, b, ph	dh, d, th		h, jh, g	i, length	gh, jh, g	i, length	
	m, a	n, a						
		r, l	r, l	y, i	a	v, u	a	
Greek	p	t	h, s, lost	k	k	p, t, k		lost
		d	z, s, i	g	g	b, d, g		
	ph, p	th, t		kh, k	a-timbre	ph, th, kh	o-timbre	
	m, am, a	n, an, a						
		l, al	r, ar	i, lost	e	u, lost	o	
Latin	p	t	s, r	k	k	kw, k		lost
		d	y, i	g	g	v, gu		
	f, b	f, d		h, lost	a-timbre	f, b	o-timbre	lost
	m, um	n, un						
		l, ul	r, ur	y, i	e	v, u	o	
Gothic	f. b, p	th, d, t	s, z	h, g, k	k, g, k	hw, gw		lost
		t	y, i, e	k	g	kw		
	b	d, t		g	lost	gw	lost	lost
	m, um	n, un						
		l, ul	r, or	y, i, e	i, e	w, u, o	a, oo	

The top row shows the phonemes reconstructed for Indo-European on the evidence of the derived languages; most of these reconstructions are those accepted by all or most specialists. A few points, marked "M. S.," are ideas of my own: (1) *z*, which seems to be indicated by some recent research, and (2) the symbols *h"* and *h"w*, used for what are commonly known as the "*a*-colored laryngeal" and the "*o*-colored laryngeal," respectively, and which are written in a number of ways (for example, H_1 and H_2 or A_1 and A_2). Three items are given with a question mark. They are omitted from other reconstructions and are mentioned here only as phonemes that might have existed in some stage of Indo-European, possibly considerably before the latest common period. Of course, no effort is made in this table to indicate the exact pronunciation of dialectal variations of each phoneme.

In the Sanskrit and other sections of the table, the phonemes are listed in positions corresponding to their Indo-European originals. If the Indo-European sound developed into more than one phoneme, according to its phonetic surroundings, all the alternates are listed. For example, in the Sanskrit position corresponding to Indo-European *m*, the listing is *m*, *a*, which means that *m* is retained in most positions, but changes to the vowel *a* if it stands between consonants or at the beginning or end of the word in contact only with a consonant. Thus the root *nam, to bow, gives the Sanskrit past participle *natá*, bowed; *natá* comes from the reduced form *nm plus -*tá*, a verbal inflection indicating past tense, *m* changing to *a* before another consonant. It is of course possible that the same phoneme may come from more than one original; so, in Sanskrit, an *a* may come from Indo-European *m* or *n*, under the conditions stated, or from either *e* or *o*. In a few cases, one of the alternates is listed as lost, meaning simply that under certain circumstances the phoneme disappeared. An example is *gh*, which is lost between vowels in Latin. Similarly, "length" is given as one of the alternative developments for *h*" and *h*"*w* in Sanskrit, and refers to the fact that any preceding short vowel is lengthened if the sequence comes at the end of a word or before a consonant. "*A*-timbre" and "*o*-timbre" mean that an adjoining vowel takes on the given quality by the influence of the consonant, even thought the latter was lost before historic times. The source of *oo* in Gothic is from the long *oo*, not from the short. If the reader wishes further details of conditional changes, he can consult specialized works on Indo-European and its branches. [*See the references listed at the end of this chapter.*]

In listing the correspondences of phonemes, it is convenient to begin with the old common language and relate to it the phonologic reflex in each of the derived languages. This is the opposite direction to the order of inference, which as I described earlier, begins with the reflexes and deduces from them what old phonemes must have given rise to them. The logic of this procedure can be seen by looking at the Sanskrit, Greek, Latin, and Gothic sections of the table, but not a common Indo-European. In the collection of probable cognates, one lines up sets of words with the same correspondences in the several languages—for instance, those that show up in the four languages as *p*:*p*:*p*:*f*—and decides that possibly *p̣* is the original sound. There are cases also of *p*:*p*:*p*:*p*; that is, labial voiceless stops in all four languages. When all such cases are examined, however, it is found that an *s* precedes the *p* in these instances and not in the others; hence one infers that the presence of the sibilant is what has conditioned the sound, so that it is preserved as *p* and does not go to *f* in Gothic. Then there are sets of *p:p:p:b*. Here it took some extraordinary scientific insight, credited to a scholar named Karl Verner and therefore called Verner's Law, to see that all the instances had the labial consonant within the word (that is, not initially and not after *s*) and that the evidence showed a lack of accent just before the labial in the old language.

Another remarkable inference (first made by Ferdinand de Saussure) deduced the original presence of phonemes lost in all the then known Indo-European languages, but still discernible from the quality and length of the vowel and from the fact that although most reconstructed roots had at least two consonants, a few had long vowels instead of a second consonant, or a vowel of set quality, *a* or *o*, at the beginning instead of a first consonant. It was almost thirty years after Saussure's suggestion that such consonants had existed and been lost that archeological work at Boğaz Köy in Asia Minor discovered tables written in Hittite, which proved to be an Indo-European language in which an *h* existed in roots where the lost consonants had been inferred. Thus Hittite *hark*, protect, shows an *h* corresponding to Latin *arceere*, protect, enclose; it is this *h* that, while still present, had caused the vowel, originally *e* or *o*, to change to *a*.

The relative figures of the phonemic systems are interesting. In common Indo-European as it has been reconstructed, there were twenty-seven phonemes, perhaps a few more or less, depending on how one resolves certain questions, or possibly only around twenty-three if one takes *bh*, *dh*, *gh* and *ghw* to be consonant clusters instead of simple phonemes. Of these all but two were consonants. In the daughter languages there are always more vowels and generally fewer consonants. There is no very strong trend, however, and it may be best to leave further discussion of this matter to later.

Indo-European has shown far more notable developments in phonetics than in grammatical structure. Key points are root form, internal inflection, inflectional categories, and word and phrase formation.

Aside from demonstratives and some other elements, which had a single consonant, the prevailing minimum root form in old common Indo-European consisted of two consonants with variable vowels. A few typical examples of roots written with the vowel *e* follow, with representative forms in derived languages (IE indicates Indo-European):

IE   **bher*, Skt. *bhar-a-ti*, Gk. *phér-ein*, Lat. *ferre*, Go. *ber-a-n*, to carry, with vowel variation in Go. *bar*, (I or he) bore, and *bor-um*, we bore, and in Gk. *phór-o-s*, tribute (that is, "what is brought").

IE   **ped*, Skt. *pad-a-m*, Gk. *pod-o-n*, Lat. *ped-e-m*, Go. *foot-u-m*, foot (given in accusative).

IE   *h''er, Lat. ar-aa-re, Go. ar-y-a-n, to plow.

IE   *deh''w, Skt. daa-, Gk. di-doo-mi, to give; Lat. dotus, given, dotaarium, dowry.

Alongside the elemental type of root there existed other extended forms, which differed from them by having an s- at the beginning, an -n- in the middle, or one or more different consonants at the end. There is reason to believe that the s preextension might have been an old prefix, possibly with intensive meaning. At any rate, forms with and without s- existed side by side in late common Indo-European and may still be reflected in English in such word pairs as *melt* and *smelt*, *mash* and *smash*, *molder* and *smolder*, *lick* and *slick*, *light* and *slight*, *lam* and *slam*, *nip* and *snip*.

The nasal infix occurs in some roots just before the second consonant, which has to be a stop; if the stop is labial, -m- appears instead of -n-. Usually the instances can be identified where otherwise identical forms are found with and without the nasal infix in different languages of the stock. Examples are Gothic *finden*, to find, as compared to Latin *petere*, to seek, from Indo-European *pent* and *pet*.

In Latin there are cases of -n- appearing in the present tense but not in the past, as in *vincoo*, I conquer, besides *viicii*, I conquered, or *ree-linquoo*, I leave, beside *ree-liiquii*, I left. The nasal infix does not show up between the first and second consonants in these cases, but between the second and third, because the Latin vowel comes from the Indo-European consonant *y*. Still, the examples are interesting for showing an infixing process with a definite meaning, that of present tense. Similar phenomena are found in Greek and Sanskrit. All infixing processes have been lost in the modern Indo-European languages.

The extension of the root by the addition of consonants after the two primary ones was apparently very common in proto-Indo-European. Examples can be cited from almost any of the descendant languages. In English we have words beginning in *fl-* or the same consonants with a vowel between them, all referring to rapid or liquid movement: *fill*, *fall*, *fling*, *flow*, *flood*, *float*, *fleet*, *fly*, *flight*, *flee*, *flit*, *flitter*, *flutter*, *flicker*. Some of these words are very old; that they may go back to common Indo-European is suggested by the fact that other languages of the family have comparable forms. For example, *flood* and *float* are based on Indo-European *ploh''w* and agree with Greek *ploo-ein*, to swim; *flood* is based on Indo-European *ploh''wto-* and agrees with Greek *plootos*, navigable. Not all of the extended forms are ancient, so that we have here evidence of a constant drift in the languages of the Indo-European stock. A certain number of extended roots existed in the period just before the present branches began to separate from each other. Some must have been lost as new ones were formed, but on the whole the direction has been toward a greater number of consonants.

If we try to project backward into a very early period of the Indo-

European community, it seems likely that the recent trend only continues an older one. Fortunately for our study, the Indo-European community divided into a number of separate parts, of which at least twelve continued into historical times. This means that there is a good chance that we will be able to reconstruct a large portion of the vocabulary of seven thousand years ago. As we continue working on the task, we find that many forms that have employed different root extensions—the prefix *s*-, the infix *-n*-, and various suffixes—are identifiable as derivatives of one and the same root. Now, after long periods of time, the connection of old derivatives tends to become less and less discernible, as a result of both phonetic and semantic changes; and in fact we can be sure that many once clearly related forms have lost their similarity so completely that we cannot even guess that a relationship exists. If, under these circumstances, the two-consonant pattern is still evident in many formational sets, the inference must be that the longer forms cannot have an indefinitely long history. This does not mean it was short. The longer form pattern may have been five thousand years old or more in the period whose forms we are reconstructing, having begun, say, ten thousand years ago. It was probably weak at first and gained momentum as time went on. Perhaps we have here a phenomenon that got started in a serious way in response to the need for an ever larger vocabulary because of the increasing complexity of society as it advanced from the local to the classic stage.

Another interesting feature of common Indo-European was the alternation of vowels. In part this was related to the accent, for unaccented syllables sometimes lost their vowels, while accented ones retained them or lengthened them; but the qualitative change between front *e* and back *o* was another matter. Here the main operating principle was semantic. An actively continuing event was symbolized by the front vowel, the state resulting from the action by the back one. Noun derivatives could be based on the active aspect or on the resultant static condition, according to their meaning. The old system was retained in Gothic in the so-called strong conjugation of the verb; but there were already many so-called weak verbs, derived by endings from the static form. The subsequent history of Germanic languages has shown a constant reduction of the number of strong verbs. In ancient Greek there were numerous verbs with vowel change, but other processes had taken over much of the work load. This was even more true of Latin, while in Sanskrit the front and back vowels had fallen together phonetically in a way that made the alternation unworkable. In all four branches, and in still others, the trend was to limit more and more the operation of alternating vowels. This came about mostly by the extension of derivative and periphrastic auxiliary formations.

Besides inner vowel change, the older Indo-European languages, and presumably common Indo-European before them, used at least three techniques of reduplication, which may be described as *e*-consonantal, *i*-consonantal, and vocalic. Sanskrit has a fourth type, which is bicon-sonantal. The three types are still found in Greek; Gothic and Latin show only the first.

The *e*-consonantal type repeats the first consonant with the vowel *e*, changed to *i* in Gothic, and often with modification of the vowel also. Here are some examples:

Latin	can-oo	I sing	ce-cin-ii	I sang
Greek	leip-oo	I leave	le-loip-a	I have left
Sanskrit	tan-oo-mi	I extend	ta-ʻtá-na	I extended

Note that *a* in Sanskrit is the reflex of Indo-European *e*, *o*, or *a*.

The *i*-consonantal reduplication employs the first consonant followed by *i*. It is required in Greek and Sanskrit for certain verbs in the present and tenses derived from it, as against other forms that are unreduplicated or which use a different type of reduplication. For example:

| Greek | di-doo-mi | I give | e-doo-k-a | I gave |

Vocalic reduplication in Greek and Sanskrit consists of setting the vowel *e* (or its Sanskrit reflex *a*) out in front of the root. Its function was to form the past tense:

| Greek | luú-oo | I loose | é-luu-on | I was losing |
| Sanskrit | vish-aa-mi | I enter | á-vish-a-m | I was entering |

The striking fact about verbal reduplication in Indo-European is that as a productive process, it was completely lost by modern times in all branches of the stock. Part of this loss took place before the classic stage, at least in some of the languages. Inner vowel change held up considerably better in certain branches. Except in Sanskrit, where it was almost completely blurred by the fusion of the two vowels of Indo-European, it still had a place in the classic languages, but eventually was greatly reduced or essentially eliminated as an active expressive device. Possibly the loss of vocalic alternation was what aided the maintenance of reduplication in Sanskrit. Everywhere, as both inner change and reduplication lost their hold, external inflection by auxiliaries or affixes took over the old functions.

The most remarkable development of all may be that of inflectional endings in the verb. If we can judge by the points that all the systems have in common and discount the features that vary greatly from one to the next, the old verbal inflection may have been relatively simple. Possibly it was built on the order of the Germanic, Gothic, or old-fashioned English systems, which have only two basic tenses, present and past, or perhaps more accurately, incompletive and completive. There was no separate future, so that "I see" served according to context for both present, as in "I see him now," and future, as in "I see him tomorrow morning." The other tense was past, "I saw him." There must have been a pattern of using certain verbs as auxiliaries, however, whether for emphasis or for giving shades of time reference. The curious thing is that Sanskrit, Greek, and Latin all developed composite tense formations based on the use of roots meaning "to be," "to become," "to go," and "to do." In Germanic the trend moved slowly, and only in relatively recent times, probably under the influence of late Latin, did it take on broad dimensions, permitting compound time phrases like "I have seen," "I shall see," "I am seeing," "I do see," and so on.

To show what happened and how it happened, it is instructive to examine some Latin conjugational formations, with a few observations relating to the other languages. One of the notable facts of Latin is that some verbs have simpler conjugations than others. They are known as irregular because of their formation and may be more limited than others in the number of their tenses and modes. Such verbs include *iire*, "to go," *fiire*, "to become," and *esse*, "to be."

"To be" is actually put together out of two roots, *es-* (with a reduced variant *s-* and the modification to *er-* before a vowel) and *fu-*. The first root is related to the third person *is*, in English. The second is closely similar to Sanskrit *bhu*, "to become." First let us compare the present and past of "to be" and with them the present subjunctive of "to go":

s-um	I am	*er-a-m*	I was	*e-a-m*	that I go
es	thou art (from es-s)	*er-aa-s*	thou wert	*e-aa-s*	that thou goest
es-t	he is	*er-a-t*	he was	*e-a-t*	that he go
s-u-mu-s	we are	*er-aa-mu-s*	we were	*e-aa-mus*	that we go
es-ti-s	ye are	*er-aa-ti-s*	ye wert	*e-aa-ti-s*	that ye go
s-u-nt	they are	*er-a-nt*	they were	*a-a-nt*	that they go

It is evident that the endings in these three sets are very similar and may indeed have been identical at one time. The second and third columns show the vowel *-a-* or *-aa-*, lacking in the first. This is a derivative suffix, perhaps identical in origin with the characteristic *-aa-* of verbs like *am-aa-re*, "to love."

Now compare the subjunctive and the future of "to be" with the present of "to go":

e-oo	I go	*s-i-m*	that I be	*er-oo*	I shall be
ii-s	thou goest	*s-ii-s*	that thou be	*er-i-s*	thou shalt be
i-t	he goes	*s-i-t*	that he be	*er-i-t*	he shall be
ii-mu-s	we go	*s-ii-mu-s*	that we be	*er-i-mu-s*	we shall be
ii-ti-s	ye go	*s-ii-ti-s*	that ye be	*er-i-tis*	ye shall be
e-u-nt	they go	*s-i-nt*	that they be	*er-u-nt*	they shall be

Here we see that the endings of "to be" in the subjunctive, except for the first singular and the third plural, are identical with the full corresponding form of "to go." The third plural -*i-nt* of *s-i-nt* could well be a simplification of *e-u-nt*, if we bear in mind that the bare root of "to go" is *ii-* or *i-*. The third plural present of "to go" and the third plural future of "to be" have the same ending as *s-u-nt*, they are. The first singular -*oo* of "I shall be" and of "I go" are identical and show one of the characteristic first person singular endings of Latin.

Let us now turn to the other root used in the inflection of "to be." The basic form in Latin is *fu-* and must have originally meant "become," if we can judge from the comparative evidence. The endings of *fu-* for the pluperfect, "I had been," and the future perfect, "I shall have been," are identical with the total forms of the imperfect and future of "to be," formed with the *er-* variant of the root. The forms for the pluperfect, in the usual order, are *fu-eram, fu-eraas, fu-erat, fu-eraamus, fu-eraatis, fu-erant*. For the future perfect, they are *fu-eroo, fu-eris, fu-erit, fu-erimus, fu-eritis, fu-erunt*.

We can now compare the one remaining tense, the perfect, of "to be" with the total form of "to go" in the same tense and, with both of them, the corresponding forms of the regular verbs "to praise" and "to warn":

i-ii	I have been	*fu-ii*	I have gone
ii-s-tii	thou hast been	*fu-is-tii*	thou hast gone
i-it	he has been	*fu-it*	he has gone
ii-mus	we have been	*fu-imus*	we have gone
ii-s-tis	ye have been	*fu-istis*	ye have gone
i-eerunt	they have been	*fu-eerunt*	they have gone
laudaa-v-ii	I have praised	*mon-u-ii*	I have warned
laudaa-v-istii	thou hast praised	*mon-u-istii*	thou hast warned
laudaa-v-it	he has praised	*mon-u-it*	he has warned
laudaa-v-imus	we have praised	*mon-u-imus*	we have warned
laudaa-v-istis	ye have praised	*mon-u-istis*	ye have warned
laudaa-v-eerunt	they have praised	*mon-u-eerunt*	they have warned

Here, all the endings are similar to the present of "to go," except that the vowel -*i*- is always short in the perfect. The third person plural is the same as the corresponding form in the future of "to be" except that the first vowel is lengthened. The first person singular is special, and there is the added element -*tii* in the second person singular, probably related on the one hand to the -*ti-s* of the plural and at the same time to the *t-* of the second person singular pronoun (*t-uu*, thou, in the nominative, *t-ee* in the accusative, and *t-i-bi* in the dative).

The characteristic mark of the perfect tense in the so-called first and fourth conjugations, as shown by *laudaa-vii*, I have praised, and *audii-vii*, I have heard, is the -*v*-, and it seems probable that this is nothing but the form taken on by *fu-* between vowels; in other words, -*vii* is a variant of the verb *fuii*, I have been. In the second declension, as illustrated by *monuii*, the sign of the perfect is *-u-*, actually the same as *-v-* in the form it takes between a voiced consonant and a vowel. After a voiceless consonant, *-ii* is added directly, as in *duux-ii* I have led, and *ceep-ii,* I have taken.

The regular future tense is apparently composed in similar fashion out of the verbal root *fi-* or *fii-,* to be made or become. Compare:

fii-oo	I become	*laudaa-boo*	I shall praise
fii-s	thou becomest	*laudaa-vis*	thou wilt praise
fi-t	he becomes	*laudaa-bit*	he will praise
fii-mu-s	we become	*laudaa-bimus*	we shall praise
fii-ti-s	ye become	*laudaa-bitis*	ye will praise
fi-u-nt	they become	*laudaa-bunt*	they will praise

The only future ending that is not absolutely obvious is the first person singular, but even here a simplification of *-bioo* to *boo* seems possible. If this is not the correct explanation, the ending would have to be due to the admixture of a termination from another part of the paradigm.

The imperfect is made with the element *-baa-,* which looks as though it might also be an amalgamated independent verb, but it must be one that no longer exists in Latin. Possibly it is related to Sanskrit *phaa,* to rise up, appear, take form. Here are the Latin forms, shown with *laudaa-:*

laudaa-ba-m	I was praising	*laudaa-baa-mus*	we were praising
laudaa-baa-s	thou wast praising	*laudaa-baa-tis*	ye were praising
laudaa-bat-t	he was praising	*laudaa-ba-nt*	they were praising

What has been shown here for Latin is essentially what appears to be the picture in other languages of the Indo-European family. Of the divisions we have been discussing, Germanic alone shows a relatively modest development of amalgamated auxiliaries. Nevertheless, it is evident that the *-d* that marks our regular past tense comes from the independent verb *do.* Saying *I worked* is therefore like saying *I did work* and goes back to a phrase like *I work did.*

The reconstructive study of such developments in the prehistory of Indo-European languages gives a notion of what was happening to them in the long period between the local and the classic stages. When we have examined a few other language groups, we may be able to draw some general conclusions.

The Semitic Languages

There are interesting and curious facts to be found in the Semitic linguistic stock. We have here one of the first languages to be conserved in writing, Akkadian-Babylonian-Assyrian; this is also the language in which the tradition of writing was maintained continuously for the longest time.

Scholars do not agree as to the exact date of the earliest Akkadian records; some say around 3000 B.C. and others 3500 B.C. or even earlier. Whatever it was, the monuments and documents in cuneiform continue for well over three thousand years, varying back and forth among the Akkadian, the Babylonian, and the Assyrian variants, until the empire was brought under Persia in the sixth century B.C. The Persians based their own writing system on the Babylonian.

The other very early instance of writing, Egyptian, was developed in a language fairly similar in structure to Semitic, and in fact recognized to be distantly related to it. Writing systems in the western Semitic languages, beginning with Sinaitic and Ugaritic and then going on to Hebrew, Phoenecian, Aramaic, Sabaean, Arabic, and Ethiopic, took their cue from late Egyptian, and used a pictogram to represent the first sound of the word it suggested. The Akkadian-Assyrian symbols, acquired from Sumeria, show syllables that are complete with vowel. The Egyptian-derived signs gave only the consonants. In the later development of such scripts as Hebrew, Aramaic, and Arabic, methods were devised for showing vowels, if desired, by the addition of auxiliary signs placed above or below the letters.

The long history of writing in Assyrian permits one to follow many details of its development. In the matter of sounds, it is interesting to note that in the course of time certain consonants blended with others and disappeared as separate sounds. Thus h, h'', G, and gh all fell together with the glottal stop. This is evident from the fact that the scribes make mistakes, confusing one sign with another, or using one almost to the exclusion of others, exactly as people tend to do when writing English words that are not spelled the way they sound. The reason for this phonetic simplification would seem to be connected with the expansion of the use of Assyrian under the Babylonian empire, when large numbers of speakers of non-Semitic languages were learning to speak it. These sounds were somewhat better preserved in Hebrew, and still better in Arabic. This seems to show that isolated desert tribes, far removed from the process of urbanization, maintained the old pronunciation. When Arabic was finally represented in writing in the seventh century A.D., a whole set of old sounds was still in use. The honor in which the old tradition is held has perhaps been a factor in conserving the old way of speaking, despite the rapid expansion of Arabic among peoples with altogether different linguistic backgrounds. Today there are many millions of people who learn a bit of Arabic as part of their religion and perhaps pronounce it badly, but most of the old sounds are still well formed in the speech of large populations. There is at present no danger that the spoken language may lose such interesting archaic sounds as the emphatic or laryngealized t'', k'', h'', g'', and d''. The only old distinction that has been lost in the spoken language, though maintained in writing, is that between the old dental and interdental emphatics, d'' and z'' in our transcription.

In matters of grammar there has been in the main a considerable conservatism in Semitic, with most of the changes being confined to minor details. There was one notable reduction in the inflectional categories between the oldest Akkadian and all the more recent languages. The dual category, referring to two objects, was originally treated as distinct from the plural. In later Babylonian-Assyrian, in Hebrew, and in the other languages, the dual formation is used merely as a variant way of expressing the plural. Another structural development was the loss of the case inflection of nouns. This had taken place by the time of the first documents in Hebrew. Arabic still retained the cases for some centuries, long enough for them to be incorporated in the literary language. Subsequently the distinction was lost in the spoken language. Today educated Arabs still write the case endings but do not pronounce them.

This trend toward inflectional simplification, manifested by the loss of the dual and of the cases, parallels the direction observed in other languages in the recent period between the classic and the world stages. We have to ascribe it to this stage in Semitic also, because Akkadian and Hebrew are definitely in the classic stage by the time of our first records of them. To get back to prior levels, we must use reconstructive inference; and we are faced with the problem that the early languages are little diverged in our earliest knowledge of them. Since there are relatively few divisions and languages in the stock, the triangulation effect from comparison among them is limited. If we look for comparisons outside of Semitic, there is the possibility of using Egyptian, Cushitic, and Berber, which scholars generally consider probable relatives of Semitic, and certain other languages, on which opinion is divided. I venture to suggest that Semitic may be as closely related to Indo-European as to Egyptian, and that the contrary impression may be due only to a few favorable coinciding isoglosses in the latter direction. This is merely a suggestion, however, and it will remain so until a great deal more effort has gone into the search. For the present, the Egyptian analogy can serve. Fortunately there are also important clues to be culled from the internal evidence of the Semitic languages themselves.

The outstanding structural trait of Semitic structure, as of Egyptian and to a certain degree of Indo-European, is the root of fixed consonants and changeable vowels. The root is made up normally of three or two consonants. By interchanging vowels, one differentiates the aspect according to a plan in which *a* typically marks present durative and *i* present momentaneous, while *u* occurs in the past and in participles. The doubling of the second consonant is emphatic, and sometimes is also required for the simple continuation of action. The repetition of the entire root expresses repeated action. Pronominal notions, voice, and derived concepts are expressed with the help of prefixes, suffixes, and infixes.

Two-consonant roots are in the minority, and do not show all of the root variation that is possible in the three-consonant ones; and yet there is some reason to believe that they are the older forms. This is suggested by many cases in which similar two- and three-consonant roots have similar meanings, as in cases like Arabic *ḍ'f*, *ḍ'ft''*, "to squeeze"; *ḍ'fz*, "to strike"; and *ḍ''fn*, "to kick." These examples seem to show that there was once a root **ḍ'af* with a meaning related to striking or applying pressure, which perhaps, according to the manner of applying the effort or its direction, was used with various additional elements. Presumably the type of combination was very typical, and in the course of time came to represent the most usual form of expression. Eventually the separate meaning of the following element faded and the combination came to be treated as a unit. The original meaning of the added consonants can be arrived at only by careful application of the reconstructive techniques described earlier in this chapter.

In all Semitic languages, four consonants, *y*, *w*, ' and *h*, show phonological peculiarities that have led scholars to designate them as "weak." By this they mean that these consonants are lost when they stand alone (that is, undoubled) between vowels, according to rules that have been recognized and described by grammarians from the oldest tradition of these studies. As the vowel structure of the root is changed to express the various aspects and derivatives, the weak consonants are conserved in a few of the forms but lost in most of them. It seems probable that, in the oldest formations, when only two consonants made up the root, the consonants were stable, and that the weakness of certain consonants developed only after the three-consonant pattern had become established. That is, as long as there were only two consonants in the root, the needs of clarity made it important to maintain the identity of each of them; when it was a matter of one of three consonants, clarity could be relaxed.

In Semitic word formation, some of the pronominal elements are used either as prefixes or as suffixes, and some also have an independent use. Thus we have in Arabic:

INDEPENDENT		OBJECT SUFFIX		SUBJECT OF NON-PAST	
'a-naa	I	*-nii*	me	*'a-*	I
na-h''-nu	we	*-naa*	us	*na-*	we
'an-ti	thou (fem.)	*-ti*	thee (fem.)	*ta-*	thou
hu-wa	he	*-hu*	him		

This variability of usage is evidently based on an earlier stage in which the pronouns occurred as independent words, capable of combining freely with other words, as most independent words can do. That is, they would sometimes be used before and sometimes after the words with which they were constructed, just as in modern English *rain* precedes the verb in "rain fell all day" but follows it in "clouds bring rain."

From these considerations we can infer at least two reasonably probable characteristics of a very early structural stage of Semitic: first, that major roots were composed of two consonants with variable vowels, and second, that the pronouns were independent. This state of affairs cannot be related to any recent period, because even the earliest Semitic languages have a majority of three-consonant roots, and because our extra-Semitic control comparison, Egyptian, also shows a good number of this type. It seems reasonably safe, therefore, to consider both characteristics as belonging well back in the local stage of Semitic, several thousands of years before our first historical records.

One more characteristic of old Semitic is suggested by the alignment of some of the vocabulary items, among which we find many roots with similar meanings and approximate agreement of consonants. They show consonants of the same broad class but not the same specific phonemes. For example, there are six dental occlusives in Arabic: *t, th, t", d, dh, d"*. Running through the dictionary under these letters, one finds the following sets of apparently related roots, with a dental as their first consonant and an identical second consonant:

talf, damage; *talif*, to perish, lose; *tlh*, perish, ruin; *t"lh"*, corruption; *t"ilal*, ruins; *dalah*, embarrassment; *dalasa*, to deceive; *d"all*, to lose, die, forget; *d"aall*, lost

tmk, raised; *t"mw*, arise; *taam*, high; *dmkh*, high

tinakh, to stop, dwell; *tana*, to dwell; *t"anab*, to stop; *dnks*, to stay home

tabbag", study thoroughly; *thaabara*, diligent; *thaabit*, firm; *t"bn, t"b*, able, wise; *d"ab*, fixed; *d"abat"*, firm; *d"abba*, to tighten

taghur, to rain heavily, gush; *t"aghay*, to overflow; *d"gh*, abundant harvest

t"ariik", road; *darag*, to go; *darg, darb*, road; *darak"*, hurry

tif, dirtiness; *taafih"*, to despise; *taafih*, small, insipid; *t"afif*, trivial, defective; *dfns*, foolish, lazy

t"away, lost, give out; *taah, tuwh*, get lost; *taakh, tawakd*, drown; *t"awaah*, to perish, lose; *dwg"*, damage; *dawii*, sick; *daag", dhawwaag"*, to dissipate

Such sets are found for the labials, for the velars, for the sibilants, and for *r* and *l*; the number of cases is sufficient to suggest an old pattern that has been preserved in scattered fossils. That is, it may once have been a regular process to modify the consonantal type with corresponding differences of meaning. When the regular alternation ceased to function as an active form of expression, there were enough examples of the variations spread through the vocabulary to remain in evidence today. If such a symbolic alternation once operated, each type of consonant—fronted or backed, voiceless or voiced, simple or emphatic—must have had a specific meaning, which may be still discoverable by careful unraveling.

Sino-Tibetan Languages

In eastern Asia the Sino-Tibetan linguistic stock offers good possibilities for knowledge of early stages of language. Some have analyzed this group as made up of two main branches, Thai-Chinese and Tibeto-Burman. Each of these falls into two parts, Thai and Sinitic, Burman and Tibetan. Sinitic is made up of five main languages, as we saw in Chapter 2; Thai has several dialects or closely related languages. Both Tibetan and Burman include a fair number of specific languages. The oldest records in any Sino-Tibetan language are of course in ancient Chinese, dating back to the second millennium before Christ. The next are in Thai, from the fourth century A.D.; Tibetan, from the seventh century; and Burmese, from the eighth. The Chinese records are in their special kind of word writing, which combines phonetic and semantic clues; to get some of the facts of the oldest language requires the use of unraveling procedures, which can fortunately combine language comparison with the careful analysis of the word signs for hints about the intention of the first scribes. Further back than this, one must proceed by triangulation, based on the divergent branches of the stock.

In broad focus, Thai and Chinese show up as strictly isolating languages (few or no inflections), which compose phrases and sentences by combining independent words in sequence. Tibeto-Burman languages are different in having prefixes and suffixes; the details vary from language to language within the branch. Ancient Tibetan and some of the contemporary languages make use of vowel variations to express aspect: *a* for ongoing action, *u* for completed action. The key problem of reconstruction is whether the Chinese type of structure is a simplification of something that was once like Tibetan, or whether the latter evolved from an older isolating type. Of course, the ancient common form need not have been exactly like either of the historical forms. In fact, there is plentiful evidence in Chinese itself for both vowel and consonant alternation, which go far beyond the patterns of historical Tibetan and have every appearance of being conserved from very ancient times, probably as far back as the common Sino-Tibetan horizon. I am referring to the variant forms of stems with indentical or related meanings which show variations in tone and in vowels, and also in consonants within a general class. The examples that follow involve velar consonants in initial position, either *k*, *kh*, or *h*. The second consonant is *m*. These examples are taken from Cantonese, which is one of the modern languages that best preserves the pronunciation of final phonemes; the tones are omitted. It will be noted that the common ideas involve closing within the mouth, pinching, or joining things together:

ham, bite, hold in the mouth, bridle bit, chin, jowl, contain, box, niche, envelope, restrain, to strike

kham, to catch, seize, arrest

    kam, to touch, seal up, bind up

    kim, to join, put together, unite, double, together, both

    khim, to pinch, hold in tongs, to nip, tweezers, manacles

    khom, to overlap, lapel, collar, sash, lockjaw, difficulty in speaking

Such arrays of forms, of which many can be cited in Chinese, lead to the deduction that there may once have been a paradigm of interchanging vowels and consonants. Though the work of unraveling has not yet been seriously attempted, one would imagine that at one time each variation of form was related to a specific semantic difference. Some part of the variations in consonants, vowels, and tones in Chinese may be related to the use of prefixes and suffixes in Tibetan; yet the latter has at least some vowel variations that are unrelated to the use of affixes. Nor is it safe to assume that all changes other than those of vowels are due to affixes. In future studies aimed at reconstructing very old Sino-Tibetan structure, it seems wisest to keep open the possibility of both consonant and vowel alternation.

Inflection is all but absent in Thai-Chinese. The one very notable instance of categorization is the classification of objects by shapes and general characteristics for purposes of counting. Thus in Chinese one says:

ih-thiau luh	one (strip) road
ih-chang chue-tsi	one (sheet) table
ih-ken kunh-tsi	one (stem) stick

In terms of actively functioning processes, not just fossil remnants, it seems that Chinese and Thai have come furthest away from the inferred older pattern. One asks if this might not be related to the fact that their area came earlier and more rapidly into the urban or classic way of life.

Fula-Bantuan

The urban or classic stage of social development began to reach western, central, and southern Africa something over a thousand years ago. There is little writing until about the fourteenth century. In central and western Africa, some graphic systems were invented on the model of the Egyptian. In southeast Africa, Arabic was introduced, and later on its alphabet was applied to the writing of Swahili, which is the Arabic name, meaning "coastal," for the main language along the seaboard. A few centuries later, European missionaries began to employ Latin letter systems for many languages, including Swahili. Because of the later introduction of writing, our information on these languages is confined to the present and a few centuries before; but there are some favorable cases for the inferential reconstruction of old protolanguages.

Most of southern Africa, as far north as the Congo and extending up along the east coast into Kenya, is occupied by populations speaking languages of the Bantuan stock. Some five hundred tongues are included, some spoken by a few thousand people, a few by millions. Some of the better known languages are Ki-Swahili, Ki-Kongo, Chi-Luba, I-si-Zulu, and Se-Suto; the prefixes are modern variants of an old prefix meaning instrument, fashion, or manner of speaking. Other members of the family use another equivalent element, as in Li-Ngala, Lu-Ganda, Lo-Nkundo. It is of interest to note the similarity of this morpheme to the Latin word for "tongue" or "language," *lingua*. It is interesting too that the Arabic equivalent is *lisaan* and the Assyrian *lishaanu*, while the Hebrew *laashoon* has other vowels. Those who speak these languages are named with the prefix *ba-* or its phonetic variants, which means "people": Ba-Kongo, Ba-Zulu, Ba-Ngala, Ba-Bangi. The name by which the whole stock is known is based on the word *ba-ntu*, "people," plural of *mu-ntu*, "person."

Glottochronological estimates give the Bantuan group a time depth of not less than three thousand years, and possibly over four thousand. Bantuan shows unmistakable ties with a number of other languages found along western Africa as far north as the Sahara. There is a series of Bantu-like languages around the Benue and Cross rivers, which have been called Semi-Bantu. Then there is a large and complicated series of interrelated stocks, known by various group names: Kwa, Guang, Voltaic or Gur, Mande, and West Atlantic. Some of the more important languages are Yoruba, Mossi, Mande, and Fula. On the basis of the languages at the northern and southern extremes, this great phylum can be called Fula-Bantuan.

An outstanding structural characteristic of Bantuan is the employment of a set of class prefixes, like *ki-*, *li-*, *ba-*, and *mu-*, which we have already illustrated in relation to the names of languages and peoples. Other prefixes refer to tree, animal, object, liquid, diminutive, abstract, substance, place, activity, one who does, and means of doing. The variations of meaning found in some of the languages suggest that some of the elements may once have had broader references than they do now. For instance, the element for "tree" may once have included objects that were stick-like, and could easily be extended to apply to any long object, even ropes or rivers. At any rate, every noun in Bantuan languages must have a prefix, which means that the conceptual world is completely divided into categories. This state of affairs is in a way quite like that in the old Indo-European languages, in which every noun must be masculine, feminine, or neuter. The class elements that refer to objects by their shape is also similar to the usage found in many languages of Asia and America in connection with numbers: the "numerical classifiers." [*Examples of Chinese numeral classifiers are given at the end of the preceding section.*]

The class prefixes of Bantuan are employed not only with nouns but also with adjectives and verbs, showing agreement with the noun that is modified or which serves as a subject. The same class prefix will thus be repeated more than once in a sentence in a form of concord even more extensive than the repetition of endings in Latin. "Those two beautiful women are singing" in Latin is *Canant illae duae feeminae bellae*; in I-si-Zulu it is *La-b'a b'a-fazi a-b'a-b'ili a-b'a-hle b'a-ya-ts!ula*. Note that each word of the sentence includes the syllable *b'a*.

Although the number and application of the individual prefixes vary from language to language in the Bantuan group, the process is so general in all of them that it must have existed in common or proto-Bantuan. The process is thus guaranteed to be at least four thousand years old. Far greater age is indicated by the fact that various languages of the Gur and West Atlantic stocks, at the opposite geographic extreme of the Fula-Bantuan phylum, also have some of the same elements, used in similar fashion except that they are not always prefixed. Such elements are suffixed in Fula, prefixed in some other West Atlantic languages and in Gur languages, and both prefixed and suffixed in certain languages of the Gur group. For example, the suffix corresponding to Bantu *b'a-*, "people," is *-b'e* in Fula, as in *Ful-b'e*, Fula people; *-ba* in Dagban-i, as in *Dagbam-ba*, Dagbani-speaking people; and a prefix, *bi-*, and a suffix, *-ba*, in the language of the *Bi-mo-ba*. Likewise the *-li* suffix for "language" can be illustrated in Dagban-i, which is a contraction of *Dagban-li*, or in Moli, the language of the *Mo-si* people. As we can see in the last-mentioned tribal name, *-ba* is not the exclusive expression of "people" in these languages, it shares this function with the *-si* endings; yet it is much used as an ending, as an enclitic or semi-independent pronoun, and as a numeral classifier. Other branches of Fula-Bantuan employ different affixes, which perhaps are reduced forms of the ones already cited. Even if they are of different specific origin, they nonetheless reflect the same general principle of noun classification.

In view of the wide distribution of classifier-pronominal elements like *b'a* and *li* in the Fula-Bantuan phylum, we can only infer that they already existed in the old common period (proto-Fula-Bantuan), eight thousand or more years ago. Were they prefixes or suffixes? Probably neither. Since they are sometimes prefixed, sometimes suffixed, and sometimes prefixed and suffixed simultaneously, we must conclude that they were originally free to be used either way. They must have been classifier pronouns that could be used by themselves or in various combinations. They then became crystallized in various ways in the derived traditions down to the present time. The present emphasis on prefixes in the south but on suffixes in the north may well reflect old regional tendencies in the common period.

Apart from these morphemes, the Fula-Bantuan languages vary between the inflectional or synthetic type and the isolating type. Bantuan, for example, includes in its verb complex suffixes of direction and voice, and prefixes of tense and aspect. Dagbani, of the Gur stock, does not incorporate any voice elements; uses suffixes for simple tenses, which may be aspectival in origin;

and expresses more varied time relations by proclitic auxiliaries. Other languages lean even more toward the isolating type of structure. The unraveling of the evidence for the common period has not yet advanced very far, but the most likely inference would seem to be that there were various classes of particles loosely combined, rather than strict affixation; and yet the germ of affixation was present in the use of these elements.

The two-consonant stem form is found in many languages of the Fula-Bantuan group. In others there are one-consonant forms, which are evidently reduced from the two-consonant form: Tamari has -*to* for "ear," but it is *tub-* or *tob-* in other Gur languages. In Bantuan and in Fula, notably, but also in various other languages, there are longer stems; the additional consonants, however, can often be traced etymologically to old affixes or stems with origins within relatively recent times. It seems possible, therefore, that most of the stem expansion belongs to the classic stage of development.

Fula, along with most of the remaining West Atlantic and a few of the Gur languages, employs a consonantal strengthening technique, which consists in changing fricatives into stops, and which serves to express certain differences of meaning. In Fula, which has one of the most extensive applications of this process, *p*, *k*, and *ch* are the strengthened forms of *f*, *h*, and *s* respectively; *b* or *g* are the strong correspondents of *w*, *d* of *r*, and so on. The process is applied principally to initial consonants, but there are also some examples in medial position. In these cases, the strengthened consonant is also doubled:

lofu	mud	*loppa*	to break up a solid in water
looha	to hunt	*lugga-gol*	stalking
tafa	to forge	*tappa*	to beat
taha	to lick	*takka*	to rub off
'tufa	to pierce	*tuppa*	to probe
uufa	to froth up	*uppa*	to swell
aala	be greedy	*ella*	to desire
saaha	to present a gift	*chakkaa-ri*	gift of food
difa	to snatch at	*dippi-ta*	to jerk away
doofa	to pull out	*doppa*	to tug at the breast in suckling
d'oya	to cough	*d'ojja*	to cough
daha	to conquer	*rakka*	to be able, to achieve

Examples like these remind one of Hebrew, in which a single consonant between vowels is pronounced as a fricative while a double consonant is kept as a stop. We can guess that there was a period in the past when Fula speakers were pronouncing all simple consonants as fricatives, but keeping the stop sound in the doubled ones, and furthermore that singles and doubles were found at the beginning of words as well as between vowels. Later on this automatic pattern of pronunciation was disturbed by the influence of words borrowed from foreign languages. In consequence a contrast between fricative and stop came to be recognized without relation to doubling. Previous to this development, the important contrast was between single and double; after it, the main contrast was between fricative and stop.

Let us turn now to the function of the strengthening process, first with regard to its present manifestation and then to its origin. To attempt to solve this problem, it is necessary to recognize that there are evidently two sources of strengthening, one of them by addition, the other by reduplication. Addition involves two consonants coming together as a result of affixation. Thus in Fula we have singular *lew-ru*, month, but plural *leb-bu*, months, in which the double *b* comes by joining the *w* of the root with the *b* of the suffix -*bu*; and *leg-gal*, tree, alongside *led'-d'e*, trees, in which the root final— basically *k*, as is evident in *lek-ki*, a variant form for "tree"—is assimilated by the *g* of the suffix -*gal* in the singular and by -*d'* of the plural -*d'e*. In the same way, when an initial spirant becomes a stop in certain verbal nouns, it is possible that some old prefix is involved, which produced a double consonant by addition. The stop became single because all doubles were simplified in initial position.

But not all the medial doubles and initial stops can be explained by the additive process. Others represent old reduplications. Those in medial position show rather clear signs of intensive meaning, "to do repeatedly or with force," as in the examples cited above. The instances of reduplication in the initial position of words have the meaning of plural, as in Fula:

wol-de	word	*bol-le*	words
suy-re	hunchback	*chu-'e*	hunchbacks
silaa-wo	basket	*chilaa-i*	baskets
rew-a	woman	*deb-bo*	women

Intensive action, repetition, and plurality are obviously related meanings, so that there is a reasonably clear indication that doubling was once a symbolic procedure with a definite significance.

In languages of the Fula-Bantuan phylum other than Fula (for example, Kabre and other closely related Gur languages), the strengthened form is also used to form the plural. In the Akan languages, a strengthening process occurs in reduplicated intensives of adjectives. In various other languages, the variation between fricative and stop crops up sporadically without immediately apparent cause; the best explanation is that the instances are remnants of an old alternation that broke down and is reflected only in scattered fossils in some languages.

Vowel alternation has been documented in some languages of the Fula-Bantuan phylum. Thus we have the Dagbani plural formations *pab-li*, lip, *piba*, lips; *nag*, cow, *nigi* cows. It is also found in various miscellaneous occurrences: *pigi*, to shell, *pugi*, to shell; *ta*, to daub, *tu*, to insert; *yaki*, to cross, *yika*, to fly; *za-*, to stand, *zi*, to carry poised on the head, and *zu-gu*, head. This is a matter that still requires systematic research, but it seems clear that vowel alternation must once have been a regular and extensive expressive process.

Tarasco-Mayan

Several languages of the New World reached the classic stage before the European invasion put an end to their advance. In North America, the Iroquois and Muskogean confederacies, the Natchez kingdom, and the southwestern pueblos were urbanized only a few centuries before European contact; but in two principal areas of present-day Latin America, Peru and a region stretching from southern Mexico to northern Honduras, high cultures appeared as early as about two thousand years ago. In Mexico, writing is known to have begun not later than the fourth century of the present era. Let us examine some languages of this region for further evidence of the development from the local to the classic stage.

We can take as our principal focus the Maya language of the Yucatan Peninsula and Guatemala. Its prehistory as far back as about 2000 B.C. can be illuminated with the help of twenty-five other languages that belong to the Mayan stock. The next nearest relationships, according to recent studies, include the Zoquean and Totonacan families and Tarasco. This last was the language of an important empire in central Mexico, a power the Aztecs made treaties with but had not conquered. The Totonacs once had a splendid culture, as archeological finds have shown, before they came under the domination of the Aztecs. The Zoquean stock includes mostly hill tribes, the "poor relations"; but at least one group, the Zoques, had a relatively advanced culture. Somewhat further removed in the order of relationship may be Uto-Aztecan, Quechua-Aymara, and other languages. When the details of their comparative linguistics have been worked out, passage from the local to the classic stage of these languages will become clear for some thousands of years back. For the present we must speak mainly of languages whose common period has been estimated about five thousand years before Christ. We shall speak of this set of languages as the Tarasco-Maya cluster, or Tarasco-Mayan for short.

In the set of four language families we are examining (Mayan, Zoquean, Totonacan, and Tarasco), there is everywhere clearly represented the typical two-consonant pattern of stems. It is the dominant type in all the languages, and there is comparative evidence to show that one-consonant forms, other than demonstratives, pronouns, the negative, and formatives, have been reduced from older two-con" nant forms. The longer lexemes, involving three or more consonants, are often analyzable etymologically into a nucleus with old affixes. Tarasco has a certain number of longer stems that cannot be analyzed, but this is quite evidently due to the fact that it has no close relatives to clarify the analysis of the complexes. Even so, the number of unanalyzable three-consonant forms in Tarasco is not over fifty or so.

There is a difference in the vocalic pattern of the root in the compared families. Totonacan and Zoquean generally have a vowel only between the first and second consonants. Tarasco normally has two vowels, one after the first and one after the second. Maya has a vowel after the second consonant in certain combinations according to an automatically operating rule: A vowel is required between consonants that would otherwise constitute a cluster in final position or which would be the last two in a cluster of three in nonfinal position. In other words, there may be one or two consonants medially and only one at the end of the word. The vowel that appears in these positions is apparently determined by the following element in certain cases, and by the preceding element in others. At the end of a root, the vowel in Yucatan Maya is in most but not all cases a repetition of the first vowel. In Cakchiquel, one of the Mayan languages of Guatemala, it is frequently different and varies from one combination to another. This state of affairs suggests that Yucatec may have come through a period of harmonization, that is, the two vowels of the roots were made to agree as a result of a definite phonologic change that took place in some period this side of proto-Mayan; proto-Mayan probably had second vowels on the same general order as Tarasco.

In Tarasco, the vowel of a suffix or the last vowel of a root may alternate with differences of meaning. The semantics of the alternations are in part general but in part depend on the usage associated with each particular stem. The simplest cases are suffixes in which the change from *a* or *u* to *o* implies reversal of direction, as in:

-*pa*-	going away	-*po*-	coming
-*ma*-	while traveling thither	-*mo*-	while traveling hither
-*ya*-	arriving there	-*yo*-	arriving here
-*nu*-	leaving home	-*no*-	returning home

The application to stems is more complicated, as may be seen in the following examples:

erá-	to face, look	*eró*	to await, expect
maná-	to wave, beat	*manú*-	to stir, mix, join
		manó-	to poke about
eshé-	to find, see	*eshó*-	to examine
kaká-	to break	*kakó*-	to bend, miss, confuse
khalá-	to sweep	*khaló*	to take out or away
paká-	to remain	*pakó*-	to resist
tzapá-	to scratch	*tzapú*-	to take in the claws

Although only a few of them are cited here, there are actually many examples of these alternations. The rounded alternate, with *o* or *u*, implies moving around, returning to a starting point, bending, or being on the lookout. The implication of *a* versus *i* or *e* is harder to discern; a few examples suggest it may have to do with a flat versus a pointed shape or diffuse versus direct action. The difference between high and mid vowels—that is, *i* against *e* or *u* against *o*— is even more difficult to fathom, probably because phonologic and dialectal factors have become mixed in with whatever original connotations may have been involved.

Besides the alternations in the second vowel, Tarasco shows some in the first vowel. Here are a few examples:

maná-	to move, shake	*mená-*	to change
talá-	to lift	*tilí-*	to hang, lift
phaká-	to push, touch	*phikú-*	unfold, separate
tepé-	to weave, join	*tupí-*	joined side by side

Vowel alternation can also be shown in other stocks making up the Tarasco-Mayan complex. Here are a few from Yucatan Maya:

bal-a-m	jaguar	*bol-a-y*	jaguar
kal	intense	*kel*	strength
kots	pull out	*kukuts*	unraveled
sip'	tumor	*sop'*	to stuff
		sup'	to make thick
bit'	to touch with the finger	*but'*	to pack, fill
p'ah	to open	*p'e'eh*	to pick open, break to pieces
k'aak'	fire	*k'iik'*	blood
net'	to cut off	*not'*	to gnaw
k'et	to twist	*k'ot-*	to twist

We spoke early in this chapter about the difficult art of unraveling. The vowel alternations of Tarasco are a case in point. Clarity in reference to its old function will surely come by making painstaking comparisons of cases in Mayan, Zoquean, Totonac, and Tarasco taken together, while carefully distinguishing instances due to vowel harmony and other purely phonological phenomena. For the present, we can infer, from the fact that examples of vowel alternation exist in all four families, that it probably existed in an older, common period. It would also seem that it expressed some pattern or patterns of shape and directional meaning.

Consonant alternation is an expressive process much used in Totonac, and weakly reflected in the other three stocks. Taking the evidence of all of them together, we may strongly suspect that there may have been two types of consonant alternation in the common period, one involving point of articulation and the other manner of articulation. In the first, the alternation was between front and back tongue contact within a general zone of the palate; in the second, it went from simple to glottalized to aspirate articulation.

Much of the first type of alternation can be demonstrated in Totonac, while parts of it can be corroborated from the other three language families under discussion. If we add the clues together, we infer the following alternations for the protolanguage:

1. *k:q* (front to back *k*), found in Totonac, with traces in Mayan.
2. *t:ts:tl* (alternation among dentals and affricates), found in Totonac, but sporadic in the other languages of the phylum.
3. *sh:s:lh* (alternation among fricatives), found in Totonac.
   sh:s and *ch:ts*, found in Mayan and Tarasco.
4. *n:l:r*, only sporadic; *r* is represented by *y* in most Mayan languages, in Zoquean, and in Totonac.

The meanings that go with the variants may be described as diminutive, but the connotation of the categories is broader than that. An *l* in Tarasco may imply vacillation or lightness; an *r*, directness or heaviness; weakness versus strength and limited action versus thoroughness are other implications. In the dental and sibilant sets, *t*, *sh*, and *n* apparently represent the neutral aspect of the quality; *ts*, *s*, and *l* are diminutive or weak; *tl*, *lh*, and *r* are augmentative or strong. In the velar set, *q* is neutral or augmentative, while *k* is diminutive. Possibly there was once a middle *k* in addition to the front and back.

Examples of this type of alternation in Totonac are:

taatah	father	*tlaatli'*	lord
aqa-luqut	horn (bone)	*qalh-, kalh-*	mouth, edge
tli'tla'qa	blackish, brown	*tsi'tsa'qa*	black

Limited examples in Tarasco are:

tsapá-	to break, to open, to plow	*chhapá-*	to cut off, remove
tshamá-	to break apart	*chhamá-*	to collapse
tseká-	to peck, knock, wound	*cheká-*	to peck, transfix, push in pointwise
shú-ma	fog	*suwá-n-da*	mist, vapor

Some Yucatec examples are:

bit'	to squeeze between the fingers	*bits'*	to thin
sak	white	*chak*	red
sit'	to jump	*shit'*	to explode
sul	to soak	*ch'ul*	wet
to'	to wrap up	*cho'*	to rub
tuch	navel	*chuch*	fruit stem

Alternation involving manner of articulation can be reflected only in Mayan and Tarasco, since Totonac and Zoquean have only one stop series. The phonemic pattern in the common period evidently included three types of stops—simple, glottalized, and aspirated. Of these, Mayan has preserved mainly two, glottalized and non-glottalized; but there are some indirect reflexes, which sometimes make it possible to distinguish the old simple from the aspirate. Tarasco has merged the glottalized with the simple, but keeps the aspirate apart, even though only at the beginning of words.

Since aspiration and glottalization involve something added to the simple stops, the alternation amounts to a kind of insertion. As such it is very similar to another form of interposition found in all four stocks of the Tarasco-Mayan complex—the insertion of glottal stop or *h* after vowels. In Totonac there are many clear cases of postvocalic glottal stop and the meaning is apparently often diminutive. In Tarasco, since there is no glottal stop, the only possible insert is *h*. The semantic content is not clear, but the same roots are found with and without it. Examples from Tarasco are:

chiká-ni	to get mixed	*chihká-ni*	dissolve, mix
katzá-ni	to grab, press	*kahtzá-ndu-kua*	leg shackles (*-ndu-*, leg)
uichú-nda-ni	close the eyes	*uihchú-hchi-ta-ni*	blink
téteká-si	strong, firm	*tehkó-n-tehkó-na-ra-ni*	emphasize, fill firmly

In Mayan languages both glottal stop and *h* are inserted, except that the *h* is lost in Yucatec, leaving the vowel lengthened. The precise meaning of the process is not evident, but it seems that words referring to general qualities, substances, and things that come in quantity are included among the words so formed. Yucatec examples are:

ya'ash	green (compare *yash*, first)
suun	sour
aal	heavy (compare *alan*, down)
booy	shadow
ka'an	heaven (compare Tarasco *kani-*, arched)
keel	cold
ko'oh	elegant
k'aak'	fire (compare Tzeltal *k'ahk'*)
so'os	tangle
me'esh	beard
lu'um	earth (compare Tzeltal *lum* without insert)

The phenomenon of alternation of manner of articulation can be illustrated with various examples that have identical meanings in some cases, different but related meanings in others. Variants in Mayan may be within a single language or between two within the family:

Yucatec *uk*, Cakchiquel *uk'i-*, to drink

Tzeltal *ot*, tortilla (thin, round, unleavened bread made of cornmeal), Tzeltal-Yucatec *ot*, skin

Yucatec *oto-ch*, house, Huastec *ot'o-ch*, skin bag

Yucatec *kush-*, to live, Cakchiquel *k'ush*, heart

Yucatec *ach*, tie tightly, *ach'*, make tight in tying

Word structure is not identical in Mayan, Zoquean, Totonac, and Tarasco; yet it is not difficult to reconstruct an earlier type that would have given rise to all of them. The first three employ both prefixes and suffixes, with the emphasis on the latter. Tarasco has only suffixes. All four join roots into compound words. Reduplication is used, but more so in Mayan and Tarasco than in the other two. Totonac has the most extensive development of word-building processes, and in many cases has derived lexemes for a meaning expressed by a simple root in the other languages. Tarasco also has quite a bit of composition and easily produces fairly long words. For the structure of the common language, an important clue is the fact that pronouns are sometimes prefixed and sometimes suffixed in each of the three languages that employ both processes, and are suffixed in Tarasco. In some Mayan languages the formations include preposed proclitics (semi-independent words) placed before the noun to express possession and before the verb to express subject and object. In Tarasco and in Mayan, the subject pronoun is not necessarily attached to its verb, but is very commonly affixed to a connective element or other particle that precedes the verb. In other words, one says *then-I sang* as easily as *sang-I*. All this adds up to a looseness of relationship, which certainly reflects an older stage in which the pronouns were independent elements, not attached to the noun and verb.

There are tense and aspect paradigms in the languages of all four stocks, but the formation is generally transparent. In some cases they can be shown to be derived from known stems with meanings like "to finish" for past, "to go" for future. This has the appearance of a secondary development out of older auxiliary verb usages. A pattern of numeral classifiers that distinguish animals from plants, long objects from flat and round ones, various kinds of clusters, and bundles and aggregates from isolates is found in varying degrees of development in Mayan, Totonac, and Tarasco. It seems reasonable to infer that it goes back to the common period.

Language Structure in the Local Stage

[*The purpose of looking at the protolanguages of several language families in various parts of the world was to obtain some idea of the characteristics of earlier stages of language. The results of this investigation are now summarized.*]

We have not had a look, by means of reconstructional unraveling, at the old state and development of the common languages of five language groupings in far-flung parts of the world. As different as these languages are today, they appear to have been structured rather similarly in the local stage to which our reconstruction has carried us. Let us consider to what extent they were alike and what this may signify. First, the common features:

The *prevailing root pattern* of two consonants for major forms and one consonant for minor ones is borne out in the main for all five of our cases.

Word structure apparently was only moderately agglutinative; that is, there were not many affixes joined into a single word. The root may have admitted the addition of some suffixes and possibly also infixes; the present evidence for this last process is confined to Indo-European and Semitic. Pronouns were apparently not affixed, nor were tense elements.

Inner changes or alternations constituted an important part of the expressive techniques. They included:

1. Alternation of vowel quality.
2. Variation of consonantal point of articulation, from front to mid to back.
3. Alternation of the manner of articulation: glottalization and aspiration as against simple.
4. Doubling of consonants.
5. Partial or total reduplication of roots.
6. Glottalic insertion in relation to vowels; that is, glottal stop or aspiration after a vowel, perhaps with repetition of the vowel.

Though some of these processes have been cited for only two or three of the five old languages, we have not yet examined all the evidence. So it is impressively clear that all five old languages had some forms of internal alternation as important features in their array of expressive processes.

The *phoneme inventories* of our common languages are characterized by three main series. There is some evidence that they may have been voiceless, voiced, and aspirate in Indo-European and Sino-Tibetan; voiceless, voiced, and emphatic in Semitic; voiceless, voiced, and glottal-implosive in Fula-Bantuan; and simple, glottalized, and aspirate in Tarasco-Mayan. In this respect the protolanguages were much more similar typologically than are languages spoken today; the latter vary from some with a single series to others with four or five. For example, Hawaiian and Algonkian have only one series: voiceless stops; English has four series: voiceless and voiced, stops and fricatives; and Indic languages also have four: voiceless and voiced, unaspirated and aspirated.

The number of points of articulation may have been nine in Tarasco-Mayan: *p, t, ch, ts, tl, k, q, kw, qw*. For common Indo-European, we can count at least six: *p, t, s, k, q, kw*, and possibly seven, if we suppose that there was a back as well as a front labiovelar. For Sino-Tibetan, there is clear evidence for at least five: *p, t, ts, ch, k*, and probably also *kw* as a sixth.

For Semitic, there may have been eight: *p, th, t, s, sh, k, q, h*". In Fula-Bantuan, we have clear indication of at least five: *p, t, ch, k, kw*. Note that there is considerable overlapping agreement in the points of articulation. The possibility that they may all be derived from a single still older system will be taken up later. We have not spoken of the possibility of tonal distinctions; our guess would be that they may well have been present in all or most of the five common languages with which we have dealt.

If we take into account the *consonant alternations*, by which the manners of articulation are variants of each other, as are to a certain extent the points of articulation, and if we consider *vowel alternation*, we can infer certain phonemes or morphophonemes as basic or primary. That is, if simple, aspirated, and glottalized sounds alternate with each other and similarly front and back *k*, then the items in each such alternating set of sounds serve to mark grammatical meanings but not to distinguish roots or affixes. To count how many such distinct basic phonemes there are in each system, one would need more information about each language than we have given in our brief descriptions, but a hypothetical figure can be given. It seems possible that it was, for each of the common languages with which we have dealt, one vowel and eleven consonants. The consonants are *p, t, ch, k, kw, h, m, n, ng, w, y*.

Since we have a notion of the shape of elements and of the number of lexically contrasting phonemes, we are in a position to estimate the *number of lexemes* existing in the common languages of the local period. Of monosyllabic elements, consisting of one consonant and one vowel, there were 11×1 possible forms, one for each consonant. For elements made up of two consonants, each followed by a vowel, there could be $11 \times 1 \times 11 \times 1$, or 121. The sum of the short and long elements could have been up to $11 + 121$ or 132 in all. It is likely that not all of the possibilities were actually used in each old language; hence the number of actual forms may have been less than the calculated figure. On the other hand, there could well have been like-sounding forms with different meaning; that is, homonyms. Thus the actual number of meaningful elements could have been more than our calculated figure, perhaps considerably more. Nevertheless, I feel justified in suggesting that the total number was probably much less than that found today in languages of all types, whether world, classic, or contemporary local.

Since the expressive apparatus for inner change or alternation was fairly rich and was evidently employed for indicating inflectional concepts, we infer that *inflection* was fairly extensive. The categories expressed may have included ideas like shape classification, nearness and farness, intensiveness and repetition, active versus static, and lightness versus heaviness.

If the expression of inflectional categories was by means of symbolic consonant, vowel, and tone alternations, apparently having some relation to the intuitional implications of the sounds, then there must have been greater similarity between the conventional and intuitional aspects of language in its earlier stages than there is today. Sound symbolism and onomatopoeia, in other words, must have been much more apparent or common.

The Direction of Growth

In the difficult art of unraveling, the chief risk is distortion: one may follow what appears to be a correct lead that does not hold up in the long run. Hence some parts of all theories need to be corrected as one digs deeper into them. In triangulating projection deep into space or time, the dangers include also undershooting and overshooting. In the case of reconstructing linguistic prehistory, this means that one may infer that a pattern existed in a certain period when it actually developed a thousand years later, or belonged to a period long before but had gone out of active use. In the projections made in this book, I am inclined to think I have both undershot and overshot. In the group-by-group reconstructions of common periods, I may have tried too hard to hold to matters that are fairly obvious, and which therefore might be expected to win the acceptance of most specialists in each group of languages. I have omitted inferences that might be attacked as unwarranted. In consequence, it is likely that some of my suggestions apply to periods this side of the local stage I have attempted to fathom.

On the other hand, in my summary I have tried to trace definite patterns applicable to all five common languages. In doing so I may have projected some that perhaps go back to the paleoglottic period. In any event, I shall be returning to these questions later.

At this point it is perhaps well to emphasize once again that the local stage in world history must have been something quite different from the existence of preliterate groups in the recent period. Ten thousand years ago the most advanced human groups had formed relatively organized societies, with significantly improved technology, in an environment in which many groups still lived as loose bands following an essentially paleolithic mode of existence. In recent times, with very few exceptions, local languages have been spoken by peoples whose neighbors were at least at the classic level and in many cases at the world level. Even where there have been no direct contacts, the effect of languages of an advanced stage may have been diffused across a series of neighbors through a number of generations. At least this is the possibility that must be left open as we go on to examine further the questions of language development.

The material we have surveyed in this chapter suggests that languages in the local stage had limited sets of phonemes available for lexical contrast, but complex patterns of alternates used in extensive paradigms of internal inflection; that the lexicon was small and the inflection complex; and that different languages were relatively similar with regard to all these features.

The development since that time has been toward a greatly increased vocabulary with a more or less drastic reduction in inflection. Often the reduction in the old internal paradigms was offset by the introduction and complication of external procedures, through the use of either affixes or adjoined words. In some places the inflections simply went by the board. The devices used for producing larger numbers of lexemes included pressing into service as lexemes what were originally paradigmatic alternants. Reflexes of this development have been used as evidence in this chapter. Another commonly used device was the fossilization of adjunct elements as parts of the roots, even though their original association had been as independent elements used in loose association. In this way old phrases became reduced to the status of simple elements. It was probably a general rule that the first language in any region to become urbanized built its vocabulary through the composition of native elements. Latecomers were able to use loan words from neighboring advanced languages. Still later, as we have seen elsewhere, all languages made liberal use of borrowing.

References and Suggestions for Further Reading

[*For techniques of historical reconstruction, see Bloomfield (1933), Hockett (1958), Hoenigswald (1960), and Lehmann (1962).*

Of the five language families dealt with here, and indeed of the language families of the world, Indo-European is by far the best described from a historical point of view. The best introduction to Indo-European historical grammar is Meillet (1937). See also Benveniste (1948), Buck (1933), and Lehmann (1952, 1962). For etymologies of English words, see Skeat (1884).

For Semitic, see Greenberg (1966). For Sino-Tibetan, see Forrest (1948). For Fula-Bantuan, see Greenberg (1966). For Tarasco-Mayan, see Kaufman (1964) and McQuown (1956a, 1956).]

Benveniste, E.
  1948. *Noms d'agent et noms d'action en indo-européen.* Paris: Adrien-Maisonneuve.
Bloomfield, Leonard
  1933. *Language.* New York: Holt.
Buck, Carl Darling
  1933. *Comparative Grammar of Greek and Latin.* Chicago: University of Chicago Press.
Forrest, R. A. D.
  1948. *The Chinese Language.* London: Faber & Faber.
Greenberg, Joseph H.
  1966. *The Languages of Africa.* Bloomington: Indiana University Press; The Hague: Mouton.
Hockett, Charles F.
  1958. *A Course in Modern Linguistics.* New York: Macmillan.
Hoenigswald, Henry M.
  1960. *Language Change and Linguistic Reconstruction.* Chicago: University of Chicago Press.
Kaufman, Terrence
  1964. "Materiales lingüísticos para el estudio de las relaciones internas y externas de la familia de idiomas mayanos." In *Desarrollo cultural de los Mayas,* ed. Evon Z. Vogt and Alberto Ruz L. Mexico City: Universidad Nacional.

Lehmann, Winfred P.
  1952.   *Proto–Indo-European Phonology.* Austin: University of Texas Press and
          Linguistic Society of America.
  1962.   *Historical Linguistics: An Introduction.* New York: Holt, Rinehart, & Winston.
McQuown, N.A.
  1956a. "Evidence for a Synthetic Trend in Totonacan." *Language* 32:78–80.
  1956b. "The Classification of the Mayan Languages." *International Journal of
          American Linguistics* 22:191–95.
Meillet, Antoine
  1937.   *Introduction à l'étude comparative des langues indo-européennes.* Paris: Hachette.
Skeat, Walter W.
  1884.   *An Etymological Dictionary of the English Language.* Oxford: Clarendon Press.

FOUR

Language Structure in the Early Local Stage

[*In the preceding chapter, some of the linguistic features of five protolanguages were reconstructed, taking us back to at least the local stage of language (in Swadesh's terminology). He argued that as one goes back in time, languages tend to resemble one another more and more with regard to certain characteristics. Now Swadesh asks if one can go back still further in time, using the reconstructive techniques of historical linguistics. With the conviction that one can, he examines the possibility of a relationship among three families or phyla: Indo-European, Ural-Altaic, and Semitic. He then proceeds to examine in detail a number of the characteristics of language (phonological and grammatical) in the very early stage, providing examples from language families all over the world.*]

Languages today vary considerably in phonetic and grammatical structure. If one were to select five languages more or less at random, one might find among them phonetic systems with from twenty to forty phonemes, each differing from the others in a variety of ways. The grammatical structures might be isolating, inflective, or agglutinative, with the use of different kinds of affixes. If we took almost at random five prehistoric languages that date back perhaps eight to ten thousand years, the situation would certainly be very different from what we found in the last chapter. Why should this be?

At least three answers seem possible. The first is that the human mind and phonetic apparatus are such that men had to adopt the same forms of conceptualization and communication. However, this notion cannot hold up in the light of the great variety of phonetic and grammatical structures known in more recent times. Contemporary diversity shows that human communication can be achieved in quite varied ways.

A second possible explanation is that the nature of human life in that period may have favored certain degrees and forms of symbolic expression. This idea seems quite plausible, since man's world was mostly the natural world, with the relatively simple modifications he was able to make in it.

115

He did not need a large vocabulary to name the multitude of new artifacts and concepts that he would invent and form in later centuries, and he was closely in tune with the varied manifestations of nature in ways that might well lead him to symbolize their associated qualities and degrees by minor modifications of vowels and consonants. And yet even these predisposing factors seem insufficient to solve our riddle.

A third possibility is that human languages were then appreciably closer to their common origin than they are today. The period we are trying to reconstruct cannot be much more than a small fraction of the two million years and more since man began converting himself into the speaking animal, but the last ten thousand years perhaps saw more diversification than a few hundred thousand years of the paleoglottic. At any rate, an examination of our five reconstructed local languages, in comparison with one another and with still other languages, should yield evidence to confirm or correct this explanation. Such a study, to be carried out fully, would require a long and complicated mass of research, far beyond the limits of this work; but we can explore it by focusing on a series of partial tests of the possibilities. Before we get properly into cases, it will be necessary to dwell on some general problems of approach.

Have We Reached the Unknowable?

In the discussion of linguistic relationship in the preceding chapter, most scholars will recognize that I have remained for the most part within the realm of demonstrated common origin. In only the last one or two cases is there as yet insufficient published evidence to permit easy verification. If I now take up questions of much deeper relationship, I do so in the face of the presumably negative judgment of many of my colleagues, with the secret applause of some, but with the open approval of rather few. This situation has a long history. In the 150 or more years since scientific comparative linguistics has been practiced, considerable progress has been made in the reconstruction of common Indo-European, Semitic, Uralic (Finno-Ugrian-Samoyed), Altaic (Turk, Mongolic, Tungusic), Malayo-Polynesian, Bantuan, Athapaskan, Uto-Aztecan, and various other clearly identifiable groupings. From time to time some scholars have attempted to unite such groups into larger units with a presumably longer history of divergence from still older common periods. This enterprise has also attracted the attention of amateurs not properly equipped for such studies, and the notion has arisen that it is fit terrain only for dilettantes. This conception seems contradicted by the famous names among those who have studied these problems—Franz Bopp, Björn Collinder, Herman Moeller, G. J. Ramstedt, Rasmus Rask, Edward Sapir, Aurelien Sauvageot, and C. C. Uhlenbeck—men known for their contributions to linguistic science, for their understanding of scientific principles, for their deep knowledge, and for their hard work and unremitting attention to facts.

While efforts at establishing remote common origin have frequently met with easy condemnation, not all critics have indulged in it. There have been a certain number of serious and careful efforts to evaluate the theories and to state plausible reasons for not accepting them. These stand as worthy efforts at rebuttal, just as meritorious as the attempts to blaze new trails. If both sides of the debate were examined by enough representative scholars, one would expect the result that should always follow such scientific endeavors—a gradual recognition of which side is right, or to what extent each one is right. Up to now, however, this scientific approach to the problem of remote common origins has not been taken.

Before we examine some of the positive evidence for deep linguistic relationships, it seems proper to examine, at least briefly, a few of the serious counterarguments that have been used against such proposals. These have been brought together here, under convenient headings, from various critical papers, each written to refute some published essay showing lists of common structural traits, common vocabulary, or both, in two or more languages or groups of languages. The criticism states that the alleged evidence does not prove the purported theory for one or a combination of the following reasons:

ERRONEOUS EVIDENCE

In offering affirmative proof, the author may have used source material that contains or may be suspected of containing errors of detail; the author may also have made mistakes in copying the data or in analyzing forms into their constituent parts. No one can deny that it is best to have accurate information, but since the best of manmade reports may contain some errors, and since the data we have for languages are not always the best, the most we can require is that scholars use the most reliable evidence available, interpreting it as they proceed. The only legitimate objection that can be made to a body of evidence is that the amount and type of incorrect information is so great or so serious as to invalidate it. Properly, we should distinguish among degrees of reliability: (*a*) occasional errors, (*b*) frequent errors, (*c*) mostly wrong information, (*d*) invented data. Situations *a* and *b* do not invalidate a case, especially if the scholar makes allowance for the possibility of errors. Even situation *c*, if handled with sufficient care, may permit effective analysis; if the correct information is carefully separated from the incorrect information, it cannot be seriously contaminated. In fact, some of our most important linguistic information from remote times and places comes to us mixed with errors, and scholars recognize that it can be used.

DIVERGENT GRAMMATICAL STRUCTURES

Since no two languages are identical in structure, no matter how closely they are related, it is evident that the presence of structural differences cannot be accepted as an absolute argument against relationship. Only if it can be demonstrated that two languages are much more divergent in structure than they might be expected to have become, even after a long period of separation, can this counterargument be valid. In my opinion, however, it has often been used in exaggerated form.

DIVERGENT SEMANTICS

Critics frequently complain that a scholar who proposes a distant relationship has compared elements whose meaning is not the same, or which are not sufficiently similar in their opinion. There is a matter of scientific judgment involved here. What is probably called for is a great deal more careful study of how far and in what ways meanings can drift apart, but this question is one of the most neglected areas of linguistic science. In the meantime, the best we can do is put in a plea for all concerned to try to take a reasonable view of the matter, and to be flexible enough not to rule out otherwise sound evidence on the basis of unproved notions of semantic stability.

INCONSISTENT PHONOLOGY

The proposed proof of genetic relationship is alleged to contain too many different assumptions about which sounds may be equated between the compared languages. In putting forth such arguments, the critics often show that they are not sufficiently aware of (*a*) the occurrence of conditional change in phonological development and (*b*) the existence of phonologic alternation among the expressive processes of languages. In this book I provide some evidence that phonological alternations were common among languages in the past; but it should not be forgotten that they exist even in contemporary languages. It is correct to want proof that such alternations existed in each particular case where they are postulated, but not to throw out of court any case for common origin because the proponent speaks of the possibility of alternations.

UNIVERSALITY

In certain cases it has been pointed out that structural traits or individual elements found between two compared languages are also found in various other tongues. From this it is supposed to follow that the agreement in the given case proves nothing at all, or that perhaps it shows that all languages are related in some vague way without indicating anything special about the matter in hand. This argument would be valid if the proof of relationship depended on one and only one point of agreement. There is more than one clue to relationship, however; and the given item can be assigned its place in the whole fabric of evidence. English *sit* and German *sitzen* are surely cognates, even though Russian and Latin have similar forms (*sedyity* and *sedeo*); and English *mother* is cognate to German *Mutter* even though *mu-khin* has the same meaning in Chinese.

NONGENETIC CAUSES

Often it is admitted that the traits or elements compared are similar enough, but it is suggested that the agreement may be due to some cause other than common origin. The two main possibilities are (*a*) borrowing and (*b*) general psychological causes, especially sound imitation. Obviously these are real and proper considerations in themselves, and the only question is whether they fit the case in point closely enough to eliminate the likelihood of common origin. It is necessary to apply some tests.

(1) *Borrowing.*

(*a*) In order for borrowing to have taken place, the languages concerned must have been in contact in the period suggested by the phonology, morphology, and meaning of the comparable words.

(*b*) The likelihood of borrowing is greater if the words in question are cultural items, known to have been introduced into one group from the other.

(*c*) If the item is widespread in the languages of one group but confined to the nearest one of the other languages, and if its form and use agree in the nearest language of the set, then it has a good chance of being a borrowing. In this way, it is possible to judge the likelihood of diffusional agreement. Borrowing must not be adduced just to eliminate someone's case for relationship, nor can one or a few possible borrowings invalidate an entire collection of evidence.

(2) *Sound imitation and common human psychology.* These are factors that exist everywhere, and they have still been insufficiently studied. If a case for relationship depends on just one or a few items of vocabulary, which may reasonably be expected to have been independently invented in this way, the case cannot be maintained. But a case for common origin cannot be thrown out of court because some of the items appear to be due to sound imitation. It is important to stress that linguists should always include such items in their evidence, since the fact that two languages have solved a similar problem of symbolization in a similar way might date back to a common period in their past, and in such a case constitute proof of common origin.

INSUFFICIENT EVIDENCE

The amount of evidence required to prove a fact ought to be objectively determinable, and should not depend on the whim of either of the claimants. Sometimes critics have argued that since a hypothesized case of common origin involves many fewer cognates than are found in a particular accepted case (for example, Indo-European), it cannot be correct. The logical fallacy of this argument should be obvious. Indo-European is a particularly favorable case for the piling up of evidence: because it is made up of a number of branches, with a large total of component languages; because the records go back from a few hundred to a few thousand years; and becuase it has been studied by hundreds of scholars for scores of years. Furthermore, although Indo-European has a fairly long prehistory, going back about three thousand years before the earliest records, there is every reason for linguistic scholars to aim at extending their range of perception far deeper into the past. This means inevitably that the amount of preserved evidence for older common unity must be smaller. What is mostly needed is a way of calculating the chance factor, to allow properly for a safe margin, and to count relationship wherever the margin is sufficiently cleared by the weight of evidence. Perhaps the best measure of chance is artificial random sampling, which can be done as follows: A list of words is prepared in two languages, so that semantically equivalent items come in the same order in each of them. One of the lists is moved up or down on the other a given number of places—five, ten, twenty, or any arbitrary number. The words that extend at the bottom of one list are matched with those that extend on the top of the other. In this way, no word is matched with another of the same meaning, but each with another that has some other meaning. One counts the number of similarities found in this way, and gets a percentage of chance agreements with reference to the total number of comparisons. The percentage found when one compares only the items of like meaning is then compared with that found by the random approach. If it is greater by what can be considered a safe margin, say twice as many or more, then one can judge that this fact is not accidental, but has a cause. If one can also rule out other possible causes, common origin can be inferred.

It should be obvious by now that linguists do not have acceptable tests for proving or disproving the common origin of languages. We all hope that such tests or criteria can be developed in the future. Furthermore, we need more knowledge of the ways in which languages develop in general, as well as much more patient unraveling of one after another strand of evidence, so that we can peer still deeper into the past.

Indo-European in Relation to Ural-Altaic and Semitic

[*Having discussed generally various arguments that have been put forth against attempting to relate language families at great time depths, Swadesh now proceeds to examine a famous case.*]

The Indo-European and Semitic language families are especially favorable means for exploring the linguistic past. To begin with, as we have seen, both give us old documentation of languages going back to about five thousand years, and they have been well studied by generations of comparative linguists. The possibilities of their common origin have been studied also, beginning over fifty years ago; and there has been gradual progress in this, despite the opposition that many scholars have shown to the enterprise. Indo-European has also been compared by serious scholars with Uralic, Altaic, Sumerian, Sino-Tibetan, Malayo-Polynesian, Eskimo, and other language families. Semitic has been compared with Sumerian, Egyptian, Cushitic, Berber, and Chadic (in Africa, south of the Sahara). Of these various comparisons, most have fallen under the general condemnation of being "speculative," with one exception: It is usually granted that Semitic is probably related to Egyptian, Cushitic, Berber, and Chadic. This complex is generally called Hamito-Semitic, a name that goes back to the Bible, since Shem and Ham were the two sons of Noah, who were supposed to have given rise to many tribes. [*But see Greenburg (1966) for discussion of the term "Hamito-Semitic."*]

For the perspective I am attempting to develop in this chapter, it should be sufficient to indicate the probable correctness of some essential portion of the relationships that bold but nonetheless scientific scholars have attempted to demonstrate. For this purpose, I shall present two samplings of evidence, one for the relationship of Indo-European and Uralic, with the inclusion of Altaic parallels where they fit the other two, and another for the relationship of Indo-European and Semitic, with the occasional inclusion of Egyptian, Cushitic, Berber, and Chadic. [*Swadesh had also intended to present evidence for the relationship of Uralic to Eskimo and Wakashan. For a sample of such evidence, see his work in attempting to demonstrate common origins at great time depth, listed among the references at the end of this chapter.*] The proper presentation of these cases would require many pages, but it should be possible to give some inkling of the possibilities even in a few pages.

Uralic is generally considered to be made up of two branches, Finno-Ugric and Samoyedic; some scholars also include Yukagir. Finno-Ugric, in turn, divides into various sets of languages, spoken in central, northern, and eastern Europe and part of Siberia. They include (1) Lapp; (2) Finnic, including Suomi, Estonian, Livian, and Veps; (3) Mordvin; (4) Cheremiss; (5) Permyak, Votyak, and Zyrian; (6) Vogul and Ostyak; and (7) Magyar or Hungarian. Samoyedic is made up of several dialects or languages spoken in northern Siberia, including the Taimyr peninsula, the northernmost land in Asia. Yukagir is also spoken in Siberia, but in the far eastern portion on the Pacific Ocean. The study of this stock has been a specialty principally of Scandinavian, Finn, and Magyar scholars. Some of these have concerned themselves with the relationship of Uralic to Altaic, apparently a distant connection, and to Indo-European, evidently even more remote.

As generally conceived, Altaic is made up of three divisions, Turkic, Mongolic, and Tungusic; some scholars include Korean also. The best known of the Turkic languages is that of the Ottoman Empire and of modern Turkey, known as Osmanli. There are numerous others, including Turkmen, Azerbaijani, Uzbek, Kirghiz, Uigar, and Altai. The oldest writing goes back to the sixth century A.D., in a runelike alphabet, replaced by other orthographies. The most important Mongolic languages are Halha, Buryat, and Oirot, and the oldest written records go back to the twelfth century. The outstanding Tungusic language is Manchu. Others are Evenki or Tungus, Lamut, and Nanai or Gold.

A noteworthy characteristic of the Ural-Altaic languages is their use of suffixes but no prefixes. The manner of joining the suffixed elements merits them the description of agglutinative, for each suffix is lightly attached to the preceding, without serious modification, so that it is quite evident where one ends and the next begins. In this respect, there is a strong resemblance to Eskimo-Aleutian and Wakashan in North America.

The kinds of elements that are suffixed are fairly similar in Uralic and Altaic. They include a sign of plurality for nouns and syntactic and adverbial case markers. The first type distinguishes subject from object and possessive. The second indicates location and interrelationship, the sort of ideas that English expresses by means of prepositions; they are therefore sometimes called postpositions. The adverbial cases of Ural-Altaic are more or less like the dative, the ablative, the locative, and the instrumental of some Indo-European languages. When nouns are compounded, the first serves to define or limit the second, just as in English and most other Indo-European languages. Verbal suffixation varies in the different languages but usually includes elements for voice, tense mode, and subject person and number.

It has been held that Indo-European and Ural-Altaic are very different structurally, but this is an exaggeration of reality, and certainly does not apply in any way that would make an earlier common period inconceivable. It is true that earlier forms of Indo-European generally had vowel alternation to express verbal aspects and to help distinguish derivatives, but much of this has been lost in the recent period, so that many modern Indo-European languages resemble Ural-Altaic in this regard. Moreover, some Ural-Altaic languages have a limited use of vocalic alternation, and there is evidence that it was once more extensive. Even though its function does not agree exactly with Indo-European, it should be remembered that the common period of Ural-Altaic–Indo-European would have to be perhaps a few thousand years before the time for which we can reconstruct Indo-European, so that the function of the vocalic alternation could have acquired different characteristics in the two separate lines of development.

That Ural-Altaic suffixing is agglutinative while Indo-European tends to be somewhat fused is no obstacle to a hypothesis of common origin. It happens that many of the close-knit affixes in Sanskrit, Greek, and Latin show signs of having been more independent in earlier times.

We think of Indo-European as being characterized by prefixes as well as suffixes, yet only limited categories of ideas are expressed by prefixes. In fact, most of the prefixes were once independent adverbs that came to be joined to their verbs. Perhaps the nearest thing to prefixation in oldest Indo-European may have been the reduplication-like augments used in forming verbal aspects and the old *s-* of causative and intensive meaning. This feature is, then, a difference with respect to Ural-Altaic, but a relatively small one. Another difference is the use of limited infixing in Indo-European.

When one comes to making comparisons of specific elements in Indo-European and Ural-Altaic, a fair number are to be found. [*Here Swadesh planned a systematic listing of cognates together with a table of phonemic correspondences. I shall list here, as suggestions or possibilities, items taken from several of his publications dealing with long-range comparisons. In addition to Indo-European and Ural-Altaic words, words from Kwakiutl (Wakashan, a language family on the northwest coast of North America) and Eskimo are sometimes added.*]

cold	English *cold*, Finnish *kulme*
ear	Sanskrit *shrautra*, Latin *auris*, Finnish *korva*
hear	Sanskrit *shru-*, Latin *audire*, Finnish *kuulla*
I, me	Latin *mee*, English *me*, Finnish *mi-ne*, Yukagir *met*
many	Latin *multes*, Finnish *moni*, Yukagir *mengeli*
meat	German *leich* (corpse), Finnish *liha*, Kwakiutl *'ls*
mouth	Latin *sonaare*, Finnish *suu*, Kwakiutl *sms*
name	English *name*, Finnish *nimi*, Yukagir *niu*
neck	English *gullet*, Latin *collis*, Mordvin *korga*, Finnish *kaula*, Kwakiutl *q'uq'un'a*, Eskimo *quŋga-siq*
stand	English *stick*, Ostyak *tyety-*, Finnish *seiso-*, Kwakiutl *tlaxw-*
think	German *sinnen*, Mongol and Turkish *sana-*, Kwakiutl *sn-*, *sin-*
this	English *this*, Finnish *tuo*, Yukagir *ting*
tongue	English *call*, Greek *glootta*, Mongol *kelen*, Finnish *kiele*, Kwakiutl *k'l-m*
walk	English *go*, Turkish *gez*, Finnish *kä-vellä*, Kwakiutl *qhas*
water	Russian *voda*, Finnish *vesi*, *vet*, Kwakiutl *'wa-p*
who	Latin *quis*, Magyar *ki*, Turkish *kim*, Finnish *kuka*, Kwakiutl *'n-kwa*, Eskimo *ki-na*

If we now compare Indo-European and Semitic, we find in the first place important grammatical similarities. Vocalic alternation is present in both and indeed has the same general function of differentiating aspects and helping identify derivatives. Both show moderate affixing, except that the relative importance of prefixing is greater in Semitic. Both Indo-European and Semitic have infixes, although the functions of the infixes are more clearly defined in Semitic. The role of prepositions is similar in both groups. As for cases, old Semitic had nominative, accusative, and genitive, as did Indo-European and Ural-Altaic, but did not have dative, ablative, locative, or instrumental. This suggests the possibility that the old common structure (Indo-European–Ural-Altaic–Semitic) did not have adverbial cases and that Indo-European acquired a few of them and Ural-Altaic even more. The order of elements in noun compounds in Semitic agrees with that of Egyptian and is the opposite of Ural-Altaic and Indo-European. In Semitic the second part of a compound qualifies the first.

In the comparison of vocabulary items, the list of possible Semitic and

Indo-European cognates is quite extensive. [*Swadesh had accumulated a long list of such potential cognates and had posited phonemic correspondences. A small part of this list is reproduced here.*]

Indo-European a-*colored laryngeal and Hittite* h = *Semitic* h" *(laryngeal* h):

Hittite *hark*, to guard; Latin *arcee-re*, to enclose, ward off; Arabic *h"rz, h"rs*, to guard, protect

Sanskrit *aarya*, noble
Arabic *h"r*, free, noble; *h"rm*, venerable

Latin *albus*, white; *albuumen*, albumen
Arabic *h"lb*, fresh milk, to milk; Hebrew *h"elboon*, albumen

Latin *amaare*, to love
Hebrew *h"aamad*, covet, desire; *h"aamal*, have pity; Arabic *h"m*, relative, friend

Greek *agoo*, to go around, do; Latin *agoo*, to drive, do·
Arabic *h"g*, go toward, pilgrimage; *h"gr*, drive away

Indo-European o-*colored laryngeal* = *Semitic* g *(pharyngeal* ayn):

Latin *op-s*, power, might, aid, weight; *opus*, work, deed, product
Greek *opis, opid-*, power or favor of the gods
Hebrew *g"uppool*. be daring; Arabic *g"frt*, astute, able

Latin *odium*, hatred; Greek *odússomai*, to hate
Arabic *g"dw*, hate, enemy

Greek *ólbios*, happy
Hebrew *g"aalaz, g"aalas"*, rejoice

Greek *oroódoo*, to fear or dread
Hebrew *g"araas"*, terrify

Greek *óros*, mountain
Hebrew *g"aar-am*, to heap up; *g"rim-aa*, heap

Indo-European bh = *Semitic* b:

Sanskrit *bhad*, good, beautiful, joyous
Arabic *bdg"*, new, beautiful

Sanskrit *bhram-*, wander about, turn, vacillate; Latin *foroo*, to bore, pierce
Arabic *brm*, twist, drill, circuit; Hebrew *bargii*, spiral; *baarag*, to screw

Latin *foras*, out of doors, forth, out
Hebrew *bar*, outside, field

Latin *feroo*, to carry; Greek *phéroo*, to carry; Gothic *barn*, child
Aramaic *bar*, son

Latin *fulgor*, lightning; Greek *phalós*, shining, white; Latin *flamma*, flame; *flaagroo*, burn, grow, flame
Arabic *blg*, shine, lightning, clear, whiteness; Hebrew *hi-bliih"*, to flicker

Indo-European d, dh = *Semitic* d, dh, d"

(Note: *dh* in Indo-European is an aspirated voiced stop, but in Semitic, reflected in Arabic, what we write as *dh* represents a voiced spirant.

Sanskrit *dashaa*, fringe; Gothic *tagl*, hair; Old English *taegl*, tail

Arabic *dhqn*, protruding edge, chin

Sanskrit *dagh-*, arrive

Arabic *dhg*, arrive from a trip

Sanskrit *daa-*, remove, part; *daatu*, portion; Greek *datéomai*, to share, cut in two

Arabic *dhh"*, to split; *dhh"g*, to skin

Sanskrit *dram-*, *dru-*, run; Greek *dromaoo*, run; Gothic *trudan*, tread
            Russian *doroga*, road

Arabic *drg*, go, walk, road; Hebrew *daarak*, tread, walk; *derek*, road

Latin *duo*, two; Greek *duoo*, two; Gothic *tway*, two

Gothic *ga-twinnans*, twin

Arabic *d"wg*, join with; Hebrew *s"aar (s"wr)*, to bind

Indo-European initial z, *medial* y = *Semitic* z; *Indo-European initial* zero, *medial*
   y = *Semitic* y:

Greek *zugón*, yoke; Latin *yugum*, yoke; Sanskrit *yuwá-ti*, tie on, hitch

Lithuanian *jáu-ti-s*, draft ox

Hebrew *zuug*, mate; Arabic *zawgun*, mate, one of a pair; *zwg*, to marry; *zwy*,
   to tie, unite

Greek *zoónee*, girdle; Avestan *yaanhayei*, to girdle; Russian *po-yasá-ty*, to girdle,
   to belt

Arabic *znr*, belt, to belt

Greek *zéelos*, zeal, jealousy

Hebrew *zaalg"aap-aa*, raging heat, indignation; Arabic *zlg"*, desire; *zalgh*,
   to burn

Sanskrit *ya*, that which; German *jener*, that

Hebrew *ze*, this

Sanskrit *yamá-*, twinned, sibling (apparently not related to Latin *geminii*);
   Sanskrit *sam-*, together; German *sammeln*, collect, gather

Greek *homós*, same

Hebrew *zimmuun*, coming together; Arabic *zm*, to tie

Prehistoric Dialect Geography

It should come as no surprise that certain features in the language groups we are comparing correlate with geography. This is exactly what happens in local variants of a language, and it is therefore what one should expect to find among languages or stocks derived from old local variants of a common language.

Some interrelations can be shown in the manner indicated below:

Ural-Altaic agrees with Indo-European in
   (*a*)   emphasis on suffixing
   (*b*)   use of syntactic and adverbial cases
   (*c*)   placement of modifier before modified in compounds
   (*d*)   distinction of singular, dual, and plural by means of suffixes

Indo-European agrees with Semitic in

(*a*)   use of both prefixes, suffixes, and infixes

(*b*)   use of syntactic cases

(*c*)   vowel alternation for aspects and derivation

(*d*)   distinction of singular, dual, and plural by means of suffixes

(*e*)   distinction of masculine and feminine by means of suffixes

Semitic agrees with Egyptian in

(*a*)   use of both prefixes and suffixes

(*b*)   vowel alternation for aspects and derivation

(*c*)   placement of modifier following modified in compounds

(*d*)   distinction of singular and plural by means of suffixes

Similar relations can be found in phonetic patterns, with the difference that in this respect Uralic and Altaic differ, while Altaic more closely resembles Indo-European.

There are, of course, features in which all the groups dealt with agree, expecially those that are most archaic. In addition to the points already listed above, vowel alternation, or traces of it, occurs in all the groups. Of course, some of the features listed apply to still other language groups, particularly but not necessarily to others geographically contiguous with those I have discussed. On the whole, I think that evidence is favorable to the notion of the common origin of Indo-European, Semitic, and Ural-Altaic in some remote period.

Phonemic Structure

[*At this point there is an abrupt shift of focus. Up to now Swadesh has dealt with the problem of the remote common origin of language families, both generally and specifically, by investigating a particular case. The hypothesized Indo-European– Ural-Altaic–Semitic relationship takes us a considerable distance into the past. One wonders what the characteristics of language in this ancient stage (in Swadesh's terms, the very early local stage) might have been. It is to this question that Swadesh now turns, dealing first with phonological and then with grammatical features.*]

We saw in the preceding chapter that ancient phonemic structures, as represented by our five reconstructed languages, had a great deal in common. It is now evident that at least two of the five may go back to a still earlier common language. [*At this point Swadesh intended to present a table showing the development of phonemes from proto–Indo-European–Ural-Altaic–Semitic into each of the descendant branches. He never completed work on this problem.*]

In setting up the system of obstruent sounds for the ancestor language, it is interesting to relate the language groups just investigated with others found throughout the world. For Altaic, Indo-European, Semitic, Egyptian, and some other similarly structured phonological systems, one might suppose that the basic set of articulation types or manners of articulation perhaps consisted of voiceless and voiced types and voiced aspirates. And yet a few of the phonemes derived from the aspirates show signs of having been voiceless. There are facts about Hittite and Tocharian of the Indo-European phylum and most Uralic languages that leave open the further possibility that the second series, instead of being voiced, might have been characterized by some other quality. Under these conditions, it is only natural to recall that languages in other parts of the world have tripartite sets that do not involve voicing at all. A common pattern in the Caucasus, in some groups of east-central Asia, and in large parts of the New World contrasts simple, glottalized, and aspirate stops. Sometimes there is a fourth set, involving fricatives in addition to the aspirates, such as *f*, *sh*, and *h* as against *ph*, *chh* and *kh*. At this stage of research, we cannot of course be sure that all these different systems came out of the same original one, but at least that is one of the possibilities.

If all the various obstruent systems we have examined in this and the previous chapter are derived from a single earlier system, then one of the most likely possibilities for the makeup of that system would certainly be a simple stop consonant occurring with and without certain added glottal features. One of the additions was very evidently aspiration, which could be either voiceless or voiced aspiration. Perhaps this last difference was strictly a matter of local variation. For instance, if we reason from the present patterns of world distribution, we might suppose that easterners tended to pronounce a voiceless aspiration, but westerners a voiced one.

The circumstances relating to the remaining stop type are quite similar. It is glottalized in some parts of the world, voiced in others, and voiced implosive in still others. Even in America, where glottalization may be strongly exploded with exclusion of all voicing in certain areas, it also has variations in which the interruption of voicing is very brief, and even some in which the oral stop is fully voiced and the glottal constriction invades the preceding vowel. Then again the typical implosive has vibration of the vocal cords by intake of air during the oral articulation, followed by a release of the full stoppage of the vocal cords into lax stoppage with vibration by means of outgoing air. Since voicing and glottalization are not necessarily separate and opposed to each other, it seems feasible to see them as features that can be equivalent, and which may once have occurred in various local variants of the same language.

Another problem is the relationship of aspirates and fricatives. In the history of sounds there are cases of the replacement of aspirates by fricatives, as in Latin, where the Indo-European aspirates have become fricatives in word initial position (for example, Sanskrit *bharaami*, Greek *pheroo*, Latin *feroo*, carry). In Germanic, where the simple stops changed to fricatives— that is, *p*, *t*, and *k* to *f*, *th*, and *h*—it is likely that the simple stops had become aspirates before they ended up as they did. This direction of change leads one to wonder whether fricativization may not have begun with aspiration as a general rule in the history of human language. It is perhaps best to think of aspirates and fricatives as displaying two kinds of breathiness, and to suppose that the one always goes back to the other.

That some phonological systems have four obstruent types does not necessarily contradict the general impression given by the bulk of languages. And the fact that some languages have only two series and others only one does not eliminate the possibility that the ancient state of affairs may have been the three-type system.

Fortunately the techniques of language comparison and reconstruction permit us to infer what the situation was thousands of years ago in group after group of languages all over the world. In some of them, the facts have been worked out in whole or in part. In others, future research will spell out the story. Let us recall the case of English. We have four sets of obstruent consonants: voiced and voiceless stop and voiced and voiceless fricative, represented for example by *t, d, th, dh* in the zone of dental contact. These are derived from the three Indo-European dentals by the rules: (1) voiceless stop becomes either voiceless fricative or (2) voiced fricative, according to position with reference to the accent; (3) simple voiced stop become voiceless; (4) voiced aspirated stop becomes simple voiced. In Sanskrit there is a four-fold system, consisting of unaspirate voiceless and voiced, and aspirate voiceless and voiced; for example, *t, d, th, dh* in the dentals. Here the Indo-European system has been changed by the addition of the voiceless aspirate, which is of low frequency. Of the elements that contain it, some are borrowings from other languages. A fair number of examples are found with the voiceless aspirate after *s*, and it is evident that this sound has provided a condition under which voiceless aspiration developed. A few examples have been traced to the sequence of stop and a following pharyngeal fricative, *h"* or *h"w*.

The Semitic languages have a fourfold stop system involving voiceless and voiced, each with a *relaxed* and an *emphatic*, the latter written *t"*, *d"*, *s"*, *s"* in our notation. Since there are strong indications that Semitic and Indo-European may be traced back to a common period, however, it follows that the Indo-European threefold system and the Semitic fourfold system may go back to one and the same older arrangement. Our evidence seems to indicate that the emphatics in Semitic are related to back-contact consonants in Indo-European, and in fact in the case of at least three of them, *t"*, *d"*, and *k"*, this is definitely one of their phonetic differences as compared with the corresponding relaxed phonemes, *t, d,* and *k*. In all cases the tongue is pulled downward and backward into the pharynx in the moment of making the oral contact. An additional differentiating mark is lack of aspiration between *k"* and *k* or between *t"* and *t*, a detail that may be of more recent development. The best conclusion that can be drawn from the facts of Indo-European and Semitic is perhaps that the special quality that is known as "emphatic" and which involves strong articulation, coupled with pharyngealization and, where possible, also back contact, is in some ways an equivalent of simple back contact. If this is the case, the emphatic would belong to a different order of variation from that involving the three fundamental articulation types.

Of the systems made up of one or two stop series, there are many interesting cases where an older stage turns out to have had three. In the first place, the classic stages of certain Indo-European languages, before the introduction of loan words from Greek and Latin, had only two series. This was essentially the case of Celtic and Slavic after the simple voiced and aspirate voiced had fallen together, and, in a more complicated way, of Hittite. In Tocharian, all three series fall into one. In these cases, however, since derivatives of common Indo-European are involved, we know that an earlier stage had the threefold system. Likewise, common Semitic, aside from the matter of the emphatics, had only two sets, and the same was true of Egyptian and common Ural-Altaic. Again, if all these groups go back to a common earlier language, the two- and threefold systems must stem from one and the same system. Now, if the threefold system is derived from the twofold system, one would expect to find evidence of a split that took place in one of the types under given circumstances. In the absence of such evidence, and with data that confirm the alternate view, we must conclude that the twofold system has come out of the threefold one by the fusing of two of the old sets, the voiced and the aspirate, in these cases just as in Slavic.

In other parts of the world, similar cases of reduction of the three to two or one are to be found. In Tibeto-Burman, Burmese has only two types, but these are evidently derived from the three still preserved in Tibetan. In the Chukchian stock of northeastern Siberia, Chukchee and Koryak have two obstruent types, voiceless and voiced, but Kamchadal, as it was reported in the nineteenth century, still had certain roots with glottalized stops, evidently a fading relic of the old common period. In the Wakashan stock of the northwest coast of North America, the Kwakiutl branch has three sets, while the Nootka has fused the nonaspirates with the aspirates. In the Algonkian and Ritwan groupings, the Algonkian languages have reduced their stops to a single series, but Yurok and Wiyot have the old three. The Uto-Aztecan languages point back to a common period, estimated as about five thousand years ago, in which the stops were already down to a single series, apart from a weak-strong dichotomy evidently based on single and double phonemes. And yet Uto-Aztecan has been shown to have a common origin with Kiowa-Tanoan, characterized by the now familiar threefold system.

In order to simplify the presentation of the general picture, I have spoken so far only of obstruent consonants. I must now add an interesting detail. There are a few languages, among them the Wakashan and Salishan languages in the Pacific northwest, which have glottalized sonorants, like *y'*, *w'*, *m'*, and *n'*. Elsewhere, for instance in Comanche, there are aspirate continuants. We have no basis for inferring as yet whether these are relatively recent innovations or holdovers from a time when tripartism was a general property of consonants in general and not just of obstruents.

There is one part of the world where a quite different type of stop sound is found. This is southern Africa, where three groups of languages—the Bushman-Hottentot or Khoisan, the Sandawe, and the Hatsa, perhaps all of them distantly related—use a differentiation of phonemes based on the contrast between simple and click consonants, in addition to the variations among voiceless, voiced, and aspirates. Clicks have also been taken from the Khoisan-Hatsa language into the south Bantuan language.

Now click sounds are found in the intuitive vocabulary of imitatives and exclamatives in many parts of the world, just as in English we make use of *p!*, *ts!*, *t!*, and *tl!* The unusual thing about the click languages is that these sounds are a part of ordinary verbs, nouns, and adjectives, as in Zulu *ts!ula*, to sing, and Hottentot *dz!ai*, strong; *ts!om*, spirit; and *t!howi*, valley. In fact, the number of Hottentot major roots beginning in clicks runs to about 70 percent of the total; interestingly, demonstratives, pronouns, and particles do not have them. The clicks may be simple, voiced, aspirate, or prenasalized, while the nonclick consonants contrast simple, glottalized, and aspirates.

The question that is posed by the click languages, and for which we have no sure answer at the present time, is whether the click effect is as old as or older than the tripartite stop sets, or whether this is a new feature that has been introduced into the conventional vocabulary from the intuitive one. Since there is every reason to suppose that intuitive and conventional vocabularies were closer together in the very distant then in the recent past, the best guess might be that we are dealing with a holdover from very long ago.

In discussing phonemic structure in the distant past, I have given considerable attention to the question of manners or types of articulation. It was necessary to make a brief survey of the world's languages in order to arrive at some tentative answers to the important question of how many such stops there were in earlier stages of language. I shall now summarize much more briefly the remaining aspects of the phonological system of ancient language. As we have already seen, there is evidence for the existence of two and perhaps three points of articulation in the general velar area in the early stage of language we are examining. Some of the evidence already given and phonological systems such as those in southern India, in Australia, and in parts of Africa and America suggest also three contact points in the dental and sibilant zones. In addition to obstruents, it seems most probable that there were also nasals and liquids, with three points of contact in the dental and the velar zones, and that there were at least two semiconsonants, *y* and *w*. Glottal phonemes may well have been glottal stop and *h*. As for vowels, the old system may have consisted of three or four: high front, high back, low, and central, which we may symbolize as *i*, *u*, *a*, and *e* respectively. At any rate, the consonant system was much more complicated than the vowel system.

Ancient Root Forms and Expressive Processes

In the five old common languages we have examined, it is evident that the prevailing root form had two consonants for major elements and one for minor ones. Adhesions of additional consonants, presumably from independent elements, had already begun before the end of the common period in Indo-European and Semitic. In fact, if we go back as far as common Indo-European–Semitic, there were already three-consonant forms that were either already set or had at least become sufficiently current as derived complexes to be reflected in both Indo-European and Semitic. Yet the instances of clear three-consonant roots pointing back to common Indo-European–Semitic are not numerous, and furthermore are usually coupled with other two-consonant forms of similar meaning, indicating that the latter are the real base of the longer ones.

Comparative linguistic research does not yet offer other cases in which the far distant past can be so clearly seen as in Indo-European–Semitic. In time it may be possible to go back much further in the line of Indo-European–Semitic to common Ural-Altaic–Indo-European–Semitic–Hamitic and even beyond. We can also increase our perspective by broadening our range of vision to other languages of the world. In this way we note that the great bulk of languages shows the two-consonant form as general and typical. There are, of course, many languages that have reduced their roots to one-consonant forms through the loss of initial, final, or medial consonants; but for these cases there is often also internal or comparative evidence to show an older two-consonant stage.

Of our two oldest recorded languages, Sumerian and Egyptian, the former is strongly biconsonantic, with instances of reduction; the latter has a limited proportion of three-consonant forms that cannot be broken down. Akkadian-Babylonian already has the characteristic Semitic three-consonant roots, with the usual evidence for earlier biconsonantism.

One of the most important approaches to this problem should be an effort to identify the added consonants and determine their meanings. If this can someday be done, it should give final assurance of what has been suggested here, that some fifteen thousand or so years ago roots did not have more than two consonants.

Whenever a scientist finds a solution to a problem, he should check it for every possible error. In this case, caution demands that I ask myself the searching questions: Could it be that I am misreading the evidence? Could it be that something in the situation works to wear roots down to two consonants or that such a principle, no longer effective under the conditions of classic and world communication, was operative up to the late paleoglottic and early neoglottic? This thought brings to mind Otto Jespersen's theory of element crystallization out of song.

Thinkers prior to Jespersen assumed an evolution of language from the simple to the complex. They held that man must have begun to communicate with monosyllables and afterward learned to combine them into longer words and sentences. Jespersen thought it might have happened the other way around. He suggested that man first expressed himself in snatches of song, which gave vent to his feelings of success or failure, joy or despair. Some of the spontaneous outbursts were repeated to recall the occasion when they were formed or to express similar events. When two songs were partly alike and partly different, the like portions became associated with the common features of two situations. In this way, words were extracted from primeval unbroken songs. Unquestionably this is a clever theory, and it fits the observed fact that some animals sing in phrases and melodies. It fails, however, to account for the fact that animals also grunt, squeal, and chirp. Perhaps some signals were crystallized out of primordial phrases, but others must have come from short bursts of voice, including one- and two-consonant monosyllables. Even the longer sound sequences of animals often consist of the repetition of syllables or syllable groups.

However this may be, we are now referring not to the dawn of language but to the late paleoglottic and early neoglottic. Well-formed meaningful elements were already present and new ones were being formed out of sound-imitative and exclamative vocables. To infer their form, we must learn to use not just theories of the primordial word, but concrete evidence realistically interpreted on the basis of a thorough understanding of the way phonemes are conserved and lost.

An essential factor in the conservation of consonants is their position in the string of phonemes that make up the word, especially with reference to the accent, but also to the length of the string. Phonemes that are accented receive more time and pressure than the others, and therefore hold up better. If they are not accented, they are more subject to wear. The principle of string and accent position tells us, as can be confirmed by comparative evidence, that the viability of consonants must have decreased when affixes were added. As words became longer, more consonants within a word were located before or after the accent, and therefore were susceptible to weakening or loss.

Consonants can also be graded as weak or strong, and therefore more easily or less easily lost. The strength of a consonant is evident in two things, first in its manner of articulation and second in its point of contact. It is weak or strong directly in accordance with the force of its articulation and indirectly according to the concentration of the effort. That is, ordinarily a simple stop is stronger than one that is voiced, glottalized, or aspirated because these movements tend to take force away from the contact. Those that are voiced pass with some ease into semivowels or blend with preceding and following vowels. If they are glottalized or aspirated, they may lose their oral contact and be retained as ' or *h*. None of this is to say that simple stops cannot be altered, since obviously they can take on aspiration or, what almost amounts to the same thing, be made into fricatives. Once having made the first change, they may move onto the next and eventually disappear. If there were no forces pushing in the opposite direction, all words would thus eventually wear down to vowels. Of the strengthening forces, one is direct compensatory reversal. That is, when sounds begin to weaken, a saving trend of strengthening may set in.

There are also grammatical influences that help preserve the component phonemes of elements. I have mentioned in another connection the doubling of consonants as a device for expressing plurality, emphasis, and repetition. This procedure at the same time helps to preserve the consonant against the tendency to be weakened or lost. In some cases it may lead to the splitting of a root into two separate items. That is, if doubling has once existed and ceases to be used, it is possible that in some instances two variant forms of the root with somewhat different meanings may live on. Still another grammatical development that may extend the life of a consonant is its joining in a sequence with another belonging to an affix. The product of two joined consonants is often a double consonant, identical with one of the components or somewhere between the two in quality. If the product is otherwise identical with the root consonant, the form of the root is strengthened and preserved. If it is not, the root will take on a new appearance, as happened with Latin *octo*, eight, when it became *otto* in Italian, thereby losing the *k* that was originally the second consonant of its root.

Another aspect of articulatory strength is evidently connected with the physiology of the articulating organs. The stops that hold up best are those made with the point of the tongue against the teeth or the gums; next come the front *k* sounds, produced with the middle of the tongue against the hard palate. Labial sounds are a bit weaker, but hold up fairly well on the whole. The weakest are the back velar and glottal sounds. It is important to recognize that these statements of "universal" phonetic developments refer only to tendencies; they hold true only in a very general way. In some languages, all sounds show an excellent record of conservation; in others, in what appears to be a capricious manner, weaker phonemes are conserved. Still, these generalizations probably cover the majority of cases.

The principle of string and accent position does not by itself solve the problem of the ancient size of the root, since obviously it could work equally well to conserve an old accented two-consonant structure or to wear down longer ones to a standard size. But the accent does not always fall on the root. It even happens with some frequency that the position of the accent fluctuates among local variants of the same language. This means that there will be differential effects upon the original items of the common language as they develop in the various descendants. Some of the latter, then, may throw light on the initial phonemes, others on the final ones, some on the root, others on the affixes, and so forth. Again, there are combinations in which each root may have been used, sometimes without affixes, sometimes with prefixes, suffixes, or infixes. Likewise, as we have seen, there are differentials of conservation according to manner of articulation, point of contact, and individual phonemes. All this means that what one may lose track of in one part of the reconstruction of old common forms may be clarified with other material. That is why I feel some confidence in concluding from the evidence that major roots had two consonants. Of course, I favor continued research, making use of these and other principles, which may help confirm or correct this conclusion.

Related to the problem of root form is that of the expressive processes. In line with my reasoning about the root form, the best inference would appear to be that prefixation and suffixation were virtually unknown in the early neoglottic, and that infixation may also have been a secondary process, coming after a period when elements were used side by side in phrases. The stringing of elements into short sentences must have existed, but the most elaborate grammatical processes in early times seem to have been those of reduplication and internal change or alternation.

Vowel Alternation in World Perspective

All five of the languages we have examined show use of expressive vowel alternation. Is this a general paleoglottic trait? One would expect it to be, if only because it fits well with intuitive language. That is, if *ping* and *bing* imitate thin, high-pitched impacts, while *bang* and *bong* represent loud, deep ones, even in modern imitative usage, then there is all the more reason to expect our paleoglottic ancestors to have allowed such expressive effects to work their way into the conventional language in their time. It is wise to hesitate before we commit ourselves completely to a doctrine, however. We must consider the possibility that the matter may be a perennial, recurrent phenomenon that through all the ages has had its outcroppings in conventional language, seeping in, as it were, from the intuitional. Not to mislead ourselves, we must examine the evidence in depth and in breadth, trying to determine whether older usage was more extensive than modern.

To define our terms, we must note that vocalic alternation may involve vowel quality or quantity, and that in the latter manifestation it may resemble glottal insert, since a lengthened vowel, like *áa*, is in a sense doubled, and so is a glottally interrupted one, such as *á'a* or *áha*. Glottal insert is dealt with in a later section; here I shall simply remark that some instances of long vowels may have arisen out of the contraction of glottally interrupted ones. In the same way, timbre or quality alternation may sometimes rest on length interchanges. In modern English sing-sang-sung-song (in my orthography *sing-seeng-sang-soong*), the old distribution of quality and quantity has been completely reshuffled. In Indo-European, this set was **seng-song-sng-soong*. In other words, the first two forms had vowels of normal length with alternation of timbre; the third had no vowel (showed the "zero" grade); and the last one had the lengthened grade of the *o*-timbre.

Now, if length differences in a language like English could have been converted into quality differences and vice versa, then it is evident that the original sound-imitative basis of the alternation must have been forgotten in the moment of these phonetic changes, at least sufficiently to permit the phonological development that occurred. There is the interesting example of old *tiine* (spelled "tine"), as documented in the fourteenth century, which gave rise to modern *taainii* (tiny), *tiinii* (teeny), and *tiin-sii* (teensy). The form *taainii* shows that the vowel went through the regular phonetic change from *ii* to *ai* that took place around the fifteenth century. The modern occurrence of *tiinii* shows renewed intuitive or sound-imitative use of the narrow vowel *ii* to represent something small. The striking thing to note in this case is that the example stands alone. If the intuitive languages predominantly controlled the conventional, there would be many such adjustments in favor of sound-imitative forms, and forms like *taainii* would be normally replaced (or not changed in the first place). Thus we see that the intuitive language breaks through into the conventional from time to time, but the conventional mostly goes its own way. Possibly in the paleoglottal period the two were much closer together.

One fact that strongly supports the idea that vocalic alternation was more important in older times is that, in all but one of our five case studies in ancient language, the trend has been markedly away from the old pattern. The exception is Semitic, where the verb is still inflected with the help of vowel changes; but even here the proportional function of the alternation process has declined with the increasing importance of nouns, both derived and borrowed, and the corresponding decrease in the use of the verb. In modern Indo-European languages, the employment of vowel alternation is at best a faint shadow of what it once was. And in the other cases, too, the active employment of vocalic interchange is limited today, while the evidence is that it was more important earlier.

If we go beyond our five case studies, one of the main difficulties is lack of information. This is because, of all the research that goes into matters of language, only a small part is historical and reconstructive; furthermore, even this work aims at reconstructing relatively recent stages of language, quite similar to contemporary languages. Even so, there are many scattered bits of evidence for ancient vowel alternations, both qualitative and quantitative, which in general support the trend inferred from our five case histories.

Certain instances of vowel alternation must be subtracted from the evidence for ancient occurrence. These include cases in which the alternation is recent and due to mechanical phonologic factors. A case in point is the mutation found in the plural, causative, and comparative in Germanic languages, and which is due to the former presence of a palatal phoneme, *y*, *i*, or *e*, in the following syllable. Examples of the mutational plural in English are:

Singular	Plural	Proto-Germanic Plural
man	*men*	**mann-i*
foot	*feet*	**foot-i*
goose	*geese*	**goos-i*
mouse	*mice*	**muus-i*

The causative mutation, based on the use of the old suffix *-ya-*, is found, for example, in:

Base Form	Causative	Proto-Germanic Causative
fall	*fell*	**fal-ya-n*
full	*fill*	**ful-ya-n*
band	*bend*	**band-ya-n*

Examples of the same changes in the comparative are few in modern English because the modified forms have been evened out. The only one still used is *elder* as the comparative of *old*, from **old-er*. Quantitative variation is often related mechanically to accent, as one might expect. The vowel of an accented syllable may be lengthened, or at least it will be retained in a normal length, while unaccented vowels may be shortened or lost entirely. Meaningful (as distinct from mechanical) length variation is involved where a vowel is given a degree of length greater or less than is normally called for in the position in which it occurs, and where this changed quantity has semantic implications.

To get at possible old meanings connected with vocalic alternation, a good way to begin is by examining the different senses in which variations are found in known languages. I shall deal first with length variations, where they occur apart from qualitative modification of where they appear to be the more important part of the change.

Recall first that lengthening is one of the factors in semi-intuitional speech. For instance, in English, an emphasis on *good* (in my orthography *gud*) will draw out the vowel, a feature we can represent by writing *gu:d, gu::d,* or *gu:::d,* to indicate different amounts of expressive lengthening. Interestingly, this protraction of the vowel does not modify its quality, and one can distinguish *gu:d* perfectly well from *guud* (*gooed*), *shu:d* (*should*) from *shuud* (*shooed*), *fi:t* (lengthened *fit*) from *fiit* (*feet*), *di:d* (lengthened *did*) from *diid* (*deed*), etc. Expressive lengthening is probably used in all languages.

The facts about formal length in earlier stages of language are not easy to find, for several reasons: because many present-day phonemic systems do not distinguish length; because, when length is distinguished, the distinction may be derived from the contraction of syllables, rhythmic conditions, and other nonoriginal conditions; and because the data may be inadequately reported. Nevertheless, it is possible to bring together some interesting facts.

The meanings associated with vowel lengthening in various languages include action in process, continuation, repetition, habitual action, extension in space, doing with energy, and trying to do. Sometimes lengthening is required with given affixes, or accompanies reduplication. Here are some very clear examples:

Nootka of Vancouver Island:

t'ichitl, strikes; *t'iichitl*, is in the act of striking
hinayi, gives, to give; *hiinayi*, is giving; *hiinayii-h*, tries to give
walhshitl, goes home; *waalhshii-h'*, tries to go home
k'u'atsshitl, acts bravely or well; *k'uuk'uu'atsa*, keeps on acting bravely

Yokuts of California:

wiya, to do; *weey'-aa*, keeps doing
k'oy'oy', bend sidewise; *k'ooy'iy'-it*, several objects bent sidewise

Arabic:

kataba, write; *kaataba*, try to write
fag"ala, kill; *faag"ala*, try to kill

Sanskrit:

vad-, to speak; *vaavad-*, keep speaking, speak energetically
-bandh-, to bind; *baabandh-*, keep binding, bind strongly
dhar-, to hold, carry; *daadhr-*, keep holding, hold strongly
shvas-, to blow; *shaashvas-*, keep blowing, blow hard
pat-, to fly; *paapat-*, keep flying

In the Kabardian language of the Caucasus there is a vocalic alternation that has been described as related to timbre, but which perhaps might better be considered as involving quantity. In one form, a short mid-central vowel is used; in the other, a low vowel. These can be written *e* and *a*, but there is actually, according to the descriptions, a difference of length, which indeed may represent the old basis of the variation. Examples are:

she	leading	*sha*	leading in
zhe	throwing	*zha*	throwing in
gye	spinning it	*gya*	getting spun
ze	one	*za*	one
s"e	three	*s"a*	three times

The meaning difference in some cases is undirected or outward action versus directed or inward action; in others, transitive versus intransitive, or numeral versus number of times. These functions may be related in some way to differences of intensity.

Certain cases of vowels lengthening in the past or perfective are found in Latin and Gothic, as illustrated by these examples:

LATIN

Verb	Present	Perfective
send	*mittoo*	*miisii*
come	*venioo*	*veenii*
flee	*fugioo*	*fuugii*
cherish	*foveoo*	*foovii*
choose	*legoo*	*leegii*
move	*moveoo*	*moovii*
cover, hide	*tegoo*	*teexii*
draw	*trahoo*	*traaxii*
see	*videoo*	*viidii*
take	*capioo*	*ceepii*

GOTHIC

Verb	Present	Past
travel	*fara*	*foor*
give	*giba*	*geebum*

Since a scattering of similar formations is found in Greek, this pattern would seem to go back to common Indo-European. In Gothic there are two types of verbs that have the long vowel in the past, some that use it only in the plural, and others that employ it in the singular also. It is a characteristic of Indo-European that length variations are commonly accompanied by timbre variations also. In the cases dealt with here, however, this factor either was not present in the common period or at least is not too closely involved. Thus Gothic examples like *fara, foor* (I travel, I traveled) show the regular derivatives of the same back vowel. In *giba, geebum* (I give, we gave), there is a like variation in front vowels; that is, in Indo-European terms, it was short *e* and long *ee*. Only in the singular *gaf* (I gave) is there a qualitative change. In cases like Latin *capioo, ceepii*, it is possible that the short *a* comes from short *e* under the influence of the back velar *q* that preceded it.

Other applications of quantitative alternation in Indo-European seem even more irregular, but may contain clues to its old function. It is to be noted in particular that derived verbs and nouns often employ the lengthened root, and that not infrequently there are variants, one with short and one with long vowel.

To help understand the function of vowel length, it is useful to examine Nootka, a language that shows an unusually varied application of this process and which surely included some reflections of archaic usage. In addition, it must be added that Nootka is unusually well developed in the use of suffixes, having a total of about three hundred. Since many of these suffixes show evidence of having once been independent words, it seems possible that forms made with them may conserve structural features that belonged to an older epoch. As it turns out, each suffix has its own rules of addition. Some are added to an unchanged stem, others to a reduplicated or lengthened stem. If we consider the aggregate of suffixes that require lengthening, this should give an insight into the archaic function of the process. The meanings expressed by such affixes include to pursue, hunt, strive for, apply effort upon, be in the act of, continue, and do from time to time. These functions or meanings are consistent with the meanings generally associated with the vowel-lengthening process which were listed above.

The vowel lengthening that accompanies some nominal derivatives in Indo-European probably also fits the general list of meanings. If the noun expresses the continuation or extension of the act, a long vowel fits the functions already noted. A verbal derivative, such as the causative, may have length if the formation was based on the noun for the extended activity. In nouns, length can be better understood if we recognize that in archaic languages nouns are primarily derived from verbs. A large proportion of our nouns, even today, are related to verbs. Although we may not actually know of such an origin for a word, it may nonetheless have had it in the prehistoric past.

Lengthening in the perfect and preterit of some Latin and Gothic verbs must have an explanation even though it is not immediately obvious. One thought is that it may go back to a time when these forms referred to the continuing state that resulted from the act. Another hint might be taken from the fact that in Gothic, the bulk of examples have length only in the plural. Conceivably the pattern began in the plural and only later was extended to the singular. If so, perhaps it was primarily an emphatic plural, with lengthened vowel to express the extension in space. And it is also possible that these long vowels are contractions from older reduplicated vowels, on the pattern of *e'e*, to be dealt with further on.

The process of vowel lengthening probably began as a feature of intuitive or imitative language but became more and more conventional with time. As a result of phonological changes together with the development of new processes, irregularities and blurring inevitably developed. Looking at contemporary languages, we see the last remnants of this long history. Much more clarity can surely be obtained by further patient unraveling of the detailed evidence.

Timbre or Quality Alternation

Qualitative vowel alternation is extensively employed today in a small number of languages. Others use it in very limited ways, and still others show only traces of its former existence. Arabic may be cited as a language that makes considerable use of the process, English as an instance of limited application, and Spanish as a language in which only fossilized remnants remain. Spanish *moler*, cognate with English *mill*, means "to grind"; *mejor*, from Latin *melior*, means "better". Both forms together show a last reflection of the old *mel-mol* alternation of Indo-European, with the relation obscured by changes of meaning that presumably originally differentiated between "soften" and "softer."

The ideas expressed by vowel alternation seem at first to be most diverse, yet it is not impossible to interpret them as variations of an archaic inter-related set of meanings. In languages spoken today, these meanings include current versus remote, small versus large, female versus male, singular versus plural, pointed versus flat or rounded, and direction toward a single goal versus random or go-and-return movement. Some miscellaneous cases can also be cited in which the relation to this set of ideas is obscure. Further, there are some apparent contradictions in the matter of which vowel expresses each category of meaning.

In order to compare the use of vowels in various languages, we have to set up a rough classification of their qualities, sufficiently broad to permit us to see which ones are comparable to which others. Insofar as possible, it should follow archaic structure. Apparently, as we have seen, archaic vowel systems were fairly simple and may have had three distinct items, including front, back, and low, and possibly also a fourth, centralized timbre. If we use the letter *e* arbitrarily for the central phoneme and the usual signs for the others, we can show this conception of archaic vowels as *i, u, a, e*. In modern systems, when there is no evidence to the contrary, we can think of an *e* as probably derived from *i*, and *o* from *u*. Rounded front vowels can be fitted into the classification only with knowledge of their history, since they may be old front vowels that have been rounded, old rounded back ones that have been fronted, or a symbolic blend of the two.

In the preceding discussion, we looked at instances of vowel alternation used for notions of time, with reference to tense or to aspect. In those examples the alternation involved the length of the vowel. In the following examples qualitative vowel alternation is used to express tense and aspect in the verb.

i or *e* versus *a, o,* or *u:*

LANGUAGE	ONGOING OR PRESENT	COMPLETIVE, STATIC, OR PAST
Gothic	*bera,* I bear	*bar,* I bore
Latin	*tegoo,* I cover, clothe	*toga,* robe
Greek	*legoo,* I speak	*lógos,* word
Apache	*-lé,* handle a rope	*-lá,* have handled a rope

a versus *o* or *u:*

LANGUAGE	ONGOING OR PRESENT	COMPLETIVE, STATIC, OR PAST
Assyrian	*i-parras,* he separates	*i-prus,* he separated
Magyar	*hal-,* die	*hol-t,* dead

The items have been taken from languages in which the vowel alternation is found either as an extensively used device or as a moderately used one, but in no case are they isolated examples that might be thought of as mere accidents. Where we have historical or comparative data, they generally substantiate, and at the very least do not contradict, the inference of the archaic origin of this process.

The next matter to be examined is the use of vowel alternation in demonstratives. Here English seems to give an excellent example, with front vowel in the near-located *this* but old back vowel in the far-located *that*; nonetheless, the history of these vowels is complicated. In the older forms of Germanic, both *i* and *a* occurred in the inflection of the demonstrative, one in the genitive and the other in most other cases. The usage was generally consistent with that of the noun endings. We can guess that the intuitive value of *i* and *a* may have favored the development of our *this* and *that*, but this case does not otherwise reflect the ancient state of affairs. On the other hand, many languages without endings that would interfere with the root vowel of the demonstratives provide examples of front-back vowel alternation used to symbolize nearness and farness.

Needless to say, I have omitted languages that do not distinguish near and far demonstratives, which do so by varying the consonant instead of the vowel, in which the facts are complicated by known historical changes, and in which the forms and their usage are too complicated to display any

Identical or related consonants:

LANGUAGE	"THIS"	"THAT, YOU"
Chinook (Oregon)	*-i-*	*-u-*
Coast Miwok (California)	*ne-*	*no-*
Yurok (California)	*k'i*	*ku*
Yaqui (Mexico)	*i*	*hu, wa*
Klamath (Oregon)	*ke-*	*ho-, ha*
Tsimshian (British Columbia and Alaska)	*gwii*	*gwa*
Guarani (Paraguay)	*tyé*	*tuvicha*
Maya (Mexico and northern Central America)	*li'*	*la', lo'*
Nahuatl (Mexico)	*iniin*	*inoon*
Pame (Mexico)	*kení*	*kunú*
Binga (Africa)	*ti*	*ta*
Zande (Africa)	*gi*	*gu*
Fur (Africa)	*in*	*illa*
Didinga (Africa)	*ici, nici, -ci*	*ica, nica, -ca*
Luo (Africa)	*-nì*	*-nó*
Tamil (India)	*idɨ*	*adɨ*
Thai (Southeast Asia)	*nii*	*nan*
Burmese (Southeast Asia)	*dii*	*thoo*
Diola (Africa)	*uré*	*urá*

Different consonants:

LANGUAGE	"THIS"	"THAT. YOU"
Piro	*ṇyi*	*tuka*
Yokuts (California)	*khi*	*t'haa*
Lake Miwok (California)	*ne-*	*ma-*
Mandarin Chinese	*che*	*na*
Apache (Southwest U.S.)	*ti-*	*'á-*
Hopi (Southwest U.S.)	*i'*	*pa-*

clear pattern. I have very occasionally run across languages that seem to contradict the pattern shown in the examples, but there can be no question that the cited examples are representative of the great majority of cases.

The diminutive function of the front vowel as against the augmentative for the back one appears as a fully active alternation in at least one language, Huave of Mexico:

a-lox	he pulls	*a-lex*	he pulls a little thing
a-or	he takes	*a-er*	he takes a little
a-guaang	he hits	*a-guiing*	he hits softly

This example is confined to one language, but it seems not impossible that further data might appear elsewhere. It is of course easy to cite occasional examples of paired forms in which the vowel correlates with size, like *little* and *large* in English, *-ito* (diminutive) and *-azo* (augmentative) endings in Spanish, *-'is* (diminutive) and *-aq* (augmentative) in Nootka, and so on, but really good data with clear historical implications can be expected only from serious research that explores the matter directly.

Examples of the use of qualitative vowel alternation in Tarasco to symbolize direction of movement were provided in the preceding chapter. It was shown that *a* expresses movement in a given direction and *o* roundabout travel returning to starting point or moving toward the speaker. I cannot now cite additional systematic instances of this pattern in other languages.

The relation of vowel timbre to object shape has been observed and analyzed in two language groups, Altaic and Wakashan. Although it is not a question of a productive process, there are enough cases to suggest that they may be fossils of older systematic paradigms. The semantic correlates of the vowels in both groups are "pointed" for front vowels, "round" for rounded vowels, and "flat" for the low vowel. In one respect the two systems differ: a cone coming to a point has the round vowel in Altaic but the front vowel in Wakashan. [*Swadesh intended here to present examples but he had not yet prepared them. See references at the end of this chapter for his work in Altaic and Wakashan.*]

Sex correlates for vowel timbres are found in the Tungusic languages, which make up a division of Altaic. The most widespread examples are kin terms, indicating perhaps that an old general system was mostly lost but maintained in this limited set of words. A few languages employ this pattern for general terms for human beings and in an occasional animal name. Curiously, there are two opposite versions, one found in most of the languages of the family, the other only in Manchu. In the first plan, the back vowel expresses female sex and the front one male sex. In Manchu it is the other way around. It is reasonable to suppose that the more widespread arrangement comes the closest to the original and that the localized one is the deviant. Hence Manchu must be the one that has departed from the old plan. This may be related to the special history of the Manchus, possibly to their contacts with China, where the emphasis is on the male side of the family. One wonders if there could be any relationship to the Chinese philosophical terms *yin*, the female principle in nature, and *yang*, the male principle.

An example of a vowel alternation that does not seem to fit the several I have dealt with is the transitivizing change of *i* or *a* to long *ee* and of *u* to *oo* in Yana, an Indian language of California. The pattern consists of changing extreme vowels to a middle quality and lengthening them. Conceivably the Yana situation may have begun as a length change and then become crossed with the quality feature. In fact, another language of California, Yokuts, though not closely related to Yana, actually has a causative formation that could be the prototype of the Yana one. In Yokuts, *ukun-*, to drink, and *ti'isr-*, to repair, make the causatives *ukuun-e* and *ti'iisr-e*; that is, a stem vowel is lengthened and a middle vowel is added. If the middle quality of the following vowel were to be carried into the lengthened stem vowel, the product would be exactly the lengthened central vowel. Whether this is what happened in Yana or not, the case may be taken as an example of the many complications that need to be studied in trying to unravel the strands of evidence for archaic general traits of language. Despite such problems, it is clear there is a thread of consistency discernible in the employment of qualitative vowel contrasts in the languages of the world.

Of the several related meanings associated with vowel quality, a reasonable working hypothesis might well be that the shape distinctions provide the general clue to them all. Let us suppose that the system began with a sharp or high front vowel to indicate pointedness, a flat or low vowel for flatness, and a rounded vowel for roundness. These distinctions could then be transferred to direction of displacement: *i* for a short directed movement, *a* for something that moves on and on, *u* for something that goes around or out and back. The application to distance of two of the vowels is simple: *i* for near, *a* for middle. For *u*, the carrying power of the timbre, as evidenced in the howling of an animal, gives it the function of expressing distance. Applied to size, the *i* is a natural symbol for small, the *a* for large. The *u* may be ambiguous and not easily separated from its shape implications; if forced into a two-term large-small dichotomy, it might go either way. In sexual symbolization, the sharp vowel can be associated with slender men and the flat one with broad-beamed women. Still, if the greater importance generally attributed to men is to be emphasized, a new symbolism may arise.

In much of the material investigated, there seems to be a pull in different directions, resolving itself in different ways. Furthermore, there are mutual contradictions between two- and three-term systems. In various specific cases, an old three-way division seems to have been forced into a two-way arrangement. In some, one sees signs of an opposite adjustment. Where the phonetic system has acquired additional vowels, with new types of timbre contrasts, the symbolic use of the vowels has in part adjusted itself to take advantage of the additional qualities and in part broken down all the more rapidly because of the new complications.

Reduplication

In the use of reduplication, one can discern two main types of application, one as a sort of special imitative vocabulary, another as part of the inflective system of ordinary nouns, verbs, adjectives, and other formal word categories. The imitative usage can be illustrated by English forms like *roly-poly*, *higgledy-piggledy*, and *mish-mash*. The inflectional use may be represented by the reduplicated perfects of Greek, Latin and Gothic. The first lives on creatively in many languages, with new expressions being invented from time to time. The other has been on the wane during all recorded language history, so that one is led to suppose that, for the most part, its manifestations are relics of an older period. For this reason, as interesting as imitative reduplications may be, the inflectional type merits especially careful study.

The reduplicative technique consists of the complete or partial repetition of an element or a word. As it appears in different languages, the process shows considerable variation, since the repeated item may be altered in form and it may occur as a prefix, an infix, or a suffix. In fact, there are languages in which two or more types of reduplication are used, and it is even possible to find two or three simultaneously present in the same word.

The meanings expressed by the process may also be varied. They include repetition, continuation, scattered distribution in space, plurality, extension or continuity in space, intensiveness, large size, and adjectival or generic quality. The common semantic element uniting all of these is evident, and one can see the analogy between the repetitive character of the process and the qualities of repetition or extensiveness in the meanings.

[*The rest of this section is dedicated to a presentation of cases that seem to deviate from the imitative or intuitive meanings that are usually symbolized by reduplication. Since this process is quite common in the languages of the world, I have added here some examples that have the regular or expected meanings.*]

Plurality:

Tsimshian (British Columbia, Alaska)	*am*, good; *am'am*, several are good
Hausa (Africa)	*suna*, name; *sunana-ki*, names
Washo (California)	*gusu*, buffalo; *gususu*, buffaloes
Comox (Vancouver Island)	*xásam*, box; *xásxasam*, boxes
Bella Coola (British Columbia)	*s-tn*, tree; *s-tntn*, trees
Nahuatl (Mexico)	*koonee-tl*, child; *kookone-n*, children

Repetition:

Karok (California)	*páchup*, to kiss; *pachúpchup*, to kiss repeatedly
	ixak, to make a noise; *ixaká-xaka*, to rattle

Intensiveness:

Hottentot (Africa)	*go*, to see; *go-go*, to look at carefully
Chinook (Oregon)	*iwi*, to appear; *iwi-iwi*, to look about carefully
Nahuatl (Mexico)	*kweyoni*, flashes once; *kwe'kweyooka*, is flashing violently or intensely

Scattered distribution in space:

Nootka (Vancouver Island)	*mah'tii*, house; *maamah'ti*, dispersed houses
Nahuatl (Mexico)	*tepe-tl*, mountain; *tetepe*, scattered mountains.
Chinese	*ping-pang*, rattling of rain on the roof

Extension of continuity in space:

Somali (Africa)	*fen*, to gnaw at; *fen-fen*, to gnaw at on all sides

Continuation:

Takelma (Oregon)	*himi-d-*, to talk to; *himim-d-*, to be accustomed to talk to
Nahuatl (Mexico)	*kweyooni*, flashes once; *kwe'kweyooka*, is flashing

Only in a few cases does one find meanings that seem to differ from the usual symbolic implications, but even in these, etymological search reveals evidence of the trail that led to the divergence.

In the Nez Percé language of Idaho and Washington, one of the Sahaptian group, one finds reduplication used to express smallness; for example: *q'eyex*, chub, but *q'eyexq'eyex*, small chub. One would expect exactly the opposite. The historic source of this apparent contradiction is to be found in just a few words, like *wána* (river), *walawála* (creek), in which there is a change in the inner form of the element. (From this word comes the name of the city of Walla Walla, Washington.) Furthermore, there are a few words in which diminution is expressed not by reduplication but by a simple change of consonant. These cases lead to the inference that the diminutive might once have been expressed by consonant change, and that the reduplication of the diminutive form implied an intensification of smallness. Later, the symbolism of the consonant alternation was lost for the majority of consonants, to be conserved only when the base form had an *n* and the corresponding diminutive had an *l*. By force of custom, the reduplication continued to be used when smallness was being expressed, so that this latter process took over the symbolism that had once been carried by consonant alternation.

This explanation implies that there must once have been diminutive modifications of all the consonants. To check the theory, one can look for additional evidence in closely related languages. And so, indeed, in Sahaptin one finds that consonant alternations are symbolic of the diminutive in such examples as these: *pshwa'* (rock), *pswa'pswa* (pebble); *átshaash* (eyes), *atsa'yatsai* (little eyes); *tu·'n* (thing), *tu·'l* (little thing, without reduplication).

To find an even more developed manifestation of diminution symbolized by consonant change, one can go on to the Wishram language of the Chinookan family, which is only very distantly related to Sahaptin. Here we find *-k'aits* (small), *-gaitlh* (large); *ílh-psh* (foot), *ílh-ps* (small foot); and *i-k'álamat* (stone), *i-gálamat* (big stone). Although the common use of similar consonant alternations in a similar sense might be explained by the proximity of the languages, since one language might have taken it from the other sometime in the not too distant past, one must also consider the possibility that the process might be so old as to have come down from the common period of Chinookan and Sahaptian, perhaps five thousand years ago.

There is another interesting function of reduplication in Sahaptian. It serves in many cases to form adjectival words or descriptive qualities, as in Nez Percé *máqs* (gall), *maqsmáqs* (yellow); *sík'em* (horse), *sik'éemsik'em* (mean, ornery); *kúus* (water), *kuskúus* (blue gray); *simux* (charcoal), *tsimúxtsimux* (black).

Interestingly, this is a phenomenon that is found in a number of languages scattered through all parts of North and South America, including Nahuatl, Tarasco, and Tzeltal of Mexico and Quechua of Peru. Tarasco, for example, has *wirhíwirhisi*, round; Nahuatl has *chilchil-ti-k*, red (from *chil-li*, chili pepper), and *xoxok-ti-k*, green (from *xoko-tl*, fruit); and Tzeltal has *silsiltik*, fringed (from -*sil*, to split lengthwise), and *tseptseptik*, very notched, as cuts in wood (from -*tsep*, to cut with a knife).

Possibly the origin of this usage was the extensive character of the qualities indicated by it—the fact that they show up all over the objects that have them. Or perhaps there was originally an alternate usage of the simple and reduplicated forms to differentiate between mild and strong characterization. However it may have begun, it resulted simply as a sign of adjectival quality.

Other applications of the reduplicative technique that are not immediately obvious are the expression of past tense in such Indo-European languages as Sanskrit and Greek. Sanskrit *jan-*, to give birth, becomes in the aorist form *á-jiijan-a-t*, she gave birth; *shnath-*, to pierce, becomes *a-shishnath-a-t*, he pierced; *dar-*, to heed, becomes *a-diidar-a-t*, he heeded; and *mar-*, to die, becomes *a-miimar-a-t*, he died. Greek *leipo*, I leave, becomes in the perfect tense *léloipa*, I have left, and *grapho*, I write, becomes *gégrapha*, I have written.

As in other parts of our complicated puzzle, there must remain some pieces whose location in the picture cannot be verified without much more patient effort than I have yet been able to give it, but there are some hints I can mention. In Greek and Latin, reduplication is used to form the past tense of some verbs. In Sanskrit there are a few verbs that reduplicate in the present, and there are a few that do so in both present and past. Finally, there are some, in Sanskrit and in other languages of the family, which reduplicate in all their forms. An interesting case is Sanskrit *bhii-*, to fear, which has both reduplicated and unreduplicated forms, but which is evidently cognate with Old High German *bibeen*, modern *beben*, to tremble. The German item is obviously based on the reduplication and there is no other form. It is reminiscent of other words with a repeated consonant, such as English *babble, bubble, totter, titter, cackle, giggle, doddle*, and even *sizzle*, which refer to repeated movements and end in -*er* or -*le*, a syllable that emphasizes the notion of this kind of repetition; it is also to be compared with more completely doubled forms, like *sing-song, teeter-totter*, and *dilly-dally*. Returning to Indo-European **bhi*, the common base of Sanskrit *bhii* and German *beben*, the old meaning may have been "tremble," while the reduplicated form would then have been the one that emphasized the repeated bodily vibration. Or perhaps the simple form carried the meaning of "to fear" and the doubled one "to tremble." At any rate, the explanation of the reduplicated form is that it is inherited from a usage that expressed repetition.

The use of the reduplicated forms, as in some Sanskrit verbs, may have begun with the repetitive aspect in the present tense and then been extended to some other tenses or aspects to express continuity. Some of the most usual cases are very short roots, including Sanskrit *hu-*, to sacrifice, and *daa-*, to give, shortened in some forms to *di-* or *d-*. There is certainly a principle at work in language history that when an element becomes very short, it tends to take to it something additional. This tendency explains why reduplicated forms, whether based on repetitive, intensifying, or plural usage, were generalized in specific cases.

Reduplicating for past tense is widespread in old Indo-European languages, including Latin and Gothic as well as Greek and Sanskrit. This could have some relation to the fact that the aorist (past) endings were very short in the first and third person singular, which would be among the most used forms (that is, reduplication was needed to lengthen these forms). Possibly the reduplication was taken over from the emphatic plural; there may be a relationship also with the use of the new prefixed "augment," that is, the syllable added at the beginning of many verbs in Greek and Sanskrit for the aorist perfect. This may be a prefix, not necessarily a form of reduplication; but the fact that such an element was used favored the employment of reduplicated forms for the same purpose.

Glottal Insertion and Joining

In various languages there are alternations or modifications that involve the addition of a glottal phoneme or feature. It may be the insertion or appending of a glottal stop (') or of breath (*h*), or the change of one or more of the consonants by adding voicing, glottalization, or aspiration. The phonetic quality in both cases is similar, but in the first, which I shall refer to as *insertion*, it is set after or between vowels; in the second, which I shall call *joining*, it is united with a consonant as a single phoneme or an intimate cluster. The two processes appear to be essentially the same, and I am unable to discern any general difference in function. As it happens, I do not know of any language that uses both of them, but there is one interesting case of two closely related languages, Totonac and Tepehua of the Totonacan family, the first of which inserts and the second of which joins the glottal-stop feature in words that are cognate in the majority of cases.

The semantic correlates are perhaps momentaneous action or minute size for glottalization and persistent action or extended size for aspiration. There is evidence that voicing in Indo-European and some other groups has the same function as glottalization. The forms without an added glottal feature are neutral. In order to find the associations of these meanings, it is necessary to operate with archaic and not secondary sound qualities. For instance, English *t*, *k*, and *ch* are aspirated descriptively but they go back, in Germanic words, to *d* and *g*, and the meanings correspond to the old voiced type, not the new aspirated one; likewise English *b*, *d*, *g*, and *j*, when they do not come from *p*, *t*, and *k*, reflect old aspirates, and the meanings fit the latter category. Similarly in other languages, voicing or glottalization may be the later products of originally neutral consonants, and might well therefore have neutral semantic implications also.

If the glottal feature is used together with reduplication, combined implication may be expressed. Glottal stop or glottalization then gives the idea of a repeated brief event, or perhaps an oscillatory or vibratory repetition; or it may express scattering in space. Aspiration plus reduplication implies emphasized continuation. Since reduplication has already been discussed, I have here only to mention a special form of this process that appears only in relation to a glottal element; in fact, our clearest examples so far show it with the glottal stop. The pattern to which I am referring is a vowel repeated with a glottal stop between the two occurrences, as in Nootka *k'a'aapk'apa*, seizing repeatedly here and there, and Yokuts *mi'ik*, to swallow repeatedly. We shall see certain cases in which original vowel doubling has to be suspected even though only one vowel has been retained, and where the former presence of a glottal stop seems to underlie what has been preserved as a long vowel.

Vibratory or extensive motion is probably expressed by glottally reduplicated vowels in certain languages. Thus Maya *k'a'ak*, fire, may have this formation because it originally referred to the flickering of the flames, while *lu'um*, earth, may express the continuity of the soil. Another meaning might have been plurality. In some languages this kind of vocalic reduplication is found in the singular of nouns, but the usage could have begun with the plural or with a descriptive word with implications of extensiveness.

The insertion of the glottal stop or glottalization is used in various languages to form the momentaneous, perfective, or active tense aspect of verbs. The following examples are from Yokuts (California), Taos (New Mexico), and Takelma (Oregon). (As in all previous examples, glottal stop is written ' and glottalization accompanying consonants is written *C'*, where *C'* is any consonant.)

YOKUTS

Base		Momentaneous	Causative or Future
meek'i	to swallow	*mi'ik'*	swallow repeatedly
yoomukh-	to frighten	*yoomu'kh-a-k'*	keep frightening
yaawal-	to follow	*yaawa'l-aa-xo*	keep following
ukun-	to drink	*uku'n-ee*	makes (him) drink
sroowon-	to swell up	*srow'on*	will swell up
ch'eenish-	to sweep	*ch'in'ash*	he will sweep
peewin-	to sew	*piwi'nee-*	makes (her) sew
poohutr-	to mature	*puh'atr'*	will mature

TAOS

Stative		Active	
chi	it is tied	*ch'i*	he tied it
p-oda	it is lost	*p'oda-nh*	he lost it
kolla	it was eaten	*k'ola-nh*	he ate it

TAKELMA

Verb Stem		Aorist Stem	
deb-	arise	*t'ebe-*	arose
duugw-	wear	*t'uuguui-*	wore
gool-	dig	*k'olol-*	dug
daag-	find	*t'ayag-*	found

In the Indo-European family, the combined evidence of component languages makes it possible to discern an old pattern of consonantal alternation. The voiced nonaspirates have the role played by the glottalized ones in American Indian languages. They express what is done quickly or lightly, or is of small size. The aspirates show slow movement, persistence, or bulkiness. The voiceless aspirates are neutral. It appears evident that we are dealing here with an old functional alternation that went out of active use early in the history of Indo-European. But even though the evidence has been obscured in many instances by altered forms and meanings, it is surprising how much of a pattern is still discernible.

Alternation in Point of Articulation

If the evidence from languages all over the world is considered, one may infer that about a dozen combinations of tongue placement and point of contact along the palate were distinguished. These fell into four sets of three each: dental, sibilant, velar, and labio-velar, each differentiating front, middle, and back. The contact points in each set served as inflectional alternants to each other. This we infer from various languages that employ such symbolisms and from fossilized examples in still other languages.

We have seen that symbolic contrasts in language often involve two and not three items, and furthermore that such intuitive or imitative symbolism is absent in many contemporary languages or at least not productive. And yet as we project backward, the evidence seems to indicate three-way contrasts.

Alternation in point of articulation in nasals and liquids is generally less frequent than in the stop consonants. To begin with, the velar nasal is found as a separate phoneme in relatively few languages, and where it occurs it is more often than not a secondary derivative of an old cluster of *n* with *k* or *g*, rather than a conserved relic. It is therefore not surprising that no cases of symbolic alternations of front and back velar nasal are known to us. There are areas of the world in which contrasts exist among front, mid, and back *n*, *d*, and *r*—some Dravidian and some Australian languages, for instance. It seems possible that research among these languages might turn up evidence of meaningful associations of the type we are studying here, but for the moment we are lacking such documentation. What we do find, in languages that do not have contact-point contrast for nasals and liquids, is fairly abundant evidence for the meaningful alternation of nasals and liquids in a three-point relationship in which *l* parallels the front alternant of the stops, *n* the neutral one, and *r* the back one. Conceivably, this was the archaic interchange, and the separate branching of *l*, *n*, and *r* was a later and secondary development in certain parts of the world. Possibly also the liquids were separate from the nasals, but *l* and *r* belonged to a single set. In this matter I can for the present only suggest alternate possibilities.

The evidence that bears on the meaning of the alternants in part spells out a natural intuitive symbolism. The central type of each three-point set is neutral; the front one indicates light weight, gentle action, smallness; the back alternant implies heavy weight, strong action, largeness. The total pattern is similar in a degree to that of the variation of the glottal elements, discussed in the preceding section, and indeed there are many cases in which the two systems intercross, reinforcing or modulating each other. That is, if front contact is joined with glottalization, the effect is of quick, gentle action—for instance, a glancing blow—while back aspirate pronunciation would imply slow, strong effort, as a heavy, crushing blow. If the opposite combinations are made, each tempers the implication of the other.

The problem of uncovering the old values of point-of-contact alternation would be simpler were it not for a sprinkling of cases that appear to be partial or complete reversals of the natural associations I have just described. In these anomalous instances, the back articulation represents the diminutive. The implications of contrary evidence are clear; the first hypothesis might be erroneous or the phenomenon more complicated than it appears. To choose between these two possibilities, we must re-examine the evidence and decide if apparent contradictions can be reconciled. In the present case, there are no substantial grounds for doubting the general correlation, and there are plausible ways in which phonological and semantic considerations may have created partial rearrangements of the symbolism.

[*Before Swadesh examines some cases that seem counterintuitive, it seems useful here to present a few examples of point-of-articulation consonant symbolism.*]

Wiyot (California)

Neutral	Diminutive	Augmentative
t	*ts*	*ch*
s	*sh*	*sh*
l	*r*	*r*

lólisw-ith, he sings; *rórishw-oots-ith* (*oots* is a diminutive suffix), he hums
tawíipa'lilh, rope; *tsawíipa'rolh-oots*, twine
chawíipa'rolh-achk (*achk* is an augmentative suffix), long cable

WISHRAM CHINOOK (OREGON)
(Changes in both manner and place of articulation)

WISHRAM CHINOOK (OREGON)
(Changes in both manner and place of articulation)

Neutral	Diminutive	Augmentative
b, p	*p'*	*b*
p'	*p'*	*b*
d, t	*t'*	*d*
t'	*t'*	*d*
sh	*s, ts*	*sh*
ch	*ts*	*ch, j*
c'h	*t's*	*c'h, j*
s	*s*	*sh*
ts	*ts, t's*	*ch, j*
t's	*t's*	*c'h, j*
g, k	*k'*	*g*
k'	*k'*	*g*
G, q	*k' (g, k)*	*G*
q'	*k' (kx̱)*	*G*
x	*x̱*	*x*
x̱	*x̱*	*x*

-*kash*, child; -*k'as*-, little child, baby
i'géch, nose; *i-k'éch*, little nose
ílh-psh, foot; *ílh-ps*, little foot
a-q'óxlh, knee; *a-k'úx̱lh*, little knee; *a-Góxlh*, big knee
i-c'híau, snake; *i-t'siáu*, little snake; *k-jíau*, big snake

NORTHWEST SAHAPTIN (WASHINGTON)

NORTHWEST SAHAPTIN (WASHINGTON)

Neutral	Diminutive
sh	*s*
tsh	*ts*
n	*l*
q	*k*
x̱	*x*

pshwa', rock; *pswa'pswa* (with reduplication), pebble
ipíx, hide; *ipíxipix*, tiny hide
tuun, thing; *tuul*, little thing

KAROK (CALIFORNIA)

KAROK (CALIFORNIA)

Neutral	Diminutive
th	*ch*
r	*n*

itáriip, fir tree; *ichániip-ich* (*ich* is a diminutive suffix), small fir
árus, seed basket; *ánus-ich*, thimble

HUPA (CALIFORNIA)

HUPA (CALIFORNIA)

Neutral	Augmentative
ts	ch
k	q
k	ky

TOTONAC (MEXICO)

TOTONAC (MEXICO)

Neutral	Augmentative
ts	ch
k	q

makan, hand; *maqan*, branch

In Hupa of California, the correlation is the normal one in two out of three matters. The thin sibilant, the *ts* type, is diminutive to the broad and back one, the *ch* type; and the velar *k* set is diminutive to the back velar *q* set. The contradiction consists in the fact that the *k* forms also serve as diminutive to the front velar *ky* series. This case is not too hard to understand if we bear in mind that the meaning of front articulation, according to our evidence, is originally not just diminutive in size, but also in general quality—light impact, perhaps also light color and still other meanings. We have to recognize that some elements may have been given front articulation for other reasons than size, and that some may have come into the language as loan words or as derivatives from the intuitional language, or may have had front articulation because they referred to an object that had been seen as the small representative of some inclusive class in an earlier period, but had since become dissociated from the originally related thing. Under these circumstances, it could have happened that objects named with *ky* lacked a possible diminutive, while others showed diminutive-augmentative variation between *k* and *q*. The originally neutral *k* might thus have acquired the association of relative smallness, leading to an interchange even with words containing *ky*. An additional possibility is that the old labiovelar may have played a role. Perhaps front labiovelar *kyw* fell together with mid *kw* before it lost its labial feature. There would then have existed a variation between back *q* and mid *k* with diminutive force to help form the present pattern. These are, of course, merely hypotheses; it would require considerable study to determine whether they actually correspond to the facts.

Yokuts and Miwok, two related language families of California, show only scattered instances of diminutive consonant symbolism. These are in the dental and sibilant zones, and have the back articulation for the diminutive instead of the expected front. These languages distinguish two points of contrast, not three, but to some extent show traces of evidence that dentals may be related to sibilants, a relationship that is also found in other language families. Perhaps the front dental became a sibilant and this led to an association of sibilant with diminutive. Under these circumstances, the back sibilant may have become used as an emphasized diminutive.

In Slavic languages, one can find instances of old front *k* sounds converted historically into modern *s* and *z*, with diminutive meaning by comparison with other forms using *k* sounds. We thus have a demonstration of the normal semantic correlation having existed in an old prehistoric period. However, one of the common diminutive suffixes is -*k*-. This is derivable either from an old back *k* or from a labiovelar, which could be either front or back. Unless it can be shown that it was definitely not from the labiovelar, the case has no necessary bearing on our problem. Even if it is not labial in origin, it does not contradict our other evidence, because it may have acquired its diminutive function after the active period of the alternation, perhaps by association with other diminutives. This Slavic suffix may be related to the *k* sound in the Latin -*culus* diminution, as in *minus-culus*, very small.

What of Common Origin?

At the outset of this chapter I asked why there seems to be so much similarity among certain ancient languages. In the discussion of a series of specific linguistic features, we have seen that many other languages, far beyond the five first investigated, also reflect important structural similarities, which appear to be based on very old patterns. This adds greatly to the possibility that many, and conceivably most or all, languages had a common origin. But the case is far from proved. One still must ask if there are specific cognates in the lexicon that support this notion and if other conditions of proof are met to bear out a common origin for all known human languages.

References and Suggestions for Further Reading

[*For some efforts toward grouping language families into larger units, see Bopp (1840), Cuny (1946), Greenberg (1960, 1966), Haas (1960), Radin (1919), Rivet (1925, 1926), Sapir (1949), Sauvageot (1924), Thalbitzer (1952), and Trombetti (1926).*

Swadesh's earlier work in long-range linguistic comparison is reported in Swadesh (1954, 1956, 1960a, 1960b, 1962a, 1962b, 1964, 1966). Jespersen's views on the role of song in the origin of language are in Jespersen (1922). The types of phonetic change that occur in language are catalogued in Bloomfield (1933) and Grammont (1965). The examples of diminutive and augmentative consonantal symbolism are from Bright (1957), Jacobs (1931), Sapir (1911), Swadesh (1966), and Teeter (1959). Many of the examples given in this chapter are from Swadesh's own work with the languages in question. Sources of examples from other languages are listed below.]

Aoki, Haruo
    1963.   "Reduplication in Nez Percé." *International Journal of American Linguistics* 29:42–44.
Berlin, Brent
    1963.   "Some Semantic Features of Reduplication in Tzeltal." *International Journal of American Linguistics* 29:211–18.

Bloomfield, Leonard
1933. *Language.* New York: Holt.
Boas, Franz, ed.
1911. *Handbook of American Indian Languages,* Bureau of American Ethnology bulletin no. 40, pt. 1. Washington, D.C.: Smithsonian Institution.
1922. *Handbook of American Indian Languages,* Bureau of American Ethnology bulletin no. 40, pt. 2. Washington, D.C.: Smithsonian Institution.
Bopp, F.
1840. "Über die Verwandschaft der malayisch-polynesischen Sprachen mit den indisch-europäischen. *Abhandlungen der Königlischen Akademie der Wissenschaften zu Berlin,* 5th series, 27:171–332.
Bright, William
1957. *The Karok Language.* Berkeley: University of California Press.
Buck, Carl Darling
1933. *Comparative Grammar of Greek and Latin.* Chicago: University of Chicago Press.
Cuny, A.
1946. *Invitation à l'étude comparative des langues indo-européennes et des langues chamito-sémitiques.* Bordeaux: Editions Bière.
Diamond, Stanley, ed.
1960. *Culture in History: Essays in Honor of Paul Radin.* New York: Columbia University Press.
Grammont, Maurice
1965. *Traité de phonétique.* Paris: Librairie Delagrave.
Greenberg, Joseph H.
1960. "The General Classification of Central and South American Languages." *Selected Papers of the Fifth International Congress of Anthropological and Ethnological Sciences,* pp. 791–794. Philadelphia: University of Pennsylvania Press.
1966. *The Languages of Africa.* Bloomington: Indiana University Press; The Hague: Mouton.
Haas, Mary R.
1960. "Some Genetic Affiliations of Algonkian." In *Culture in History,* ed. Diamond.
Hoijer, Harry, ed.
1946. *Linguistic Structures of Native America,* Viking Fund Publications in Anthropology no. 6. New York: Wenner-Gren Foundation for Anthropological Research.
Jacobs, Melville
1931. *A Sketch of Northern Sahaptin Grammar,* Publications in Anthropology no. 4. Seattle: University of Washington Press.
Jennings, Jesse D., and Norbeck, Edward eds.
1964. *Prehistoric Man in the New World.* Chicago: University of Chicago Press.
Jespersen, Otto
1922. *Language: Its Nature, Development, and Origin.* London: Allen & Unwin.
Mandelbaum, David G., ed.
1949. *Selected Writings of Edward Sapir in Language, Culture, and Personality.* Berkeley: University of California Press.
Newman, Stanley
1946. "The Yawelmani Dialect of Yokuts." In *Linguistic Structures of Native America,* ed. Hoijer.
Radin, Paul
1919. "The Genetic Relationship of the North American Indian Language," Publications in American Archaeology and Ethnology 14, no. 5, pp. 489–502. Berkeley: University of California Press.

Rivet, Paul
  1925. "Les Australiens en Amérique." *Bulletin de la Société Linguistique de Paris* 26: 23–63.
  1926. "Les Malayo-Polynésiaines en Amérique." *Journal de la Société des Américanistes de Paris* 18:141–278.
Sapir, Edward
  1911. "Diminutive and Augmentative Consonantism in Wishram." In *Handbook of American Indian Languages*, pt. 1, ed. Boas.
  1915. *Noun Reduplication in Comox, a Salish Language of Vancouver Island*, Department of Mines Geological Survey, memoir 63: Anthropological series no. 6. Ottawa: Canadian Government Printing Bureau.
  1921. *Language*. New York: Harcourt, Brace.
  1922. "The Takelma Language of Southwestern Oregon." In *Handbook of American Indian Languages*, pt. 2, ed. Boas.
  1949. "Central and North American Languages." In *Selected Writings of Edward Sapir*, ed. Mandelbaum.
Sauvageot, A.
  1924. "Eskimo et Ouralian." *Journal de la Société des Américanistes de Paris* 21: 296–97.
Swadesh, Morris
  1939. "Nootka Internal Syntax." *International Journal of American Linguistics* 9: 77–102.
  1954. "Perspectives and Problems of Amerindian Comparative Linguistics." *Word* 10:306–32.
  1956. "Problems of Long-Range Comparison in Penutian." *Language* 32:17–41.
  1960a. "On Interhemisphere Linguistic Connections." In *Culture in History*, ed. Diamond.
  1960b. *Tras la huella lingüística de la prehistoria*. Mexico City: Universidad Nacional.
  1962a. "Archaic Doublets in Altaic." *American Studies in Linguistics: Uralic and Altaic*, series 13, pp. 293–330.
  1962b. "Linguistic Relations Across Bering Strait." *American Anthropologist* 64: 262–91.
  1964. "Linguistic Overview." In *Prehistoric Man in the New World*, ed. Jennings and Norbeck.
  1966. *El Lenguaje y la vida humana*. Mexico City: Fondo de Cultura Económica.
Teeter, Karl V.
  1959. "Consonant Harmony in Wiyot (With a Note on Cree)." *International Journal of American Linguistics* 25:41–43.
Thalbitzer, William
  1952. "Possible Early Contacts Between Eskimo and Old-World Languages." In *Selected Papers of the 29th International Congress of Americanists*, pp. 50–54.
Trager, G. L.
  1946. "An Outline of Taos Grammar." In *Linguistic Structures of Native America*, ed. Hoijer.
Trombetti, Alfredo
  1926. "Le origini della lingua basca." *Memorie della R. Accademmia della Scienze dell'Institutio di Bologna*, series 2, nos 8–9, pp. 1–164.
Tucker, A. N., and Bryan, M. A.
  1966. *Linguistic Analyses: The Non-Bantu Languages of North-Eastern Africa*. London: Oxford University Press.

FIVE

Out of Animal Cries into Language

[*Up to this point, Swadesh has used the techniques of historical linguistics to project backward in time, trying to reconstruct the characteristics of earlier stages of language. Now he jumps back to man's evolutionary predecessors to see if their systems of communication provide insights into.the origin of human language. A number of features seem to be shared by both animal and human communication.*]

The fossil and other evidence demonstrating that the present human species is an evolutionary development out of simpler earlier forms is powerfully convincing. Fifteen million years ago our ancestors were not in any great degree more dexterous or more intelligent than other animals. It was as a result of a combination of circumstances that early characteristics were improved in what eventually turned out to be revolutionary proportions. Today a run-of-the-mill man like me can write about communication in the various species; but no other species on this planet has specialists studying its own and man's behavior, calculating the distances between the stars, or building art museums. Let us consider why this is so.

As animals peopled the earth, they fitted into and adapted to certain environmental niches. Some survived because of strength, others by swiftness or toughness. But there was also room for weak animals who could endure because they were too small a morsel to attract the largest beasts, or because they knew how to hide. Among these were the early tree-dwelling primates, which gave rise in time to the shrews, the tarsiers, and the tailed and tailless monkeys; among the latter were the ancestors of man. In their adaptation to life in the trees, they developed grasping fists, capable of hanging onto branches, but also of picking up objects, whether food to be carried to the mouth, their own young when they started to wander off, or sticks and stones to be used as tools and weapons. The eyes looked forward, perhaps because they ran in hordes; a number of individuals could be looking in different directions and give out cries of warning in the event of danger. Since they

157

fed on fruits, berries, nuts, bugs, and worms, they had no need for penetrating
teeth, like the cats and canines, but developed grinding molars instead.

Man's ancestors were neither the largest nor the smallest primates. The
tiny ones could escape from danger high in the trees. The really big ones
could give battle with their great strength. Early hominids were among those
that moved back and forth from the trees to the ground, according to
need. On the ground they were handy with sticks and stones. In the course
of many centuries they learned a trick that made up for their lack of penetrating teeth: splitting stones by banging one against another. A freshly
split stone has a sharp edge, very useful in a fight or for cutting a vanquished
enemy into pieces convenient for eating. Such artifacts have been found
associated with one of the earliest known forerunners of man, *Australopithecus*,
whose fossil bones have been found in Olduvai Gorge in Kenya in Eastern
Africa.

Of course, no fossil cries were found in Olduvai Gorge, because sounds
do not turn to stone, but it is a safe bet that *Australopithecus* used his voice.
This can be inferred from the very fact that he was a primate, since all
species in this order have some kind of sound-production apparatus, and
from the fact that his more or less lineal descendants have voices. The
voice was an instrument of survival. We can be sure that if our ancestors
did not at least know how to scream, they would not have survived.

From these few items of information we can draw some conclusions. Early
hominids were not well endowed in regard to strength and natural weapons,
such as claws and teeth; but they knew how to use their hands and to mold
tools to their purposes. They used teamwork and could signal to each other
by vocal signs. Struggling to survive with the aid of these few skills, they
had to improve them. This required sharpening their wits, and increased
intelligence gave them new opportunities to keep ahead in the struggle for
existence. In the hundreds of thousands of years since those hominids
walked Olduvai Gorge, man's skills and organization have developed
enormously, and his intelligence has increased to previously unheard-of
proportions. The screams that helped him survive in those days have given
rise to language as we know it today.

Intuitive Language

Some scholars in recent decades have complained that it is impossible to
understand how articulate human speech could have developed out of the
formless cries of animals. I venture to suggest that they exaggerate the
problem. Animal communication is structured. Furthermore, there seem to
be some features that are shared by animal and human communication
systems. If we study these common features, we may discover how the gap
was bridged.

To begin with, man has not completely abandoned the simpler animal cry. Sometimes, when we are suddenly hurt or frightened, we let out a scream without forming words. Or if we do utter a word, it may be so filled with anguish that this makes itself felt much more than the dictionary meaning. In either event, the tone and quality of sound serves to bring help or warn others of danger. In similar fashion, the fulfillment of a fervent wish may bring forth a cry of satisfaction, understood by others regardless of the consonants or vowels that give it form. In fact, it can be set down as a general rule that whenever a human being speaks, two streams of communication are conveyed, one by the meaning of the words and another by the manner of speaking. A normal rhythm and melody tells the hearer that the person speaking is relaxed. Rapid speech with sharp variations of tone show that he is excited. Slow and weak talking indicates that he is ill, tired, or discouraged. Various rhythms, emphases, and tonal qualities convey friendliness or anger, hope or fear, interest or boredom, generosity or greed, amusement or impatience, and many more shadings and mixtures of feelings. The speaker may be unconscious of what he is revealing, conscious but indifferent, aware and distressed, or actively hoping to create a given impression. It is usual for human beings to be aware of the effect of their manner of speaking, and people are generally expected to keep it within socially appropriate limits. Even though these matters respond in some degree to social norms, however, it is evident that they constitute, in their general outlines, a broadly intuitive form of behavior, comparable to the vocalization of lesser animals.

In addition to the emission of uncontrolled cries and the general patterns of voice, tone, and quality, there are various other aspects of language that fit in with intuitive behavior. One is the fact that every language includes a certain number of purely interjective vocables that have no logical meaning and do not form syntactic constructions in the ordinary way, but serve to carry exclamative voice qualities. Such items in English include: *ah, aw, bah, boo, dum-dee-dum dum, ha, hello, hurrah, oh, ooh, oops, ouch, ow, rahrahrah, tra-la-la-la, whee, whoops, wow, yay, yippee, yoohoo, and yow.*

[*These forms are not usually reported by linguists in their language studies. An interesting exception is Sapir's Takelma grammar, which lists many, including* aaa, *surprise, generally joyful or weeping;* ooo, *sudden recollection, admiration, wonderment, call;* he^n, *scorn, threat;* mm mm, *gentle warning, pity;* waaa waaa *(loudly whispered), cry for help;* jah, *disapproval, warning;* ha-i, *alas.*]

Some exclamatives have unusual phonetic forms, not like those of ordinary words in the language. For example, they may have consonants without vowels, such as English *mm, pst, sh,* and *sss*; some are written as though they had vowels, but are actually pronounced without any, such as *humph, pshaw,* and *whew*. Some have nasalized vowels, although English does otherwise use this class of sounds, such as *aha, uhhuh, uh-uh*. Many use a glottal stop, a consonant sound produced between the vocal cords, shown by the hypen in *oh-oh* or *uh-uh* (in my orthography, *o'o* and *u'u*). Another class of special sounds used in English exclamatives is that of clicks, as in the vocables generally written *tsk*, *tut*, and *tut-tut*. (In my orthography, these forms are *ts!*, expressing pity; *t!*, surprise; and *t!t!*, disparagement.) Some exclamatives admit variation of phonetics with some features held constant. For example, the affirmative grunt may be not only $a^n ha^n$, but also *aahaa*, *ehe*, *mhm*, *nhn*, and *nghng*; the negative, $a^n a^n$, *aa'aa*, *e'e*, *m'm*, *n'n* and *ng'ng*. [*Sapir points out that in Takelma too, interjections have a phonetics all their own.*]

There is a repertory of exclamatives that have the form of real words, but are used without reference to their ordinary meanings, such as *boy-oh-boy*, *oh man*, *oh my*, and *oh me*. We may count here the imprecations that are holdovers from the ancient practice of calling on the supernatural powers, the same thing applied with reference to the Christian religion, and the parody forms made up in imitation of the old style: *by Jove*, *by Jupiter*, *by the stars*, *by the great horned toad*, *by the saints*, *oh God*, *oh Lord*, *for heaven's sake*, *for land's sake*, *ye gods and little fishes*, *damn*, *blast it*, *bless it*, *darn*, *mercy*, *mercy me*, *goodness gracious me*. We also have forms with modified phonetics which are considered less offensive than the real words, such as *gawd*, *gosh*, or *golly* instead of *God*; *gee* instead of *Jesus*; *lawzee* for *lord*; *dad rat it* for *God damn it*, and so on.

It is interesting to note than many of the meaningless exclamatives are more or less conventionalized in their phonetics even while they convey their real content by the tone of voice. Thus in English the conventional syllable for expressing pain is *ow* or *ouch*, in German it is *ach* (pronounced *akh* or *ahh*), in Spanish *ay*, in Korean *aya*, in French *ai*, and in Nootka *ishkatakh*. Yet in the stress of the moment, the expression of pain may take whatever phonetic form the position of the mouth happens to give it.

Conventionality of phonetic form also applies to sound-imitative words. In English dogs say *bow-wow*, in French *wa-wa*, in Spanish *gua-gua*, and in Russian *af-af*. Actually, a reasonably good imitation of a dog can be produced by employing the right tone, rhythm, and voice quality, regardless of what speech sounds they may accompany.

The vocabulary of imitatives in any language is quite extensive. It includes forms for representing animal cries, the sound of wind and water, the impact of various kinds of objects, musical instruments, and machines. They are not necessarily used for sounds. Patterns of movement may be suggested by the rhythm of the syllables or by making sounds that might be brought forth during the particular type of movement. Roundness may be shown by using rounded vowel sounds like *o* and *oo* (phonetically written *ou* and *uu*). Largeness may be shown with broad vowels, like *aa*, smallness by narrow vowels like *ee* (phonetically *ii*). Sibilant sounds, *s*, *z*, *sh*, and *zh*, imitate rustling or rushing noises and sometimes rubbing or slipping.

L sounds are often associated with lightness, glancing contact, and flexibility; *r* sounds tend to show heaviness, crashing impact, hardness, and harshness. Voiceless stops at the end of the word imitate the contact of hard objects; voiced stops, soft impact. Nasals reflect resonance, as of musical percussion. Various consonant sequences, like *mp*, *shr*, and *sl*, are used for their combined effect. These imitative symbolisms are found not only in interjective particles, but also in verbs, nouns, and adjectives. Some examples from English will serve to give an idea of the extent to which this type of word crops up: *moo, meow, to-whit-to-whoo, squall, squeak, tick-tock, slap, slam, peep, pop, sip, chirp, cheep, lap, tip, clip, rip, drip-drop, clip-clop, slip-slop, trippety-trap, flip-flop, flippety-flop, lickety-split, pat, flit, flutter, mutter, chit-chat, chatter, crackle, crack, creak, click, clink, cluck, crickety-creek, quack, flick, flicker, whack, pad, paddle, blob, glob, dab, jab, sag, gurgle, bubble, trickle, budge, gasp, trudge, nudge, hodge-podge, rasp, rustle, whistle, fuss, terse, tense, wince, course, fizz, whisk, wheeze, ooze, buzz, wheeze, sneeze, drizzle, sizzle, fizzle, swish, slush, slash, lash, brash, splash, smash, crash, crush, crunch, scrunch, huff, huffy, gruff, puff, woof, biff, cough, bark, caw, bray, neigh, guffaw, bam, boom, zoom, roar, groan, grunt, honk, twang, bang, ding-dong, rrring, gong, singsong, boing, clang, bump, thump, tamp, stamp, plink, plunk, grumpy, lilt, trill, drawl, howl, fft, brrr, whirr.*

Some sound-imitative words may derive from an earlier use in which they had no such implication, but acquired it later, perhaps because their phonetics seemed to suggest certain environmental sounds. Other words that may once have been imitative have acquired semantic associations that take them out of their earlier sphere of use. The use of sound imitatives is evidently such a living tendency that people feel free to make them up. Yet there are already so many that it is rare to find a completely new one formed.

Evidence of the active role of sound imitation in ordinary speech is the common practice of emphasizing or dragging out those sounds that best fit the meaning pattern of what is being said. For instance, in saying, "The wind blows," the speaker may emphasize the rounded semiconsonant *w* of *wind* and the rounded vowel of *blow*. In speaking of a rustling of leaves, a person given to talking dramatically is likely to drag out the *s*. There are also ways of working sound features into the flow of speech, such as by talking nasally, hoarsely, raspingly, breathily, liltingly, in a singsong fashion, in a monotone, and so on. Military drill commands in English use a drawled effect for the preparatory call and abrupt glottal closure for the final signal, often with modification or omission of some of the sounds, such as *fooord haar'* for *forward, march*; *baaau, hei'* for *about face*; *tennn-shan'* for *attention*; the cadence count may be made *ha' tu' hri' hooo* for *one, two, three, four*.

People talk loudly or shout to make themselves heard or to waken those who are sleeping; they speak softly or whisper so others may not hear. They speak rapidly and with emphasis to stir others to action or calmly to quiet their fears. In all these ways they make language express many and very important things that are not necessarily implicit in the words themselves.

Verbal and Nonverbal Communication

While people talk they may produce a continuous sequence of gestures, with hands, facial muscles, head, sometimes also shoulders, feet, and the body as a whole, which may add to the verbal communication. Sometimes these gestures are used alone, without words; and thus we see even better how effective they are for conveying ideas.

As a general rule gestures need to be seen to be understood; hence they lose their effectiveness in the dark or around corners. But some can be heard indirectly. Turning the body and face in the direction of the person addressed is a very effective manner of indicating just whom we are speaking to; moving closer to him adds to this impression. The effect of this gesture holds to a large extent even in the dark. There are also audible gestures, like clapping the hands, slapping one's side or any handy object, or stamping the foot. Noisemaking with objects or special instruments is properly not gesture as such, but may be a further extension of the communicative process, as are also the handling of objects for their visual effect and physical contact, in the form of pushes or caresses, with the person one is addressing.

Some nations and some individuals are more given to gestures than others, but everyone uses them to some extent. After all, frowns and smiles are gestures, and so are gritting the teeth, winking, shutting the eyes or opening them wide, taking a step backward or forward, nodding or shaking the head, shrugging the shoulders, pointing with the hand or foot, turning the face toward something to which one is calling attention, scratching the head, swaying the body, shuffling the feet, and so on.

Many gestures are spontaneous and seem to be almost instinctive, but man is subject to social norms and often suppresses or modifies his spontaneous tendencies so as not to merit censure and in order to win friendly responses. We laugh not only because we are amused, but also to show friendliness and good spirits. Sometimes we control our laughter because it would be impolite to someone we cannot afford or do not want to offend.

Man is normally both a speaker and a gesturer. Except for those few unfortunate people prevented from speaking by physical defects, all men have and employ the power of speech from early childhood on, and all men are also given to gesturing. It is common to use both forms of behavior together, but sometimes one is partially or completely suppressed while the other takes over. When the Bushmen of the Kalahari Desert are out on the hunt, they use gestures in order not to give their presence away to their hoped-for prey. They have silent signs for each of the animals they hunt, and they indicate direction and distance by gestures; they can also indicate silently important other facts; whether the animal they are stalking is sleeping or eating, proposed tactics for heading it off, and the direction of the wind. The American Plains Indians had, and many of them still employ, a flexible sign language capable of saying about as much as a spoken language. It served them on the hunt and on the war path, and also for communicating with members of other tribes. In many situations they talked while they gestured. For parleying with strangers, they usually spoke the words in their own language while making the hand signals. It was even common for orators addressing their own tribe to duplicate their words in signs for the purpose of emphasis. The practiced sign talker was able to express himself in this medium with as much ease and spontaneity as in his spoken tongue.

The Bushmen and the Plains Indians are merely outstanding exponents of practices followed in varying degrees everywhere in the world. An interesting example of wordless signaling is involved in the direction of traffic. A primitive form, still in use, is that of the hand signals of the traffic policeman, who in the United States says "stop" by showing the palm of his hand, "go ahead" or "turn" by waving motions, and "hurry" by making the movement more rapidly. In Mexico the traffic policeman has it easier. He raises the arm only to indicate that the signal will change and waves mostly when he wants people to hurry or when there is only one car to send in a given direction. Mostly he stands still, with his face and back in the direction of the halted traffic and his sides in the direction of moving traffic; the drivers thereby know if they must go or stop. In other countries, too, there may be minor differences in the signals; but this means of communication, silent except for the warning whistle, everywhere is understood and carries out its purpose. And yet it can be and frequently is replaced by automatic signals with a different symbolism based on lights: red for stop, green for go, and amber for change, with illuminated arrows for the turns. Some traffic signals add printed words to the lights, especially "walk" and "wait" directed toward the pedestrian. The whole matter of traffic signals points up the equivalent and complementary functions of various forms of communications. Speech, writing, gestures, colors, arrows, schematic pictures all can be made to work efficiently once the signals are generally known among the people who are to react to them.

If one tries to classify gestures into types according to their meaning, the most important dichotomy is probably that of *demonstrative* and *associative*, just as for spoken language; but the relative importance may be different. The possibility of pointing out things within view or directions of movement is always present in face-to-face communication, and the meaning of the indication is generally at once evident. There are a number of ways of showing what we are talking about; one may point with the finger, with the chin, with pouted lips, with the eyes, or with any other portion of the body. Pointing at people with the finger is sometimes considered discourteous, so one nods in their direction instead. Some groups of people seem to prefer the use of pouted lips and others the lifted chin; but all these gestures have something in common—movement in the required direction. In consequence, the demonstrative gesture is universally understood. This is more than can be said for the spoken demonstratives, which by themselves are ambiguous, and often require a gesture to clarify their reference.

In spoken language, there are interrogatives, such as *which* and *where*, corresponding to the demonstratives. Gesture language has no simple equivalent for these, but there are ways of indicating doubt: the wide-eyed look, turning to one side and then the other as though searching for something; the hunching of the shoulders, to say "I am at a loss"; turning the open palms outward as though saying "I have nothing" or "I lack information." A combination of a question gesture with pointing in different directions may be equivalent to saying "Which one?"

Negation is not always expressed in the same way. Shaking the head is widely used, but Greeks lift the head backward, and Mexicans prefer to wag a finger from side to side. Affirmation by nodding the head is fairly general.

Gestures for movement are closely related to demonstratives. When necessary, a difference is made by extending the gesture through space or by repeating it. "Come" and "go" are fairly universal, but there are some differences. Mediterraneans make the "come" signal downward, while northern Europeans make it upward; Mediterraneans use the whole hand, northern Europeans sometimes use one finger. The Mexican's "good-bye" looks like "come" to the American, and vice versa; the Mexican's "good-bye" is made with the hand sidewise, and the fingers are waved toward himself. The one-fingered "come" generally is puzzling to the Mexican who sees it for the first time, but he may figure it out from the context.

It is evident that gestures are in part spontaneous but contain a large element of conventionality, sufficient to puzzle people in cross-cultural communication. Yet there can be no doubt that gesture language has much more universality than formal spoken language; it is therefore constantly resorted to in interlinguistic contacts, along with sound imitation and expressive exclamations.

In general the imitative sign is very evident in gesture communication. Shapes are shown by holding the hands in corresponding positions or by drawing an outline in the air. Actions are shown by acting out or imitating instruments and movements with the hands.

In the use of gestures as practised by any human group, there are always some conventionalized features, most of which do not hide their basic imitative nature, but a few of which may appear to be completely arbitrary. This is not at all surprising in view of the fact that gestures must have been in use for many thousands of years, sufficient time for the origin of some of the signs to be lost. Certainly specific meanings have come not from elemental actions of man as an animal, but from mythical and religious conceptions or from historical facts. The sign of the cross as a protection from evil has such an origin, which can be understood only by Catholics or by people who at least know Catholic traditions. The American Indian sign for white man is the palm of the hand held up to the head and moved across the forehead: white men wore hats with flat brims. The use of the colors red and green for stop and go must also go back to some ancient belief or practice.

Some gestures are derived from features of formal spoken language. For instance, in Mexico touching the elbow signifies stingy. This comes from Mexican Spanish, in which *codo*, elbow, is a slang substitute for *codicioso*, greedy, avaricious. The two words are similar only in their recent history, since *codo* goes back to Latin *cubitus*, elbow, and *codicioso* is a derivative of *cupidus*, eager, desirous; they fell together because of the loss of consonants, *b* in one and *p* in the other, and the change of *t* to *d* between vowels, all incidents in the development of Spanish from Latin.

There are also hand alphabets with manual representations for each of the letters, used by the deaf and dumb and others. During World War II the manual sign for V came to be used as a gesture for victory, and naturally was extended to the meaning of success and good fortune in general.

The Nature of Communication

The word *communication* is related to *common*. It means the act of making common, and applies especially to information and feelings, the only form of gift that remains with the giver even after he has passed it on to another.

Language, spoken and written, is man's chief instrument of communication, but it is not the only one. Gestures have a similar role, as we have seen, and so do other forms of symbolism. A gift normally conveys friendship of the desire to be well thought of. The choice of gift adds overtones to the general idea being expressed, especially when it is interpreted in accordance with its association in a given community. American Indians used a ceremonial pipe as a symbol of peace. In medieval Europe a glove was a challenge to a duel. Wearing a particular kind of clothing or ornament is a device for making known one's affiliations and loyalties. Flowers have meanings, and there are fine points of symbolism that make up what has been called the language of flowers. The kind of house one lives in, one's possessions, the places one goes, and the things one does all carry meanings to one's fellows. Thus, in sum, communication is a pervasive manifestation with many forms. My concern here is primarily with spoken language, but to understand it fully we need to see how it relates to other communicative behavior.

Communication is normally and typically an intentional, planned activity; but sometimes we say things we do not mean to say, or our tone of voice tells things we had not planned to reveal. If we follow communication back to the lower animals, we find there can be such a thing as *instinctive com-munication*. If one member of a species experiences pain, fear, or any other emotion because of a physical stimulus and utters a cry, makes a grimace, or moves away, and if this reaction evokes an analogous or related emotion in other individuals, an act of communication has taken place, whether or not any conscious intention has been involved. If the reaction pattern follows a strict inborn tendency, it is instinctive. If the tendency is generalized and is subject to conditioning by experience, it may be better described as *intuitive*, a term I have used to label simpler forms of human speech be-havior. Insofar as a code has developed, requiring considerable learning and involving many arbitrary associations between the signal and its mean-ing, we are dealing with a *formal system*. Human spoken languages con-stitute such codes, as do systems of mathematical signs, traffic markers, and numerous others used among human beings.

The form of messages and the meaning they convey depends a great deal on context. A given remark in some instances may be an understatement; in other circumstances, an overemphasis. Under certain conditions it may be friendly and kind; in others, antagonistic and cruel. Much depends on who says what to whom, what happens or was said just before, and what the reasonable expectations for subsequent actions are.

Words and tones have the property of bringing to mind associations with things and ideas, and communication is possible to the degree that the speaker and hearer have similar associations. Words and tones are therefore symbols with meanings. Since context determines and modifies the under-standing of what is said, we must attribute meaning potentials to the context also.

When we want to know the meanings of words nowadays, we can look in a dictionary. Or we can ask someone who we think might know. There is another way to get at meanings, however, and that is to observe the con-texts in which people use the words. Much of the child's learning of language consists of such observation. Another method is experimentation. When a child has heard a word a few times, he is likely to use it himself. If people react the way he expects, his use of the word is confirmed. If they act con-fused or respond in unexpected ways, the child becomes aware that some-thing is wrong, and may modify his future use accordingly. The semantic associations of a word are generally complicated and vary according to context. However complicated the matter may be, people do learn to use words with relative effectiveness.

The meaning of the linguistic symbol is not the formal definition listed in the dictionary. It is the sum total of its associations in the minds of those who speak the language. It is not a rote phrase, but a complex reaction potential in the community.

[*Up to this point, Swadesh has discussed generally some of the characteristics shared by animal and human communication, both verbal and nonverbal. Now he proceeds to investigate more particularly some aspects of the communicative systems of a number of animals.*]

The Question of Animal Language

It is evident that man's symbolic behavior today is related to his evolved intelligence, and that it must have developed out of far simpler earlier forms in keeping with his cerebral capacity in earlier stages of his evolution. Two million years ago it could not have been much more advanced than that of the chimpanzee. At some still earlier level it must have been inferior to the present-day ape species; and still further back, it must have been at levels comparable to those of the simpler animals. Thus, if we want to comprehend how present-day human language came to be, we are well advised to consider animal communicative behavior with as much understanding as we can muster.

It is sufficient to observe the visible and measurable facts of animal interaction in order to recognize that the individuals of many species behave in company with each other differently than when they are alone, and that audible sound effects have a definite correlation with their behavior. To mention a single simple instance, researchers have placed two dolphins in adjacent tanks with provisions to permit or impede the carrying of sounds from one to the other. They found that the dolphins from time to time emitted sounds even when they could not hear each other, but they did so far more frequently when they could; furthermore, most of the sounds followed immediately after others, often in a chain of take and give. This and other abundant evidence show that the making of sounds is related to the conditions of interchange, or, in other words, that it is social. Many other observations show that vocal and nonvocal behavior are correlated. There is also evidence that vocal activity at times leads to adjustments to external conditions and that to some extent it tends to favor survival. Animals also adopt stances and carry out incomplete acts or feints with similar correlations, roughly comparable to some of man's gesture behavior. Thus, without violating strict scientific caution, we can safely say that many animal species demonstrate social interaction connected with vocal or silent muscular activity. To find clues as to how human language and gesture communication evolved, it will be necessary to examine some specific instances of animal interaction.

In my investigation of animal communication here, my aim is not to exhaust the subject, but to indentify some essential characteristics that may help us understand the genesis of human speech. For this purpose it is sufficient to examine a few typical manifestations.

Let us take, as our first illustration, the behavior of the mother hen who strolls out to forage with her brood. She moves forward in leisurely fashion, clucking at short intervals. The chicks spread out around her, each repeatedly peeping as he goes along. Both hen and chicks search out and peck up bits of food. If the mother finds something big and juicy, she changes the tone and frequency of her clucking and the chicks come running up. When the food is eaten, they resume their open formation with its clucking and peeping. In the hen's movements, one notes a characteristic turning from side to side. If one of the chicks strays away from the mother, she clucks faster and louder and turns in the direction of the stray; the small one responds by running toward the mother, peeping as he goes. Sometimes the straying chick is the one who first takes alarm and peeps louder and faster, till the mother responds and they restore contact. If a chick gets stuck in the weeds, he sounds the alarm with raised pitch and louder and faster or drawn-out peeping. The mother's voice is raised as she comes running to the rescue, pecking and pushing to extract her babe; if the danger is animal, the mother attacks, squawking. The rest of the chicken colony may remain indifferent to the hen and her brood, until and unless she and they sound a serious alarm. In that event, they all come running and join in common action to save the threatened member. Observers of bird behavior have noted a difference between a cry of alarm and a cry of despair. The first brings the flock hurrying to the rescue; the second, emitted by a fowl in the clutches of a hawk, a fox, or a human, sends them scurrying away to save themselves or freezes them in protected locations.

The social behavior of pigs is somewhat similar to that of hens. In the barnyard, the various species generally keep apart, but occasionally there is interaction, especially when cries of alarm or despair are uttered very close by. Then the cry of the pig may alert the chickens, and vice versa. Flocks of different animal species that are together for the first time are less likely to respond in a communicative chain. This seems to show that response is partly conditioned by previous experiences. If a single individual has received such conditioning, he may serve as the link between the species.

A hen without chicks feeds as part of the adult flock. Her relationship to other adults is much looser; for example, she does not announce the discovery of food unless the find is extremely plentiful. When she has laid an egg, she announces it loudly; and the rooster may second the announcement. It may be hard to persuade oneself that the hen and the rooster are thus informing the farmer of their usefulness, so he will not elect them for cooking, even though farmers are generally influenced by these considerations. The physiological reality is surely related to the flow of hormones, so that cackling and crowing are expressions of sexual vigor. When the hen comes into the brooding stage, however, her behavior is quite different, including its vocal manifestation. She seeks a hidden spot to make her nest and does not announce the laying of eggs. The farmer thus does not easily find them and the hen has the opportunity of hatching them. In this farmyard drama we need not imagine that the hen engages in a process of cogitation that leads to her elusive behavior. It is rather that she experiences a marked emotional change and her normal tendencies to cackle are restrained. This form of behavior is probably older than the practice of keeping hens, and must have favored the survival of the species against the inroads of egg-stealing hawks and beasts in an earlier period.

The conduct of dogs is in certain ways very different from that of chickens. When the mother moves about with her young pups, they cluster about her without constantly talking back and forth. This seems to be related to the species' superior sense of smell, which gives them a silent means of keeping together and which is part of their innate hunting skills. Still there is a fair amount of signaling back and forth between bitch and pups; and the adults are much given to growling, barking, and occasionally howling in ways that help cooperation under the special behavior mode of the canines. Dogs and their kindred species, wolves, foxes, coyotes, and so on, are far-ranging. They often hunt individually or in small groups, yet are able to bring together a pack when there is worthwhile prey to be brought down. The canines can stalk silently, but often hunt with loud barking, which in part serves to make their prey nervous and in part facilitates cooperation among their own kind or with their frequent hunting partners of the human species.

The behavior code of dogs apparently calls for answering the distant bark and running to join the hunt. The domestic dog probably reflects this old behavior in an inhibited fashion when he responds to barking next door, even though ·he may not go running over there. Howling is apparently a form of canine communication that is geared to great distances and perhaps serves to inform the lone animal where his nearest fellows are.

It is evident that different animal species show different forms of vocal and gesture behavior. One of the most remarkable species is the bee, which is capable of communicating with great accuracy the location of a find of nectar by carrying out a series of motions, which have been described as a dance. The bee moves in alternate directions around a constant axis, so as to describe an approximate figure 8. The axis of movement indicates the direction of the find, the speed of the circling is related to the distance, and the agitation of the animal reflects the abundance of the find. While the dance is being executed near the hive, the other worker bees form a circle around the dancer. After witnessing his movements a few moments, they make off in the proper direction and fly the correct distance before descending to the flowers. Another form of bee communication occurs when part of a colony is ready to swarm. The bees assemble at a convenient point outside the hive apparently long enough to establish a center of operations. Then workers go off in different directions. Those bees that come upon a suitable location return to the main group and indicate by their excitement that they have found a site. Bees that fail to find a suitable location also return. If favorable reports come in from a number of directions, the swarm shows indecisiveness, moving to one side and another until a weight of opinion has formed in favor of one of the locations. In their communicative behavior bees do not employ vocal sounds, but the buzzing made by the vibrating wings apparently plays a role in conveying excitement and emphasis, perhaps comparable to degrees of conviction in human beings.

Another interesting form of vocal behavior is imitative. There are several classes of birds that engage in sound imitation: the mockingbird, the myna, and many orders of parrots. There is no very evident reason for their sound imitation as far as conservation of the species is concerned. Perhaps it is merely an exceptional manifestation of the echoic tendency common, in lesser degrees, to many animal species. Imitation usually occurs within species. When one individual utters a sound, others are likely to answer with a similar sound. The special feature of the imitative birds is that they have exceptional ability to produce assorted vocalizations that echo the sounds of other species. Their only match among mammals happens to be the human being. Some of the other primates—for instance, the chimpanzee—have some imitative power, but apparently far less than the parrots or man. That other animals are not entirely without imitative abilities has been demonstrated by those animal trainers who have taught seals, dogs, and horses to "sing." Apparently the trainer achieves this result by first imitating the animal and then getting him to respond to his voice. Once this has been accomplished, the trainer can introduce variations in pitch and quality within limits that the animal can follow.

The human being is apparently the only species that has made abundant use of other-species imitation to add to his survival power. In hunting, he does this in two ways. He imitates the call of his prey to bring it close, especially by using the call of one of the sexes to attract the other. And he uses animal cries to signal to other hunters, so as not to betray the presence of humans. In either event, men increase their ability to obtain game by the use of animal imitations. It seems at least reasonable to suppose that man has been using this skill for a long time, and that it may have been one of the adaptive devices that helped him survive difficult periods in the early history of the species.

Another interesting form of vocal behavior is the continuous outpouring of sound practiced by many birds, frogs, and some insects, alone or in chorus. The manifestation here is an expression of an emotional state, generally of well-being, as may be seen by the fact that sick individuals do not participate or do so weakly and intermittently. Expressions of pain are rarely prolonged. Occasionally states of melancholy or uneasiness give rise to long wailing or howling. The species vary greatly in the extent of this form of behavior, its frequency and duration, and its social implications. Man is one of the species most given to it, but there are individual and group differences according to cultural division, age, sex, weather, and other factors. Man's communicative behavior takes the form of singing (individually and in groups), conversation, speechmaking, and ritual.

Analogues for at least some of these forms can be found among the lower animals. In particular, the patterns of friendly conversation have a fairly close parallel in the chattering of various species of monkeys, who gather in large trees in the early morning, swinging and playing about and giving vent to shouts and answers, which fill the air for protracted periods.

Men's custom of greeting each other on meeting has its analogue in some animal behavior. Dogs greet strangers of their species by wagging their tails when circumstances do not evoke suspicion or rivalry. They ratify their recognition by sniffing and end up by running together or playing. When bands of chimpanzees meet in their natural habitat, they have been observed to go through a procedure of eyeing each other with accompanying grunts, then touching and pawing each other, then dancing about, and finally resuming the customary activities of food-gathering, exploring, resting, sleeping, and so on. The bands generally separate again later. If they join forces, the relations of individuals have to be defined in accordance with a complicated social organization, in which one male is dominant in the band and each other individual has his place in a descending hierarchy.

Animal Phonetics

Most animals have relatively rigid speech organs or lack the nerve controls to permit extensive adjustments. The cow, for example, has a crude velum, a large tongue of limited flexibility, and nearly immovable lips. The velum in man permits him to make either nasal or oral sounds. That is, if the velum hangs down, the air passes through the nose; if it is lifted, the nasal passage is cut off and the air passes through the mouth. With the mouth wide open and the velum raised, one says *aa*; with the velum dropped he says *aa*^{n}, as in *aa*^{n}*háa*^{n}, or as in the *ã* vowel of Portuguese. The cow rarely opens the mouth sufficiently to say *aa*^{n}, and instead says *ïi*^{n}. If the mouth is closed, the sound in *mm*; if the mouth opens during the vocalization, the result is *mmïi*^{n}. And these are just about all the vocalizations a cow can make. The cow that says *moo* does not really exist. To do this she would have to round her lips, a trick that is too much for her. When we imagine the cow is saying *moo*—phonetically *muu*—she is probably just saying her very characteristic *ïi*^{n}. This does not prevent her from being fairly expressive; she can make the *ïi*^{n} either short or fairly long, or give it an upward-gliding tone or a level or falling one. She does not have much pitch variation, but she can manage a few tones up and down. She also varies the spacing of the vocables, sometimes emitting a single isolated *ïi*^{n} and sometimes a continuous sequence of them in quick or slow rhythm, maybe letting free breath escape, producing sounds like *ïi*^{n}*hh*, *mh* and *hm*. The use of free breath is more characteristic of the male of the species, whose voice is also hoarser, and who uses more falling tones than the female.

The cat is also a nasal animal, but her tongue is more flexible than the cow's. Although we represent her as saying *meow*, she actually does most of her vocalizing with the mouth open, which means that there is actually no *m*, but just nasalized vowels. Her usual way is to begin with the tongue held in the front of her mouth, but then she tends to pull it backward, so as to say *iiïⁿ*, *eeaaⁿ*, or something in between. Vocal flexibility also appears in the fact that the mouth may be opened little or much, producing both close and open vowels. The cat also varies the length and tone of her mewing in ways that seem to reflect emotional states. There is the soft version in a level medium tone, the unhappy drawn-out plaint in a slow falling tone, or the angry voice with sharp drop of pitch. The use of open vowels is related to the more intense emotional states. In anger and in combat the cat uses voiceless sounds, particularly the spitting sharp aspiration, made with the lips drawn back and the teeth bared, which we imitate as *fft*. In quiet repose, the cat purrs with a continuous vibratory sound that has no analogue in the human species. The whole emotional gamut of vocalizations may be canceled and all sounds suppressed in the intense concentration that characterizes the cat's silent stalking behavior.

Pig phonetics has some relation to that of the cat in its nasality and movement of the tongue, except that the pig's tongue movement goes from back to front. The sound of the pig in the relatively relaxed state is typically very short, ending in glottal closure; it well merits the description "grunt." The typical phonetic shape is *ïï'*, and the tone is low and level. Under the stress of discomfort and fear or anger, the grunt is lengthened to a squeal, and the tone may rise and fall.

Dog phonetics is not very complicated, but the dog's vocal behavior is much more noticeable than that of other animals because of its range of loudness, from restrained to very strong, capable of carrying for miles. The voiced vocal effects include the growl, the bark, the yelp, and the howl. The growl is definitely of short carrying range. It may be made with the mouth closed or somewhat open, so that the phonetics may be *mm* or *ïïⁿ*, and the sound may be protracted. The growl may be preliminary to barking, as though the animal were making up its mind. The bark is made with the mouth fairly fully opened with each vocal emission, and a powerful push of lung air throws the sound out with force; it is made with vibrating vocal cords but may end in free breath. It is commonly repeated from a few to a great many times. The simple phonetics may be shown as *'ah 'ah 'ah 'ah* . . . but the closing of the mouth with each bark may give an effect like *'aïh 'aïh 'aïh*. Despite its simple phonetics, the bark seems to be fairly expressive. Depending on the rhythm and tone, it is apparently possible to distinguish whether the dog is warning of an intruder, uttering the cry of the hunt, or announcing that the prey is cornered. The yelp is a scream of pain that may be dragged out and may show marked tonal modulation. It has relatively little carrying power. The howl, on the other hand, reaches great distances. The sound begins with the open-mouth *aa* and ends in a narrow-mouth *ii*. It is drawn out long and passes from low tone to high and then falls gradually. The length and tone of the howl contribute to its carrying power, and so does the lung power behind it. When a dog wants to howl, he prefers to do it out in the open on high ground, and he projects his voice upward; all this helps keep the sound from being muted by the ground and thick vegetation. In taking these measures, the dog is responding to instinct rather than the engineer's manual; but the result is nevertheless very effective.

Ruminants, canines, felines, and most other animals use the outgoing breath to set their vocal cords vibrating and to produce breathy unvibrated sounds. Some of the rodents use the indrawn breath and the vacuumatic click sound. The squirrel, for example, compresses his cheeks and lips against his teeth and gums, then brings the breath inward, perhaps by the click technique, to make a cheeping sound as the breath squeezes through the tightly narrowed space. As a click sound, we can write it perhaps *fs!* to show that both lip-teeth friction and sibilant effects are involved.

Some animals use percussion sounds; for example, the rabbit drumming the ground with his hind feet and the beaver slapping the ground with his tail. The rattlesnake carries a musical instrument on his tail and hisses through his mouth. Insects have a variety of techniques, involving, among other things, the rubbing together of parts of the body.

Man's closest relatives include some of the versatile soundmakers, but not all the anthropoids and monkeys are equally capable in producing sounds. The howler monkey has a spectacular noisemaker in his cartilaginous vocal organs, which produce a noise of tremendous volume; but it is his only form of vocalization, generally employed only for a relatively short period each evening. Certain monkeys specialize in click sounds, smacking the lips, clicking with the tongue, and so on. The chimpanzee and many of the tree monkeys are very vocal, with both clicks and outbreathed sounds, and make beating and rubbing sounds with whatever may be at hand. As few other animals, they can shape their lips to make rounded sounds. Their sounds vary between voiced and voiceless, and their velum operates something like man's, permitting nasal, oral, and orinasal sounds. Their inferiority in relation to man is probably far more mental than physiological. It is conceivable that man's ancestors three million years ago had no more physical soundmaking ability than the more clever of his cousins today, and that his improved use of language came only with increasing mental power. Any mechanical advantage he has would consist only in the relatively shorter mouth and tongue, which may permit easier control of movement; the lighter jaw; and small teeth. Yet these physical facts by themselves are not determinative. An important part of the difference must be in the acuity of the ear, and this may well be related to the practice of imitating the sounds of the environment. This property of man must be a refinement of the generalized tendency to echo, found in various degrees in different species but raised to a high degree in man by long practice.

If one compares man's phonetic ability with that of lower species, it may appear vastly different; and this will certainly be true when man is contrasted with the least articulate of the animals. In comparison with the parrots and some monkeys, however, the contrast is less marked. Many animal species pronounce only vowels, and perhaps only one or a few particular ones; some manage one or another consonant, especially fricatives of out-going breath. The ability to produce stops is far less frequent, and the com-bination of stoppage and vibration of the vocal cords may be entirely lacking. Man's superiority consists in being able to manage a great number of resonant, fricative, and stop consonants; to make click and inbreathed sounds as well as outbreathed ones; and above all, to produce complex combinations and sequences of varied sounds. His abilities go far beyond the demands of any single language, as is evident from the richness of exclamative and imitative sounds in all languages (with phonetics that go beyond that of the language in question) as well as the ability to learn foreign words.

There are unquestionably a number of important points of relationship between man and other animal species in respect to the use of sounds. To begin with, man shares with many other species what appears to be by nature essentially a sound-producing mechanism, the vocal cords, consisting generally of a pair of muscles on either side of the windpipe, which, when brought close together, loosely vibrate to the passage of air from the lungs. Coordinated with the sounding mechanism is a receiving mechanism, the ear, with nerve connections to the brain.

The glottis is often a fairly flexible instrument. Relaxed and open, it permits the free passage of the breath, which is relatively silent but can be heard at short distances, especially when the breathing is energetic, or when the glottis is not opened to its fullest. In man there is an additional position of the glottis, in which the vocal cords are closed but a space is left between the arytenoid cartilages, which gives the whisper effect. The vibration of the vocal cords can be stopped abruptly by complete closure, the *glottal stop*, which is one of the most common consonants among animal species. Many human languages also employ it as a regular phoneme, while others use it only in exclamatives and imitatives. The vibrating glottis, in man and many other species, is capable of giving a wide gamut of tones, by adopting different degrees of tenseness or by movements that lengthen or shorten its vibrating length. Different volumes of sound are produced by modifying the force of air pressure delivered to the vibrating glottis by the lungs.

Man and most animals instinctively, even at very early ages, use the sound-producing apparatus in correlation with emotional states: in relaxed manner in conditions of well-being, in strained manner when ill at ease, and with animation or in desperation under the influence of stronger emotions. Yet there are also emotional conditions that suspend all vocalism, as when the animal is stalking prey or when it fears detection by a dangerous enemy.

There are times when man and some other animal species seem to be making sounds for the sheer pleasure of it; and some animals, including man to some extent, guide themselves by the echos of their voices. Many species respond to sounds of their own species almost automatically, unless they are under an inhibiting influence. Response is the basis of group cohesion in some species and in some situations; the giving and receiving of signals serves to locate each individual with reference to the group and to permit the individuals to modify their movements so as not to become separated from each other. This favors species survival because it permits the individuals to come to each other's assistance in case of need, to share food finds when they are more than one individual can eat alone, and to find sexual partners in time of mating. There is evidence that nearness to their own kind has an emotionally beneficial effect on gregarious animals. In some cases signaling back and forth seems to be a device for defining territories, to remind other individuals within the group not to encroach on alien land and to warn away members of other groups.

To signal location, an animal may increase the volume of his sound, or direct it toward an area where friends are likely to be, or turn in various directions, repeating the signal in each. Even more sophisticated, apparently, but within the capacity of some lower animals, is the selection of locations acoustically favorable for signaling. With this goes behavior like raising the head and pointing the mouth upward, and even adopting vocalic qualities and tones that carry great distances.

Correlated with the behavior of projecting sounds are the directional and distance-gauging capacities of the ear. Animals have one mouth with which to make sounds but two ears for hearing. Placed at either side of the head, the ears are able to judge with relative efficiency the direction from which a sound is coming. The animal typically turns from side to side until it is facing directly toward the source of the sound. This behavior works out well because of the repetition of the signal at intervals by the transmitting animal. The receiving individual, after he has zeroed in on the signal, gives answer with a repeating signal, which permits mutual location.

The maintenance of group contact is important. It provides the framework within which further signaling can be carried on to the advantage and satisfaction of the individual and with survival value for the species.

But communicative behavior is also directed at rivals and victims. Many animals growl and scream as they attack. The purpose may be to frighten the enemy into rash behavior, to throw him off guard, or perhaps to paralyze him with fear. In any one of these cases, advantage is gained. Yet when stealth gives an advantage to either the hunting or the hunted animal, all cries are suppressed. Man is particularly expert in using cries that will help him in the hunt. He knows that a sudden shout will make a rabbit freeze in its tracks and give him the time to strike him with a missile. He also, somewhat in the style of the canines, makes a great hue and cry to send his prey scurrying in the opposite direction, straight into a trap, over a cliff, within striking range of other members of the hunting party, or into panic or exhaustion, so it can be easily picked off.

We have seen that imitation of sounds in one form or another is probably practiced by quite a number of animal species. Man exhibits the apparently instinctive behavior known as *echolalia*, which consists of automatic repetition of a sound that has startled him. More usual forms of imitation include the repetition of a sound the individual himself has uttered or the cry of others belonging to one's own species. Man's special capacity, which he shares with the imitative birds, is that of reproducing, approximately, the sounds of other species and those of nonanimate origin.

Divergent repetition or imitation is apparently practiced as a game among some primates in their behavior known as *chatter*. It consists of saying something that is partly the same and partly different from what has gone before. That is, instead of saying *ayii ayii ayii*, one says *ayii ayuu ayii*. This is a form of play, which would seem to be extremely important for the development of language.

The Structure of Intuitive Language

Research has shown that animals do not emit large numbers of unanalyzable cries, but have fairly small repertories of basic ones that vary along a limited number of lines of differentiation. Leaving aside the spit, the purr, and any other generalized signal he may have, the cat really has one basic mew, which varies in loudness, pitch, length, vowel opening, voice quality, and patterns of repetition. Each of these variables expresses a corresponding range of meaning or emotion, based essentially on the way various emotional states affect the acoustic properties of the sound and reflecting indirectly the kind of things in the life of a cat which give rise to the emotions. Joy, relaxation, and indifference are degrees on an emotional scale; malaise, fear, and terror form another sequence. Abundance and lack of food, the presence of enemies, and the sex drive lead to specific emotions, and it is always possible that two or more of these situations may present themselves at the same time. A proper analysis of the way in which conditions determine emotions, the way the emotions influence cat mews, and the way mews affect cats would give the structure of feline language.

We can also get some insight into the communication of cats if we examine understandingly man's own intuitive language; that is, if we recognize that the various modes of the mew will have some relation to the stress, tone, length, voice quality, and repetition patterns of exclamatives like *oh*. The next step is to note some analogies between intuitive language and formal language.

In the vocal behavior of the cat, different degrees of mouth opening, from the narrowest iii^n to the broadest $eeaa^n$, express different degrees of intensity of feeling and might indirectly reflect the size of a menace faced by the individual cat. In the behavior of primates it is possible that vowel opening might reflect the physical size of an animal being observed or the distance at which it is located. Now, as we have seen, there are some human languages —for instance, Huave of Mexico—in which vowels express size, *i* being used for small things and *a* for large. In English, *this*, with close vowel, and *that*, with open vowel, indicate nearness and distance. The variation between *sit* and *sat* similarly indicates present and past, which amounts to nearness and distance in time.

There are other cases in which the symbolic transfer of pronunciation is less clear or even appears to be arbitrary; but in any event, it is conceivable that the most primitive applications of any phonetic features might have been along intuitive lines. Thus relative loudness or stress is a differentiating principle, for example, in English, in which *hold out*, with stress on both words, is a verb, but *holdout*, with the main stress on the first syllable, is a noun. Nasal versus oral quality distinguishes vowels not only in intuitive but also in formal language in Portuguese, French, and other languages. Pharyngeally narrowed consonants in Arabic form a special class; aspirated stops form a class in English, Chinese, Hindi, and many other languages. In the preceding chapter I suggested that these and other now arbitrary or formal phonetic contrasts may have developed out of old intuitive symbolisms, and examined evidence for this proposition.

There is a fundamental difference between intuitive and formal language in their utilization of phonetic qualities. In the expressive vocalization of intuitive language, there are continuous gamuts between the shortest and the longest possibilities, the highest and the lowest, the weakest and the strongest, the narrowest and the widest, and so forth. In formal language, the units are discrete; along any dimension or continuum, generally two but sometimes more degrees of variation are employed. Thus sounds are either rounded or unrounded, voiced or unvoiced, glottalized or unglottalized, and so on. There remain, then, intermediary or extreme degrees on each dimension which may function when intuitive overtones are combined with the formally valid types. Sounds may be *more* rounded, *more* voiced, *more* glottalized.

Early Demonstratives, Imitatives, and Syntax

Animals react to things they see, smell, or otherwise detect in their surroundings; and such things are often the basis of communication between individuals. Chimpanzees, for example, utter cries and gesticulate when they encounter other animals or noteworthy objects. Such attention-calling behavior is comparable to saying, "Look at this!" The excitement of the pointing animal communicates the importance he attaches to his discovery. Although the reports on chimpanzee behavior have not yet clarified such matters, it seems likely that something in the demonstrative vocalism may reflect the nearness or distance of the object. This would represent an early manifestation of the almost universal distinction in formal languages between close and far demonstratives. I suppose size might be reflected by similar techniques.

The type of object involved in imitatives is reflected in human intuitive language. It seems reasonable to suppose that this sort of thing may have appeared far back in the evolution of our behavior. Conceivably the scientists who devote themselves to the study of animal behavior and communication will yet discover similar symbolic imitation in some of the lower species.

The shape of objects is imitated in human gestures and from there passes into vocalization. This is due to two circumstances. One is that, in humans as in other primates, the lips are flexible and can be used to copy shapes, such as round or flat. The other is that the passage of air through spaces gives a resonance that is related to their shape. The wind passing through or across the opening of a hollow gives a characteristic resonance, which can be approximately imitated by producing a rounded vowel sound.

Any signals developed in intuitive attention-calling behavior had the possibility of one day entering formal language as demonstratives. Imitative vocables of the intuitive language could one day become part of formal language as verbs and nouns.

The basis for the development of patterns of meaningful elements—that is, syntax—must lie in the running together of intuitive signals. In the lowest animals, the usual thing is the single cry, which appears also in spaced sequences. More intelligent animals are sometimes also more garrulous, frequently bringing their vocables close together, especially under conditions of excitement.

The Evolution of Language

In the evolution of species a sounding apparatus develops in relation to breathing and comes to be coordinated with the sound-sensory equipment. The sound-production and hearing complex is not isolated but has a close relationship with other forms of producing and perceiving stimuli, including the visual, tactual, and olfactory. Sounds produced by some means other than breath also correlate with the auditory equipment: external rubbing and banging.

Whatever the mechanism, many species have come to produce and to respond to perceptible interaction stimuli. These come to be important media of interaction, serving as the basis of social existence. The stimulus-response mode of interaction gives a species advantages in proportion to the degree of intelligence employed. The highest effectiveness of interaction involves consciousness, intention, and discriminatory judgment. At the lower end of the scale, the reactions are instinctive. An individual receives an impression from something in his environment. This causes a glandular secretion, or emotion, which gives rise to a muscular contraction that shows itself in a movement, a grimace, a cry, or perhaps even the emission of an odorous secretion. Other individuals of the same species who see, hear, or smell the outward emotional manifestation react emotionally and physically in a way that is related to the original reaction, it is perhaps generally similar to it but not necessarily identical. There may also be emotional reactions that inhibit or modify the outward manifestation that might otherwise take place. The mechanism by which one individual's sensations may bring forth reactions in others, especially of the same species, constitutes communication.

Two main levels of communication can be distinguished: the *instinctive-intuitive*, found in all animals, and the *formal, conventional,* or *arbitrary,* found only in man. In the former, there are relatively few elemental signals, even though each may vary along one or more axes of magnitude; also, to a greater or lesser degree, signals may be joined simultaneously or strung together. In formal systems of communication, a limited number of points on each axis of variation serve as contrastive features, with rules of combination that permit the distinguishing of relatively large numbers of elemental signals, which can be employed with relatively neutral intuitive variables or with all the degrees of intensity of the intuitive component, except insofar as this may be preempted in the signal proper. The formal systems of communication in man include gestures, language, and pictorial symbols. Art forms are complex behavior systems involving features of intuitive and formal communication. The formal systems of communication must have crystallized out of the intuitive, and very primitive art forms may have played a role in the process.

Just how the formal systems of communication developed out of the intuitive can be best understood with the help of evidence about early stages of language. Here we note that different animal species have different levels of instinctive-intuitive communication and that the higher levels provide clues to the development of the formal system. Among the features that probably marked the advance toward language are the differentiation of demonstrative (pointing) signals from diffuse, attention-calling ones and the advanced use of sound imitation in play and in expression. The combination of gesture and voice communication probably also played an important role in language development. The ancestors of man progressed in intelligence because of a series of circumstances: the education of the hands in grasping as a result of tree dwelling; subsequent adaptation to life on the ground; the lack of effective teeth for fighting and hunting, which required compensatory behavior, especially the use of tools; effective social cooperation; and strong competition in the struggle to survive. Increased effectiveness of communication was aided by and in turn aided the general development of intelligence. The approach to and the entrance into the stage of formal systems of communication was an inevitable consequence of the growth of intelligence in a species that had already achieved an advanced use of intuitive forms of symbolic interaction.

References and Suggestions for Further Reading

[*For the relationship between human evolution and the evolution of language, see Hockett and Ascher (1964) and the accompanying bibliography. The Takelma exclamatives are from Sapir (1922). For sound symbolism and onomatopoetics in language, see Bolinger (1950), Brown (1958), Brown, Black, and Horowitz (1955), Emeneau (1969), Jespersen (1922), Marchand (1959), Miron (1961), Newman (1933), and Sapir (1949). For an analysis of nonverbal communication, see Birdwhistell (1952).*

Swadesh's discussion of animal communication is extremely general. He was apparently not aware of the research that has been undertaken in this area in the last few years. For this research, see Sebeck (1968). In addition to the recent interest in animal communication and its relation to human communication, there has been an interest in the nature or defining characteristics of language and the processes involved in its acquisition. These questions are discussed in Chomsky (1967, 1968), Darley (1967), Hockett (1959), Lenneberg (1964, 1967), and Smith and Miller (1966).

It seems useful to note here that recent work in generative-transformational linguistics has pointed to such general or abstract properties as levels of structure, transformations, and the ordering of rules as defining characteristics of language. There is a possibility, however, that these properties are not specific to language, but rather are basic features of human and perhaps animal intelligence, as aspects of cognition or perception, for example. In this regard, see Chomsky (1967, p. 84), and Lenneberg (1967, pp. 296–302, 324–26). It is not with these general properties, however, that Swadesh deals in this book. Rather, as we have seen, he is concerned with the origin of particular linguistic concepts and processes, and areas of vocabulary.]

Birdwhistell, Ray L.
    1952. *Introduction to Kinesics: An Annotation System for Analysis of Body Motion and Gesture.* Washington, D.C.: Department of State, Foreign Service Institute.
Boas, Franz, ed.
    1922. *Handbook of American Indian Languages,* Bureau of American Ethnology bulletin no. 40, pt. 2. Washington, D.C.: Smithsonian Institution.
Bolinger, Dwight P.
    1950. "Rime, Assonance, and Morpheme Analysis." *Word* 6:116–36.
Brown, Roger W.
    1958. *Words and Things.* Glencoe, Ill.: Free Press.
Brown, Roger W.; Black, A.; and Horowitz, A.
    1955. "Phonetic Symbolism in Natural Languages." *Journal of Abnormal and Social Psychology* 50:388–93.
Chomsky, Noam
    1967. "The General Properties of Language." *Brain Mechanisms Underlying Speech and Language,* ed. Frederic L. Darley. New York: Grune & Stratton, 1967.

1968. *Language and Mind.* New York: Harcourt, Brace & World.
Darley, Fréderic L., ed.
1967. *Brain Mechanisms Underlying Speech and Language.* New York: Grune & Stratton.
Emeneau, M. B.
1969. "Onomatopoetics in the Indian Linguistic Area." *Language* 45:274–99.
Hockett, Charles F.
1959. "Animal 'Languages' and Human Languages." In *The Evolution of Man's Capacity for Culture*, arr. J. N. Spuhler. Detroit: Wayne State University Press.
Hockett, Charles F., and Ascher, Robert
1964. "The Human Revolution." *Current Anthropology* 5:135–68.
Jespersen, Otto
1922. *Language: Its Nature, Development, and Origin.* London: Allen & Unwin.
Lanyon, W. E., and Tavolga, W. N., eds.
1960. *Animal Sounds and Communication*, publication no. 7. Washington, D.C.: American Institute of Biological Sciences.
Lenneberg, Eric H.
1964. *New Directions in the Study of Language.* Cambridge: MIT Press.
1967. *Biological Foundations of Language.* New York: Wiley.
Mandelbaum, David G., ed.
1949. *Selected Writings of Edward Sapir in Language, Culture, and Personality.* Berkeley: University of California Press.
Marchand, Hans
1959. "Phonetic Symbolism in English Word-Formation." *Indogermanische Forschungen* 64:146–68, 256–77.
Miron, Murray S.
1961. "A Cross-Linguistic Investigation of Phonetic Symbolism." *Journal of Abnormal and Social Psychology* 62:623–30.
Newman, S.
1933. "Further Experiments in Phonetic Symbolism." *American Journal of Psychology* 45:53–75.
Sapir, Edward
1922. "The Takelma Language of Southwestern Oregon." In *Handbook of American Indian Languages*, pt. 2, ed. Boas.
1949. "A Study in Phonetic Symbolism." In *Selected Writings of Edward Sapir*, ed. Mandelbaum.
Sebeok, Thomas A.
1963. "Communication in Animals and in Men: Three Reviews." *Language* 39: 448–66.
Sebek, Thomas Albert, ed.
1968. *Animal Communication: Techniques of Study and Results of Research.* Bloomington: Indiana University Press.
Smith, Frank, and Miller, George A., eds.
1966. *The Genesis of Language.* Cambridge: MIT Press.
Spuhler, J. N., Arr.
1959. *The Evolution of Man's Capacity for Culture.* Detroit: Wayne State University Press.

SIX

The Origin of Vocabulary

[*After a one-chapter interlude in which he discussed some similarities between animal and human communication, Swadesh continues to investigate the characteristics of the very early stages of language. Here he looks at various areas of vocabulary and, by considering languages from all over the world, tries to explain their origin and development. By Swadesh's own admission, some of the interpretations presented here are quite bold. Nonetheless, the facts on which they are based are intriguing and lead one to wonder whether similarities of vocabulary are due to common origin, language universals or tendencies, or chance.*]

Millions of years ago, when the ancestor of man was still low on the evolutionary ladder, he had the power to cry out, and he could instinctively modify his cries in intensity, length, rhythm of repetition, and a few other ways. His utterances had a great range of variation, but they were all interrelated, so that they might be best thought of as a single root word with many inflections. As man evolved, the first important change in his sound-using patterns may have been the more or less consciously controlled use of imitation, so that the imitative system came to be separated from the exclamative one. The exclamative system may then have split into two parts, a purely expressive paradigm and an attention-calling or demonstrative one. With the first elaboration of such a signaling complex, man was in the *eoglottic* stage, which may have been roughly contemporaneous with his first use of crudely modified sticks, bones, and stones, the level of artifacts known as the *eolithic*.

Our understanding of the eoglottic stage derives from the consideration of the vocal manifestations of subhuman animals and of the subsequent stages of language development in man himself. In tracing human language development we have to work backward, from the present and the historic past into the prehistoric, by the careful sifting of the combined evidence of the languages we know. So far we have been investigating matters of linguistic

182

structure; we must now come to grips with vocabulary. Perhaps the way to do this is to take up special categories or areas of words. Interesting results may be obtained from an investigation of numerals, kin terms, negations, demonstratives, pronouns, color terms, and words for big and little and various noises, actions, and shapes. The order in which I shall treat these categories is a matter of convenience. I shall begin with the numerals because we have reason to believe they were among the last to take on their present character. In each category I shall look for evidence of development from an earlier state. A guideline is the statistical fact that vocabulary has grown, at first slowly and later at an explosive rate. Since the final stage is fully known and some of the preceding ones partially so, we can concentrate on the period between the late *paleoglottic* and the *neoglottic*, or, within the more recent past, between the late *local* and the incipient *classic* stages. We may suppose we are dealing with a time span in which vocabularies developed from a few hundred to a thousand or so elements and in which composite lexemes began to be important.

At all times we must base our deductions mainly on the actual evidence of words existing in historic language or inferred on substantial grounds to have existed in a common period. At the same time, we can often make good use of the known relationship between formal vocabulary and quasi-intuitive or imitative symbolization. In other words, while recognizing the arbitrary nature of the sign in formal language and the strongly conventional nature of even imitative words, we must not reject clues that come from observation of the intuitive implications of each class of speech sounds.

The Evolution of Numeral Systems

The first adding machines were adapted to the decimal system of counting, but the most powerful modern computers operate on a binary system. The reason for using a system of two is that it simplifies matters of wiring and transfer of electrical charges, effecting a considerable saving in complicated electronic apparatus, while the possibility of practically unlimited multiplication at lightning speed permits the efficient handling of very large quantities. It is interesting that in the process of making more complicated computers, man has in a sense reversed the primitive history of mathematics, because there is reason to believe that man's first precise counting went only from one to two. The resemblance between the ancient and the modern binary systems is only partial, of course, since primitive man could not go far beyond two, while for modern computer science, two is not a limit, but rather a step toward rapid calculation.

Decimal counting, by far the most widespread system in the world today, is based on the fingers of both hands. In English we call each simple number a "digit"; the same term is used for the finger or toe, just as the Romans used the word in its Latin form, *digitus*. In many languages the word for "five" is identical with or similar to the word for "hand"; "ten" is frequently "two hands" or "pair of hands" or "the upper part"; "twenty" is in some languages called "all digits," "hands and feet," "the whole man," or something of the sort. There are also expressions for the numbers from six to nine which are clearly based on finger counting, since they say for "six" something like "one on the left hand," for "nine" perhaps "one short of two hands."

[*Swadesh intended to list here many cases from different languages of words for numbers which are related to words for parts of the body. The following examples are taken from several of his publications and from various grammars.*]

Chukchee:

rílhirkin, to count = to finger
ming, hand; *ming-ítken,* ten (belonging to the hands)
klik (obsolete), man; *qlikkin,* twenty (belonging to a man)

Greenlandic Eskimo:

tallimaṭ, five (derivative of *tallīq,* arm)
arfiniq, six (derivative of *arfaq,* the outer side of the hand)
qulĭ, something on top; *qulĭt,* ten
inuk naallugu, twenty (man finishing)

Tlingit:

kéejin, five (*ke,* up, and *jin,* hand)
jínkaat, ten (*jin,* hand, and *kat,* across, upon)
tléeqa, twenty (*tleeq,* one, and *qa,* man)

Takelma:

ha'ii, in the hand; *ha'iimí's,* six = one (finger) in the hand
ii-x-, hand; *íxdiil,* ten
yap'à, man; *yap'amí's,* twenty (one man)

Maidu:

maa, hand; *máawika,* five; *máasoko,* ten

Nahuatl:

ma-i-tl, hand; *ma-kwili,* five

Mayan:

winik-, twenty = man

Diola:

ka-banan, twenty = finished man (*ban,* finished, and *an,* person)

Acholi:

ching, five = hand

Sumerian:

i, five = hand

In modern English the words "eleven" and "twelve" seem to be un-analyzable, but in earlier Germanic they were apparently *ain-lif* and *twa-lif,* meaning "one leave" and "two leave," probably based originally on objective finger counting and not on abstract decimal concepts.

Since some numbers, either obviously or after analysis, are derivable from finger counting, one wonders to what extent the others might not have a similar origin. Careful examination of the evidence often leads to interesting hints.

The word for "ten" in Indo-European, on the basis of Latin *decem,* Greek *deka,* Gothic *tehun,* and other forms, has been reconstructed as **dekmtóm.* The last part, *-kmtóm,* could be a formation out of the root **kem,* in its reduced grade **km,* and is perhaps related to the Latin prefix *com-,* together, the preposition *cum,* with, and Greek *koinos* (from *konios,* based on *kom-i-o-s*), common. The word **km-tó-m* would then be a past participle meaning "joined together." Since it is reasonable to expect phonetic simplifications in very old compounds, we can now analyze the Indo-European word into *dek-km-tó-m* or *deg-km-tó-m* and explain it as "fingers taken together." The root is present in Greek *dak-tu-lo-s,* finger, and probably also in Latin *digitus,* which may be a transpositionally assimilated form of an older **deg-yet-o-s.*

The word for "six" in Indo-European reconstructs to **seks* or **sweks,* and it is a reasonable guess that the first is a simplification of the second. It is even conceivable that the earliest form may have been even more com-plicated, maybe **sh"weks.* This last shape could be analyzed as *s-h"we-k-s.* Except for the first consonant, it could then be identified with Old English *waksan, weaksan,* to wax or grow larger, and Latin *augere,* to increase. The first element is then surely to be identified with certain forms for "one" in Indo-European languages, including Hittite *sa-ni-s* and Greek *he-m-s* from **se-m-s;* also *hé-te-ro-s,* one of two, different. Indo-European "six" would thus be "one added," a strictly hand-and-finger designation for the numeral.

A noteworthy coincidence is the fact that "two" in Uralic languages and "four" in Indo-European are essentially identical. Thus Magyar *keet* and Vogul *kit*, two, may well go back to the same original root form as Indo-European **kwet*, seen in Latin *quattuor*, Greek *tettares*, and Russian *chetíre*. Such a relationship can be explained in terms of finger counting, because in some regions the custom is to begin with the little finger and in others with the thumb. The index finger would thus be the second finger, or "two" in one system and the fourth, or "four" in the other. Now, **kwet* evidently means "point" in such formations as Latin *tri-queet-ru-s*, three-cornered, triangular, and old English *hwaet*, sharp, and *hweettan*, to whet or sharpen. Hence "two" in Uralic and "four" in Indo-European would both appear to be called "pointer," or "index finger." Similar words for "two" and "four" in different languages are shown in the following examples. In some cases, the identity of the forms depends on a possible phonetic development of labiovelar to labial, that is, of *kw* to *p*. Such languages include Egyptian and the great Malayo-Polynesian phylum.

"Two"		"Four"	
Slave (Canada)	*oki*	Latin	*quattuor*
Zuñi	*kuilin*	Javanese	*pat*
Cofan (South America)	*kuangi*	Lycian (Asia Minor)	*kadr-*
Cheremis (Russia)	*koktot*	Ancient Egyptian	*fdw*
Avar (Caucasus)	*k'igo*	Hausa (Africa)	*hu'du*
Basque	*bi*	Etruscan	*huth*
Karen (India)	*ki*	Berber	*okkoz*
Maya	*ke*	Mocha (Africa)	*gutto*
Migibu (Central America)	*Kubu*	Galla (Africa)	*afur*
Jívaro (South America)	*katu*	Pomo (California)	*joto*
Khmer (Cambodia)	*pir*	Paya (Central America)	*ka*
Tasmanian	*pie*		
Tahitian	*piti*		

The element that expresses "four" in Uralic is **nel*. If the second consonant is a suffix, there remains **ne* or **neh* as the root, an old alternant of **nek*. This element occurs in Uralic with meanings like "push against, straight toward," and in other languages with the meaning "inside" or "between." Since "two" in Uralic seems to be based on a name for the index finger, then "four" must correspond to the ring finger. "Inside" is certainly a possible old name for this digit. A similar name might be expected for "two" in Indo-European, and it so happens that **dw*, the root of "two," is also found in forms that mean "between," such as German *zwischen*, English *between*, and Latin *dum*, while, meanwhile. Scholars have generally treated these other meanings as either derived from the idea of "two" or as unrelated, but it seems to make better sense to suppose that "between" is the primary sense.

The root of "four" in Semitic is built on *rab*, found also in words for "lord," "captain," and "lookout, sentinel." Although there is no direct connection with the idea of "index," or "pointer," there might be some relation with the idea of directing or dominating. Perhaps, then, there is here an old name for the index finger as the leader, in which case the derivation would be a little like that of Indo-European.

The common Indo-European word for "five" appears to have been **penkwe* or **peenkwe*, as shown by Greek *pente* and Sanskrit *paancha*. A variant form **pempe* is reflected in Gothic *fimf*; and another, **kwenkwe*, in Latin *quiinque*. The labiovelar (*kw*) in Latin may be due to the influence of the *kw* in the second syllable and at the same time to its presence in the word "four," *qwattuoor*, because it precedes "five" in the count. In the same way, the labial in "five," Indo-European *p* and Germanic *f*, may explain the *f* of Gothic *fidwoor* and English *four*. Indo-European "five" appears to be related to Gothic *fingrs* and English *finger*, but the idea of "five" must be based on all the fingers of a hand rather than on "finger" as such. The fact is that words for "finger" and "hand" not infrequently interchange in meaning.

If the simple numbers are named for the fingers, "three" would be represented by expressions appropriate to the middle digit, no matter which direction one takes in counting. The name might be "tall," "thick," "big," or a related notion. A few forms that might have such an origin involve velar plus liquid, dental plus liquid, and sibilant plus labial nasal: *ker* or *kel*, *ter* or *tel*, and *shem* or *srem*. The following examples fit the three types either quite obviously or after allowing for phonological changes:

KER, KEL		TER, TEL		SHEM, SHREM	
Basque	*hirur*	Latin	*trees*	Cherkess	*shya*
Mongol	*ghur-ban*	Hittite	*tri-*	Egyptian	*xmt-*
Hausa	*uku*	Old Tahitian	*toru*	Sumerian	*esh*
Finnish	*kolmä*	Samoan	*tolu*		
Magyar	*haarom*	Mota	*ni-tol*		
Esselen	*xula-p*	Nengone	*tin*		
Mixtec	*'uni*	Fula	*tati*		
Mapuche	*kɨla*				
Jívaro	*kala*				

The striking thing is the large number of languages that conform to these three types, even though at times only approximately.

It should be clearly emphasized that the connections we find between numerals and other words suggestive of their origin are often not obvious. Thus, in seeking an explanation for "three" in Ural-Altaic, we have to consider forms like Finn *kolmä*, Magyar *haarom*, Samoyed *naa-q ir*, Mongol *ghur-bar*, and Tungus *il-an*; and we can compare these with Finnish *korkea*, high, tall, and *karttu-a*, to grow; Hungarian *kor*, old age, and *koros*, old; Mongol *kulk*, tall; *kür*, thick, fat; and *il*, exceed; and Nanai *gulde-* and Lamut *gil-de-*, lengthen. The phonological variations in the world for "three" overlap those for "big," "long," and "fat" in their phonetic manifestations sufficiently to suggest a common origin. A complete demonstration, eliminating all possibility of any misreading of the evidence, might well result from thorough research. For the present, we can only claim a strong preliminary case, which, alongside the many cases of unquestionable analysis of numerals into phrases or derived words, supports the notion that numerals are generally based on concepts of finger counting.

An important limitation of the digital principle has to be recognized for certain large portions of the world. In a series of languages extending from Borneo and New Guinea to Australia and Tasmania, and in a region in South America including parts of Bolivia and Argentina, the basic count, at least before modern contacts with the outside world, was "one" and "two." The next two numbers could be expressed by addition, such as "two and one" and "two and two." Any quantity above four had to be pieced out by circumlocution, gesture, or any of various devices that varied from community to community and according to the ingenuity of the individual speaker. Cases are reported of comparing the number to clusters of leaves or petals on certain plants, of showing a corresponding number of fingers as a mute gesture without using any specific numeral word, of giving the names of all the individuals composing a group that is being described, or of stating how far a collection of persons or animals would reach in a single file. There was a strong tendency, however, simply to avoid statements as to exact numbers. In recent times the speakers of these languages have generally adopted numerals from other languages, or developed new terms out of native expressions. An interesting instance is that reported for the Noub language of Papua, where the count goes (1) one, (2) two, (3) one-and-two, (4) index, (5) thumb, (6) fist, (7) forearm, (8) elbow, (9) upper arm, (10) shoulder. This is an anatomical solution, comparable to the use of finger names and possibly inspired by knowledge of that practice.

Still other groups of languages have a quinary or decimal system of counting, but on closer examination they show clear traces of the former existence of a one-two system. Notable cases include the Hokan languages of the western United States and northern Mexico, Huave and Manguean of Mexico and Central America, and Sumerian of the ancient Middle East. This evidence would seem to indicate that the one-two count must once have been widespread and probably represents human usage before the invention of finger counting.

Even in Indo-European, where decimal counting must go back at least seven thousand years, one of the roots for "one" seems to go better with a simpler system. That is the sibilant element reflected in Hittite *sa-ni-s* and Greek *he-i-s*, one, and Latin *se-mel*, once, and identical with an emphatic demonstrative also found in Sanskrit *sa-n-u-ta-r*, for oneself, English *s-un-de-r*, to separate, Gothic *si-k*, oneself, and *s-l-boo-n*, self, and Latin *see*, oneself.

The emphatic character of the *s* demonstrative has been lost in some of the forms, such as Latin *i-s-te*, this, and Greek *ho*, the. It is perhaps also present with strengthened meaning in the Latin prefix of verbs like *see-paraa-re*, to separate, and *see-duuce-re*, to lead apart. Greek *hé-te-ro-s*, one of two, other, is particularly suggestive of an older system in which the sibilant demonstrative may have been used as one of the words in a one-two count. It would be interesting if we could identify the second item of such a set. Possibly it is the root of Gothic *an-tha-r* and Latin *al-te-r*, other, which might conceivably have been a demonstrative; old **ho* or the major root **h"on*, to change; or related to the root **hak* or **hok*, found in other parts of the world. Another possibility is the old element of Gothic *bai*, Latin *amboo*, Greek *amphoo*, Sanskrit *u-bhaa*, and Russian *o-ba*, all meaning "both," and Latin *ambi-*, *amb-*, around, and Greek *amphi*, around, on both sides. This element might be **bhy*, contained in Sanskrit *bhid*, to split. It is tempting to relate this element with a characteristic form of the word for "two" with labial stop in a number of languages of south Asia and southward, including Khmer *pir*, Santali *bar*, and Tasmanian *pie*, but at this stage it is best to recognize that these are mere possibilities, with nothing that can be regarded as even partial proof of relationship.

A particularly interesting case is that of Sumerian, which combines a one-two count with the word for "hand" used to express "five" and another, possibly related form for "ten." The analysis of the system is not obvious in some of its details, so I shall present here the actual forms, with some possible suggestions of etymologies.

1. *ash*
3. *esh*
   (the word for "one" with vowel change)
5. *i*
   ("hand")
7. *i-min*
   ("hand plus two")

9. *i-limmu*
   ("hand plus four")

2. *min*
4. *li-m-mu*
   ("two" with prefixed elements and vowel change for a double)
6. *ash*, probably *aash*
   (contraction of *i-ash*, hand plus one)
8. *us-su*
   (perhaps from *esh-mu*, twice four, with first vowel assimilated to second)
10. *u*
    ("hand" with vowel change for "double")

It should be remembered that the Sumerians were among the first mathematicians and astronomers. Their language was put into phonetic writing around 3000 B.C., and their advanced culture began about two thousand years before that. Since the indications are that counting to two antedates more elaborate systems, it seems likely that their mathematics evolved under the stimulus of cultural advance, begun while they were still using a one-two count.

The Sumerian *ash* for "one" resembles the archaic element in Indo-European in that both contain a sibilant, and it is conceivable that the Sumerian form may have been derived from an earlier compound demonstrative, *a-she* by the loss of the second vowel. It is furthermore noteworthy that sibilants are generally common for the first numeral in the languages of the world. Some examples are:

Nahuatl	*see*	Puelche	*chia*
Pawnee	*as*	Misupa	*maskoki*
Wichita	*wi-'as*	Desaña	*sika^n*
Cherokee	*soķwe*	Tunica	*sa-hky*
Huron	*eskate*	Keresan	*iska*
Oneida	*onskah*	Bella Coola	*smaw*
Nootka	*ts'awaa-k*	Taruma	*oshe*
Chemakum	*ch'amiish*	Macusi	*chewne*
Seri	*ta-sho*	Guató	*chenay*
Pomo	*ch'a*	Guarao	*isaa*
Shasta	*chaa'a*	Paya	*as*
Chinook	*ish-t*	Old Zapotec	*cha-ga*
Uru	*chi*	Panoan	*achu-bi*
Ono	*sows*	Paez	*yas*
Tehuelche	*chanke*	Shavante	*simisi*
Rama	*sai-min*	Nengone	*sa*
Cagaba	*ai-sua*	Ainu	*shine*
		Tibetan	*g-chigs*
Cureto	*chuyu*	Circassian	*zī*
Piro	*sa-ti*	Kabardian	*si̇*

If we bear in mind that the numeral "six" is often expressed as "one added to five," "one on the second hand," or still other terms of expression involving "one," it is interesting to note cases of sibilants in "six" also:

Seri	*isnaapka-shoh*	Sumerian	*aash*
Zapotec	*ssho'oppa'*	Egyptian	*syir*
Paya	*sera*	Hebrew	*shisshii*
Mochica	*tsalhtsa*	Basque	*sei*
Quechua	*suqta*	Berber	*sedis*
Indo-European	**seks, *s-weks*	Paez	*sanki*

Words for "five," "ten," twenty," and "one hundred" may also have a bearing on the matter, since these notions may be derived from "*one* hand," "*one* full count," and "*one* large count." Some examples of words for "five" which contain a sibilant are:

Avar	*shu*	Gondi	*sai*
Samoyed	*sombila*	Lenca	*tsaihe*
Tungus	*sunja*	Nengone	*se-dongo*
Berber	*semmus*	Korean	*tasot*
Ainu	*ashik*	Galla	*shan*
		Turkish	*bosh*

This collection of numerals containing sibilants can be considered as suggestive of the onetime existence of a sibilant element for "one" which began to be used very early, and which was retained in or spread to many languages. I do not feel that I have proved this hypothesis, but I do believe I have demonstrated that it is not wholly fanciful. The number of cases of numerals for "one" with sibilants seems much larger than could reasonably be expected on the basis of chance alone.

In parts of the world in which a one-two count occurs, the first number is not necessarily a sibilant. In the area of the Indian and Pacific oceans where that type of counting prevails, the usual word for "one" is *me*, *pe*, or *pak*. These may be old words for "hand," left over from expressions like "this hand," and seem to be related to phonetically similar demonstratives. Another problem is what term or terms were paired with "one" when the one-two system prevailed. Present data show that in at least some cases it was something like *hok* or *hak*, or had a labial consonant.

In general the evidence seems to support the existence of the one-two count before the invention and spread of finger counting. Presumably the idea behind this very ancient numeration was the contrast between just one and the combined or joined hands. The second element may have been a demonstrative, like the first, or it may have been an expression descriptive of the union of hands.

Nasal Murmurs and Grunts

In the languages of the world the nasal consonants are generally not the most frequent phonemes, and yet they are very common in certain categories of elements. These include words for mother and woman, for suckle, for the negative, for demonstratives and pronouns, and for other notions that can·reasonably be supposed to have been taken from these.

In many languages the word for mother has the form of or is similar to *mamma* or *nana*. The first is most common in Africa and Europe, the latter in Asia and America; but not infrequently both forms are found in languages of the same family or stock. Thus in Indo-European, alongside *mother* and *ma* in English, Albanian has *nene*, and Sanskrit has *maataa* as the formal expression, equivalent to and cognate with *mother*, but *nanáa* as the familiar expression, corresponding to English *ma* or *mom*. Words with *m* and *n* are also found for aunt, grandmother, nurse, woman, and girl. At times they turn up in general words for person, including old person and baby or for the male companion terms to each of the female personalities. Some examples are: Wintun *win-tuun* and Patwin *pat-win*, person; Nisenan *win*, man; Mixean Copainalá *win*, person, body; Mayan *winik*, man; Quechumaran *warmi*, woman; Yamana *win*, person; Misupan Misquito *waynka*, male; Xilenca Lenca *wana*, person; Sonchonan Moseten *wenci*, husband; Mapuche *went"i*, man, *mawon*, woman, and *weñi*, child; Coahuiltecan Cotoname *wawnahe*, man; Tocharian *onk*, man; English *wench*, girl; Sanskrit *wrsan* and Greek *arséen*, male; North Melanesia *mwana*, boy; Basque *anre*, lady; Tamil *pen*, woman, and *aanak*, grandmother; Hano-Tewa *meme*, mother's brother, elder clansman; Georgian *máma*, father; Kocch *mama*, uncle; Tamil and Telugu *mama*, mother's brother; English *nana*, nurse; Blackfoot *ninnah*, father; Greek *nennos*, uncle; Rashad *om*, person; and Cuna *puna*, sister.

To explain the prevalence of such words, one may think of Latin *mamma*, female breast, and Finnish *nisa*, teat, and *nänni*, nipple. The influence would then be that a mother was thought of as a woman suckling her baby. The origin may be sound-imitative, since babies frequently make nasal sounds in the midst of suckling. The action itself does not require nasality, since the child closes his lips on the teat and at the same time presses it between the forward part of his tongue and the upper gums. The sucking vacuum is formed between this double closure at the front of the mouth and the back of the tongue held tight to the back palate. If the baby vocalizes while suckling, or when he has set his mouth in anticipation of it, the most likely sound to be produced is a nasal, made while the lips, gums, and palate are pressed together. Under these circumstances, the effect is like *m*, *n*, and *ng* combined. The hearer can associate the sound with any one of these nasals, or if his language has a nasal phoneme of double contact, *ngm*, the latter will come closest to the actual sound. The name given to the mother and based on the suckling murmur will apply equally well to the wet nurse and can pass by association to the grandmother, aunt, elder sister, or any female who looks after the child, even though she does not actually suckle it. Sense transfer can also account for the application of the same terms to persons in a protective role regardless of sex, and may eventually even become separate from the idea of protection.

Still, to explain all the words for mother as due to the baby's murmur while suckling would be to oversimplify matters. The English word *mother* goes back to common Indo-European **meh"-to-r*, whose root would seem to be identical with that of Greek *maakros*, large. "Mother" might therefore be etymologically "big one." The most reasonable inference may well be that in the course of the development of each language, the word for mother came to resemble various other elements in the language. If the meanings seemed at all fitting (from a sound-symbolic point of view), an association was established which could even lead to the modification of one or both of the similar forms, so that they would then be even more alike than before. Phrases and derivative formations were probably also produced which emphasized the description suggested by the phonetic similarity. In this way, some modern terms for mother may derive from different roots, which resembled the earlier terms. On the other hand, some of the descriptive expressions may have originated independently and only later taken on the function of the kin term.

The explanation for the relative frequency of nasal consonants in the negative, in demonstratives, indefinites, and interrogatives, and in personal pronouns must be somewhat different. The most widespread consonant in the expression of "not" in the languages of the world is *m*; next comes *n*. In demonstratives and third-person pronouns, *n* is very frequent and *m* is not uncommon. The *m* is frequent in interrogatives and indefinites. In the pronominal elements for first and second person, some languages have the same nasal in both, with differences in the vowel. Many, especially in America, have *n* in first person and *m* in the second; some do it the other way around. There are pronominal expressions that have nasals in only one of the two persons, or that employ them in the singular but not in the plural, or vice versa. A peculiarity of Indo-European is that it uses the nasal *m* in the oblique cases of the first person singular, while the nominative has a velar stop: *g* or *gh*. It is hard to find a language that does not have a nasal in at least one form of the first and second person pronouns.

The use of nasal phonemes in the negative in so many languages of the world must in some way be related to the prevailingly nasal character of the grunt. In English, the vocable of denial is almost always nasal; but it can vary from a nasalized vowel to any of the three nasal consonants: *an'an*, *én'en*, *ón'on*, *m'm*, *n'n*, *ng'ng*. When it is a nonnasal vowel, such as *a'a*, it can still be recognized by the duplication of the syllable with its glottal separation, accent on the first syllable, and the characteristic tonal drop. Why is nasality so common? Surely because it results from the relaxation of the velum. We might indeed note that the most usual position of the velum is down, and that the most relaxed form of grunt is nasal. The prevalence of nasals in the negative and the demonstratives may therefore be due to the fact that they are based on grunts. The difference between negation and demonstration must originally have been mainly one of tone. Similarly, tone may have distinguished interrogatives from demonstratives. Hence the inference is that negation, interrogation, and demonstration was a matter of inflection, principally tonal, based upon a single root. Conceivably at one time the difference among the several specific nasals, *m*, *n*, and others, was of minor importance. In an earlier epoch or in certain regions it may have had some special significance, but probably not anything connected with the matter of negative or interrogative as against demonstrative. As I suggested in the two preceding chapters, degrees of closeness and distance have at one time been distinguished by vowel quality; but at a still earlier stage they may have been related even more to the contact point in the mouth.

Apparently the same grunt words, with prevalence of nasals, were also used for the personal pronouns of the first and second persons. Presumably the first person was expressed as a near inflectional grade of the demonstrative and the second person normally as the removed but not distant grade. The distinction between a reference to the speaker and an object very close to him may have depended on context or the use of manual gestures. The use of the lips as against the point and root of the tongue must also be thought of as a form of gesture. Pouting gives the lips a shape adequate for pointing, and the tip of the tongue can also serve as a pointer. When the lips are not actually pouted and when the tongue remains in the mouth, the sounds may still convey the implication of the visible gesture.

Since the epoch when inflectional alternations were used to designate interrogation, demonstration, and negation, the major change has involved the replacement of the inflectional symbolization by distinct lexical items. At a deeper level, probably belonging to the paleoglottic period or possibly even before, the various nasals may have been in inflectional-alternation to each other.

Mamma, Papa, and Other Kin Terms

The relationship of *mamma* and *papa* in English, French, and other European languages is parallel to that of *naná* and *tatá* in Tarasco and other languages of Mexico. In each case the nasal of a given contact point, labial or dental, expresses the female parent, while the corresponding stop consonant designates the male parent. Symbolically, this can be understood as relaxed velum for the feeding parent, tensed velum for the loosely associated parent. Another interpretation, based on the prevailing physical characteristics of the sexes, might be nasal for the soft parent and stop for the tough parent. Examples from various languages are:

	"Mamma, Mother"	"Papa, Father"
Greenlandic Eskimo	*anaana, anaanaq*	*ataataq*
Crow	*masake*	*birupxe*
Yokuts	*no'om*	*nophoph*
Dakota	*ena*	*ate*
Nahuatl	*naan*	*ta'*
Yucatec	*nan*	*tat*
Tiv	*ng*	*ter*
Luo	*mama*	*baba*
Hebrew	*ima*, mommy	*aba*, daddy
	em, mother	*av*, father
Eastern Arabic	*'imm, 'immayaat*	*'aabaa*
Burmese	*qaméi*	*qaphéi*
Sanskrit	*nane*	*tatá*
Tamil	*ammaa*	*appa*
French	*mère, mama*	*père, papa*

The mother is one of several females with whom the child has contact, the others being sisters, aunts, grandmothers, and so on. The father similarly is one of a group of male associates. To distinguish specific relatives in each set, inflection may once have been used. Certain vowel and consonant alternations were apt devices in some languages in some periods, but might later have ceased to be used inflectionally. Modern kinship systems surely reflect a mixture of older periods, while being dominated by the lexical contrasts that have replaced the older inflectional ones.

Consider the following four terms of Russian kinship: *maty*, *máma*, mother; *babushka*, grandmother; *bába*, old woman; *otéts*, *pápa*, father; *ded*, grandfather, old man. There seems to be a general outline of a consistent plan of alignment, especially if we take the present forms back to a far earlier stage when they were, say, **ma*, mother, **ta* or **pa*, father; **bha*, grandmother; and **dha*, grandfather. The older generation is designated by aspiration, the immediately related generation by nonaspiration. Nasal is for the feeding parent, stop for all others. What was originally a vowel difference separates *otéts*, father, and *tyótya*, aunt, perhaps formerly referring to the father's sister. *Dyádya*, uncle, from earlier **dhee*, if we reconstruct the aspiration, may have originally indicated the father's older brother; one would expect so from the symbolic value of aspiration. The junior uncle may have been indicated by **de*, with the diminutive symbolism of the voiced stops. English *dad*, going back to Indo-European **dhodho*, may preserve the aspiration in a different application of its symbolic significance, since the form could be based on the respectful usage. The familiar and affectionate implication of *dad* as against *father* may be a more recent association with what was originally a reserved form of reference.

It is interesting that the stops in kin terms tend to be of the neutral type, even in languages that also have glottalized or voiced and aspirated ones. Interrelationships involving different articulatory types, as in Russian and English, are therefore exceptional. The reason for the predominance of the neutral type of stop may be that the usage reflects infant pronunciation, which tends to pass over the subtler phonetic distinctions. It may also be an archaic feature, in that the oldest alternations, reflected in the kin terms of many languages, might well have been those between stop and nasal and among the various contact positions.

As is well known, kin terms show certain special structural features. These include especially reduplication, as shown by Spanish *mamá* and *amá* for mother, *papá* and *apá* for father. It is also common to have formal terms beside familiar terms, such as English *mother* and *ma* or *mom*. The formal expressions in many cases seem to be based on the familiar terms by the addition of affixes such as those used in the non-kin part of the vocabulary. In other cases, the familiar expression seems to be an abbreviation of the formal one.

Demonstratives

The interesting fact about demonstratives is that most languages have a variety of them, greater than needed to distinguish near and far and all the other demonstrative designations recognized in the language. Only in a few languages do most of these forms have distinct references. Such is the case of Eskimo and Aleut, in which usage depends on the position of the object referred to and its level in relation to that of the speaker. The following demonstratives are from Aleut.

Seated: *wa-n*, directly at my side; *ji-ngá-n*, the next; *ga-Gá-n*, in the next to the last place; *qu-ká-n*, the farthest; *qa-kú-n*, directly in front; *qi-kú-n*, farther in front; *ja-ká-n*, on top; *ji-ká-n*, farther up; *u-k-ná-n*, farther down; *a-ká-n*, at a little distance; *i-kú-n*, in second place toward the door.

Standing: *i-qú-n*, at my side; *ja-kú-n*, at a distance.

Walking: *a-wá-n*, at my side; *ji-kú-n*, to one side; *a-kú-n*, at a distance.

Indifferent position: *u-ká-n*, inside the house; *sa-dá-n*, outside the house; *a-ma-ya*, this one (not visible); *u-má-n*, *ja-má-n*, that one (absent or not visible); *na-má-n*, this (in general).

In other languages the various forms are used arbitrarily, as in English, in which an *s* root is found in *so* and *such*; a *y* root in *yes* and *yet*; an *n* root in *now*; and a vowel initial, deriving from glottal consonant (*h* or '), in *as*. Furthermore, there is the all-purpose *dh* in *this*, *that*, *there*, *then*, and so on; the *h* of near location in *here* and with no special implication in *he* and *her*; and the *wh* or *h*, from old *kw*, in interrogative and relative *what*, *which*, *how* and others. Moreover, the apparent meaning of each demonstrative root in English is not borne out in other languages of the Indo-European stock. The implication, then, is that in common Indo-European there was already a variety of demonstrative elements of miscellaneous use. We can suppose that at one time each form had a specific function, but this must have been a long time before the late stage of common Indo-European usually revealed by comparative linguistics. After the specific functions were lost, they were all more or less equivalent to each other, and could easily shift in details of usage and meaning.

The following listing shows various modern functions of common Indo-European demonstratives. It suggests that the various consonants had early lost the specific values they may once have had and had become vaguely equivalent, possibly with different uses in the local variants of common Indo-European.

COMMON INDO-EUROPEAN FORMS	DIVERSE MEANINGS IN VARIOUS INDO-EUROPEAN LANGUAGES
*te, *to, *too	Russian *ta-k*, so, *ta-m*, there, *to-t*, that one; German *doch*, nevertheless; English *though*
*ye, *yo, *yoo	German *yetzt*, now; English *yet*; Sanskirt *ya*, the one that; German *ya*, yes; Polish *ya-k*, how, as; English *yon*, yonder
*n-u	Russian *nu*, well, then; Latin *nunc*, therefore; English *now*

*kwe, *kwo	Latin *quo-d*, what; English *which;* Sanskrit *cha*, Latin *que*, and
*se, *soo	Gothic *sik,* himself; English *so;* German *sie*, she, they; Sanskrit *saa*, that (feminine)
*ke, *ko	English *he, her;* Latin *cis-*, on the near side; English *here;* Greek *kai*, and

[*For further discussion of the nature and origin of demonstratives, see Chapter 4, where examples are provided of front-back vowel symbolism used to mark near and far demonstratives.*]

First and Second Person Pronouns

In the languages of the world in general and often within a single stock or family, or even within the vocabulary of a single language, there is often disagreement in the basic consonants used for the pronouns of the first and second persons. The Indo-European languages present quite a complicated picture in this respect. In the first person, the nominative has a velar consonant, which may be voiced or aspirate (Latin *ego* but Greek *ekhoo*); and yet the other cases and derivatives have *m*, such as English *me* and *my*. The plural verb ending of the first person generally has *m*, as in Latin *amaa-mu-s*, we love; and in Russian the independent plural also has *m* in the nominative *mi*, we, but the Russian plural accusative and other forms have *n*, as in *nas*, us, and *nashiy*, our. English has *w* in the first person plural, *we*; but Latin has *w* (spelled *v* or *u*) for the second person plural, *voos*, you. The second person plural in Germanic has *y*, you, as in Gothic *yu*, ye. The usual form for the second person singular independent pronoun is *t*, as in Latin *tuu*, thou, but in the verbal ending Latin uses *-s*, as in *ama-s*, thou lovest.

Pronominal variation in Indo-European is perhaps greater than in many language groups, but it is not entirely exceptional. There are other languages that have about the same amount of variation or even more. In some cases it is possible to trace the origin of particular instances of inconsistency. Sometimes it is phonological. For example, when a consonantal pronominal sign was in final position in one form but intervocalic in another, it may conceivably have been retained in one but shifted in the other, or changed in different ways. Again, the characteristic consonant may be lost through the operation of a phonological process, in which case the meaning may become attached to some associated element. This happens, for example, in languages in which the pronouns are formed by adding pronominal endings to a neutral pronominal base, as in Tzeltal *ho'o-n*, I, consisting of the general demonstrative stem *ha* with the affixation of *-n*, the sign of the first person; at the same time, the vowel is changed to *o* and reduplicated with insertion of glottal stop. In Zuñi, "I" is *ho*. In Tarasco we have *hi*, I, and *hu-cha*, we,

with -*cha* identifiable as a pluralizer. Thus it would seem that Tarasco and
Zuñi have lost the first person ending, but have transferred its function to
the originally neutral base. In Tzeltal, "we" is *ho'o-tik*, in which -*tik* is the
plural ending and *ho'o-* the old base, but the -*n*- of the first person has been
lost in contraction. The notion of first person now is carried by the vowel
o, as against *a* used in the second and third persons.

There are cases where the second person element has come to be used as
the sign of first person in the plural, all based on the use of a combined
reference to "thou and I," a category designated the "inclusive" in grammars.
Beginning with this usage, a combined "thou and I" form may come to be
understood as "we" in general, whether it refers to "thou and I" or "he
and I." The last step in the chain of events is that the plural form "we"
may become associated with the meaning of first person regardless of
number. That is, it may end up as the equivalent of either "we" or "I."
If at the same time the phonetic form is worn down until the only part
retained is the one that originally represented the second person, then the
shift is complete. An original second person has come to be applied to the
first.

Even after one has recognized all cases of phonetic change and the ways
in which the pronominal function may be transferred, there still remain
other instances in which some other explanation is called for. In the last
analysis, there seems to be evidence for pronominal variability, which
leads one to suspect that the difference between first and second persons may
once have been a matter of inflection, similar to that noted for third person
demonstratives. Hence it may well be that what are nowadays the concepts
of first and second persons may once have been just two special ways of
using the demonstratives. Possible additional support for this inference is
the fact that the persons are differentiated by alternating vowels or tone
in some languages. [*Here are some examples of vowel alternation used to symbolize
pronominal person in a number of languages, most of them African.*]

	"I"	"You"	"He"
Katla	*nyong*	*ngang*	*ngung*
Otoro	*ngi*	*nga*	*ngu*
Rashad	*-rang, -rïng*	*-rong*	*-rung*
Krongo	*a'a*	*u'u*	*i'i*
Tabi	*aane*	*oone*	*iine*
Lango	*án*	*(y)ín*	*én*
Yana	*-ni-, -tsi*	*-nu-, -tsu*	
Tamil	*naan*	*nii*	

Evidence of consonantal alternation of an inflective character is perhaps
to be seen in the fact that the first person is more commonly expressed by
a nasal than the second person. In many languages the first person has a

nasal and the second a stop. [*Here are some examples, mainly from American Indian languages.*]

	"I"	"You"
Eskimo	*-nga*	*-it*
Algonkian	*ne-*	*ke-*
Yurok	*nek*	*ke'l*
Taos	*'a^{n}n-*	*ka^n-*
Nahuatl	*ni-*	*ti-*
Cuna	*ani-*	*pee-*
Sidamo	*ani*	*ati*
Somali	*aan*	*aad*
Alagwa	*ana*	*ku*

The symbolic interpretation may be that the nasal marks first person because of its relaxed character, while the stop is appropriate for the second person because of its relative tenseness.

As for the specific nasal or stop used, this appears, in recent times, to be mainly an areal phenomenon. In some parts of the world a labial is more usual for the first person, while the second person tends to be dental. Elsewhere it tends to be the other way around. In certain regions the velar nasal appears, especially for the first person.

Paleoglottic Alternations and Symbolism

[*This section serves to summarize the categories of vocabulary just discussed (kin terms, demonstratives, and pronouns) by characterizing the nature of the grammar in which they developed. Swadesh stresses the importance of the role played by consonantal and vocalic symbolism in the early stage of language he is considering. See Chapters 3 and 4 for a further discussion of this characteristic of language.*]

The evidence of the demonstratives and other similarly treated elements seems to indicate that, before the neoglottic period, perhaps in the paleoglottic, fewer phonemes were differentiated than in contemporary languages, and all were in alternation with each other. There may have been horizontal interchange among dental, palatal, labial, labiovelar, velar, and glottal. Each of these positions must have had its own symbolic significance, which cannot yet be clearly discerned but which we can hope to understand better when the matter has been properly studied. I can offer some tentative suggestions, however, based on hints from preliminary exploration of modern usage and from the symbolic trends evident in imitative vocabulary. The glottal position perhaps was undefined or neutral in emotional tone. Velar may have suggested what is very close, perhaps within the speaker; labial, what is farther off; and dental, what is near. The palatal may have been a variation of the dental or a compromise between it and the velar;

its semantic implication may have been nearness with contact. The labio-velar, combining the labial with the velar, perhaps implied extension from near to far or from one extreme to another.

The alternation of phoneme types or manners of articulation, as has already been shown, probably expressed emotional overtones. Simple nasality expressed relaxation and contentment. Joined with laryngeal constriction, it signified rather displeasure or frustration. Aspiration, as in its more modern manifestations, expressed energy and the force to resist or continue. Voicing may have expressed weakness, nonopposition, and there-fore also friendliness or affection. In contrast to vacuum sounds, it perhaps gave the idea of movement away from the speaker. Clicks and implosives may have given the notion of movement toward the speaker, the first being perhaps more forceful. Rubbing—that is, converting a stop into a fricative—must have had a symbolism similar to that of aspiration but with increased force. Glottalization gave the effect of quickness or abruptness.

Even before the dawn of human language, a system such as this was potentially present, because the symbolism is based on animal gestures and analogies to reality. Man's mental capacity to discriminate implications had not yet developed, however. Hence his reactions could not be clear and consistent. Under these circumstances, the differentiated implications of contact position could not have had much effect. Perhaps we can suppose that all nasals were approximately the same in their effect, and likewise all stops, all fricatives, and so on. It is also very likely that in-between or blended sounds were infrequent and did not lead to differentiated reactions.

We may suppose that in the earliest formative stage of human language, the *eoglottic*, man began to discriminate sounds, to react and to communicate in terms of different symbolic significance to the general main zones of articulatory contact, and to appreciate subtler distinctions and combina-tions of sound types and features. In this period, too, he began to improve in his capacity to imitate sounds heard in his environment. He learned to copy not only largely vocalic animal cries, but also the noise made by various objects striking against each other. Down to the present time, in the intuitive language, the stops reflect sharp impact, in different degrees and varieties according to the manner of articulation: voiceless, voiced, aspirated, or glottalized. Nasals represent resonant vibration. The fricatives naturally echo the continued rubbing and ongoing sounds of a nonresonant vibratory character. The vocalic timbres are usually associated with shapes corres-ponding to the form that the mouth must assume to produce each of them; that is, approximately sharp, flat, and round, respectively, for *i, a,* and *u.*

The imitative value of the separate points of articulation depends upon the subtle acoustic overtones they produce. Man today is able to sense when a noise sounds more like *p, t,* or *k,* or, if it is resonant, *m, n,* or *ng;* and it is likely that he was even more sensitive to these subtleties when he depended upon them for communication. The crystallization of an imitative code, with a notable amount of conventionalization of many of the syllables to reflect the sounds made by certain objects as they struck each other, may perhaps have been readied by about a half-million years ago. By this time there may have begun to develop a new phonetic subtlety, leading eventually to the system of three subzones in each principal zone of articulatory contact and the new alternations among the phonemes of each set of three. It is also possible that the manners of articulation were reduced and simplified. By neoglottic times there presumably was a basic inventory of roots, subject to the inner inflection described in Chapter 4. Some of our evidence indicates that the pattern in which the triple contact sets developed and the simplification of the articulatory manners or types took different directions in different parts of the world.

When imitative sounds had begun to be used in addition to expressives and demonstratives, human language had acquired its first differentiated vocabulary. It consisted perhaps of two roots, one the demonstrative expressive, the other the imitative vocable. Each of them had many variations, but if I am correct in my inference that these were all manifestations of just two generalized symbols, than all the specific forms were inflectional. Language had a minimum of lexemes, but a large internal inflection.

The later steps of language evolution involved converting inflective into independent roots. That is to say, when certain syllables came to be associated with the sounds made by definite classes of objects on impact, it became possible for each imitative vocable to symbolize that impact, the action leading to the impact, or one of the objects involved. These new lexemes were ratified in part by the new internal inflections, based on subzones of contact, and by a greater formalization of the number and associated meanings connected with the articulatory types. Presumably the final ratification of independent lexemes was brought about by the evolution of syntax—that is, the joining of two or more roots, both demonstrative and imitative, into expressive combinations.

The process of making meaningful lexemes out of old inflective forms was repeated in the later history of language, the neoglottic period; in the passage from the neoglottic to the recent periods, the classic and world stages; and in the many smaller steps that went into each successive major transformation. The first lexemes were necessarily produced out of alternants showing changed consonants and vowels. Later on, when inflections had also developed out of combinations of elements, the stage was set for the formation of new lexemes out of paradigmatic forms containing affixes.

Each general sweep in the direction of independent elements endangered the older inflective system. Not all of the old inflection had to disappear, as is evident from the fact that some limited symbolic alternations are still retained in a number of languages spoken today.

When scholars make comparative studies of languages that appear to have derived from the same earlier one, they often encounter difficulties involving words of similar meaning which do not quite fit the posited phonological correspondences. (For example, the words might have *n:l* where the expected correspondence is *l:l.*) The easy solution, adopted by rigid scholars, has been to disregard these cases, saying that the items are unrelated. More subtle scholarship has felt that there are problems still to be solved. We now see that the difficulty may arise from the fact that the languages in question were undergoing inflectional change in the period when their local variations were developing and deepening. In consequence, different alternants of the same root show up as the nearest semantic equivalents in the related descendant languages. Or, on the other hand, the forms that correspond phonetically may have meanings that differ sharply. In either case, the common origin of the items compared is less obvious than in instances where old alternations and dialect variation are not involved. (The scholar must be prepared to reconstruct not only single words, but also, to the best of his ability in view of the nature of the evidence, old alternations or inflections in phonology and lines of semantic change. He may also infer some information about old dialectology.) Unless we are prepared for patient unraveling, we may lose the thread.

Color Terms: An Example of the Need to Separate Ancient and Recent Vocabulary

In our efforts to penetrate ancient vocabulary, it is absolutely essential to understand what kinds of words are old and what kinds are new. This is related in part to the history of invention and in part to the evolution of vocabulary out of inflective forms. In both areas we know from the outset some of the more obvious facts. In other matters the comparative study of vocabulary in related languages can reveal many things that we might otherwise only suspect or which may even come as surprising revelations. I have already spoken of the linguistic evidence for the evolution of numerals from one-two counting systems through finger counting into modern mathematics. Let us now examine some additional categories of vocabulary.

In modern world languages there has been a tremendous buildup of color terminology, which now runs into hundreds of expressions distinguishing all sorts of shades and hues. The multiplication of color names is most active in the paint and dye industries, with some of the finer distinctions appearing in relation to cosmetics, ladies' hose, gloves, and so on.

In every recorded language, whether world, classic, or local, one can distinguish between basic color words and secondary descriptive ones. In the latter we may include technical terms, everyday nonbasic expressions, and casual figures of speech or phrases made up on the spur of the moment or already in use but not altogether general. Some of these may be used today and forgotten tomorrow, or be popular in one generation and unused in the next. Other casual uses become fixed everyday terms and acquire precise meanings. One characteristic type of phrase is made up of a conventional color term together with the name of an object or substance that displays some distinctive shade of the color: *golden orange* and *canary yellow*; *jade* and *chartreuse green*; *coral*, *wine*, and *rose red*; *chestnut* and *chocolate brown*; *gunmetal* and *ash grey*. Once the expression becomes general, the color reference may be dropped, and the name of the object alone be used as a color term: *gold, orange, canary, jade, chartreuse, coral, wine, rose, chestnut, chocolate, gunmetal, ash*. Some of the secondary terms have been in use so long that their origin has been completely lost. An outstanding example is *purple*, which we have from Latin *purpura*, and Latin in turn from Greek *porphura*, originally the name of a shellfish used to obtain a dye.

The names of the cardinal colors in most languages have so long a history that their origin may be completely lost to common knowledge. Yet there are some cases in which the etymology is still obvious, or in which at least an association of ideas is still evident. In English, *yellow* is evidently connected with *yolk*, an association especially clear in the dialectal pronunciation *yelk*. The relationship of *yellow* to *gold* and *gall* is not apparent in modern English but still more or less so in German, in which the words are *gelb*, *Gold*, and *Galle*. A relationship between words meaning green or yellow and gall or bile is evident in many languages. In others, the similarity is between green and leaf or grass. In the same way, white may go with snow or bone; black with charcoal; and red with blood. These are only some of the interesting associations found in various languages.

[*Some examples from Nahuatl are* ista-k, *white, from* ista-tl, *salt;* shoshok-ti-k, *green, from* shoko-tl, *fruit;* kwil-ti-k, *green, from* kwili-tl, *greens;* tliil-ti-k, *black, from* tliil-li, *ink;* kos-tli, *yellow, gold;* es-ti-k, *red, from* es-tli, *blood; and* chil-ti-k, *colored, from* chil-li, *chile. In the Torres Straits language of New Guinea we find* kulka-dgamulnga, *red, purple, from* kulka, *blood, plus* -dgamulnga, *it looks like;* mur-dgamulnga, *yellow, orange, from* mur, *yellow ochre;* il-dgamulnga, *green, blue, from* il, *gall bladder; and* malu-dgamulnga, *green, blue, from* malu, *sea.*]

The transfer of meanings in the recent period has mainly been from the names of objects and substances to colors, but the opposite also occurs. When we speak of the white of an egg, or when Latin called it *albumen*, from *albus*, white, it is the color that has gone to name the substance. It is quite possible that English *yolk* goes back to an old root word for "gall," and even more probable that all these expressions originated in something altogether different. Possibly their beginning can be traced to an old period when inflection by consonantal alternation was widespread. This is suggested by the fact that most Germanic basic color terms are very similar one to another in two main sets, one with velar and liquid consonants, the other with labial and liquid. With first consonant *g* or *y* in English, going back to Indo-European *gh*, and with *l* or *r* as second consonant, we have *yellow*, *green*, *gray*, and *grime*. The German word *hell*, bright, belongs with these. *Red* and *light* are also related if they originally began with the velar fricative *h"*, which would have been lost long ago. In this case, *red* would then be cognate to Latin *ardere*, to burn, and *light* would be cognate with Latin *albus*. However, it is also possible that there was another set of alternation forms, *new*, *rew*, and *lew*, and that from them there came *red* and *light*. A third possibility is that two old roots existed, and that the English words in question developed in association with both of them. At any rate, the color words derived from Indo-European *gher*, *ghel*, *kel*, *h"el*, and *h"er*, found reflected in Germanic, Italic, and other branches of Indo-European, apparently came from expressions for glowing and burning. Other related forms in English include *glow*, *gleam*, *glisten*, *lukewarm*, *hearth*, *hard*, and *char* (the last may have another origin). Many more examples could be given from other Indo-European languages to support the association with fire, light, and related concepts, but it may be sufficient to cite just three more: Latin *calidus*, hot, and *clarus*, clear, and Russian *goryaty*, to burn.

Another set of basic color terms in English has a labial as first consonant and a liquid as second: *black*, *blue*, and *brown*. It has been said that *brown* derives from the animal *bear* because of the color frequent in the species, but as we have seen in other cases, it could have been the other way around. At any rate, it is quite possible that *brown* may be connected with *burn*, *brimstone*, and *bright*, and with Latin *fervere*, to boil, and *frigere*, to fry. *Black* and *blue* can be compared with *blaze*, *blush*, *bleak*, *blank*, *blind*, *flare*, and *flicker*, and with Latin *flamma*, flame, and *flagrare*, to blaze up. This is another set of words having to do with fire, with a range of meanings that is somewhat different from the *ghel* set. The idea of black color is derivable from that of fire if we think of the color of soot and things that have been burned. Thus the different meanings may derive from the same original one as a result of a sequence of semantic shifts, sometimes moving in opposite directions, as is already evident in Old English, in which *blaec* is "black" but *blac*, with no other phonetic difference than that in the vowel, is "pale."

Changes of form and meaning in some thousands of years have greatly blurred the old state of affairs, but it seems nonetheless evident that basic colors were once expressed as shades of lightness and darkness in an alternating inflective paradigm. There is apparently no language today that handles the matter of color as purely paradigmatic. But the conceptual scheme connected with the old pattern may still be preserved in a large part of the world, while the phonetic relations continue to be evident (or reconstructable) in many scattered language groups, including English.

In the simplest terminologies of basic colors, found in much of Africa, Oceania, and South America, two or three concepts are recognized, which may be translated "light," "dark," and "colorful." The first includes white in varied forms, light gray, and all very light hues. The second includes black, dark gray, and all very dark hues. The third covers saturated bright colors. In some of the languages, blues and greens, if they do not shade into violet or yellowish, are conceived as dark, while all but the lightest and darkest yellows and reds are considered colorful.

[*Torres Straits has two basic terms:* mialalunga, merkalunga, *white, and* kubikubinga, *black. Jalé of New Guinea also has two basic terms:* sing, *black, and* hóló, *white. Tiv of Africa has three basic terms:* ii, *dark;* pupu, *light; and* nyian, *colorful. And Tshi of Africa also has three basic terms:* tuntum, *black;* fufu, *white; and* koko, *red (Berlin and Kay, 1969).*]

The peoples who use such basic color terminology are not color-blind or insensitive to shades and hues. In fact, they may have highly developed traditions in textiles, pottery, or basketry. They are known to describe shadings of color in words, particularly by making analogies with flowers, leaves, kinds of clay, organic substances, and the like, or by mentioning two or more colors that appear to be contained in the one to which they are referring. It is only their gamut of basic color terms that is a little more restricted than those of some other languages, and which may preserve the memory of a very ancient scheme.

The phonologic outlines of old color paradigms seem to be reflected in many language groups, especially of Eurasia, Australia, and America. The forms have mainly stops for the first consonant and liquid for the second, but there are also cases of nasal or continuant for the first. They often agree with words for fire and light. The inference to be drawn is surely that the origin of the expressions is at least as old as the paleoglottic. The consonantal types, then, refer to shapes: the first consonant to the base of a burning mass, the second to the characteristic fluctuating point of flame. The roots beginning in a labial consonant symbolized the broad burning bush or the large bonfire. The velar initials, by far the most numerous, may be based on the small-appearing stars. Where the second consonant is *l*, the implication is of light; where it is *r*, the implication is of intense heat or the bleakness of a burned-over field. Alternation of the first consonant according to the neoglottic inflection—that is, among the subzones and articulatory types or manners—with the meanings associated with these interchanges is common.

Big and Little

Just as interesting as color terms, and in many ways very similar, are those for size, weight, strength, degree, number, and other quantitative implications. In the recent period there exist many expressions based on nouns and verbs referring to objects and actions that represent outstanding instances of the quality concerned. Big things are called *gigantic, colossal, titanic, monstrous, elephantine, mammoth, herculean, gargantuan, monumental,* and *astro-nomical.* For small things we say *lilliputian, bantam, dwarfish, pygmy, midget, toy,* and *microscopic.* These terms are based on ideas from mythology, literature, folklore, or common knowledge. Others are simply descriptive, like *overgrown, puffy,* and *swollen,* and *stunted, reduced,* and *infinitesimal.* Still others seem to refer to size alone, but this is often because the etymology has been lost to sight. *Big* is an interesting example. Traced back to Indo-European, the root was **bheu-gh-,* to blow or puff out, represented in Latin by *bucca,* swollen cheeks. *Small* apparently comes from the same root as *mill, meal,* and *mellow,* whose reference therefore appears to have been to grinding things into fine particles or making them soft.

Three general facts result from any broad study of size and quantity words: (1) They are likely to be many and varied in any one language. (2) In a group of distantly related languages, there is likely to be considerable disagreement in their vocabularies in this respect. (3) Some of the expressions are likely to show sound symbolism of the neoglottic type, and as one goes farther back in the recent millennia, the more evidence there is of this feature. All of these facts help reveal the history of words expressing size. In the beginning, the developing human species reacted to large things by opening the mouth wide and thus making open sounds, by letting the tongue make contact farther back in the mouth, or by opening wide the vocal cords and letting the breath out in puffy aspiration. To small things the reaction was the opposite: narrow vowels, front articulation, and voicing or glottalization. For thousands of years there were no separate words to express size in the abstract, but only inflectional alternants with this quality built in. The evidence of the old state of affairs has not been lost, and in fact it is still being reinforced in some ways, even as it is being obscured in others, by the living use of sound symbolism in the intuitive language and the tendency to enrich the formal language from this source. In consequence, any list of words for big things and large amounts, even in languages spoken today, is likely to show a predominance of *r* rather than *l,* of open vowels like *a* rather than close ones like *i,* of aspirates rather than voiced or glottalized sounds, and of back- rather than front-articulated consonants within a zone. Insofar as recent phonological changes have shifted matters around, what look like specific contradictions to any one of the main symbolic features may be found, but the trend is still generally there.

We should not expect much correlation of size with open and close vowels in English, because their use in Indo-European went through a phase of redistribution on the basis of tense aspect and derivation. The only correlation possible as to point of contact of consonants is that *r* represents the back or large type and *l* the small. As for articulatory type or manner, *b, d, g,* and *y,* being derived from aspirates, should correlate with large, and *t* and *k* or *ch* with small; *f, th,* and *h* are neutral. *Big, broad, far, grown, great,* and *grand* fit the rules for large things; *small, little, light, slender, tiny,* and *child* fit

the rules for small things. The idea of "long" in many languages is expressed
by words of mixed phonology; that is, with one consonant symbolizing
"big" and the other "little." The English word is said to be derived from
Indo-European *dloon-gho*; the two first consonants then symbolize "small"
but the last one symbolizes "big." The explanation of the mixed symbolism
in words for length perhaps lies in the conception of bigness in one dimension
and smallness in the other.

Noise, Action, and Shape

[*Swadesh concludes this chapter by discussing the notion of sound symbolism and
internal inflection in general. We have already seen in the preceding sections how these
processes apply to particular areas of vocabulary. Finally, Swadesh suggests some
phonological-semantic formulas as hypothetical roots of a very early stage of human
language.*]

The development of language can now be roughly divided into three
stages: (1) totally inflective, (2) zonally inflective, and (3) externally
inflective or noninflective. The first stage corresponds to the first emergence
of human language, just above the lower animal threshold. All of language
was essentially intuitive, even though the basis of its use involved a certain
amount of intelligence and consciousness. The number of root words was
possibly no more than two, one a one-consonant demonstrative expressive
element and the other an imitative made up of two consonants; their
inflections did not coincide. A notable fact that applied to both elements,
however, was that they were highly inflective by means of tone, rhythm,
point of contact, articulatory type, and glottal accompaniment. From the
viewpoint of modern formal language, the most notable fact was that *t*,
ch, *p*, *kp*, and *k* were alternants of each other and also of *n*, *ny*, *m*, *ngm*, and
ng and of *l*, *y*, *w*, *gw*, and *gh*. In the zonally inflective stage, corresponding
presumably to the paleoglottic period, all these basic contact points and
articulatory types became more or less separated from each other and each
became the focus of a new inflection involving three subzones—front, middle,
and back—within its general area. In this way, independent root words
arose out of what was originally a single all-embracing inflectional variation.
Eventually the zonal inflections were weakened or lost in consequence of
the development of external inflection, and again there was a multiplication
of root words built up with fragments of the zonal paradigms. The most
significant growth of vocabulary was based on impact imitative roots.

Man's very first imitation must have been mostly of animal sounds.
Since he had used the vocal mechanism in such ways for a long time, this
was neither very difficult nor radically educational. It was when he began
to imitate the vibration of inanimate things, and especially the impact of
one object on another, that he had to develop very different perceptions

and skills. The most important novelty was that once he learned to imitate noises, he could later use these sounds not only to portray the noise in question, but also to symbolize the action that produced it and the shape and makeup of the object or objects involved. Eventually he would learn to name things more or less arbitrarily or by agreement with his fellows, but the important advance was the basic art of imitating the noise of contact and the vibration of bodies of various shapes and sizes.

Today our problem is to recapture these first beginnings by reconstructive techniques. Fortunately, we can use for this purpose the evidence of contemporary intuitive imitation as well as the elements of the many formal languages. Expanding and bringing together hints we have developed in previous discussion, we can formulate a hypothetical manual of sound imitation:

1. Stops represent hard impact, nasals soft impact or resonant vibration, continuants free vibration.
2. Vowels indicate shape, presumably in accordance with the kind of vibration that goes with each form of resonance space.
3. Labials (p, m) give the effect of flat surfaces slapping together, dentals (t, n) the contact of a point, velars (k, ng) that of blunt objects, labio-velars (kp, ngm) hollow or cupped contact, sibilant (ch) liquid or sliding contact.
4. The two consonants of a vocable permit the definition of a complex sound, from first contact to final fading, the shape of each of two colliding objects, or a three-dimensional shape defined by its form at each end.

The job of recognizing old roots in recent languages begins with the recognition of similarity and possible common origin in a number of words or underlying roots in various languages or language families. By taking into account the more recent inflectional alternations, it may be possible to understand variations of form and meaning that might otherwise wreck the comparison, and in fact to obtain even stronger evidence of cognancy and a more accurate notion of the earlier basic form. As one works in this manner, it is usual to find more and more forms in each language, and at the same time more and more languages, families, and stocks, which show the same element with recognizably similar meanings. Because of the semantic variation connected with inflectional alternation and because of transfers of sense that came about after the weakening of inflection, it is common to find sets of related meanings that cluster about a core idea or which trail off in one or a few directions from it.

The gathering of patterned sets of forms is a research procedure whose value should be neither exaggerated nor underrated. One must not expect magical results, such as finding that all forms in all languages fall quickly into place in the sets. There has to be a patient reconstruction of old forms and meanings, of trying one and another arrangement, and of modifying early conceptions in the light of new evidence. When forms just do not fit, it is best to set them aside, assuming that there must be some explanation, perhaps that the pattern is not yet properly understood, that the given form is etymologically different from what it appears to be, or that something special in its history accounts for its unusual form or meaning. Setting aside some items, then, one sees if others fit. If a reasonably promising pattern seems to be developing, the work may go on.

Some of the problems are phonological; that is, not enough is yet known of the ways in which the sounds are interrelated from language to language. Others are semantic; that is, we are still struggling with means of defining each pattern of interrelated ideas. But if we continue to work at both types of difficulties, matters are likely to improve.

To give a concrete notion of this form of approach, I shall list some of the elements that seem to crop up in many languages in various parts of the world with what appear to be the last echoes of a common meaning. Several such items are listed in abstracted form, with a suggested meaning and a series of instances taken mostly from modern English. This is not intended to represent proof of the reconstruction, which is a far more difficult matter, but an indication of the sort of thing with which I have tried to deal.

pek — Flat base to blunt point, impact of flat on blunt (or the opposite); principally associated objects and qualities: bone, hard, white.
Examples, *pack, peck, pick, bicker, fight, fickle, patch, pact, face, speck, back, fang.*

mek — Soft and broad set on something hard, associated with buttocks, belly, cheek, big.
Examples: *mackle* (spot), *main, magnanimous, mega-, might, mass, match* (to pair).

pet — Flat base to pointed tip, flat contact against something pointed or stiff.
Examples: *pat, pad, pet, pit* (as of fruit), *bat, foot, feather, pintle.*

pen,
pel,
per — Broad base tapering to soft point, broad and soft, movement from a firm base into vibrating motion, flat touching soft.
Examples: *fen, penis, pin, fly, flit, fall, flame, prod, press, prop, bribe.*

men,
mel,
mer — Vibratory sound, broad soft base to soft point, woman's breast, and extended: soft, vibratory motion, mind.
Examples: *moan, milk, mel* (honey), *mildew, milt, mire, marsh, mer-* (for sea, as in *mermaid*), *mild, mill, mind, memory.*

tek — From pointed to blunt (or the opposite).
Examples: *stick, tack, toggle, dog* (because of pointed snout), *dig, dagger, tag, tick, tickle, touch.*

nek,
lek,
rek — Soft point against something hard, soft point placed on something hard, and extended: tongue, nose, eye, see, light, hearth, inside.
Examples: *nose, nick, lick, next, night* (sun in inside, or neutral light), *latch, lingual, in.*

kep   Blunt against flat, opening out from narrow to wide, taking in open hand or mouth and closing together flatly, and derived: fist, ball, head.

Examples: *gable, cabin, ship* (Old English *skip*), *capture, keep, give* (cause to keep), *heft, haft, cap, cape, cabbage, capitol, shape.*

kew   Narrow at base and opening wide; curved or vaulted.

Examples: *curve, cave, cove, cup, excavate.*

kem   Sounding with closed lips, blunt against soft, narrow at mouth and closing softly, blunt to broad and soft, together.

Examples: *hum, hammer, hem, comb, hump, camel, com-* (prefix, "together," as in *com-press*).

The test of whether such sets add up to a safe demonstration of the form and meaning of old roots of a very old common language, possibly the forerunner of many historic languages, depends on careful compilation of data. [*Here Swadesh intended to list words from various languages which seemed to him to be derived from the old roots he posited above. I shall provide here some examples taken from other publications of his.*]

pek   French *bec*, beak; Mayan *p'ek'*, dog; Latin *pectus*, chest; German *Backe*, cheek; Tarascon *phaká*, pat.

mek   Tsimshian *mik*, mature; Alsea *makst*, long (in time); Takelma *maháy*, Nisenan *muk*, big; Nez Percé *mexshem*, mountain; Yawelmani-Chukchansi *moxlo*, old; Mixean **mɨha*, big; Totonac *maqat*, far, *maqaa's*, of long duration; Yucatec Mayan *muk*, of long duration; Tzeltal *muk'*, big; Quechumaran Quechua *maqma*, broad, *maqhu*, mountain; Sonchonan Moseten *meke*, mountain; Old Irish *mochtae*, large; Hittite *makkes*, big; Tokarian A *maaka*, much.

pet   Siuslaw *lhput*, Patwin *pute*, Nisenan *butuy*, Sumu-Ulua *butu-*, feather; Misupan Cacaopera *pit-*, feather, wing; Greek *pterón*, Sanskrit *páttra-*, Latin *penna* (**pet-na*), English *feather*, Hittite *pattar*, wing; Russian ptitse, bird.

pen,
pel,
per   Rumsen *capur*, Santa Clara *tiprek*, Clearlake *poolpol*, Tarasco *hapónda*, lake; Mixean Oluta *piyɨk-*, Misupan Misquito *plapa-*, flow; Alakaluf *aperas*, rain; Coahuiltecan Chontal *pána'*, river; English *float, flow;* Latin *pluwius*, rain; Sanskrit *pláwa-*, Greek *pléoo*, swim; Tsimshian *pyelst*, Nisga *plist*, star; Santiam *pyan*, sun; Mayan Huastec *pil*, firefly; Tsimshian *plkwa*, feather; Alsea *pluplu*, hair, fuzz; Siuslaw *lhpnat*, bird; Kanpanan Guambia *palayi*, Paya *opra*, fly; Quechumaran Quechua *pharpa*, wing; Sonchonan Moseten *pañ*, feather; *fin*, hair; Tokarian *plu*, German *fliege*, English (*house*)*fly;* Lithuanian *sparnas*. Lettish *spàrns*, German *flügel*, wing; Latin *plumma*, Lithuanian *plùnksu*, Russian *pyeró*, feather; Sanskrit *parná-*, feather, leaf; Indonesian **bulu*, feather, hair; Basque *biloa*, hair; perhaps borrowing from Late Latin, Tibetan *phir-*, fly.

men,
mel,
mer   Samoan *malu*, soft; Basque *malba*, weak, *malso*, slow, *malsho, mardo*, soft; Arabic *mals*, smooth, soft, *mald*, soft; Chehen *meelin'*, weak; Tamil *mel*, fine, tender; Latin *mollis*, soft; Russian *myíliy*, kindly; English *mild;* Cholon *-cman*, know; Tarasco *minzi-ta*, mind, heart, stomach; Sanskrit *mánas-*, Latin *menti-*, English *mind;* Tokarian A *mnu*, Gothic *muns*, Lithuanian *mɨntìs*, thought; Sanskrit *mánya-*, think: Armenian *imanam*, understand.

The forms above were collected by a broad sweep; the question is whether they give the impression of interrelationship. Next we must ask if there are other such sets, sufficient to add up to clear evidence for a common human language, thus supporting the hypothesis of Chapter 4.

References and Suggestions for Further Reading

[*For earlier work of Swadesh on the origin of vocabulary, ancient root forms, and early gram-matical structure, see Swadesh (1960a, 1960b, 1964, 1966).*

There is a tradition in anthropology and linguistics of interest in the origin of numeral systems, either within a single language family or geographic area or in language in general. See Dixon and Kroeber (1907), Hymes (1955), Salzmann (1950), and Tylor (1871). For the phonetic shape of kin terms in various languages, see Freire-Marreco (1915), Jakobson (1962), Jespersen (1922), and Murdock (1959). There has been little interest in recent years among anthropologists and linguists in the origin of vocabulary. An interesting exception is the work of Berlin and Kay (1969) in the development of color terminology. For phonetic symbolism in language, see the references to Chapter 5. Many of the sources for the examples used in this chapter are listed below.]

Berlin, Brent, and Kay, Paul
    1969. *Basic Color Terms: Their Universality and Evolution.* Berkeley: University of California Press.
Boas, Franz, ed.
    1911. *Handbook of American Indian Languages,* Bureau of American Ethnology bulletin no. 40, pt. 1. Washington, D.C.: Smithsonian Institution.
    1922. *Handbook of American Indian Languages,* Bureau of American Ethnology bulletin no. 40, pt. 2. Washington, D.C.: Smithsonian Institution.
Diamond, Stanley, ed.
    1960. *Culture in History: Essays in Honor of Paul Radin.* New York: Columbia University Press.
Dixon, R. B., and Kroeber, A. L.
    1907. "Numeral Systems of the Languages of California." *American Anthropologist* 9:663–90.
Freire-Marreco, Barbara
    1915. "A note on Kinship Terms Compounded with the Postix 'E in the Hano Dialect of Tewa." *American Anthropologist* 17:198–202.
Hoijer, Harry, ed.
    1946. *Linguistic Structures of Native America,* Viking Fund Publications in Anthropology no. 6. New York: Wenner-Gren Foundation for Anthropological Research.
Hymes, Virginia Dosch
    1955. "Athapaskan Numeral Systems." *International Journal of American Linguistics* 21:26–45.
Jakobson, Roman
    1962. "Why 'Mama' and 'Papa'?" In *Selected Writings,* vol. 1:*Phonological Studies.* The Hague: Mouton.
Jennings, Jesse D., and Norbeck, Edward, eds.
    1964. *Prehistoric Man in the New World.* Chicago: University of Chicago Press.
Jespersen, Otto
    1922. *Language: Its Nature, Development, and Origin.* London: Allen & Unwin.

Murdock, G. P.
   1959. "Cross-Language Parallels in Parental Kin Terms." *Anthropological Linguistics* 1, no. 9:1–5.
Salzmann, Zdeněk
   1950. "A Method For Analyzing Numerical Systems." *Word* 6:78–83.
Swadesh, Morris
   1960a. "On Interhemisphere Linguistic Connections." In *Culture in History,* ed. Diamond.
   1960b. *Tras la huella lingüística de la prehistoria.* Mexico City: Universidad Nacional.
   1964. "Linguistic Overview." In *Prehistoric Man in the New World,* ed. Jennings and Norbeck.
   1966. *El Lenguaje y la vida humana.* Mexico City: Fondo de Cultura Económica.
Tucker, A. N., and Bryan, M. A.
   1966. *Linguistic Analyses: The Non-Bantu Languages of North-Eastern Africa.* London: Oxford University Press.
Tylor, Edward Burnett
   1871. *Primitive Culture.* London: Murray.

SEVEN

The Progress of Babel

[Having presented in preceding chapters his conception of the origin of language and the nature of its various stages of development, Swadesh intended to provide in this last chapter a general classification of the languages of the world. Unfortunately, the sections concerning language classification were only sketched. I am therefore including here only those sections of the chapter that Swadesh did complete, together with two charts representing his last views on the classification of the world's languages.]

When man's ancestors still lived only instinctively, their cries were determined by their muscles, nerves, and glandular secretions. If we call their vocal behavior "language," as a figure of speech, we can say that they spoke just one language. Individuals then, as now and in other species, were not identical, so there must have been differences in their vocal behavior, but they were not deep. In addition to individual differences, there could have been variations by subspecies and by locality, but all within essentially one "language." Just as breeds of dogs may run together in miscellaneous packs or interact as individuals when they chance to meet, in that distant past man's ancestors could all understand each other when they met and vocalized. Even when our ancestors developed greater skill in vocal communication and doubled their vocabularies by adding two-consonant impact imitation to the simple expressive, communication continued to be closely bound to the instinctive-intuitive symbolism of sounds and muscular tensions, and there was still little room for the development of local traditions. Very, very gradually the human species developed in intelligence to the point where individual memories could be shared, and common-consent signals could play a role in communication. Man was moving to a stage where local languages could exist.

Some centuries before the present, philosophers had the wisdom to state a problem: Did all languages come out of one, or was language invented more than once in different parts of the world? Single origin or multiple origin?

213

Or, in scientific terminology derived from Greek by way of Latin, *monogenesis* or *polygenesis*? The debate was long and often exciting, but mostly just talk, because no clear answer was possible until people learned to think of man as a species that has evolved from a creature incapable of real language to one fully capable of it. Even when this conception had been achieved, it was still necessary to develop a proper understanding of the relationship of evolved human language to the simpler forms of animal communication. This has come slowly, and we surely still have far to go. Nevertheless, in this last chapter I finally feel I can come reasonably close to a satisfactory answer.

It is clear that, if we go back to the days when prehuman communication was not yet really language, there could be only one system common to our evolving species, albeit with minor individual and subspecies differences. Furthermore, only when a fairly definite and sizable degree of conventionalization had come about was it even possible for different languages to exist. This sort of vindicates the Tower of Babel story, which suggests that, as long as men lived simply, they spoke one language. When they acquired wisdom and yearned to raise themselves to heaven, their language developed local variations and there arose different, mutually unintelligible forms of speech. The problem is still not solved, however, because we must ask if separate languages arose only by gradual divergence out of the commonly evolving species communication or by separately developed traditions of formal language. Or, again, could there not have been fresh starts that became disconnected from earlier traditions? Some philosophers, trying to explain the existence of so many languages in the world, thought that youngsters every once in a while got lost from their elders and invented new languages among themselves. To the first of these possibilities, my answer must be that the normal tendency was surely always to build on what existed before. When appreciable numbers of arbitrary symbols came to exist in human communication, they must at first have represented only a small part of the total communicative behavior. Individuals of two early hordes would certainly still have had much in common in their speech, not only in the relatively large instinctive-intuitive part of the system, but also in the fact that most of the arbitrary associations must have been very natural out-growths, built upon the intuitive base in such a way that each could still sense the other's meaning. Furthermore, formal language must have deve-loped very slowly, and there was time for innovations to spread from one horde to the next. There would then be a graduated divergence in the dialec-tal pattern. With man still closely bound to habitats he could cover on foot and to natural conditions with which he could cope, there was not much possibility of complete and continuous long-term isolation of one human group from another. If such a situation ever came about and was main-tained sufficiently long for a totally different language tradition to develop, and if the language so derived should have continued down to our time, it should be possible to demonstrate this fact by means of linguistic comparison. Youngsters getting lost from their parents and starting up their own language would be another special mode of language creation, if it ever actually occurred.

Another important problem is that of chronology. We must ask when men had developed sufficiently as language users to be capable of having distinct languages. I already gave this question a provisional answer when I drew the analogy with tool using. The principle is that the first experimental steps are the hardest. There is no special reason, then, to suppose that there was any marked amount of language divergence until half a million or so years ago. Indirect evidence from archeology and physical anthropology supports this hypothesis. For example, there is not much evidence of strongly localized material cultures or religious practices so long ago. Also, the size of fossil brain cases only gradually exceeds what is found in some of the other anthropoids. With regard to the problem of the age of language differentiation, we have to seek any evidence that can be found in the comparison of known languages. This is the approach I shall use in the remainder of this book. The questions to be dealt with include the classification of the world's languages, the evidence for the common origin of the historical languages, the degrees of likeness or unlikeness among them, the date of original divergence suggested by the existing divergence, and other related problems.

A World Network of Languages

In preceding chapters we have come across evidence pointing toward an earlier uniformity of language with regard to phonology, grammatical structure, and vocabulary. We must now come to grips with the possible implications of our findings. If the pertinent clues are followed up, will it be demonstrated that all historical languages have come out of just one? Or will there be revealed a large number of parallel but separate developments of formal language out of the primordial instinctive-intuitive vocal communication? Or, finally, between these two extremes, will it turn out that some small number of common traditions lies back of the separate languages?

For the present, there is no final solution to this problem, but the second possibility, that of many different origins, seems to be definitely eliminated, while the case for a single beginning seems fairly strong.

The reader will recall from earlier chapters the processes of linguistic diversification that have been observed in the historic period. Knowledge of these processes makes it possible to sift clues and make correct inferences of common origin in cases of relatively recent diversification. When languages have developed out of a single earlier form in the last two or three thousand years, as in the case of the Slavic, Romance, and Germanic languages, we can always count on being able to recognize this fact on the basis of agreements, in form and meaning, of a sizable portion of the vocabulary, along with structural similarities. With greater time depth the matter is more difficult, and we are dependent either on favorable circumstances or on exhaustive and skillful use of data for certainty of common origin. If the languages involved have suffered few radical changes of a kind that might seriously blur the similarity of forms, successful comparison is easier, as it is if they have been conservative in retaining old vocabulary. It also helps if there are a large number of languages involved in the same group, since evidence that happens to have been lost in one language may be preserved in another. With a good combination of favorable circumstances and thorough study, it should be possible to demonstrate common origin as far back as six thousand years or more.

Another means of tracing common origin involves the proper utilization of patterns of divergence, including especially the interlocking arrangements found in language nets and chains. (See Chapter 1.) This intergrading effect, as we have seen before, is present almost everywhere in language. It can be especially helpful for reaching great time depths in every instance of a graduated sequence in which the first language or language group is too distantly related to some others to permit satisfactory direct comparison, but when there are intermediate languages that link or bridge the gap. For example, the comparison of Chukchian with Eskimo-Aleutian and of the latter with Wakashan is far more favorable than the direct comparison of Chukchian with Wakashan.

[*Possible cognates are taken from Swadesh (1960, pp. 143–44).*]

CHUKCHEE AND ESKIMO

Chukchee	Eskimo	Meaning
-t	-t	you
-uri	-ut	we
ringek-	tingmi-	fly
meki-	a-miglasuu-	many, much
nanqin	naaq	belly
ngegne	qaqqaq	hill
pi'a-	paniq-	dry
inging	qingaq	nose
rilit-	nala-	lying down
mi-kin-	kina	who
-riraqen	taki-	long
miqik'i-	miki-	small
gitka	itigak	foot
nute	nuna	earth
nikirit	unnuaq	night
mimil	imiq	water
ngeu-	agnaq	woman

ESKIMO AND KWAKIUTL (WAKASHAN)

Eskimo	Kwakiutl	Meaning
-nga	nu	I
-ngi-laq	k'is	no
miki-	'ma	small
suluk	ts'lts'lk	feather
kigut	kke	tooth
qunga-	q'uq'un'a	neck
kii	q'k	bite
nuia	'nw'i	cloud
kina	'n-kua	who
malguk	ma'ss	two
auk	'lku	blood
asshait	'ay'asu	hand
tinguk	t'iwana	liver
taku-	tuqu-	see
atiq	tliq-	name
ishi (from q'isi)	qyaqs	eye
tuni-	ts'o	give

Using this approach, one may make the easier comparisons first and then go on to the more divergent ones, or make all at the same time in such a way as to take advantage of the interlocking evidence.

With the combined help of all possible factors, it should be possible to double the time-depth penetration in even limited relational complexes. Someday, when enough research has been done, we should be able to understand this problem much better; but even now we can hope for some clarity with regard to the question of common origin. In effect, my efforts up to now strongly suggest that all or most of the languages of the world have had a common origin and that they are related in a continuous network that stretches from Africa through Eurasia to Oceania and the Americas. In order to obtain the grouping of languages in the world network, lexicostatistic divergence measures were taken. Groupings and subgroupings were made by using arbitrarily selected break points of forty and fifty *divergence centuries*. Languages were included in the same stock, or *division*, if they were found to be related to at least one other included language at not more than forty divergence centuries; in the same way, the *phylum* or *major net* consists of languages related to at least one other included language at not more than fifty divergence centuries. Insofar as measures were obtained, the links between one major net and the next proved to be of not more than seventy divergence centuries. The evidence is not yet complete at all points, however. In some instances the lexicostatistic counts had to be made with insufficient data, and in others no measure has as yet been reported. Our picture, then, is admittedly tentative.

The tentative world linguistic net is shown in Figure 7.1. It consists of eleven component nets: *Macro-Khoisan*, *Macro-Saharan*, and *Fula-Bantuan* in

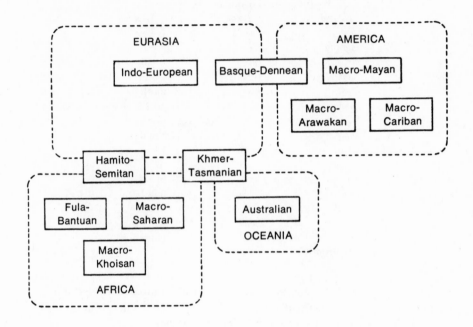

Figure 7.1. **The World Linguistic Net**

Africa; *Hamito-Semitan* in Africa and extending into Asia Minor; *Indo-European* in Eurasia; *Basque-Dennean* in Eurasia, extending into America and Oceania; *Khmer-Tasmanian*, extending from Asia southward to Tasmania; *Australian* in Australia; and *Macro-Mayan*, *Macro-Arawakan*, and *Macro-Cariban* in America. There are several isolated languages or families that do not fit into the large nets, or at least have not yet been fitted into them. They include several in America, such as Beothuk, Nambicuara, Tinugua, and Omurano. There are also some language isolates in the ancient world, particularly Sumerian.

[*At this juncture Swadesh intended to discuss each large grouping or phylum in detail, covering the following topics:*
1. *The member languages and divisions and their geographic distribution.*
2. *The types of grammatical categories and processes, including dialectal differences within the phylum.*
3. *Possible points of contact with other phyla.*]

Tracing the Flow

As I remarked earlier, linguistic differentiation tends to occur and language varieties to develop in every situation of reduced contact among the various parts of a language community. If all or part of the population moves, differences will appear more rapidly or more slowly in proportion to the degree of isolation or contact that results. Intercourse with outside groups can influence the details of development, depending upon both its nature and its duration.

Wherever languages have similarities in phonetics, vocabulary, or grammatical structure, it is possible that they have had a common history— either that they were dialects of a single language or that the people who spoke them were neighbors for a substantial period of time. To read the evidence correctly, we must recognize that other things than intimate or recently shared history may also produce similar end products; they may be due to general similarity of basic underlying conditions. The fact that two compared groups are both human, with similar physiology, instincts, and needs, may be sufficient to direct them toward solutions that are partly alike. This means that in each specific case it is necessary to examine the facts surrounding each similarity to determine to what extent it gives evidence of common history. It seems worthwhile to take up a few specific examples, in order to illustrate the type of reasoning that one might use.

Voiced stops are found in various languages of the world, but their relation to the corresponding voiceless stops is not always the same. In Zapotec of Mexico, the voiced stop changes to voiceless if it is doubled, as happens in the formation of the causative. This is one bit of evidence showing that at an older stage of the language the contrast was not voiceless versus voiced, but strong or double versus weak or simple. This is confirmed if one compares Zapotec with more distantly related groups. A similar explanation for the series of voiced stops or of voiceless fricatives is possible for other linguistic groupings, among them Eskimo-Aleutian and some Uralic languages. We do not yet know all the places in which the voiced-stop series has such an origin, but presumably we can find out by means of patient and intelligent research. On the other hand, there are languages and language groups in which voiced stops can be shown to be due to very different causes. Thus the voiced stops of Indo-European turn out to be of two old classes, simple voiced and voiced aspirate. The comparison of Indo-European and certain Amerindian groups leads one to the conclusion that the simple voiced stops of Indo-European are equivalent to the glottalized set in languages like Wakashan, Mayan, and Quechuan, with regard to ancient symbolism. The overall comparison of the languages of the world suggests that doubling of consonants is an old and widespread process, as are the contrastive types that gave rise to the simple and glottalized or unvoiced and voiceless stops. This means that the mere presence of a voiceless-stop series is of little significance in language comparison if we know nothing of the background of its development. Any evidence of old doubling, even though the details may have changed, counts as evidence of old common history. For this reason, doubling, or strengthening, in Fula, Semitic, Uralic, Gilyak, Eskimo, and Zapotec may well be evidence of an ancient relationship.

For an example from another area of language, let us consider the traces of shape and gender classification in various parts of the world. Instances of such classification are found in areas so far apart that it is impossible to consider them as due to any recent common history. Can this trait be a matter of instinct or fundamental human drives? Perhaps so, since all beings who respond in associative fashion to their environment engage in some kind of classification of the things about them. Following this bent, man must have developed classifications based on shape and other qualities quite early. As language got further and further away from the instinctive, the classification could take on different forms of expression, and we must try to group the facts within sets of languages in order to see how they connect and what they reveal about past history. The study of this phenomenon is not yet sufficiently advanced to give final answers, but we can attempt some guesses and try to make them as realistic as possible.

The geographic spread of form, shape, and size classification is broader than that of sexlike gender. It also occurs in more varied forms, such as numeral classifiers, noun classes, and verbal application. This all suggests great time depth, since diversification and geographic spread increase with time. Sexlike gender may well have been a later development out of the earlier system and therefore did not spread quite so far. And yet it did go fairly far, and can be thought of as following close behind the first distinction. The absence of classes is found in part in languages at the ends of the earth, and in part in great areas of each of the continents in languages whose earlier stages are known to have had or which can be suspected of having had some type of classification. There is reason to believe that the classifying mode is a formalization, by the use of affixes and particles, of old inner inflections that were expressed earlier by means of vowel and consonant alternation.

Consideration of the above examples should show that an explanation of the distribution of a linguistic trait is a complicated matter. The only way we can achieve solid results in the long run is to examine all factors together carefully, interpreting them in the light of degrees of linguistic relationship, patiently discovered. Interlocking patterns of agreement are useful insofar as they can be revealed, and the use of statistical measures of degrees of relationship is helpful. In this way I have arrived at the mesh or net grouping of languages shown in Figure 7.1. When we compare this classification and subclassification of the world's languages with their distribution on a map, we can begin to infer the movement and expansion of various peoples. The hints we can get from the study of linguistic relationships need to be considered together with all other available evidence, geographical, geological, biological, archeological, historical, and legendary.

Slower and Faster Expansion

In various parts of the world, one finds remarkably wide extensions of certain linguistic families, in sharp contrast with others that occupy modest or very reduced territories. There are striking cases of the rapid expansion of single languages in recent centuries: Latin in a large portion of Europe; Arabic over a considerable part of northern Africa; Russian across thousands of miles of Siberia; Spanish and Portuguese in the Western Hemisphere; and English in Australia, South Africa, India, and America. In each case there were circumstances that led to territorial growth. The languages that subsequently reached out far beyond their old boundaries were spoken by prosperous communities. Their populations increased, their commerce was active, and their armed forces fought in distant lands and brought back captives to expand the home population. The new lands were penetrated in a series of waves, usually at first commercial, then military, political, and religious, not necessarily in a precise order but in a way that led to eventual domination. The spread of the language into new territory resulted not only from the vitality of the expanding language community; it varied also according to the characteristics of the linguistic community it penetrated. In particular, if the invaded population was relatively small and divided among a number of local languages, the new language was likely to win out.

Although it is normal for a language to have local variations in its original home, there is a marked tendency toward uniformity as the language moves out of its old limits, as we have seen. That is, among the individuals organized into commercial missions, armies, religious orders, and so on, it is usual that one or a few of the linguistic variants become predominant. Under these circumstances, individuals tend to drop the ways of speaking peculiar to their home areas and begin to use, to a large extent, the dominant forms. In consequence, the new territory is likely to be more uniform in speech than the old one was. Once the initial period of growth is past, however, local differentiation may set in once again.

Detailed knowledge of historic cases of language expansion helps us to understand the traces of more or less similar events in the past. Let us consider, for example, the Bantu languages of central, southern, and eastern Africa. There are at least four hundred of them, some with very large and some with very small territories, but all clearly similar in a degree that indicates about three thousand years of divergence. The evidence would suggest that there were several periods of expansion involved in the history of the Bantu, but that some important part of it was surely under way before the time of Christ. Indirectly, the expansion may have been the outcome of the cultural developments in the classical world. That history has not preserved the record of the expansion of Bantu can be due only to the distance that separated the region in which it was spoken from the regions in which writing had come to be used. The early expansion of Bantu could not have been exactly like that of Latin, even though its territorial effect was even more drastic. The Bantu-speaking peoples did not move with steel-armored legions against tribes just beginning to use iron, but with simply organized tribes against primitive hordes. The nature of the outcome was due to the relative superiority of the new over the old.

Something similar took place in Oceania, possibly at about the same period as the Bantu explosion. This was the spread of the Austronesian languages. The number of languages in this group is even greater than the Bantu—over seven hundred. The land territory is great, and it is even more impressive because it is scattered among islands separated by vast expanses of ocean.

One of the great American expansions is that of the Athapaskans in northern and western North America. About thirty languages can be distinguished, and their time depth is about sixteen to eighteen centuries. Another group is Algonkian in central and eastern North America, including about a dozen languages with divergences in the neighborhood of two thousand years. The Siouan group includes some two dozen languages, and the divergence for the greater part of this group is about three thousand years. Uto-Aztecan involves a similar number of languages, with a time depth of over four thousand years.

In Central and South America the geographically great groups are Chibchan, Arawakan, Tupian, and Carib. The numbers of languages are about thirty, sixty, forty, and thirty respectively. The depths of divergence run from three thousand to five thousand years.

We thus see that the territorial expansion of language communities is uneven; it sometimes progresses rapidly and sometimes slowly, depending to a large degree upon social, cultural, and political factors. Breaks in the continuity of language interrelationships are often created by the expansion of one group in a way that displaces and eliminates intermediate languages.

The Bulging Hub Principle

When the world's languages are compared and the degrees of interrelationship are used for setting up a meshed intergrading classification such as that suggested here, an interesting pattern of distribution is revealed. From a vaguely marked central area in the region where Eurasia meets Africa, four large phyla extend outward in three directions: far south into Africa, west across Europe, and northeast and southeast across Asia and Oceania. From what we know of linguistic distributions in earlier historic times, the pattern was once simpler and less intercrossed. At that time Babylonia was the approximate juncture of Fula-Bantuan, Hamito-Semitan, Indo-European, and Basque-Dennean. Indo-European and Basque-Dennean had not yet intercrossed each other's territory to the extent that they do in historic times. The pattern formed by the four phyla is approximately that of four broad spokes projecting from the hub of a wheel. As one moves outward to the rim of the wheel, the continuity of language interrelationships is more scattered, and it is there on the rim that the greatest number of isolated languages and smaller groups are located. I think it may be possible to trace the causes of this pattern.

It is evident that the center of the wheel coincides with that general area of the world in which agriculture first developed and in which subsequently the first urban centers arose. It is also apparent that the farther one gets from the main centers of cultural development, the slower was the technical development of the early populations. The reason for this is easy enough to see. Man's technical progress has always been related to communication, because it depended on the accumulation of ideas. In this process the central areas had the advantage over the outlying ones, and it was there that skills and economic capacity mushroomed. This in turn made for more abundant means of livelihood, denser populations, and the outward push of people and ideas. These developments were not even and constant, but the general trend over a long period of time was sufficiently marked to give the effect I have described.

We have to suppose that up to some period, the four spokes of the wheel were outward extensions of the common hub, and that the language groupings showed intergrading relationships. The fact that Semitic, Indo-European, and Ural-Altaic have clear points of similarity is the last reflection of this earlier state of affairs. However, new circumstances apparently changed the situation in a way that modified the graduated nature of the relationships. What caused this must have been the establishment of new centers of culture growth in scattered places around the old center. Asia Minor, Babylonia, Persia, India, and even Egypt and Greece may be thought of as examples of such new focal points. At any rate, each such locale represented a nucleus from which population and cultural advances moved outward. Intermediate language types would tend to be eliminated, so that the frontiers of newly formed languages showed sharper contrasts than those of their predecessors. Thus abutting separate spokes took form in place of an old continuity of hub and spokes.

Farther out on each of the spokes, areas of relative discontinuity developed because of the more active push of populations in some places than in others. Far out on the periphery, the trend must have been for the relatively isolated extreme linguistic types to disappear. This does not mean that all peripheral speech forms withered away at an even rate, but rather that they were only more exposed to the risk of being lost as new populations spread from the center. The peripheral populations would become mixed with the new-comers, and there would be a strong tendency for the older populations to adopt the new languages.

The operation of such trends can still be seen in historical situations. Thus the earliest history of England tells of the Picts being replaced by the Celts, and eventually Pictish ceased to be spoken. The Celts, who began to move from the continent to the British Isles a few centuries before Christ, once occupied all of that area, but they later had to share their territory with Germanic settlers, and eventually to cede the dominant role to them. The spread of Asians through Oceania and of Europeans into America also illustrates the trend of populations from the center outward. Although the forms of movement were necessarily different in earlier times, the general direction from the center outward must have been similar. Only in the most recent centuries have there been real departures from this pattern.

Divergence Cast Off

There are languages in the world today that differ enormously from each other, so much so that speakers of two languages, except to the extent that they rely on intuitive forms of communication, cannot understand one another. And yet, as we have seen, there may still be noteworthy similarities between the languages that reflect their ancient common history. If we try to gauge the differences not in relation to understanding or lack of under-standing, but rather in relation to the degree to which the old sameness is still reflected, what kinds of conclusions can we draw?

At the dawn of language, when the devices of human communication were close to the instinctive, communicative forms must have moved apart only very slowly. Differences must have existed, for that is a law of life, but individuals of our species could understand each other to a great extent in instinctive and intuitive fashion. When language began to develop new means of expression and prehumans began to use it with growing cleverness, local traditions began to manifest themselves. Diversification must have occurred slowly at first, however, and may even have continued for hun-dreds of thousands of years. Eventually language reached a stage of develop-ment in which local forms could become differentiated at a certain rate limited only by the needs of maintaining communication from generation to generation. We have seen, however, that the extreme divergences on the farthest borders of the inhabited world tended to be lost. We can then ask: How much of the diversification produced in the history of language has been maintained to our time?

Lexicostatistic time estimates are roughly satisfactory for periods up to about five thousand years. Readings of between five thousand and ten thousand years are more uncertain. For example, in a set of languages in

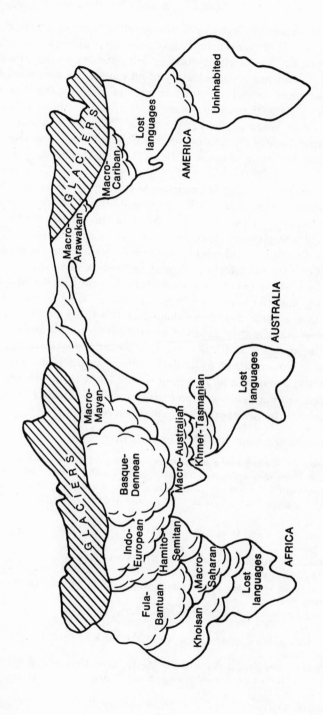

Figure 7.2. **The Theory of Linguistic Waves** (Hypothetical Scheme About 25,000 B.C.)

which one might expect divergences in the neighborhood of about eight thousand years, some language pairs may give readings of about six thousand and some of about ten thousand. Possibly, by using the knowledge of intermediate languages and much careful study of all details, we may someday be able to make more reliable readings in greater time depths. For the present, we can only say that we get readings of up to ten thousand or so years for the extreme languages within the major phyla in the world. One might suppose that some of the positive scoring may be forced, and that the true readings may be better assumed to be in the neighborhood of twenty thousand years.

Applying lexicostatistic dating to languages from far portions of the world network, we sometimes get readings in the neighborhood of ten thousand years, and sometimes far more than that. Most of this variation must be due to the difficulty in recognizing cognates under the circumstances. Here also we can hope that future studies will permit better counts. For the present, we can only say that the time depth indicated for the languages of the world may be somewhere above twenty thousand years. We can suspect that this time is too short, and the better readings may come closer to twice that much and perhaps a great deal more than that. There seems to be little reason to suppose that the time depth of diversification for all known languages should be as much as 100,000 years, however. Even if we bear in mind the probable slower rate of vocabulary change in earlier time periods, 100,000 years is still a generous figure. And we are left with the notion that most of the diversification that could have developed in language must have been cast off around the periphery of the inhabited world.

References and Suggestions for Further Reading

[*For other publications by Swadesh dealing with language classification at great time depth and with the mesh, net, or intergrading approach to this problem, see Swadesh (1960, 1962, 1964). For other, more traditional or conservative classifications of the languages of the world, see Bloomfield (1933), Gleason (1961), Lehmann (1962), and Muller (1964).*]

Bloomfield, Leonard
    1933.   *Language.* New York: Holt.
Gleason, H. A., Jr.
    1961.   *An Introduction to Descriptive Linguistics.* New York: Holt.
Jennings, Jesse D., and Norbeck, Edward, eds.
    1964.   *Prehistoric Man in the New World.* Chicago: University of Chicago Press.
Lehmann, Winfred P.
    1962.   *Historical Linguistics: An Introduction.* New York: Holt.
Muller, Siegfried H.
    1964.   *The World's Living Languages.* New York: Frederick Ungar.
Swadesh, Morris
    1960.   *Tras la huella lingüística de la prehistoria.* Mexico City: Universidad Nacional.
    1962.   "Linguistic Relations Across Bering Strait." *American Anthropologist* 64: 1262–91.
    1964.   "Linguistic Overview." *Prehistoric Man in the New World*, ed. Jennings and Norbeck.

Appendixes

Morris Swadesh: From the First Yale School to World Prehistory

Morris Swadesh was born January 22, 1909, in Holyoke, Massachusetts. Like many great linguists, he was a "linguist" in the popular sense as well. His parents had come from the south of Russia, and from them he learned Yiddish and a little Russian. As an undergraduate at the University of Chicago, he concentrated on languages (German, French and some Russian). Later he was to work in Spanish and Tarascan, and to write guides to the learning of Russian, Chinese and Burmese.

Swadesh's progress through degrees was rapid. He received the Bachelor of Arts, and election to Phi Beta Kappa, at twenty-one (1930). Continuing, at Chicago, he took the Master of Arts in a year (1931) working with Sapir on a project of comparative semantic analysis for the International Auxiliary Language Association and using Sapir's materials for his thesis on aspect in Nootka. When Sapir then went to Yale, Swadesh went with him. (Provision for Swadesh and Stanley Newman, also then at Chicago, is said to have been one of Sapir's conditions for accepting the call as Sterling Professor). As research assistant at Yale for the next two years Swadesh devoted himself to "a searching study of Nootka structure" (Sapir, in Sapir and Swadesh 1939:10), completing his doctorate at twenty-four (1933). He had already been published as junior author of a pioneer semantic monograph (Sapir and Swadesh 1932). A year after receiving his degree he had achieved intensive field experience with four languages in five successive summers; had joined in the orthographic changes (1934c) that were to symbolize the generation of Americanists emerging around Sapir and Bloomfield[1]; had published the first systematic description of an American Indian language based on phonemic principles (1934b), and the first

1. Boas found the changes "quite unnecessary" (1947: 208, n. 5).

systematic American statement of phonemic method (1934a; cf. Joos 1957:37), the principle that was to be central to the development of linguistics as an autonomous discipline in the United States in the next decade. And he had presented a paper to the annual meeting of the Linguistic Society of America (December, 1934) concerning his work on Sapir's project in English grammar. This energy, enthusiasm for languages and the capacity for hard and detailed work on them, and the sense of pioneering in a cooperative enterprise, were to be characteristic throughout his life.

The First "Yale School"

Swadesh's career must be seen against the background of these years as student of and collaborator with Sapir. One hears of the "Yale School" of linguistics in reference to Leonard Bloomfield, who went to Yale as Sterling Professor in 1940, and more particularly in reference to the "neo-Bloom-fieldian" scholars who dominated American linguistic discussion in the nineteen-forties and early nineteen-fifties. They published through *Language*, edited at Yale, and regarded Bloomfield as the founder of a scientific approach to language. From 1931 until his death in 1939, there existed an earlier "Yale School" centered around Sapir.

The two "Yale Schools" of linguistics differed in several respects. The concerns of Sapir's circle were more similar to those of linguists today than those of the intervening neo-Bloomfield era. Some possible misapprehensions must be forestalled, however. The two "schools" were not sharply opposed. In neither case was there homogeneity of view, but rather a great deal of close collaboration and discussion among persons diverse in background, outlook, and subsequent career. In neither case were all adherents present together at Yale. Elective affinity could be involved, in Bloomfield's case especially—his influence was far more through his book *Language* (1933) than through his teaching. Both Sapir and Bloomfield taught at the Linguistic Institute (in the summer of 1937 for Sapir, the summers of 1938–1940 for Bloomfield).[2] Certainly Sapir and Bloomfield held each other in high respect (cf. Sapir's choice of title for his paper, "The concept of phonetic law as tested in primitive languages by Leonard Bloomfield," and Bloomfield's remarks about Sapir in the dedication in Hoijer et al. 1946).[3] A number of linguists studied with or were influenced by both men, and some admirers of Sapir shared in the outlook and concerns that dominated

2. For some indication of the impact of Sapir at the 1937 Institute, see Joos 1967: 9 (regarding effect on Bloch) and the dedication (p. 3) and pp. 53–54 in Pike 1967; for the 1937 and 1938 Institutes, Sturtevant 1940: 304.

3. I am indebted to R. A. Hall, Jr. and C. F. Hockett for comments on this point.

the "neo-Bloomfieldian" era. In particular, it would be anachronistic to read into the period before the Second World War the atmosphere that prevailed for a time after it, when the elevation of Bloomfield into a scientific savior was accompanied by a down-grading of Sapir as "intuitive" and "mentalistic" (derogatory terms then)—a genius, to be sure, but only that (cf. Joos, 1957:25, 31, 115; also 96, and 80b at end).

It remains to identify the group particularly associated with Sapir. The contributors to the volume in his memory (Spier, Newman, Hallowell 1942)—Hoijer, Voegelin, Haas, Swadesh, Whorf, Trager, Newman, Herzog, Emeneau—and the contributors to Hoijer et al. 1946—Hoijer, Swadesh, Voegelin, Haas, Li, Newman, Trager, Whorf, and Halpern, a student of Hoijer—serve as indication, as does the multiple authorship of "Some Orthographic Recommendations . . . " (Herzog, Newman, Sapir, Haas, Swadesh, Voegelin). Five had followed Sapir from Chicago to Yale (Walter Dyk, Mary Haas, Stanley Newman, Morris Swadesh in 1931, and George Herzog in 1932). Two had already obtained degrees at Chicago (Hoijer, Li). Li was later to visit Yale as Visiting Professor of Chinese Linguistics in 1937–39. Others were post-doctoral students at Yale (Emeneau, a Sterling Fellow in 1931–32 after his doctorate there in 1931; Voegelin in about 1933–35; Trager in 1936–38); one was non-doctoral (Whorf). Two men, Zellig Harris and Kenneth Pike, were never at Yale, but knew Sapir from professional meetings, the 1937 Linguistic Institute, and through association with others of the group.

The founding of the Linguistic Society of America (1924) and the launching of its journal *Language* (1925), Sapir's "Sound Patterns in Language", and Bloomfield's "A Set of Postulates for the Science of Language" (*Lg.* 1:37–51 [1925] and *Lg.* 2:153–164 [1926]—both in Joos 1957:19–25, 26–31) can be taken as starting points for the development of structural linguistics and its successors (or transformations) in the United States. In the second quarter of the century, then, the prospect for young linguists, especially those inspired by Sapir, included these tasks:

(1) to develop the methods of the nascent structural linguistics and to test their application in the analysis of both exotic and well known languages;

(2) to sustain the profession of linguistics, where almost no recognition existed so far as departments, chairs, specific courses, and autonomy of the discipline were concerned;[4]

(3) to·continue to rescue disappearing languages;[5]

---

4. Bloomfield "always, on principle, advised inquiring students to specialize in other subjects than linguistics, on the ground that paying positions in the latter field were very few" (Sturtevant 1940: 304).

5. The mission was unequivocally supported by Bloomfield. In a statement for the conference and bulletin discussed below under (3), Bloomfield spoke of "future work: a national duty. If we fail, we shall be shamed before the judgement of posterity: we may be certain that it is by this kind of thing that future generations will judge us" (Letter in Freeman 1977; quoted in Voegelin 1949: 138).

(4) to pursue proof and establishment of genetic relationships among languages;

(5) to relate the results and methods of linguistic inquiry to other things— to other disciplines in the humanities and social sciences (Sapir once remarked that "Linguistics is the 'chemistry' of the humanities and the social sciences" [see p. 27–28 below; cf. Sapir 1929a]); to particular problems within these disciplines—such as cultural symbolism and patterning or personality and verbal art; and to practical affairs, such as education.

Other possibilities existed, especially the application of dialect geography to American English and the relating of the new discipline to the traditional philologies of both language and literature. The five possibilities sketched above pretty much define the framework within which those who looked to Sapir were to work. The focus of each might differ and change over time, but each was likely to see his or her own path as carrying out the heritage of Sapir. Certainly it was so with Swadesh. While he is best known now for his work on the relationships among languages, he contributed to all the other tasks sketched above, sometimes centrally.

STRUCTURAL METHOD

Swadesh was a leader in the first generation to develop modern linguistic analysis in the United States—the generation that came to the analysis of linguistic structure as something with a distinct methodology to be developed and learned. Boas' general methodological stance and his interest in grammatical categories as mental phenomena had led him to clear away a priori approaches in favor of inductive analysis. Most immediately in the United States, as one scholar has put it, there was a man and a disembodied book, Sapir and Bloomfield's *Language* (1933), twin foci for a sense that something new was happening.[6] And there was the small number of young scholars who chose linguistics, rather than languages, literatures, philology or some other aspect of anthropology, as their uncertain career.

Phonology. It is said that young linguists today read nothing from the years before 1957 (the date of Chomsky's *Syntactic Structures*). Certainly the rejection by many of an autonomous sphere of phonology, and even of a distinct phonemic zone for the representation of utterances, may make it difficult to grasp the idea of phonemic pattern as a "breakthrough" and to appreciate a major contribution to institutionalization of the idea as significant. Yet in the earlier period (as in part later), theoretical controversy,

6. There was also knowledge of Trubetzkoy and Jakobson, already at work in Prague to develop the new approach systematically. Young Americans perhaps did not then read de Saussure, whose posthumous book had set the goal of synchronic analysis of structural relations, but Sapir and Bloomfield had read him, and Trubetzkoy and Jakobson were obviously a development from such a base.

alternative conceptions of science and the goals of linguistics, and the future of linguistics itself centered on the concept of the phoneme. These existed in Europe an international group to promote the phonological description of languages (with Roman Jakobson as secretary), and to promote the same goal and cooperate with the international group, there was formed a Group for Phonemics within the Linguistic Society of America (headed by Sapir as Chairman, with Kurath, Twaddell, and Kent). As late as the 1940's the notion of phonemic (phonological) analysis was controversial. It is not that its opponents had in mind a superior conception of phonology. The point is rather that phonological analysis constituted a revolution against a study of language without it. In important part it was, as Sapir's "Sound patterns in language" makes clear, a revolt against dichotomization of the synchronic study of language into two disjunct realms, one a natural science *(Naturwissenschaft)* of phonetics, the other a social or human science *(Geisteswissenschaft)* of grammar. Phonology was the sphere in which structural analysis achieved its first recognized success, a success the consequences of which are still spreading (cf. Lévi-Strauss 1945).

Swadesh's central role may be indicated by a few citations:

"I am indebted to Edward Sapir and Morris Swadesh for instruction in phonemic theory and its application to the Shawnee language" (Voegelin 1937:23, n.1).

"The early work of Sapir, showing how two different systems could be created from a single set of phonetic elements . . . , the careful discussions of Bloomfield . . . , and the methodological work of Swadesh showing how phonemic principles were to be applied and how interpretation of long long consonants grew out of such principles . . . largely comprise the basis upon which my own understanding of phonemics grew." (Pike 1967: 345–6; cf. 54.)

In the study that was to be the starting point of epistemological debate, Twaddell, (1935) despite their methodological differences, conceded that Swadesh's (1934a) was: "the most comprehensive and methodologically lucid treatment of the phoneme with which I am acquainted. Swadesh has recognized and avoided many of the palpable weaknesses of earlier writings on the subject" (in Joos 1957:66). Other papers that were to be seen as fundamental to the later development of the "neo-Bloomfieldian" position acknowledge his influence. In "Phonemic Overlapping" (1941), Bloch cited Bloomfield, Swadesh, Twaddell and Trubetzkoy for general principles, and Swadesh (1934a, 1937b) on pattern congruity (n. 1, n. 7). In "A System of Descriptive Phonology" (1942), Hockett cites Trager and Bloch for chief stimulus, Mary Haas for specific criticism, and also "Morris Swadesh for many suggestions in the past" (n. 1). A paper to which Swadesh contributed the methodological insight (1939c: 2) has been cited as one of "the two germinal papers in American morphophonemic theory" (the other being Bloomfield's "Menominee Morphophonemics" of the same year in Hockett 1967: 208, n. 2).[7]

In these years the phonemic interpretation of the syllabic nuclei of English was a particular focus of discussion, and to a great extent a symbol of the new linguistics. In a constructive critique of Bloomfield's treatment, Swadesh (1935a) analyzed the syllabics as all unit phonemes, as Trubetzkoy was to do shortly afterward. This short paper, arising out of work on Sapir's English grammar project, for some years defined one position (cf. Pike 1947a). Swadesh continued to be concerned with this question, and an incident reported from the 1941 meeting of the LSA in Indianapolis reveals something of the man and of his part in the climate of the time.

"While the room was being prepared for lantern-slide projection, it was agreed at the suggestion of Mr. Swadesh to devote half an hour to a special discussion of the syllabic phonemes of English. Mr. Bloch was requested to lead the discussion and to present in condensed form the interpretation set forth by Mr. Trager and himself in a recent article in Language 17: 227–46. Mr. Ward . . . [Sturtevant, Allen, Jr., Swadesh, Bloch, Hockett, Trager, Harris] and Mr. Kent participated in a lively discussion, which it was necessary to interrupt in order to continue the meeting, but which it was agreed should be continued at the close of the session if time permitted" (*LSA Bulletin* 15: 24(1942)).

Swadesh was persuaded by some of the evidence put forward by Bloch and Trager to accept analysis of the syllabics, but not to analyze the non-short vowels into vowel plus consonant, nor to assume a vowel variant of h in syllable final. In the course of this argument, Swadesh presented the first published version of what was to become famous as the "overall pattern" of nine elementary vowels for English:

7. Hockett's note begins: "Although not published until 1944, Newman's description of Yokuts was essentially completed by 1936. This antedates the two germinal papers." This generous tribute to Newman for priority of merit, if not of influence, misses the fact that the Swadesh and Voegelin paper was itself "written some years earlier" (Harris 1951: 293, n. 10) and was presented at the Philadelphia meeting of the LSA in December, 1937. Swadesh and Voegelin themselves remark (1930: 2–3) that "Swadesh, having learned the use of formulae in synchronic phonology from Sapir in his work on Nootka." [Swadesh (1934a: 129) had already used the notion and term "morphophoneme]." Newman (1944: 6) notes that his first published account, written shortly after the field trip of 1930, is brief and schematic (IJAL 7: 75–89 (1932)) —it indicates vowel formulae for stem forms (88), but is paradigmatic in format like Hockett's 1967 restatement, not abstractly morphophonemic; that in 1932 a short grammar was submitted as a dissertation at Yale; and that the Yokuts grammar in its present form was largely completed by 1936, as a revised and expanded version of the doctoral dissertation. In short, his abstract morphophonemic treatment was arrived at while working at Yale with Sapir, where he was a Research Fellow of the Institute of Human Relations 1932–37, in the same period that the formulaic morphophonemic treatment of Nootka was arrived at by Swadesh also working at Yale with Sapir. Indeed, in 1934–36 Newman and Swadesh were working together with Sapir on the English language project, and in a wellknown review article of Newman's Yokuts, Harris (1944: 196) described the grammar as an example of Sapir's mature methods. In sum, American abstract morphophonemics would seem to have its origin in the "First Yale School" in the post-doctoral collaboration about 1933–36 of Newman and Swadesh with Sapir. Newman deserves the credit that Hockett gives him, but as part of a larger scene.

"The number and nature of the short₊bound [bound, as occurring always before another phoneme] syllabics vary from dialect to dialect, but it is nevertheless possible to give a composite maximum pattern that covers all the types ordinarily found in English. This is a nine-vowel scheme of three levels (high, mid, low) and three front-to-back series (front unrounded, central, or back unrounded, back rounded):

i	ə	u
e	ʌ	o
ɛ	a	ɔ

"In our general survey of English syllabics, we found . . . an overall maximum system of nine short-bound elements. However, it is unlikely that any one dialect will be found to illustrate the full range of types" (1947c: 142, 143).

The origin of the nine-vowel maximum pattern may have been with Trager, since Swadesh, surveying patterns of Scottish, Greenville, S. Carolina, Chicago, New Jersey, and Southern British, makes use of information from Trager for the New Jersey variety (and from Raven McDavid for Greenville). Indeed, the first published mention of Trager's changed view appears in a footnote by Swadesh.[8] Referring to Trager and Bloch (1941), Swadesh writes: "The description published there has been supplemented by additional information received in correspondence and discussion with Trager. (Note that although Trager and Bloch originally posited only six vowel phonemes, they now recognize a maximum of nine." (1947c: 141, n. 6.)

Swadesh himself proposed an analysis of complex English syllabics as consisting not of vowel plus semi-vowel (w y h) but of vowel plus vowel.

Grammatical semantics. To focus on phonology, however, is too much the sort of history victors write, and only part of the story. Influence on what was seen as important after the war, continuity and cumulation, are important; but there was discontinuity as well. During and after the war the dominant spirit of American linguistic analysis was to reject formulations of linguistic relations in terms of process, and to reject "mentalism" and "intuition" in one's work. Process formulations were a spirit driven out by Sapir's disciple Harris, as Joos (1957: 115) would have it, only to return with a vengeance with Harris' disciple, Chomsky, along with trust in the

---

8. Swadesh's paper is cited anonymously in the 1950 presidential address of the Linguistic Society (Haugen 1951, n. 21). The Trager and Swadesh analyses of English are given as prime examples of the complaint that "the difficulty of nailing a purely distributional analysis down to anything concrete has been evidenced in the constant change of conclusions concerning given language systems by practicing analysts". The complaint ignores the fact that Trager and Swadesh had encountered new facts, that Swadesh explicity states the facts and considerations that convinced him he had been wrong, and that a criterion of phonological identity (Haugen's main concern) as well as distribution was in fact used by Trager and Bloch and was a basis for Swadesh's alternative.

judgments of native speakers and in intuition. This turn of the wheel, associated with phonology and Sapir, is well known. Process formulations, intuition, and trust in native speaker judgments were the controversial hall marks of Sapir's work. It is little known that Sapir's mentalism in phonology was matched by a serious "mentalistic" attempt to deal with *semantic* description, in terms both of categories specific to languages and of features and logical relationships that are universal. Both concerns, the specific and the universal, were part of the Boasian approach. Boas developed the first in his own work; Sapir and members of the "First Yale School" developed the second.

An inspection of grammatical sketches by Newman, Swadesh, Haas, and Whorf in a volume planned by Sapir (Hoijer et al. 1946), as well as of their separate treatments of Yokuts, Nootka, Tunica, and Hopi, will show attention to semantic definition of formal categories, such as the semantic features inherent in the unmarked verbal stem, and particular attention to aspect. (Cf. Swadesh 1931, Whorf 1936b, 1938, and the flurry of discussion of a 1935 LSA paper on verbal aspect joined in by Haas, Newman, Swadesh, and Whorf [*LSA Bulletin* 9: 4(1936)].) Whorf's famed treatment of Hopi arose not only out of his experience as an insurance inspector and his analysis of Hopi, but also out of a collaborative ambience at Yale. Swadesh's prior work on aspect, and a general interest in the category of aspect on the part of Sapir, may have influenced Whorf, who made much of the prevalence of aspect and absence of tense in Hopi. In his revised Nootka study Swadesh states: "The semantic interrelation of the Nootka aspects may be summarized in terms of the three processes, namely, linearization, punctualization, pluralization." (1931–32.) All three were to be important dimensions for Whorf in his study of Hopi. Whorf's "A Linguistic Consideration of Thinking in Primitive Communities," written in late 1936 (Carroll 1956, Hymes 1964), acknowledges the tradition of Boas and Sapir, and in its notes cites Haas, Newman, Swadesh and Trager. His "Grammatical Categories," written at Boas' request late in 1937 and published posthumously in 1945, states (n. 1): "The author wishes to acknowledge his indebtedness to his colleagures, Dr. George L. Trager and Dr. Morris Swadesh, with whom some of these questions of category have been discussed" (Carroll 1956: 87). Besides well known languages (Sanskrit, English, Latin, French), the paper cites the American Indian languages analyzed by Sapir and his students: Algonquian (Voegelin), Southern Paiute (Sapir), Tubatulabal (Voegelin), Taos (Trager), Navaho (Sapir, Hoijer), Nitinat (Haas and Swadesh), Yana (Sapir), Aztec (Whorf) and of course Hopi (Whorf). A collective body of knowledge seems to have been drawn upon.

The impression has sometimes been given that Whorf was an extreme relativist, or at least interested only in the distinctive differences of languages. A reading of his work (Carroll 1956) shows that impression to be false. Whorf, like Sapir and Boas, was concerned to do justice both to what was distinctive and to what was universal in a language. With Boas, Sapir, and Swadesh, he was concerned to develop more systematic and precise ways of describing the semantic structure of particular languages, and to do so in ways that would make comparison and universal statement possible as well.[9]

Swadesh's principal personal contribution to this work, *The Nootka Aspect System* (1931), was never published. This study, the comparative part of his paper on Chitimacha derogatory verbs (1933b), and his work in 1930–31 on the ending point relation in English, French and German, are part of a major impulse given by Sapir to "detailed study of the variety of ways of expressing logical relations in language" (Sapir and Swadesh 1932 p. 3), with an understanding of universal characteristics as the practical and scientific goal. But the rise of a self-conscious, autonomous, linguistic science around phology, morphology, and syntax was to make semantics for a generation appear part of some other science, or at best, part of an interstitial field such as "ethnolinguistics". Anti-mentalism and divorce from meaning may have been popular in part as convenient ideology to shelter the working out of the formal descriptive problems of immediate interest. The post-war climate of opinion, however, did not eradicate its predecessor, so that Chomsky was both to inherit a conception of meaning as secondary and to look to the seventeenth and eighteenth centuries for precedent for his mentalistic interests. There is a precedent just as reasonable not more than a generation back, in the views of Sapir and the work of the nineteen-thirties at Yale.[10]

A LINGUISTIC PROFESSION

Swadesh joined the Linguistic Society of America when he began graduate school in 1931, becoming a Life Member in 1937. He was an active member,

9. Cf. "Language: Plan and Conception of Arrangement," circulated among colleagues in 1938 and intended as a supplement to the *Outline of Cultural Materials* prepared by Murdock and others at Yale (Carroll 1956: 125–133), and the conclusion of the 1937 paper on "Grammatical Categories" written for Boas, referring to "generalizations of the largest systemic formations and outlines found in language when language is considered and described in terms of the whole human species." (Carroll 1956: 101).

10. Note that Sapir carried on a tradition that distinguished between "surface" and "underlying" grammatical relations, just as he distinguished between observed and "underlying" phonetic relations. In his Takelma grammar—the fullest and finest published Amerindian grammar before the rise of selfconscious structural linguistics—he noted, for example (1922: 181): "It is the logical unexpressed subject of a passive sentence, not the grammatical subject (logical and formal object), that is referred to by the reflexive possessive in –gwa." Just these sorts of observations "provide the primary motivation and empirical justification for the theory of transformational grammar" (Chomsky 1965: 70). Sapir did not know or develop the formal machinery for handling such relations on other than a case-by-case basis, but the fundamental insight continued into his work on the logical relations underlying the overt expression of notions such as "ending-point." His Takelma grammar, indeed, served as model for at least one of his students, Harry Hoijer (personal communication). It would seem to be the concern with distributional relations of the 1940's that drove out the "spirit" of underlying relations, not as a necessary consequence but because of the empiricist ideology accompanying it.

presenting papers[11] and participating frequently in the discussion of other papers, as shown in the accounts of meetings in *Language* and the *Bulletin* of the LSA.[12] At the age of thirty he was elected to the Executive Committee. (Because of his work in Mexico, he was represented at the 1939 December meeting by Trager and McQuown.) He was a member of both special interest groups formed within the LSA in 1937, the "Group for Phonemics" and the "Group for American Indian Linguistics".[13] He served, on the Managing Committee of the latter with Franz Boas as Chairman, Leonard Bloomfield, Alfred L. Kroeber, and Edward Sapir. His belief in cooperative effort to meet the needs of linguistics and his willingness to work hard to this end are evident in these early years. The proceedings of the 1935 meeting of the LSA (*Bulletin* 9: 16 [1936]) report of this young Ph.D. that: "Mr. Swadesh called attention to the need for cooperation in bibliographies,

11. Papers given: "The Phonemic principle," Washington, D. C., December, 1933 (*Lg.* 10: 81 [1934]); "English Parts of Speech," December, 1934 (*Lg.* 11: 65 [1935]); "Proverb Displacement in Chitimacha," Philadelphia, December, 1937 (*LSA Bulletin* 11: 4 [1938]); (C. F. Voegelin and ———). "Morpho-phonemics and Variable Vowel-length in Tubatulabal," Philadelphia, December, 1937, (*LSA Bulletin* 11: 4 [1938]); "Composite Words in Chitimacha and English," December, 1936 (*LSA Bulletin* 10: 17 [1937]); "Problems of Mohican Phonology," December, 1938 (*LSA Bulletin* 12: 25 [1939]); "Foreign Influence: The Bifurcation of Phonemes, as illustrated by Recent Tarascan and Middle English", December, 1941 (*LSA Bulletin* 15: 25 [1942]); "On the Analysis of English Vowels," Chicago, December, 1946 (*LSA Bulletin* 20: 16 [1947]); "Synthetic Trend in Nootka," New Haven, December, 1947 (*LSA Bulletin* 21: 19 [1948]); "An Experiment in Remote Comparative Linguistics," New York, December, 1951 (*LSA Bulletin* 25: 6 [1952]); "Mosan as a Problem in Remote Common Origin." Bloomington, Indiana, August, 1952 (*LSA Bulletin* 26: 5 [1953]); "Time Depth Problems in the Classification of American Languages." Cambridge, December, 1952 (*LSA Bulletin* 26: 20 [1953]).

12. Interventions by Swadesh occurred on many topics—phonemic method, American Indian languages, Indo-European and Hittite, child language. Recall the incident quoted above from the 1941 meeting regarding English syllabics, and see the Proceedings of the annual meetings of the LSA in *Language* and the *Bulletin* of the LSA:

1932 *Lg.*9: 104, 105 (2 papers), 113, 115 (1933);
1933 *Lg.* 10: 70 (2), 72, 81 (2), 82 (1934);
1934 *Lg.* 11: 54, 63, 64 (3), 65 (1935);
1935 *Bull.* 9: 4, 5, 17 (2), 18 (1936);
1936 *Bull.* 10: 16 (3), 17 (1937);
1937 *Bull.* 11: 4, 6 (2), 20 (2) (1938);
1938 *Bull.* 12: 21, 22, 23 (2), 24, 25 (3) (1939);
1941 *Bull.* 15: 24, 25 (4), (1942);
1946 *Bull.* 20: 16 (5), 17 (2) (1947);
1947 *Bull.* 21: 18 (3), 19 (2) (1948);
1948 *Bull.* 22: 16 (2), 17 (1949);
1949 *Bull.* 23: 21 (1950);
1950 *Bull.* 24: 16 (4), 17 (1951);
1951 *Bull.* 25: 16 (2), 17 (4), 18 (1952).

13. The careers of the two groups are outlined in the reports of their establishment (*Lg.* 13: 257, 258 [1937]) and in a few comments in the Report of the Secretary of the LSA, until the first decided to discontinue for the time (*Bulletin* of the LSA 15: 16 [1942]), and the second was discharged with thanks (*Bulletin* 22: 11 [1949]). The membership of each was published at the end of the general membership list of the Society: *Bulletins* 11: 53–54, 12: 61–62, 13: 67, 14: 62, 15: 57–58 (1937–41) for the Group for Phonemics; *Bulletins* 11: 54, 12: 62–63, 13: 68, 14: 63, 15: 58, 16: 44–45, 17: 42–43, 18: 45–46, 19: 43–44, 20: 45–46, 21: 49 (1937–1948) for the Group for American Indian Linguistics.

especially in linguistic bibliographies, so as to cover the field completely, and also to eliminate needless bibliographies and those of poor quality." As part of the surge of effort to support work on American Indian languages, Swadesh sought to implement his own advice, launching in *Language* a program that was intended "to furnish complete annual lists of books and articles on American Indian languages, with brief indication of contents" (*Lg.* 14: 319 [1938]); cf. *LSA Bulletin* 12: 10 [1939]). Readers were asked to supply omissions, authors to send offprints, especially such as might be overlooked, and all cooperation was appreciated. When funds for the *International Journal of American Linguistics* seemed lacking, he conceived a plan for a dues-paying society to continue it. At the Chicago meeting of the LSA in 1936, at the request of Chairman Sapir, he acted as secretary to the group that discussed a proposed Society for American Indian Linguistics (*Bulletin* 10: 17 [1937]). From this grew a major though little known effort in the following year.

After ten years of existence and in the midst of a depression, the Committee on Research in American Native Languages found supporting funds running out. Since launching it under ACLS sponsorship in 1927, Boas had been able to sponsor a considerable amount of work by a considerable number of new recruits to linguistics and the Amerindian field (mostly students of Boas and Sapir). In 1935, 1936 and again in 1937, however, there were no funds for field work. Prompt working up and publication of materials was also frustrated by lack of funds.[14] The ACLS appropriated $1000 for a conference on April 25–26, 1937, to consider the state and needs of the study of native American languages and to formulate plans for further work (*LSA Bulletin* 10: 17 [1937]). The American Anthropological Association and the Linguistic Society both selected representatives. From this meeting came a request for discharge of the old Committee, organization of a new Continuing Committee (listed above as a group of the LSA) (*ACLS Bulletin* 27: 64–65 [1938]), and a series of recommendations and decisions, including the preparation of a comprehensive statement for possible publication by the ACLS as a bulletin (*AA* 39: 733 [1937], *Lg.* 13: 257–8 [1937]). Swadesh was Secretary of the new Committee, and most of the work, including the bulletin, fell to him. He devised an outline for a general statement of the history, character, importance and needs of the scientific study of aboriginal languages of America, together with appendices on several topics to be contributed by Sapir, Bloomfield, Herzog, Reichard, Cassirer, and others (Boas to Swadesh, June 14, 1937). Swadesh wrote for contributions and information (to Kroeber, Michelson, and others),

14. In his report for 1935 he listed urgent needs for 1936–7, all six of them projects of completing analysis for publication (*ACLS Bulletin* 25: 88 [1936]). "In regard to Nos. 4 and 5, until October 1936, Newman and Swadesh will be engaged in the project of English Grammar of Sapir. I am exceedingly anxious that they should go back to their field notes and work these out."

integrated the replies,[15] and prepared the final manuscript. On November 22, 1937, Boas wrote to Swadesh in his usual terse style: "Will you be good enough to let me know about the status of the work you did for the committee on Indian Languages, whether the MSS are completed, in process of completion, or ready for the printer, and what they are?" On February 21, 1938, Boas wrote again: "At the meeting of the Council of Learned Societies it was decided not to print the report submitted by our Committee, but to prepare another report especially designed to interest foundations in our work and Professor Bloomfield was requested to prepare such a report. Yours very truly, Franz Boas." In the end, the *ACLS Bulletin* carried a trenchant statement by Boas and a succinct history by Kroeber.

The *Bulletin of Information on the Scientific Study of Aboriginal Languages* (Swadesh 1937a) remained in Boas' possession and came with his papers in 1943 to the Library of the American Philosophical Society. Two of the appendixes prepared for it were separately published, Bloomfield's "Philosophical Aspects of Language" (1942), and posthumously, Sapir's "The Relation of American Indian linguistics to General Linguistics" (*South-western Journal of Anthropology* 3: 1–4 [1947]). Swadesh's own text remains unpublished, testimony to a young man's energy and devotion in an effort to sustain part of the tradition of Boas, Kroeber, Bloomfield, and Sapir, and to the role assigned him at age twenty-eight in recognition of those qualities.[16]

FIELD WORK

From the time he became a graduate student in linguistics in 1930, every year of the ensuing decade saw Swadesh engaged in fresh field work, during almost every summer season and at other times as well. In the summer

15. E.g., "RFD a, St. Helena, Calif, 6/28/37. Dear Swadesh: Your outline looks fine. I enclose the data you ask for. Will you have them typed and send me a carbon for my record? I shall be up here till August 20, then back at Berkely. Sincerely, A. L. Kroeber."

16. The *Bulletin* and associated materials are to be found as Freeman 1977, 497.3/ B63c/Anc, and in Boas Papers, Miscellaneous B/B61 (the relevance of the latter was noticed by Dr. Alexander Lesser, to whom I am indebted for calling it to my attention). I have used also the reports by Boas, "Reports of Progress, 1931" *ACLS Bull.* 18: 74–77 (1932), and correspondingly, 20: 88–89 (552–553) (1933), 22: 112–114 (242–244) (1934), 23: 88–90 (455–457) (1935), 25, 85–88 (743–746) (1936), 26: 74–77 (74–77) (sic) (1937), and 27: 633–635 (219–221) (1938) for years 1932, 1933, 1934, 1935, 1936, 1937. (The pagination in parentheses is the continuous pagination of the volume, that before parentheses of the issue.) See also Boas 1939 and Kroeber 1939.

17. C. F. Voegelin was also in the group; c.f. Jacobs 1931: 87, 97. Materials from the Nez Percé (and some Sahaptin) work are deposited in the Library of the American Philosophical Society; see entries 567, 568, 2397 in Freeman and Smith 1966. (The "Cayuse" of the heading and main entry for 567, 568 is Nez Percé, as the note to 567, "Nez Percé Language as Used by Cayuse Indians of Oregon" but not to 568, explains. Despite Jacob's efforts to locate Cayuse speakers, the language was by then extinct.) Materials in the Library of the APS from subsequent field work of Swadesh are identified by the short form "Freeman" and the entry number in brackets. I have identified entries, partly because under "Swadesh . . . Field Notes," the Freeman index indicates only a portion of the entries that represent his field work, and partly to call attention to this important source of information.

of 1930 he worked on Nez Percé at Umatilla Reservation, Oregon, under
the auspices of the Laboratory of Anthropology (Santa Fé) and the direction
of a leading Boas graduate, Melville Jacobs.[17] In the summer of 1931 he
and Mary Haas Swadesh worked in southern British Columbia on Nitinat
[Freeman 2401], a "remarkably deviating dialect [actually, a separate
language] of the Nootka" (Boas, *ACLS Bulletin* 18: 74 [1932]). The summers
of 1932 and 1933 were spent near the Gulf of Mexico in Louisiana, salvaging
Chitimacha [Freeman 730–736] from its last two capable speakers, the
best of whom died in 1934 [Freeman 730–736].[18] Some Penobscot and
Malecite material was obtained in 1933 with C. F. Voegelin [Freeman
2102, 2946]. The summer of 1934 saw work in New Haven with Alex
Thomas, Sapir's Nootka informant, producing a "large amount of new
material—lexical and grammatical" (Sapir, in Sapir and Swadesh 1939a:
10). In September, 1934, Swadesh and Mary Haas Swadesh collected
Atakapa, Alabama-Koasati, Creek, and Biloxi materials in a survey
conducted through southern Louisiana, East Texas, and eastern Oklahoma
(Haas 1968; Freeman 423, 1890, 463; Haas had worked on Tunica in 1933
while Swadesh worked on Chitimacha, and had recorded some Chitimacha
herself). The years 1934–36 saw work on Sapir's project, "A Descriptive
Grammar of English," to which Swadesh contributed at least analyses of
parts of speech and of vowel nuclei.[19]

At some point in 1936 an Eskimo came to New Haven and Swadesh
promptly obtained material that was to become the basis—together with
his "Structural Restatement" (Voegelin 1954: 441) of Kleinschmidt's
nineteenth century Greenlandic material (1946a)—of an important series
of papers on Eskimo (1951c, 1952c, d, e, f; Freeman 1355–1358). The first
of these papers reveals something of his method of work:

> The Unaaliq material was obtained from James Andrews, who visited New
> Haven, Connecticut in 1936 as a participant in the Sportsmen's Show. Since
> Mr. Andrews had only a few days to spend, it was not possible to obtain more
> than a vocabulary of about 500 words, a few paradigms, and a short text. Following
> my usual work procedures, I recorded rapidly, reserving the verification of subtle

18. Freeman 731 refers to texts from 1931, and 736 to cylinder records from 1931, while 735
identifies field notes as 1930–34. All other information available to me gives the summers of
1932 and 1933 and some portion of 1934 as the time of Swadesh's work on Chitimacha. (*ACLS
Bull.* 20: 88 [December, 1933]; *ACLS Bull.* 22: 112 [October, 1934]; Swadesh 1933b: 192;
Swadesh 1934b: 345, n. 2; Swadesh 1937g: 76). The notebooks now in the APS themselves
contain no indication of date. The typed sheet and external writing appear to be in the same
form as other materials indexed by Swadesh about 1950 for the Library and in part in his own
hand. I cannot explain this discrepancy.

19. Swadesh's part is reflected in his paper at the December 1934 meeting of the LSA,
"English Parts of Speech", (*Lg.* 11: 65 [1935]). Cf. Sapir's Report of Progress, 1934 (*ACLS Bull.*
23: 125–127 [June 1935]), in which stress and parts of speech are noted. See also "The Vowels
of Chicago English", *Lg.* 11: 148–151 (cf. Sapir's Report of Progress, 1935 *ACLS Bull.* 25:
117–120 [1936]). The other published result of the project known to me is Stanley Newman's
"On the Stress System in English", *Word* 2: 171–187 (1946).

phonetic details for later check and recheck. However, the brief period of work with Mr. Andrews prevented a final check of all points. Some errors remain, particularly in the distinction of palatal . . . (1951c: 67).

The pattern is typical of Swadesh—to push ahead while frankly confessing limitations, regarding perfection vs. silence as a false choice. His work on Eskimo was in fact to make clear for the first time the existence of a language boundary between *two* Eskimo languages, and to substantiate the classification, maintained on authority alone, since Powell's time (1891) of Eskimo-Aleut (1951c).

During this period Swadesh had of course been engaged in intensive analysis of Nootka, with an eye on Nitinat (Haas 1969: 109, n. 8) as well, and had been analyzing and preparing for publication his material on Chitimacha. After six years at Yale,[20] he accepted a position as Assistant Professor of Anthropology and Linguistics at Wisconsin. There he worked for two years on Mohican, an Algonquian language, collecting his own materials and making interlinear translations of earlier liturgical literature [Freeman 2080–2083]. He also obtained field notes on the Siouan language, Catawba, on Algonquian Potawatomi (1937—Freeman 551, 3020), and on Algonquian Chippewa and Menominee (1938—Freeman 2546, 2166–67);[21] Bloomfield prepared a summary of Menominee inflections for his use [Freeman 2161]. At some point he found time to record Chinese from the anthropologist Li An-che (celebrated for his view through non-Western eyes (1937) of the Zuñi made famous by Ruth Benedict's *Patterns of Culture*), and to work up a phonemic sketch as his contribution to the memorial volume for Trubetzkoy (1939e). He suggested that his mode of presentation would be useful for the proposed phonemic survey of the languages of the world.

In 1939 Swadesh began work on an Iroquoian language, Oneida, but his work was cut short by a sudden opportunity to go to Mexico. There, while plunged into a new and demanding role (see below), he managed to collect vocabularies in a variety of languages: Huichol (Freeman 1601), Kickapoo (Freeman 1888), Mixteco (with Norman McQuown [Freeman 2255]), Nahuatl (Freeman 2349 and 2350, the latter with Adrian León), Papago (Freeman 2647), Tzeltal (Freeman 3826), and Zapotec (Freeman 3975–3977).

RELATIONSHIPS AMONG LANGUAGES

Swadesh first undertook a comparative study, so far as I know, at the time

20. In 1931–33 as research assistant to Sapir; 1933–34 as ACLS Fellow; 1935–36 as associate on Sapir's grammar of English (an ACLS project); 1936–37 as Instructor.

21. Swadesh apparently was of some assistance to Hockett in the latter's field work on Potawatomi during the summers of 1937 and 1938 (Hockett 1948: 1, n. 1). He also heard Menomini with Bloomfield before beginning his own work; a letter from Bloomfield to Bloch (28, December 1940) states in an answer to questions about the language: "Swadesh, recording more accurately as to ear than I, and not knowing the language, confirmed the above in main outline "(Hockett 1970: 368).

of his Mexican work as part of the preparation in 1941 of a chapter published later (1949a), collecting himself many of the vocabularies and paradigms used (1947d: 220, n. 1; cf. Freeman 3974). His major historical work followed the Second World War, and will be discussed as a whole below. It followed Sapir's death, but was a continuation or revitalization of one of Sapir's major interests and contributions. Whorf and Trager had made some advance in the 1930's along lines sketched by Sapir in Uto-Aztecan and Tanoan and gone on to link that group with Penutian, but the work lay dormant. The two great periods of intense progress in Amerindian linguistic relationships had been at the Bureau of Ethnology under Powell and Henshaw in the 1880's, and around Kroeber at Berkeley, Sapir at Ottawa, and others of the newly emerged academic generation of anthropologists in the 1910's. In the post-war period, with neither government nor academic post, Swadesh was to be the controversial center of a third.

OTHER RELATIONSHIPS

Like Boas and Sapir and their other students, Swadesh was from the first attentive to social and cultural data that emerged in the course of linguistic work and interested in the relation of linguistic features to cultural patterns of expression (cf. 1933b). His article on verbs of derogation viewing linguistic form from the standpoint of an expressive function is of a kind rare among American linguists. Indeed, his historical work has an extra strength not usual among Americanists in its attention to expressive symbolism (e.g., in 1960j, 1962c; note support in the findings of Hymes 1957: 86–87 and Jacobsen 1969: 142–3, 144 for proposals by Swadesh [1956b and 1953a, respectively]). His studies of the patterning of phonetics among bilinguals (1941c) and of obsolescent languages (1948e) are pioneering contributions, and his work in the analysis and presentation of Nootka songs (1955d) and texts, including an ethnographic analysis on a topic of some general importance (1948c), is invaluable.

It would be incorrect to speak of a systematic "ethnolinguistics" or "sociolinguistics" for Swadesh, or others of the first Yale school, but it is important to note their readiness to notice and pursue a point of cultural pattern or social relevance. A concern for the relation of linguistics to public and practical affairs can be found throughout Swadesh's work. Such a concern was no stranger to the linguistics of the thirties. There was Sapir's semantic work for an international auxiliary language, and Bloomfield's development of a method of teaching reading on a linguistic basis. In a related vein, Sapir observed at the 1937 meeting on American Indian linguistics [Freeman 1977]: "Linguists do not realize the interest of scientists in various fields in matters of language. These scientists on the other hand do not realize that scientific linguistics concerns itself with matters of interest to them. They have a notion that linguistics is hopelessly exotic, whereas actually our interests overlap theirs to a large extent . . . Linguistics is the 'chemistry' of the humanities and the social sciences." Whorf interpolated, "Linguists should take it on themselves to make these things known by articles placed in various journals." One can glimpse the beginning of Whorf's famous series of articles in *The Technology Review*.

Swadesh wrestled with the relation of scientific work to social relevance in writing the main text of the Bulletin commissioned by that meeting (pp. 5–7, on "Practical Value"). A year or two later his concern reached print: "In one thing the Mexican Institute differs greatly from the glottologic interests in this country; its goal is social as well as scientific . . . Practical value and scientific interests are not necessarily contradictory" (1939m: 120). His main opportunity to act on his concern was to come shortly. At Wisconsin he had initiated a WPA Language Project in 1939, but it was left in the hands of Floyd Lounsbury when he accepted a call from the government of President Cárdenas of México to head a program of Indian education, undertaken by the new Department of Indian Affairs (Departamento de Asuntos Indígenas).

The next two years laid the foundation of Swadesh's long and intimate association with linguistics and anthropology in México. They were extraordinarily active years. He was Professor at the Instituto Politécnico Nacional de México and the Escuela de Antropología (1939–1941), Director of the Consejo de Lenguas Indígenas, Director of linguistics in the Departamento de Asuntos Indígenas, and President of the Linguistic Section of the Twenty-Ninth International Congress of Americanists (México City, 1939); he gave "Cursos de Técnica de enseñanza para profesores en zonas indígenas" [Course in instructional techniques for teachers in indigenous zones] and "Cursos de alfabetización para alumnos indígenos" [Course in alphabetization for indigenous students] for the Departmento de Asuntos Indígenas [Department of Indian Affairs] in Pátzcuaro, Michoacán (1939–40), and lectured at the Universidad de Primavera, Morelia, Michoacán in 1940. All the while his central concern was the Tarascan Project, a pioneer effort in literacy and fundamental education. To be able to teach Tarascans, prepare Tarascan materials, and administer the project, Swadesh learned Tarascan (the principal Indian language of Michoacán) and was instrumental in launching a Tarascan newspaper. He had not previously known Spanish, so within his first year he mastered that language, to the point of preparing *Orientaciones lingüísticas para maestros en zonas indígenas* [*Linguistic orientation for teachers in indigenous zones*] (1940a) and of lecturing in Spanish at the Universidad de Michoacán on linguistics and its practical applications ("Cursos IV Centenario," 1940). These lectures formed the basis of his first major treatment of linguistic theory, *La nueva filología* [*The New Philology*] (1941).

In these works there was much that was inseparable from the character of the man. There was his delight in seeing to the detailed work himself. His father·had taught him the printing trade as a child, and in Mexico, having persuaded a representative of a linotype company to create a new Amerind type font, Swadesh himself set publications in type in Tarascan on a hand press in the Indian Boarding School in Paracho. He set the text of *La nueva filología* himself on the linotype in the offices of the Mexico City newspaper "El Nacional" (McQuown 1968: 755, 756). There was his assumption of mutual responsibility with "informants." Through his Nootka work with Alex Thomas, Swadesh had been inducted into the Boasian practice of teaching Indians to write their languages. It was a tradition of work in a collaborative, even collegial spirit.[22] The Oneida publication (1941b) was prepared by Floyd Lounsbury as a repayment of sorts to the Oneida community for their assistance to the WPA language project that Swadesh had launched (the title page statement, "F. Lounsbury né detolisdohlalak" means equally correctly "he printed it" or "he typed it"). Toward the end of the Tarascan literacy project, when money was not forthcoming from Mexico City, Swadesh sold his car and whatever else he could convert into cash in order to pay his staff of Indians and teachers before leaving.

The approach of war brought Swadesh back to the United States. Called into service, he received officer training and became a first lieutenant in the Signal Corps. Serving in the Language Section of the Army Service Forces in Washington and New York (at 165 Broadway, an office where many American structural linguists were concentrated) and in the Office of Special Services, he edited dictionaries, prepared linguistic analyses and teaching materials in Spanish, Russian, Burmese (he visited Burma briefly), and Chinese, and taught courses in these languages. His books on learning Russian (1945) and Chinese (1947) were among the results.

After World War II

A concern for the application of linguistics to human problems (McQuown 1938) and a desire to make linguistics useful and to interpret it to the man in the street (Newman 1967) continue throughout Swadesh's career. All his general books (1940a, 1941a, 1960a, 1966a), and many other publications and activities attent to this, and there is no reason to think that he regretted his contribution to what for him was honestly a war against fascism. Yet altogether, the Oneida project, the Tarascan project (1939–1941), and the war work (1942–46) had taken eight years of his life. It is not surprising that, a civilian once again, he returned to the field of his first commitment

---

22. See Sapir's discussion of such experiences with Southern Paiute, Sarcee, and Nootka in his famous essay, "The Psychological Reality of Phonemes": "The most successful American Indian pupil that I have had in practical phonetics is Alex Thomas . . . and it is largely from a study of his texts that I have learned to estimate at its true value the psychological difference between a sound and a phoneme" (1949 1933: 54). Cf. Swadesh 1954f: 640.

and first training with Sapir and resumed the program of research on Nootka language and culture left incomplete at Sapir's death in 1939.

The changes brought about in linguistics and anthropology by the Second World War and its aftermath are not well understood. Only now, as a new climate of opinion emerges, are the years from about 1942 to 1965 beginning to be seen as one period, significantly distinct from what preceded and what is beginning to follow. It was a period of academic expansion and of cold war. Anthropology reorganized its professional association and a new generation came to leadership. Linguistics was institutionalized in separate departments for the first time and grew greatly in numbers and influence. The relation between linguistics and anthropology, once so obvious and intimate, came to seem a problem, as methodological developments absorbed the attention of linguists and made their work and talk esoteric to many anthropologists. The unity of anthropological disciplines implicit in their common study of the American Indian broke down as American anthropologists followed, if not the flag, then trusteeship, trade, and new power through much of the rest of the world, and as the classifications of Amerindian tribes, races, languages, culture traits, and archaeological traditions that had once been common knowledge became one body of special lore among many others.

Within this novel scene, there was continuity and piety. Manuscripts by Sapir and Whorf were retrieved and posthumously published; a volume planned by Sapir and a mature example of his methods were published in an anthropological series (Newman 1944, Hoijer et al. 1946); Boas' *International Journal of American Linguistics* was revived; and the 1937 meeting Swadesh served as secretary was looked back to as defining a subsequent decade (Voegelin 1947). The role of Boas' ACLS Committee on Native American Languages was taken up by the Library of the American Philosophical Society, where the Boas papers were housed, with first Zellig Harris and then C. F. Voegelin serving as Library Research Associates; Swadesh in 1945 added a gift of papers from Sapir (Lydenberg 1948: 124–5; Harris 1945:97, n. 2). But the men who had made Amerindian languages and anthropological work inseparable from the advance of linguistics (Boas and Sapir) were gone, and their tradition was to seem marginal to a "linguistics without meaning" and a study of "culture without words" (to quote from the somewhat exaggerated title of an article by Voegelin (1949b)).

Of the five tasks identified for the preceding period, the first, development of method, has preoccupied linguists from the war until today. The 1940's saw a flurry of methodological papers on morphology and syntax (see papers 12–26 from 1942–1948 in Joos 1957), and the students of Sapir were marginal to this activity. Swadesh contributed to the debate on English phonology (1947c) as described above, but in continuation of an old involvement, and did not take further part in discussions of method. Nor did he engage in what became a focus of concern for linguistics in relation to other fields, the discussion of the relationship between linguistics and ethnographic method and the attempts to extend linguistic method to analysis of the rest of culture. The seed of such an effort can be seen in Boas' claim that the clarity of the unconscious patterning of language could be a key to the solution of ethnological problems, and Sapir (1929) explicitly stated that linguistic method had a lesson for the social sciences. This notion was taken up actively in the 1950's, especially among students of Sapir and those who shared in the Sapir tradition like Kluckhohn (who had contributed the first discussion of cultural patterning on the analogy of language to the Sapir memorial volume [Spier et al. 1941]), Voegelin, Trager, Pike, Lounsbury and Goodenough. Discussion of a substantive relation between language and culture, focussed upon the writings of Whorf, also was concentrated among such scholars (Trager, Hoijer, Kluckhohn, Newman, McQuown, Voegelin). The Nootka work did as a byproduct furnish a test case for George Kingsley Zipf's "principle of least effort" (Zipf 1949: 78–81; AA 51 [3]: 533 [1949]). But for Swadesh, linguistic method seems always to have been a practical way of dealing with language, and the connection between language and culture obviously lay in meanings, not in methods or form.

Swadesh indeed stood consciously apart from the dominant attitudes of the post-war years; the concentration on method, form and formal symbolism. The only published expression of his view is an article written in support of critiques of behaviorist psychology in linguistics by Margaret Schlauch (1946, 1947). The debate continues the discussion that began before the war (1935b). Pointing out inconsistency in the effort of Bloomfield, Bloch and Trager to avoid meaning, Swadesh analyzes the difficulty as evidence of a struggle "between the fact that meaning is an inseparable aspect of language and the fetish that anything related to the mind must be ruled out of science" (1948f: 254). Against Bloomfield's view that linguistic meaning must wait upon definition in scientific laboratory terms, he points out that "languages are spoken by people who have no such minute and verified knowledge of the whole universe" (256). With regard to method he goes on to observe: "It is characteristic of the linguistic mechanists that they have great confidence in the scientist and none in the native speakers of the language" (256). On the contrary, "the judgment of the speaker proves to be valuable to the scientist even in the case of the subtler problems" (258). The charge of "circularity" against relating linguistic facts to human minds is answered first by noting that the objectionable inferences from observable behavior to unobservable "mind" are quite similar to the inferences from known to reconstructed languages practiced by behaviorist scholars and second by noting the inadequacy of such a "philosophy of science" on its own grounds: It is not considered "mentalistic" to speak of atoms and alpha particles, even though they are known mainly by their effects.

A note of personal pique perhaps creeps into this paper when Swadesh notes that a writer on a French creole had written *lapoht* (corresponding to French *la porte*) "under the impression that this was the standard mode of analyzing and representing long vowels among all modern linguists," and when he describes the use of parallel slanting lines to indicate phonemes as a "functionless esoteric device . . . mostly a peculiarity of the journals *Language*, edited by Bloch, and *Studies in Linguistics*, edited by Trager . . . not . . . without qualification . . . the general practice of linguists" (259). Overall, the article upholds the tenets of the Sapir approach in terms that were to be accepted as a devastating, unanswerable critique of the fallacies and inadequacies of "anti-mentalism" a decade later.

Except for an ethnographic field trip to the Nootka on an SSRC grant-in-aid in the summer of 1949 (Freeman 2406–7)—like English vowels, a continuation of an earlier interest—Swadesh did not undertake sustained field work again except as it related to his historical concerns. Of the five substantive tasks identified earlier, the only one to which he had not made major contributions before the war, relationships among languages, was to become his central concern and to be the basis of the contribution he would make to all the others.

The building of a profession of linguistics continued to involve Swadesh as it had in the United States and Mexico before the war. In 1945 the Linguistic Circle of New York launched a journal, *Word*, and with its second volume (1946), Swadesh became editor for four years. The Circle and its journal were international in composition and orientation, reflecting the concentration in New York of scholarly refugees from repression and war in Europe. They stood apart from the "anti-mentalism" that came to be associated with "native American" linguistics and with some of the major contributors to the Linguistic Society's journal *Language* during this period.[23] It offered space to a wider range of contributions, sometimes uneven, but often more interesting. *Word* was for a time the place for unorthodox thoughts and concern with semantics, literature, creole languages, and the like. It is symptomatic that Swadesh was editor, for if simple rather than "sophisticated" in manner and taste, he was always cosmopolitan in outlook.[24]

What Swadesh might have further contributed to the profession in the United States as editor, organizer of research, and teacher—he was an absorbing and inspiring teacher—was not to be known. In 1948 he was

23. I use "native American" advisedly. When Roman Jakobsen arrived in the United States, he was housed by Franz Boas, but some of the linguists at 165 Broadway circulated a petition (or signed a dollar bill—stories differ) to complain about carpet-bagging foreigners—presumably a joke.

24. Swadesh was joined at *Word* by Andre Martinet for Volume 3 in 1947. Vols. 3–5 list both Martinet and Swadesh as Managing Editors on the cover, but Vols. 3–4 list only Swadesh on the inside front cover as Managing Editor for receipt of mss. Vol. 5 (1949) lists Joseph Greenberg and Martinet on the inside front cover, not Swadesh.

appointed Associate Professor of Anthropology at the City College of New York. There was a student strike, and Swadesh openly supported the students. He was not reappointed.

The "Swadesh Case"

The onset of the cold war and of "McCarthyism" in the academic world had already begun to affect anthropology.[25] The Swadesh case was to play a prominent part in shaping the stance that the American Anthropological Association (AAA) would adopt, and the basis on which it would respond twenty years later to a new series of appeals. Fresh from a reorganization with new powers that made some members apprehensive, the Executive Board of the AAA reported proudly that it had taken "immediate action" with regard to the proposed dismissal of a Curator at the Ohio State Museum for alleged Communist associations (*News Bulletin II* [3]: 37–38 [June 1948]), referring to its own "celerity and vigilance in protecting the interests of Fellows of the Association and the name of anthropology." (The Board had also successfully protested a disparaging comment by Drew Pearson about government appointment of an anthropologist to a position concerned with the Pacific Trust Territories.) But it shortly took notice of objections that it should not take a stand on anything other than professional competence ("The Morgan Dismissal and the Powers of the Executive Board," *News Bulletin II* [4]: 51–51[September 1948]) and agreed with its critics, pointing out that it had not tried to judge the merits of the case or apply sanctions, but merely to secure a fair hearing. It adopted the view that the case was "a civil matter, lying outside strictly professional interests of the Association, that . . . [it was] in such a matter not empowered by the Constitution to take action that would commit the membership without an opportunity for it to express its collective wishes" (*News Bulletin II* [5]: 72–73 [November 1948]; *American Anthropologist* 51: 347 [1949]; both reporting the meeting of the Executive Board of July 1, 1948).

Matters did not rest there; "new pressures and other cases that have been

25. In the same issue as an official notice regarding the Morgan case (see below) and a communication by Voegelin (1950) suggesting the separateness of language from culture, some problems of the larger context of mobilization for the war and of large-scale government support afterward were presciently noted by Embree (1950).

The war caused many social scientists not only to lose their objectivity in regard to the cultures of enemy nations, it revived in them serious acceptance of the white man's burden. . . . The whole philosophy presents a striking parallel to that of French and British colonialists who have devoted their lives unselfishly to administration of the affairs of their little brown brothers. . . . Just as America, now the richest and most powerful nation on earth, must learn some self restraint, if she is not to ruin the peoples and cultures of the rest of the world, so American anthropologists who have so many opportunities for intellectual leadership must be aware of falling in love with their own culture and their own professional folkways to such an extent as to lose sight of their primary object: to study the nature of man and his culture, of the relations between men and their cultures.

mentioned as cognate" (*AA* 51: 347 [1949]; Board meeting Dec. 27, 1948) led to putting the matter on the agenda of the annual meeting of the Council of Fellows, which, after lengthy discussion, passed a Resolution on Professional Freedom. Contrary to a narrow view, it resolved:

> that the American Anthropological Association go on record as favoring investigation by the Executive Board in cases where the civil rights, academic freedom and professional status of anthropologists as such have been invaded and take action where it is apparent that injustice has resulted that affects their rights as citizens and scientists.

A Committee was to be appointed to recommend what action should be taken in such cases (*News Bulletin III*[1]: 1 [February 1949]; *AA* 51: 370 [1949]).

The report of the Committee on Scientific Freedom (G. P. Murdock, Chairman; E. G. Burrows, A. I. Hallowell) and Swadesh's case were both to come before the Council of Fellows at its next meeting (November 1949), and to be linked together. Swadesh's part in the 1948 and 1949 meetings and their character and conflict are barely suggested in the published report of actions taken. The Board reported:

> Under date of June 29, 1949, Morris Swadesh, whose appointment as Associate Professor at CCNY was not renewed as expected, addressed a letter to the President [A. Irving Hallowell] asking the intervention of the Association on his behalf. Subsequent to lengthy discussion, correspondence, and examination of various documents and letters the following minute was unanimously adopted at the September meeting: 'The Executive Board of the AA has examined the facts in the case of the failure of City College of New York to reappoint Morris Swadesh as Associate Professor in the Department of Sociology and Anthropology for 1949–50. The Executive Board finds that the By-Laws of the Board of Higher Education of New York City do not require notification of intention not to reappoint individuals on one-year appointments and that therefore no violation of civil rights or legal forms is involved. The Executive Board sees no grounds for further action in this case, although it believes that the By-Laws of the Board of Higher Education and the proceedings of City College of New York may not be in accordance with the best practice in institutions of high academic standing.' (News Bulletin III [4]: 3, [October 1949]; *AA* 52: 136–137 [1950]).

At the next Council of Fellows (November, 1949), Murdock, after presenting the recommendations of the Committee on Scientific Freedom, "made a number of remarks concerning the circumstances under which the Recommendations were drawn up by the Committee, with particular reference to the action of the Executive Board during the past year in the case of Morris Swadesh, a Fellow of the Association"[n.b., not in the case of the Curator in Ohio] . . . [and] then moved that the actions of the Executive Board during the past year [e.g., in the case of Swadesh] be sustained by the Council. . . . After considerable discussion from the floor, President Hallowell called for the question and in a standing vote of the Council the motion was carried . . . 76 yeas, 6 noes, 26 abstentions." The recommendations of the Committee itself were carried without dissent on a voice vote (*News Bulletin IV* [1]: 1–2 [January 1950]; *AA* 52[1]: 152–3 [1950]).

The climate of the time can be glimpsed in the wording of a resolution condemning dismissals at the University of California that became symbolic of the new situation:

"The Executive Board of the American Anthropological Association [one member dissenting] deplores the dismissal in August, by a bare majority of the Board of Regents, of members of the faculty of the University of California, all of them free of suspicion as to communist sympathies." *(News Bulletin IV* [4]: 7 [1950]; not published in the *AA*).

Morris Swadesh was not a man free of suspicion as to communist sympathies. Nor was he inclined to be silent, on linguistic or on social matters, where he believed principles to be at stake. Newman recalls: "As a result of this episode (the CCNY strike] and of other less publicized ones, he became labelled unambiguously as a 'leftist' during the noisiest period of the McCarthy Era, and university administrators were unwilling to take the risk of hiring him" (1967: 949). True, his sympathies were not misunderstood by colleagues who knew him and his work. As editor of *Word* (1946–49), Swadesh preferred certain simplifications in spelling English words. Twitted in an editorial meeting that the Soviet Union, which had once endorsed them, no longer did so, Swadesh observed, "Now they are wrong" (or words to that effect). The leading eminent theoretical linguist of the period recalls with some amusement that he rather resented Swadesh's reputation as a great radical. He himself had arrived at a particular position through agonizing consideration of the alternatives posed in the intellectual debates of the time, whereas for Morris it was simply a matter of family and what was right. There were, to be sure, enemies. It is reported that a motion of censure was introduced *against* Swadesh at the 1948 AAA meeting by the chairman of his department and that a leading anthropologist temporarily refused nomination to chairmanship of a committee pending its passage. In the end, he was not to have employment or to be able to teach for seven years, and not for more than a decade, and then only as a visitor, in the United States.

Swadesh managed to continue his research. After the Nootka field trip in the summer of 1949, he worked in the Boas Collection in the Library of the American Philosophical Society, and had some support from the Phillips and Penrose Funds of the Society over the next few years, with the encouragement of Carl Voegelin and Zellig Harris. The Library had decided to specialize its Phillips bequest in the American field of linguistics, ethnology, and archeology (Lydenberg 1948).

The Library was proud of its program in these years, as well it could be.

Since the inception of the new policy with respect to the use of the Phillips Fund, established in 1946, the projects centering around American Indian linguistics and archaeology have been among the busiest and most fruitful of the Library's activities. Under the supervision of C. F. Voegelin and Z. S. Harris a program for comparative studies in the Iroquoian languages . . . together with plans to improve the quality and usefulness of that collection is well advanced. Under this program, the Boas Collection has been completely reclassified and catalogued by Morris Swadesh (*APSY* 1950: 88–89 [1951]; *PAPS* 95 [3]: ii [1951]). Results from the Phillips Fund projects prove again the justification for specialization in the American field of Indian linguistics and ethnology. (*APSY* 1951: 87 [1952]; *PAPS* 96 [4]: i [1952]).[26]

Possibly there is a connection between the sense of accomplishment in these years and the contrary report for 1953—after Swadesh had left—that activities had slackened and that after ten years a reevaluation was needed to chart future policy *(APSY* 1953: 88 [1954]; cf. *APSY* 1954: 85 [1955]). In any case, during these years Swadesh not only completely classified the Boas Collection, but augmented it as well. Some 82 entries in the index to the Indian manuscripts of the Library (Freeman 1966: 486) represent his donations at this time. In addition to Nootka and Yana work of a descriptive sort sponsored by A. L. Kervelor, as Library Associate, he carried on the research into the relationships and rates of change among languages that was to lead him into the linguistic prehistory of mankind as a whole.

The Linguistic Approach to Prehistory

Swadesh's work in the history of language represents a second career, as it were, begun as he neared forty. All his published historical work comes after the Second World War[27] His 1941 study of Proto–Zapotec was revised then for publication (1947d), but this the first published work in this vein was based on his knowledge of Chitimacha (1946e, 1947a). The connections of Chitimacha and Atakapa were not pursued further at the time, perhaps because Mary Haas was at work on the deeper relationships in the Southeast. In any case, Swadesh turned to the other language with which he had worked most intensively, Nootka, investigating its relation to

---

26. For activities of the Library in this period, especially with reference to Swadesh, see the "Report of the Committee on the Library", *PAPS* 93 (2): iv–vii (1949), *PAPS* 94 (3): i–ii (1950), *PAPS* 95 (3): i–iii (1951), *PAPS* 96 (4): i–iii (1952), *PAPS* 97 (5): i–iii (1953), *PAPS* 98 (6) i–iii (1954); and the more extended "Report of the Committee on the Library" (although often with the same language with regard to Amerindian Linguistics and archeology) in *APSY* 1953: 87–99 (1954), *APSY* 1954: 83–99 [1955]. See also the "Note on the Papers in American Indian Linguistics and Archaeology" by W. E. Lingelbach opposite p. 367 in *PAPS* 96 (4) (1952), the issue containing Swadesh 1952a.

27. In reviewing Andrade's Quileute (1935c), Swadesh had included 10 likely Nootka-Quileute comparisons, after observing, "In phonetics and morphological structure it [Quileute] has a close resemblance to the Nootkan dialects, but lexical resemblances are not easy to find. Still one finds enough good comparisons to feel that the possibility of an ancient historical connection between Chimakuan and Wakashan may be worth investigation" (219). The same general methodological perspective was expressed in his review of Bunzel's Zuni two years later (1937f: 255)—see n. 30.

Kwakiutl within the long-recognized Wakashan family (comprising also Nitinat and Makah). Suddenly, within a few years, Swadesh had invented glottochronology, reinvented lexicostatistics, proposed new criteria of proof of relationships, and published path-breaking comparative studies of four different major language families (Mosan, Eskimo–Aleut, Na–Dene, Penutian), the last of which led him on to comparison on a continental scale. Just as he had pioneered in communicating the phonemic approach and in drawing others into its use (cf. 1937e), so he was now pioneering in communicating the new historical approach that he had largely discovered himself and seeking to draw others into its cooperative development and use. All this came to fruition in years when he was without academic position of any kind.

THE USES OF BASIC VOCABULARY

His work on linguistic relationships and the development of lexicostatistics and glottochronology were intertwined. Common to both is the pattern of setting out on a path opened up by Sapir and making discoveries of unforeseen scope.

The initial choice to study Amerindian relationships derived from Sapir's proposals of a generation before. Despite much new data and much work, the "official" classification of Amerindian languages north of Mexico remained that of Powell for which the evidence had never been published and which later evidence clearly superseded. The sense of fixity introduced by Powell's classification persisted until after the Second World War, abetted by an illusory sense of conflict between the extremes of Powell's 55 stocks, based on lexical inspection, and Sapir's 6 phyla, based on intuition, or at best on grammar alone. In fact, Sapir published a good deal of evidence, both grammatical and lexical, for some of the new relationships he proposed, and his six ultimate units were clearly presented as a set of hypotheses. Lost from sight was an intermediate classification in his famous 1929 article, assembling the results of collective Americanist effort in the 1910's and 1920's. That classification recognized some twenty-three groups, and had that scale of classification been advertised by a map (as were Powell's 55 and Sapir's later 6) it would have proved a sensible basis for further work after the war.[28] As it was, some of Swadesh's work appeared daring and controversial only because its continuity with a previous consensus was overlooked and the nature of the work on which it was built misunderstood.

Swadesh clarified the basis of Sapir's historical practice (1954f: 641–2, 1955f, 1961a) on such points as Sapir's requirement of both lexical and grammatical lines of proof.[29] Sapir's proposed Na-Dene family, joining

28. See discussion in Hymes 1963, and Darnell ms.
29. Cf. Swadesh 1937f; 255, noting that despite the striking structural resemblances of Zuni to Uto-Aztecan and Kiowa-Tanoan, lexical resemblances do not obtrude themselves, and "serious attempts at comparison will have to wait until a dictionary appears." He later (1955k: 377) found lexico-statistic criteria to show that Zuni has no special affinity to Kiowa-Tanoan; cf. 1967c: 295–301, and 1969b for other affiliations of Zuni.

Athapaskan, Tlingit, and Haida had been the focus of a famous controversy with Boas as to the possibility of detecting remote genetic relationship and distinguishing it from resemblance due to borrowing. Swadesh undertook a methodological experiment, assessing what could be shown of the connection, through Indo-European, of English and French, and whether the evidence of genetic connection ("archaic residue") could be separated from "diffusional cumulation" (1951b). The results were applied triumphantly to Na–Dene, and the old objection that grammatical structure showed convincing connection but that much of vocabulary did not, was met by the fact of elapsed time. (Cf. the situation in Wakashan, as noted by Sapir in footnote 32). Received opinion since Powell had seen only one Eskimo language from Greenland to Alaska. Carrying on his Eskimo work, Swadesh used lexicostatistical criteria to demonstrate a language boundary in eastern Alaska, thus validating an observation only now recalled from the explorer Rasmussen, and in the process christening the two "new" languages (Yupik, Inupik). With Marsh he gave substance to the Eskimo–Aleut relation traditionally accepted since Powell (1951d; cf. 1952a: 452–3, 5). Mosan had been privately suspected by Sapir, publicly suggested and named by Frachtenberg, and then given a wider possible link to Kutenai and Algonkian by Sapir, a generation before (cf. Swadesh 1953: 27–28). Mosan itself was proposed as comprising the families of Wakashan (Kwakiutl, Nootka, Nitinat, Makah), Salishan (many languages in British Columbia and Washington with an outlier in Oregon), and Chemakuan–Quileute, Hoh, Chemakum). Swadesh had glimpsed some connection early in his work with Nootka (see n. 29a). Now he approached it through study first of two of its branches, Wakashan (1948g, 1948k), and Salishan (1941b, 1950a, 1952), and then built on earlier comparisons of particular branches by others (Chemakuan–Quileute [1955h], Nootka–Quileute [1953c], Salish-Wakashan [1953g] and himself (Nootka–Quileute [1935c—see n. 29a], Salishan–Coeur d'Alene [1949b]), in a detailed study of lexical and grammatical connections (1953a, f). One purpose was to smooth the way for examining more distant relationships, "including particularly Sapir's Algonkian–Mosan hypothesis" (1953: 27). Sapir's barely sketched conception of Penutian became the framework of further methodological experiments (1956h, i, presented in 1952), and of a field survey (1954b), leading to broader, "Penutioid" perspectives (1954d, 1955k, 1956b, 1957b, 1957c).[30]

As evidence of connections in basic vocabulary accumulated, Penutioid deepened into a comparative study of the languages of the New World (1958a, 1959j), and Swadesh's knowledge and exploration of languages of the Old World led further into a glimpse of remote connections in the lexical stock of all or most existing languages (1960c, 1960i, 1964f, 1965b).

Glottochronology, in the sense of a method assuming a standard rate of

---

30. In a letter to me of May 12, 1957, he wrote: "Pretty soon, I hope to send you a chart of Penutioid, which is much more oid that ever and I wish I had a better name for it."

replacement in basic vocabulary, came about by accident. Swadesh began with a statement from Sapir's famous monograph on time perspective that diversity among related languages is related to time, and that the more diverse related languages are, the longer they have been diverging from their common ancestor. To this common-sense assumption Swadesh joined the standardized use of a basic vocabulary. The notion of basic vocabulary is at least as old as comparative linguistics. It has long been noted that words for common features of human experience—such as body parts and functions; phenomena such as water, fire, wood, sky, bird, fish, lake, smoke, mountain, rain; sense experiences and dimensions such as long, small, red, hot, cold, etc.—are valuable in tracing relationships among languages. Such words can be found in any language, are less often borrowed from another (there being no semantic gap to fill), and tend to persist longer in a language than other words. The fact of relationship and the relative degree of relationship among languages often has been assessed by the comparison of vocabulary of such kind. Obviously, to infer that languages which share more basic vocabulary are more closely related than others implies that the persistence (or replacement) of such vocabulary is a function of elapsed time. If the relation to time were random, no such inference could be drawn.

Swadesh became. famous and controverisal for attempting to make this traditional use of basic vocabulary precise. Stimulated by the discovery of radio-carbon dating, he began with the expectation that the rate of change in basic vocabulary had a definite maximum (1952: 454, referring to 1948g). The rate of change in language was known to be relatively slow, and the needs of communication between generations would impose a limit. His first experiment compared the percentage of basic vocabulary in common between English and German to the percentage in common between Nootka and Kwakiutl, obtaining an estimate of the time depth of the latter relationship. If 59 percent of basic vocabulary was common between English and German, known to be separated about 1,100 years, Nootka and Kwakiutl, having 30 percent in common, must have had a much longer period of divergence. "In this way historic knowledge .serves to clarify prehistory" (1952a: 454). In the absence of any native written records or dated monuments, such an inference of time depth is quite useful, and a reasonable estimate is better than none at all.[31]

Working at the Library of the American Philosophical Society in the fall of 1949, Swadesh extended his experiments to Salishan, using the percentages

31. It is interesting to compare Sapir's earlier impressionistic judgment. "In regard to vocabulary Kwakiutl and Nootka differ greatly. Considering the very stricking morphological agreement between them it is somewhat disappointing to find comparatively few stems held in common. It is highly important, however, to note that many of these are rather colorless in content and thus hardly to be suspected of having been borrowed in post-Wakashan times. . . . By careful comparison of the two Wakashan branches one can in part reconstruct a Wakashan 'Ursprache' but the actual differences between the Kwakiutl and Nootka are in fact very great; they differ perhaps as much as Slavic and Latin." (Sapir 1911: 19, 15).

of words retained in English from Old English (about 1000 years older) as a convenient yardstick. When the rate of change in the test vocabulary among Salish languages was repeatedly found to be consistent, he decided to try the technique on languages of known history. By the time his second Salishan study appeared in print (1949b, 1951a; cf. 1952: 455, Voegelin and Harris 1951: 324–326), several colleagues had joined him in making such studies. Robert Lees undertook to provide a general statistical analysis and mathematical basis (1953; read as a paper at the Linguistic Institute, summer 1951), and the technique was incorporated provisionally into Swadesh's comparative study of Eskimo–Aleut (1951d) and his study of Na–Dene (1951b). In the next year a full-fledged presentation of the approach was published (1952a) and quickly became a focus of discussion and cooperation among anthropologists (cf. 1953h, 1954e, the companion papers in the special issue of IJAL [1955i, 1956f], and the special session held at the 1955 meeting of the AAA in Boston.)

In all this, Swadesh was conscious of his predecessors. He edited and published their work to give them credit and to show the continuity of his work with theirs (Mosan, 1953c, 1953g cf. 1953a; 278); Penutian 1953b, 1964c). He referred to lexicostatistics as having had to be "reinvented," after its earlier discovery by Dixon and Kroeber (1950b, 1956b). And as the scope of the horizon opening before him grew, he became more than ever conscious of the need of collaborative work. With support from the Columbia University Social Science Research Fund, he collaborated with Joseph Greenberg in studies of several linguistic stocks in Africa, Australia, and America (cf. Greenberg and Swadesh 1953, Greenberg 1953, and Swadesh 1952: 455). Through Greenberg the same fund also supported his survey of Penutian vocabulary. With a small grant from the American Philosophical Society, he undertook to enlist the aid of others in obtaining the vocabularies that had become the tool of exploration:

At the outset the grantee had a collection of about 30 diagnostic vocabularies, including 17 in the Penutian phylum. It was necessary to find a way of rapidly assembling similar material from other Amerindian languages, ideally from all of the 1,500 or so languages of the New World. He undertook to accomplish this by communicating, by mail or personally, with linguists, ethnologists, teachers and missionaries, wherever he knew of anyone in a position to provide the needed material. Each was requested to furnish a list of 200 selected words, and also phonetic and grammatical notes of each language. The project has been met with widespread interest, and responses have been received from individuals and institutions working on Indian languages of Canada, United States, Mexico, Honduras, Guatemala, Costa Rica, Panama, Colombia, Venezuela, Brazil, Bolivia, Peru and Chile. About 100 vocabularies have been submitted and many more have been promised. They are being published by the grantee in a series called Amerindian Non-Cultural Vocabularies (in mimeographic form), which is being distributed to individuals, educational institutions and libraries (1955h).

In 1953 Swadesh moved to Denver, Colorado, for the sake of the health of his second wife, Frances. The Amerindian Non-Cultural Vocabularies (1954a) were launched there, from the basement of his home. Many scholars and field workers received Swadesh's encouragement and help in return for accepting copies of word lists with a promise to fill them out.[32] The method was evidently capable of gathering a complete collection for the hemisphere. As the APS report goes on to say, however, "the grantee, with a minimum of clerical assistance, is unable to keep pace with the large volume of correspondence and editorial work." Almost without research funds, Swadesh could not keep a typist consistently employed or meet requests for copies of vocabularies without outside assistance. He worked with help as it could be found. A little money from the Department of Anthropology of the University of Chicago enabled him to analyze the individual persistence rates of words in the diagnostic list and to revise the list itself (1955i).

Fresh field work in Amerindian languages was at a low ebb outside California, while for many languages the number of speakers continued to dwindle. For the sake of anthropology, Swadesh suggested that scholars reverse their usual priorities and publish first not a grammar, but a dictionary with a brief description of phonetics and structure as an aid to its use "the exhaustive grammar can be left to future generations, if necessary" (1954f: 640–1). And he urged that the shortage of manpower be met by reviving the training of gifted native speakers, and by welcoming and encouraging (not discouraging) the contributions to lexical work of ethnographers, missionaries, and scholars in other fields (1954f: 640).

In the spirit of the Boas Committee on Native American Languages, Swadesh sought funds in 1955–56 for an ethnolinguistic survey of native America. He envisioned it as a program that would provide basic data for systematic historical work and would salvage a usable minimum of information, including the diagnostic list, from the many languages on the verge of extinction. At the same time, aware of hostility to the new methods, he stressed general goals and benefits, and judged that the Survey, however valuable it would be to Americanist studies, would fail if notably associated with glottochronology or himself.[33]

Some impetus to the Survey came from the Consejo de Lenguas Indígenas [Council on Indigenous Languages] in Mexico, and the plan was given the

---

32. From a postscript to a letter to me of March 26, 1954: "In a letter I just got, Carl [Voegelin] mentions you among his students who have had field experience and who might be willing to fill out vocabularies for my collection. So I enclose blank sheets with my request that you give me whatever vocabulary or vocabularies you may have . . . I can repay your kindness in vocabularies."

33. Plans for a small volume on glottochronology, to include the discussions at the 1955 Boston meeting of the AAA, were suspended by a university press with the apology that they had not realized linguists and anthropologists were so divided on the subject; other evidence reaching Swadesh suggested that a colleague had introduced political considerations as well. (Letter to me of February 20, 1956).

blessing of Alfred Kroeber and Clyde Kluckhohn, as well as other colleagues. It failed to find funding, probably mainly because the study of disappearing languages, although it cannot be deferred, often strikes sources of funds as the last thing that needs doing at the time.

MEXICO AGAIN

In 1954 Kluckhohn had tried to bring Swadesh to Harvard. The proposal was supported by anthropologists, but characteristically opposed by the head of the linguistics group there. During these years, Swadesh visited Mexico a number of times, and in 1956 he returned permanently to Mexico as Research Professor of Prehistoric Linguistics in the Institute de Historia of the Universidad Nacional Autónoma de México, and as Professor also at the Escuela Nacional de Antropología e Historia. He resumed an active part in the linguistic and anthropological life of Mexico. The number of publications in Spanish signed "Mauricio Swadesh" naturally increased, as did studies of Mexican languages.

Swadesh's concern for practical, efficient means in the face of the great scope of the work to be done, found expression in prehistory as in phonemic field work (1937e, 1965d, 1965e). At the time of the 1959 meetings of the AAA in Mexico City, he had discovered the computer and had begun to cooperate with an interested engineer. One midnight, when no one else was there to mind, he commandeered me to spend several hours punching cards for a Chinookan–Tsimshian comparison in the University electronic center. The former printer did some punching of his own, and investigated the way in which the card sorter and print-out might work. His concern to overcome the bias introduced into prehistory by the accident of what language a scholar knew well or thought to compare. He wanted to develop a general method of comparing language for special affinity at any level of relationship (cf. 1963b, 1966d). His involvement with computer work also led to his taking responsibility for coordinating a project for the decipherment of Mayan hieroglyphics (1968b).

The opportunity to work continuously in Mexico gave Swadesh fuller acquaintance with its major language families and a broader foundation for his exploration of the connections of Amerindian languages as a whole (1964e, 1967c, 1967d, 1969b). The center of gravity of New World linguistic relationships is indeed in Latin America, and only from the standpoint of the major families found in Latin America can the deeper problems of New World linguistic prehistory be properly posed and solved. Penutian was leading Swadesh into the Mexican connections partially detected earlier by Sapir; and in Mexico, his habit of relating his work to the interests of those around them meshed with the natural development of his own explorations. And Mexico brought him personal happiness and collaboration in many studies with Evangelina Arana.

Swadesh was never a parochial scholar, but Mexico gave him a special

opportunity to be fully cosmopolitan and to contribute more effectively to
an international perspective on linguistic prehistory. It was there that his
conception of the "world linguistic net" developed (1960c, 1960i, 1964f).
It was through this work, and his analyses of the basic lexical stock of some
major Mexican languages (1965a, 1966b, 1967a, 1969a), that much of his
conception of the evolutionary history of human languages emerged (1965b).

In his teaching and research in Mexico Swadesh was to be judged "the
only linguist who from this country has made theoretical and practical contributions to his discipline, and the only one who in Mexico has formed a
school of linguistic anthropology which he himself took charge of activating
and stimulating" (Wigberto Jiménez Moreno, quoted 1968a: 7). He
attracted students from the United States as well (cf. Troike 1969: 183, n. 1).
He lectured for brief periods at several Mexican and Latin American
institutions (e.g., Universidad de Nuevo León (1956), Universidad San Luis
Potosí (1958), Universidad Iberoamericana (1959–60), Universidad Central
de Venezuela (1959), Colegio de México (1964)), and in the 1960's he
began to be invited to teach in the United States, first at the Linguistic
Institute at the University of Washington (summer, 1962), then at Columbia
University (summer, 1964) and Syracuse University (fall, 1965). He was
also invited to teach in Canada at the University of Alberta (summer,
1966 and spring, 1967). In early 1965 Swadesh spent several months working
on lexicostatistic relations among West African languages while at the
Institute of African Studies in Ghana. With his usual energy and enthusiasm
he soon had a large group of colleagues assisting him. There followed travel
in Europe, with lectures at Hamburg, Berlin and Prague, and consultation
with colleagues and books in Paris, Tervuren, and elsewhere in further
pursuit of his studies of linguistic relations.

On July 20, 1967, while awaiting the arrival from the airport of Sapir's
youngest son, he died suddenly of a heart attack at his home in Mexico City.

His colleagues and students had been planning a volume on the occasion
of his sixtieth birthday, then two years away. A series in his honor has now
begun with the new edition of *La nueva filología* (1968c). Tributes at a
memorial meeting of the Sociedad de Alumnos de la Escuela Nacional de
Antropología e Historia (August 24, 1967) are to be included in a book in
the series, and the April 1969 issue (vol. 35, no. 2) of the *International Journal
of American Linguistics* was dedicated to his memory.

The Man and the Work

One can only speculate on what would have followed for Swadesh, for
linguistics, and for anthropology, if he had remained in or returned to the
United States and worked at an appropriate institution. To dwell on the
loss to linguistics and anthropology in the United States betrays a certain

ethnocentrism. Certainly there were economic and personal difficulties for Swadesh. Yet he can be seen as a student of Sapir who effectively broke the barrier of parochialism that characterizes the organization of American Indian linguistics in the United States. He was to become so fully a part of Mexican work that the writer of a preface to one of his books referred to the years from 1942 to 1956 as a temporary interruption.[34] In an elegy, the West Indian poet John Figueroa was to find himself quoting Mauricio in Spanish and using Spanish for the refrain.

It is coincidental but appropriate that Swadesh returned to Mexico and renewed involvement with its languages and their speakers just before the enlarged Joint Committee on American Native Languages, of which he was a member (1949–1956), was reduced to a few official representatives of organizations, and the journal that Boas had launched to contribute to the study of native poetry (among other things), was nudged onto another course. Increasingly, the concern of the journal became the relation of the study of American Indian languages, not to the study of the American Indian, but to the study of other languages, such as those of Oceania and Africa. Its unifying principle thus became a particular method of work, the field recording and analysis of little known languages, and the relation of a language to its culture was replaced by the relation of a linguist to his data.[35]

It is safe to say that such was not Swadesh's way of working. In the academy and in the field, he saw the work as collaborative, and the speakers of languages as his partners and ultimate beneficiaries. (One incident relates that a year after the Penutian survey, an old man in Florence, Oregon, spoke warmly of the good times he had with Swadesh during the few days they worked together). He could be commandeering and certainly was bold, yet always with a directness and simplicity based on confidence in sharing a worthwhile goal. Figueroa speaks justly in his poem of "Mauricio el suave." Though he was *engagé*, it is a striking fact that in the controversy over his linguistic work, disparaging remarks are to be found only in the writings of others. His work in glottochronology and lexicostatistics has to defend itself against claims it did not make, pretensions to which it did not pretend, arguments repeated after they had been answered, the turning of technical corrections into invented controversy (cf. Hymes 1969: 33, n. 12), and outraged denials that mathematics and statistics could have anything to do with language (cf. some of the comments on van der Merwe 1966).

34. "La labor del Dr. Swadesh se halla íntimamente ligada a México, donde ha permanecido, con breves períodos de ausencia, desde 1939" [The work of Dr. Swadesh has been intimately tied to Mexico, where he has permanently resided with brief periods of absence since 1939.].

35. The organized advisory board of IJAL has since been replaced by an ad hoc Conference on American Indian Languages, convened by an editorial board that continues to have no representative of the ethnology or folklore of the countries and languages where most American Indian languages are spoken today (Canada, Latin America), or indeed, of those who speak them.

Sometimes a note of bitterness would appear momentarily in private, but Swadesh invariably tried to see in what way another's work or approach could contribute to the general goal.

This indeed must sometimes have been unintentionally infuriating. Swadesh always acted as if there *were* a common goal; that if everyone would try his best, it could be reached; that details would be corrected later, and that all would come right in the end. The essential thing was to be working together as practically and efficiently as possible, getting the main lines clear. He saw himself as the patient secretary of a commune devoted to prehistory.

It was not the time for such a commune. It is accidental but significant that Swadesh returned to Mexico just before the work of Chomsky initiated a revolution within structural linguistics in the United States. In the early 1950's the achievements in structural phonology and morphology, and to some extent syntax, were sufficiently taken for granted that a number of extensions of linguistics and linguistic method were beginning to be revived and explored. In these years came the beginnings of paralinguistics and kinesics, of Greenberg's work on typology and universals, of kinship semantics (Goodenough, Lounsbury) and folk taxonomy (Conklin, Frake), and of linguistically inspired models for the analysis of social structure and myth (Lévi–Strauss). The initial interest and excitement attendant on lexicostatistics and glottochronology was part of a scene in which new discoveries and departures into spheres of general anthropological concern were quite expected.

The Chomskyan revolution displaced these trends, so far as the central participation of linguists was concerned. They remained alive and well in anthropology to varying degrees. Without judging the relative merit or importance of these trends, one can suggest an explanation for their differential success in the succeeding period. Lévi–Strauss's proposals for the analysis of social structure and myth have become central to the study of these two subjects. Kinship semantics and folk taxonomy have prospered. Transformational generative grammar itself can be placed in this category, for the data it required were in the heads of the linguists it inspired. In each case the initial impetus was a new approach to data already in hand or accessible. Where a new kind of data was required, success was slow or interrupted. Such has been the case in linguistics itself, where the sociolinguistic approach of Labov has had to win its way slowly because it depends on social and linguistic data from the community as well as on a linguist's introspection. Such was the case with paralinguistics and kinesics, because a continuing body of workers was not developed, and the initial specification of features did not progress to an independently usable method (or to an organized description of the relation of features to social meanings that others could use). A similar difficulty befell the work of Whorf, developed by Hoijer, and the work of Swadesh. The parallel is instructive.

WHORF AND SWADESH

Both Whorf's proposals as to the relation of language to habitual thought and Swadesh's proposals as to linguistic prehistory can elicit prejudgment and some of the passion reserved for heresy. Pointing out the fallacy of extreme positions is the stock in trade of many an introductory course, and "Whorf" and 'Swadesh" are sometimes used as tags in this way. Just as Whorf has been taken as having said that language wholly determines thought and world view and that language worlds are incommensurable, so Swadesh has been taken as having said that all of language changes at the same rate, that it is always at constant rate, and that lexicostatistics and glottochronology displace other methods. If the straw men attacked under these two names were collected, one would have fodder for all the cows in Kansas.

Both men pushed their insights and inferences as far as they could go. When these end-points are taken in isolation, it is easy enough to regard them as idiosyncratic, or impinging upon anthropology and linguistics from some other sphere. Original and inventive as both men were, however, their work grew naturally out of the tradition of Sapir. Their work is bold, but fledgling linguistics and Sapir were bold. In the post-war era the two men seemed unique perhaps because the climate of opinion in which they and their kind of boldness had developed had largely disappeared from view. Some of their statements or inferences taken in isolation appear extreme because the general experience from which they stem is not grasped; because their ideas require a supporting structure of work that has not been forthcoming; and perhaps because others are unwilling to draw the logical conclusions of what are in fact shared experiences and observations.

In Whorf's case, the observations are first of all that languages differ as they are used. In other aspects of life the instruments that are used are accepted as conditioning what is done, We see the relation of hand tools to what is made, and what can be made, at a given place and time, and we accept this dependence without concluding that a technology wholly determines a culture. For reasons apparently having to do with the history of philosophical and ideological debate in our culture, we resist the parallel that words and sentences are "mouth tools" conditioning what is done and thought, and what can be done and thought, at a given place and time. Yet if children growing up in a community are not in a position to substitute a different technology, neither are they in a position to substitute a different set of means for storing, reporting, and manipulating information. The differences among languages in vocabularies, grammatical categories, and grammatical relations are evidence that different communities have adapted their linguistic means to facilitate doing and thinking some things rather than others. New participants in a community (children) adopt and adapt to those means largely as given. Languages do change and adapt, shaped by the creative responses of their users. But the community's principal tool for handling information is necessarily functionally connected with the assumptions and activities of its way of life. This fact is perhaps hidden when one thinks in terms of a relation between "language" and "culture," if one understands by the terms a grammar abstracted from meanings and use and an ethnography abstracted from speech. Whorf worked to develop modes of semantic description and saw the need for a kind of description cutting across the usual categories of grammars, a description of "fashions of speaking" that represented the adaptive edge of a language's engagement in social life. His ideas came to the fore, however, after the Second World War, at a time when almost no semantic description was being done or contemplated—little has been done in the delineation of ways of speaking until the recent emergence of sociolinguistics.[36]

In the case of Swadesh, the development of his work depended upon meanings in a different respect. Recurrent patterns of semantic change and expressive symbolism became familiar to him as part of the "apperceptive mass" with which he assessed evidence (Cf. 1953a: 29, 1956: 30–32, 1960c: 139–140, 1962c, 1967c: 297–300 on "oblique cognates"). There was nothing in this to startle one familiar with the shapes and shifts of roots, stems, extensions and ablauts in the reconstructed etymons of the standard-bearer of comparative work, Indo-European. To workers coming from primary training in descriptive grammar, where segmentations, identifications, and patterns were evident and clearly present or absent, the flexibility required of prehistoric detective work could seem strange and rash. (Just so, Sapir's use of a sensibility trained in Indo-European detective work appeared "intuitive" and idiosyncratic to an earlier generation of Americanists conditioned to regard comparative grammer as a rigid machine from exposure only to its neatest examples.)

As evidence accumulated of lexical connections throughout both the Old and New World, Swadesh's conviction of the unity of the whole became firm. (Just such a conviction of the unity of the whole, stronger than conviction as to the specific affinities of particular parts, has been acquired by others who have explored connections of this scope and depth.) The main problem then came reasonably to be to work out the sub-classification; the alignments

36. Whorf has been further discussed with regard to the "First Yale School." Note that he contributed to all the tasks indentfied here. He developed a model of the structure of English phonemic distributions; his description of his own dialect of English was part of the discussion of English syllabics; he contributed to the development of concepts and methods for the description of gramatical categories and relationships; he sought to show others the value of support for linguistics; he worked with Hopi and Aztec with support from the Boas Committee on Native American Languages; he joined with Trager in reconstructing Uto-Aztecan-Tanoan and broaching wider relationships; and of course he sought to discover the relation between linguistic and cultural patterns, a quest in the anthropological climate of the time, where the notion of patterning and the relation of cultural patterns to personality (and personal experience) were major concerns. For an explication and socio-linguistic critique of the tradition developed by Whorf, see Hymes 1966: 114–123, 1957–8. For the prior development of such notions by Sapir, see Hymes, 1970.

within the whole. From the standpoint of those who were not yet persuaded of a particular relationship and who did not bring to the evidence the same world-wide "apperceptive mass," Swadesh's proposals could seem arbitrary. To those who felt that the near-to-hand must be wholly secure before one could explore at a deeper level, Swadesh's assumptions could be infuriating.

What was missing was the participation of many scholars in developing etymologies of a middle range. But just as Whorf's ideas seemed reduced to grammar versus behavior, so Swadesh's ideas seemed reduced to the statistics of a 100-item word list versus systematic sound correspondences. Some of the work of each could lend itself to such an interpretation. Yet the context of the whole clearly shows Whorf to have been concerned with language and culture together in a common historical matrix, and Swadesh to have been concerned with explorations by basic vocabulary as one line of evidence to be checked, corrected, and integrated with others. He said so many times. Because the fact has been so often overlooked, some of these statements, spanning his comparative work, are given here:

"Relationships are manifested in many facets of language. Percentage of common basic vocabulary is but one of many lines of evidence bearing on the problem. Morphologic and phonological isoglosses can be examined with profit. So too, specific vocabulary isoglosses—the distribution of specific words both native and borrowed." (1950a: 167)

"Lexicostatistic data must be coupled with other evidence, including that of archaeology, comparative ethnography, and linguistic paleontology. The separate lines of study serve to verify or correct one another and to fill in details of the story." (1952a: 453)

"All the time depths given here have to be regarded as provisional in greater or lesser degree. This follows, first, from the fact that the lexicostatistic method has not yet been developed to its maximum reliability (it cannot be until more research has been done on control cases): second, the test lists are much too limited in some cases; and finally the phonological formulas and structural reconstruction necessary for maximally reliable identification of cognates in each pair of languages has not been sufficiently worked out." (1954e: 36)

"Preliminary time-depth estimates have been made for all the language groups for which vocabularies are available. This serves to indicate which languages are closer to each other, to set the general scale of each grouping, and thereby to provide a frame of reference for phonological and other detailed analysis. More carefully drawn chronologies, which are possible after phonological and structural studies." (1955k: 377)

"Clues as to additional and apparently closer affinities of Zuni came about ten years ago from exploration by means of diagnostic wordlists. However, by now such study has been supported by various other tests." (1967c: 296)

The essential thing is to see Swadesh like Whorf, as someone who pioneered within a tradition, whose work has stood out for a time as a dramatic manifestation of that tradition, but whose own desire would be, not to be judged as having heroically (or foolishly) sprung forth full armed, but as having contributed to furthering that tradition and its goals, even in unpropitious times.

SWADESH'S PLACE IN THE TRADITION

Swadesh's effort was one that should have been sustained by substantial funds over a long period of time. As it was, he accomplished much by his own effort, energy and commitment. Many scholars have discussed the classification and prehistory of American Indian languages. Of Swadesh it may be said that his work showed him to be the most serious man among them, the one who, having accepted the goal, made it his life work.

Swadesh's contributions to the methodology and results of language classification remain controversial. This is not the place to discuss technical problems in detail. Let me say only that I have sometimes expressed reservations, but that I believe his work to be the most significant since that of Sapir for an understanding of the linguistic prehistory of the world, matched only by the contributions of Greenberg (with whose procedures Swadesh's work has much in common). Without detracting from the merit of Greenberg's work, it is historically revealing to compare the reception of the classifications of South American languages by the two men. The two classifications agree on the essential unity of the languages of the New World, differing on various internal groupings. Greenberg's classification was obtained with a list of 30 to 40 glosses, Swadesh's with a list of 100 glosses (both sometimes obtaining less information for a language than they wanted). Greenberg published the result without supporting data, backed essentially only by personal authority. Swadesh presented an explicit account of his procedures, endeavored to make the data available, and regularly revised his findings in the light of new evidence and research. The classification based on authority without supporting evidence has been reprinted often in anthropological textbooks and journals; the work presented as an explicit, continuing scientific enterprise has not.

To some extent the controversy attaching to Swadesh was a product of the style of the man and of his work. The anthropological audience for work in linguistic prehistory wants general classifications, but generally does not want to understand the data and procedures either as part of a general theory of cultural change and historical inference or as the result of a particular process of inference. It wants simple answers and definitive guide-lines. For Swadesh, the work was a continuing process in which the published results were not authoritative gestures, but progress reports inviting revision and collaboration. The linguistic audience often prefers to dispute details rather than consider the general thrust of the case, and to argue for the primacy of one line of evidence as against others (a habit that clouded understanding of Sapir's work until his approach was clarified by Swadesh [1961]). Proof of a single relationship is sometimes seen as the ultimate goal rather than as a means to other ends. More detailed reconstruction and inference, is gingerly postponed. Some want to work where the data is rich and provides many familiar types of problems—that is in relationships of little time depth—and avoid long-range comparison altogether. Some refuse to accept probabilistic inference, or set criteria of proof that exclude long-range relationships. Few besides Greenberg see the methodology of linguistic prehistory as itself a possible object of experimental inquiry, of basic research; many see the methodology as already fixed (since the nineteenth century perhaps). What was such an audience to make of a man who would sacrifice an occasional point of detail for the sake of a larger mass of evidence, a larger picture? Who considered all usable lines of evidence relevant? For whom a proof of genetic relationship was a means to an end? For whom the remotest past of language was in principle accessible? For whom the presumably long-established methodological foundations of linguistic prehistory were indeed a field requiring basic research?

To repeat an important point: some linguists have wanted to work as if each level of relationship had to be fully reconstructed before a deeper level of relationship could be broached, and as if the penetration of the linguistic past could be accomplished only in an additive, unidirectional, mechanical way. (The parallel to "phonology first" description is apparent.) I believe this approach to be demonstrably wrong. Certainly it was not the way of working of Sapir and Swadesh who moved back and forth between the immediate and the remote levels of prehistory, finding the two mutually illuminating. (Swadesh has pointed out that Sapir's correspondence with Berthold Laufer on the possibility of a Sino-Tibetan connection for Athapaskan is instructive on this score.) But it was just this strength (from the standpoint of discovering significant phenomena) that troubled and confused an audience wanting one neatly wrapped result at a time. An audience barely ready to consider evidence for a relationship between New World and Old World languages when the languages in question were geographically near each other (Eskimo and Chukchee) was not ready for glimpses of the interrelationship of geographically more distant languages of Asia and America. In fact, the editors of Swadesh's article on "Linguistic relations across Bering Strait" required him to omit these glimpses. While necessary in the circumstances, this omission deprived readers of a unique contribution.

When one understands Swadesh's work as that of a pioneer, an explorer of new terrain, one recognizes it as indispensable. Swadesh, like Sapir, was somewhat of an intellectual buccaneer. His work often troubled more cautious colleagues just because it could not be dismissed; it seemed to go too far, and yet it made substantive discoveries that could not be ignored or explained away, but had to be taken account of. There was just too much evidence that the paths he blazed did go somewhere, and that one would eventually have to follow them out. The lexical sets and morphological processes he uncovered as pertinent to world linguistic prehistory are indeed pertinent, even if, by linking both the Old and New Worlds, they go beyond what we are able to incorporate in ordinary classifications at the present time (1960i). These data demand explanation, and it is to Swadesh that we are indebted for their discovery and for the first steps toward answering the problems they pose.

Swadesh's work has often been criticized in terms of detail, such as the mistaking of the analysis of a suffix in Tsimshian in the course of showing a relationship between Tsimshian and Chinookan. I am concerned about Tsimshian and Chinookan, their relationship and their suffixes; they are languages on which part of my life has been spent. It is too much to expect many others to be concerned, unless some more general question is thereby illuminated. It is Swadesh's great merit that he made many American Indian languages assume world importance through their role in his studies. His work can be corrected on details, like the Tsimshian suffix, but in point of fact, Tsimshian and Chinook are related, as he said they were, in the light of all the evidence, much of which he assembled. Moreover, in relating the two languages he brought them into the context of general questions of method and of relationships that extend to the Mayan languages of Mexico and Guatamala and beyond.

Swadesh's methodological explorations have been much discussed in the extensive literature on lexicostatistics and glottochronology (cf. references and comments in Hymes [1964]). Here it can only be said that future generations will honor him as one who saw the possibility and necessity of transcending ad hoc controversy and partial views in linguistic prehistory by converting its assumptions into explicit parts of a basic science subject to empirical test. His studies of rates of change, rates of borrowing, lexical versus grammatical retention and borrowing, basic vocabulary, persistence of similarity in phonological shape, and the like were not radical innovations in subject matter, but radical only in proposing to treat explicitly and systematically what had usually been treated implicitly and incidentally. Swadesh's methodological explorations tended to be part of the study of a concrete problem. Just as he put structural linguistics to work in describing languages rather than concentrating on methodology itself, so he constantly put to work the existing state of knowledge of lexicostatistics and glottochronology in problems of actual relationship. Once something serviceable was developed, he used it as the best tool available rather than postponing substantive work until methodological problems were resolved.

In recent years mathematics adequate to the problems of lexicostatistics and glottochronology have been developed and applied (van der Merwe 1966, Sankoff 1971). The empirical foundations of the subject need now to be restudied on this basis as part of the general problem of persistence and rate of change in language, a problem which has many implications in addition to those of prehistoric dating. In the preponderance of cases, basic vocabulary is replaced at about the same rate and can be useful in historical studies (cf. Troike 1969). The 100-item test list has become a standard international instrument, known familiarly as the "Swadesh list." But Swadesh's most distinctive contribution inheres in his vision of linguistic prehistory as a whole. As he himself said of his conception of a world linguistic network, the whole is stronger than the parts. Working at frontiers of knowledge, he could not always be sure of details, and sometimes went too far and too fast for many of his colleagues to follow. He died before all could be woven together. Yet his explorations and the new dimensions he discovered have permanently extended our knowledge and conception of the contribution of linguistics to the understanding of the human past. Above all, Swadesh posed the true problem of linguistic prehistory in the context of an emerging world society. He saw that linguistic prehistory is ultimately justified by addressing itself to the problem of the unity of mankind.

References

ACLS
  Bulletin. Washington, D. C.
ACLS
  1963   Recipients of fellowships and grants, 1930–1962. A biographical directory. Washington, D. C.
Berlin, Brent
  1970   A Universalistic-Evolutionary Approach in Ethnographic Semantics. In *Current Directions in Anthropology*, 3–18. Ann Fisher, ed. (Bulletins of the American Anthropological Association, 3 (3), Part 2). Washington, D. C.
Bloch, Bernard
  1941   Phonemic Overlapping. *Am Sp* 16: 278–284. [In Joos 1957].
Bloomfield, Leonard
  1933   *Language.* New York. Holt.
  1942   Philosophical Aspects of Language. In *Studies in the History of Culture. The Disciplines of the Humanities.* 173–177. Menasha, Banta, for the ACLS.
Boas, Franz
  1911   Introduction. In *Handbook of American Indian languages, Part I.* (Bureau of American Ethnology Bulletin 40). Washington, D. C.
  1939   A report of the Committee on Research in American Native Languages. *ACLS Bull.* 29: 105–115.
  1947   Kwakiutl Grammar, with a Glossary of the Suffixes. Edited by Helene Yampolsky with the collaboration of Zellig S. Harris. *TAPS* 37, Part 3.
Carroll, John B. (ed.)
  1956   *Language, Thought and Reality. Selected Writings of Banjamin Lee Whorf.* Cambridge, M. I. T. Press.
Chomsky, Noam
  1965   *Aspects of the Theory of Syntax.* Cambridge, M. I. T. Press.
Darnell, Regna
  ms.   The Classification of American Indian Languages, 1879–1920. Paper read to the Linguistic Society of America, San Francisco, December 1969.

Embree, John F.
   1950   A Note on Ethnocentrism in Anthropology. *AA* 52: 430–432.
Freeman, John E. (compiler) and Murphy D. Smith (consultant)
   1966   A Guide to Manuscripts Relating to the American Indian in the Library
           of the American Philosophical Society. (*APS*, Memoir 65). Philadelphia,
           APS.
Greenberg, Joseph H.
   1953   Historical Linguistics and Unwritten Languages. In *Anthropology Today*.
           A. L. Kroeber et al. 265–286. Chicago, University of Chicago Press.
Gursky, Karl Heinz
   1969   Benjamin L. Whorf: the Uto-Aztecan Stock/Azteco-Tanoan/Macro-
           Penutian. (*Abhandlungen der Völkerkundlichen Arbeitsgemeinschaft*, 22). Nortorf,
           Germany.
Haas, Mary R.
   1968   The Last Words of Biloxi. *IJAL* 34: 77–84.
   1969   International Reconstruction of the Nootka-Nitinat Pronominal Suffixes.
           IJAL 35: 108–124.
Harris, Zellig S.
   1946   American Indian Linguistic Work and the Boas Collection. *APS-Y* (1945).
           96–100.
   1947   Developments in American Indian Linguistics. *APS Library Bulletin* (1946).
           84–97.
   1951   Review of Mandelbaum (ed.). 1949. *Lg.* 27: 288–333.
Haugen, Einar
   1951   Directions in Modern Linguistics. *Lg.* 27: 211–222. [In Joos 1957].
Hockett, C. F.
   1942   A System of Descriptive phonology. *Lg.* 18: 3–21. [In Joos 1957].
   1948   Potawatomi I. *IJAL* 14: 1–10.
   1967   The Yawelmani Basic Verb. *Lg.* 43: 208–222.
   1970   *A Leonard Bloomfield Anthology*. Bloomington, Indiana University Press.
Hoijer, Harry et al.
   1946   *Linguistic Structures of Native America*. (Vicking Fund Publication in Anthro-
           pology, 6). New York, Wenner-Gren Foundation for Anthropological
           Research.
Hymes, Dell
   1957   Some Penutian Elements and the Penutian Hypothesis. *SWJA* 13: 69–87.
   1960   Lexicostatistics So Far. *Current Anthropology* 1: 2–44.
   1963   Notes Toward a History of Linguistic Anthropology. *Anthropological
           Linguistics* 5(1): 59–103.
   1964   *Language in Culture and Society*. Dell Hymes, ed. New York, Harper and Row.
   1966   Two types of Linguistic Relativity. In *Sociolinguistics*. William Bright, ed.
           114–158. The Hague, Mouton.
   1968   Mauricio Swadesh. (1909–1967). *A de A* 5: 213–224.
   1970   Linguistic Method of Ethnography. In *Problems of Method in Linguistics*.
           Paul Garvin, ed. The Hague, Mouton.
Jacobs, Melville
   1931   A sketch of Northern Sahaptin Grammar. *University of Washington Publi-
           cations in Anthropology* 4(2): 85–292. Seattle, University of Washington
           Press.
Jacobsen, W. H.
   1969   Origin of the Nootka Pharyngeals. *IJAL* 35: 125–153.
Jiménez Moreno, Wigberto
   1968   Lección Inaugural, IV Simposio, Programa Interamericano de Lingüística

y Enseñanza de Idiomas, México, D. F. [Cited by Daniel Cazes, in Swadesh 1968a: 7].

Joos, Martin (ed.)
1957   *Readings in Linguistics. The Development of Descriptive Linguistics in America since 1925.* Washington, D. C. *ACLS.*
1967   Bernard Bloch. *Lg.* 43: 3–19.

Kroeber, A. L.
1939   An Outline of the History of American Indian Linguistics. *ACLS Bull.* 29: 116–120.

Lees, Robert B.
1953   The Basis of Glottochronology. *Lg.* 29: 113–127.

Levi-Strauss, Claude
1945   L'Analyse Structurale en Linguistique et Anthropologie. *Word* 1: 1–21.

Li An-Che
1937   Zuni: Some Observations and Queries. *AA* 39: 62–76.

Lydenberg, Harry Miller
1948   The Society's Program in American Linguistics and Archaeology: 1. American Linguistics. *PAPS* 92(2): 124–126.

Mandelbaum, David G. (ed.)
1949   *Selected Writings of Edward Sapir.* Berkeley and Los Angeles, University of California Press.

McQuown, Norman A.
1968   Morris Swadesh 1909–1967. *AA* 70: 755–756.

Newman, Stanley
1944   *The Yokuts Language of California.* (Viking Fund Publications in Anthropology, 2). New York, Wenner-Gren Foundation for Anthropological Research.
1967   Morris Swadesh. *Lg.* 48: 948–957.

Pike, Kenneth L.
1947a   On the Phonemic Status of English Dipthongs. *Lg.* 23: 151–159.
1947b   Grammatical Prerequisites to Phonemic Analysis. *Word* 3: 155–172.
1967   *Language in Relation to a Unified Theory of the Structure of Human behavior.* The Hague, Mouton.

Rendon, Juan José
1967   Mauricio Swadesh 1909–1967. *América Indigena* 27(4): 735–746.

Sankoff, David
1971   Lexicostatistics: Mathematical Bases. In *Current Trends in Linguistics* 11. T. A. Sebeok, ed. The Hague, Mouton.

Sapir, Edward
1911   Some Aspects of Nootka Language and Culture. *AA* 13: 15–28.
1921   *Language.* New York, Harcourt, Brace.
1922   The Takelma Language of Southern Oregon. In *Handbook of American Indian Languages* 2: 1–296. Franz Boas, ed. (Bureau of American Ethnology Bulletin 40). Washington, D. C., Government Printing Office.
1924   Culture, Genuine and Spurious. *American Journal of Sociology* 29: 401–429. [In Mandelbaum 1949].
1929a   The Status of Linguistics as a Science. *Lg.* 5: 207–214. [In Mandelbaum 1949].
1929b   Central and North American Languages. *Encyclopedia Britannica* 5: 138–141. [In Mandelbaum 1949].
1931a   Conceptual Categories in Primitive Languages. *Science* 74: 578. [In Hymes 1964].
1931b   The Concept of Phonetic Law as Tested in Primitive Languages by

Leonard Bloomfield. In *Methods in Social Science: A Case Book*. Stuart A. Rice, ed. 297–306. [In Mandelbaum 1949].

1933   La Réalité Psychologique des Phonèmes. *Journal de Psychologie Normale et Pathologique* 30: 247–265. [In Mandelbaum 1949].

Schlauch, Margaret

1946   Early Behaviorist Psychology and Contemporary Linguistics. *Word* 2: 25–36.

1947   Mechanism and Historical Materialism in Semantic Studies. *Science and Society* 11: 144–167.

Spier, Leslie, S. S. Newman, and A. 1. Hallowell (eds.)

1941   *Language, Culture, Personality. Essays in Memory of Edward Sapir*. Menasha, Banta. [Republished, Salt Lake City, University of Utah Press. 1960].

Sturtevant, Edgar H.

1950   Leonard Bloomfield. *APSY* 1949: 302–305.

Swadesh

All references to Swadesh are to the bibliography at the end of the book.

Trager, G. L. and Bernard Bloch

1941   The Syllabic Phonemes of English. *Lg.* 17:223–246.

Trager, G. L. and Henry Lee Smith, Jr.

1951   An Outline of English Structure (Studies in Linguistics, Occasional Papers, 3). Norman, Oklahoma.

Troike, Rudolph C.

1969   The Glottochronology of Six Turkic Languages. *IJAL* 35: 183–191.

Twaddell, W. Freeman

1935   On Defining the Phoneme. (Language Monograph 16). Baltimore. [In Joos 1957].

Van der Merwe, Nicholas

1966   New Mathematics for Glottochronology. *Current Anthropology* 7(4): 485–500.

Voegelin, Carl F.

1937   Shawnee Phonemes. *Lg.* 11: 23–37. [Voegelin has kindly sent me Sapir's letter of comment on his paper].

1949a   A Decade of American Indian Linguistic Studies. *PAPS* 93(2): 137–140.

1949b   Linguistic Without Meaning and Culture Without Words. *Word* 5: 36–42.

1950a   Magnetic Recording of American Indian Languages and the Relationship of This to Other Kinds of Memory. *PAPS* 94(3): 295–300.

1950b   A "Testing Frame" for Language and Culture. *AA* 52: 432–435.

1952   The Boas Plan for the Presentation of American Indian Languages. *PAPS* 96(4): 439–451.

Voegelin, C. F. and Zellig S. Harris

1951   Methods of Determining Intelligibility Among Dialects of Natural Languages. *PAPS* 95(3): 322–329.

Whorf, Benjamin Lee

1936a   A Linguistic Consideration of Thinking in Primitive Communities. In *Language, Thought and Reality: Selected Writings of Benjamin Lee Whorf*. John B. Carroll, ed. Cambridge, M. I. T. Press.

1936b   The Punctual and Segmental Aspects of Verbs in Hopi. *Lg.* 12: 127–131. [In Carroll 1956].

1938   Some Verbal Categories of Hopi. *Lg.* 14: 275–286. [In Carroll 1956].

Zipf, G. K.

1949   *Human Behavior and the Principle of Least Effort*. Cambridge, Addison-Wesley Press.

What Is Glottochronology?

The history of recent centuries is conserved in books and written documents. For the history of periods of time previous to the adoption of writing (usually called *prehistory*), we have to search by means of indirect methods that permit us to read, almost as though they were written in books, the traces of the past that are found hidden beneath the earth and conserved in some form in the living customs of diverse human groups. The techniques that have been developed for uncovering pregraphic history are already varied and are being expanded and improved little by little. Since 1949 these techniques have included lexicostatistic glottochronology. In spite of its impressive technical name, it is in essence basically simple. I shall try here to explain what it is, how it used, up to what point the validity of its findings have been established, its imperfections, and the possibilities for correcting its deficiencies and converting it into a precise instrument.

Some idea of what this prehistoric technique is comes to use from its name. Chronology, from Greek *kronos*, time and *logos*, concept, ought to be "the science of time," but in the study of history the term is generally used for the relationship in time of a series of events; in other words, the order in which things have happened. Glottochronology, formed from "chronology" prefixed by Greek *glotta*, language, is the sequence in which stages in the history of a language have appeared or the history of the separation of a language into local dialects, and the differentiation of these in a more or less gradual fashion into distinct languages. The glottochronological method with which I am dealing here is lexicostatistic because it is based on the counting of similar words among vocabularies of related languages, according to the following criterion: Under similar conditions, the lower the number of agreements, the longer the dialects have been separated. For

From Morris Swadesh, *Estudios sobre lengua y cultura* (Mexico City: Instituto Nacional de Antropología e Historia, 1960); translated by Joel Sherzer.

reasons· I shall discuss in a moment, this simple principle aids substantially in revealing the facts of prehistory.

Glottochronology exists only as part of the established science of comparative linguistics; it is a technique for rendering more exact the chronological indices obtained by this science. The utility of comparative linguistics to prehistorical research lies in the fact that it permits the reconstruction of earlier stages of languages and of the words that formed their vocabularies. Wherever we find people who speak the same language, we know that they belong to a single existing community, or that such a community existed not too long ago. For example, all the non-Iberian countries in which Spanish is spoken today have undergone strong influence from Spain in a recent period of history. If we can show by means of comparative linguistics that various peoples spoke a single language sometime in the past, although they now may have languages very different from each other, we can infer their previous identity or a very intimate and very extended ancient contact. Furthermore, if we are able to determine where and when this speech community existed, we have in hand some data essential for the reconstruction of prehistory and a base that, when taken together with other information (archeological, geological, and so on), aids us in the reconstruction of still more facts from the past. Finally, by means of the words that existed in the previous period, we can learn something about the objects and ideas that were known and possessed by the ancient community.

It may seem that the science that permits us to know where, when, and how languages now greatly transformed were previously spoken is magic; but it is easy to prove the contrary by taking an example well known from recent history. French, Spanish, Italian, Romanian, and some other languages are by no means identical today; yet in the many similarities of their vocabularies and inflections they reveal that some centuries ago they were indeed identical. Even if we did not have the documented history of Rome and Europe to confirm this statement, we would still be able to state it as a fact. Furthermore, from the present geographic distribution of the languages, taking into consideration their marked local variations in Europe and their relative uniformity in America, Africa, and so on, we would judge that their homeland must have been Europe, and probably southern Europe. By taking into consideration the degrees of differentiation among the various Romance languages, the experts in such matters can estimate the date of their separation. And finally, the study of cognates would indicate many details of the life of the ancient community. For example, a series of words like Spanish *harina*, French *farine*, Italian *farina*, Romanian *farina*, flour, varied in form but always recognizable as related, indicates that the use of cereal was already known in ancient times. Furthermore, the reconstruction of this and other words related to agriculture in the original vocabulary reinforces our belief that we are dealing with a temperate region.

At times phonetic changes go so far as to conceal the original identity of words. Among divergent languages that separated relatively recently, such as the Romance languages, most of the cognates are easily recognizable; they are only exceptionally as different as Spanish *hecho* and French *fait*, fact, which are derived from late Latin *factu*. Naturally, when dialects have been separated by many centuries, the difficulty of discovering cognates and proving common origin is increased. Nevertheless, more than a century ago a surprising discovery was made, which enabled the establishment of original identity even when there was an enormous divergence in the sounds of words. This was the so-called law of phonological regularity; that is, the fact that when a given sound in a language changes, it always tends to change in the same way in all words in which it is found or in all those in which it occurs in a similar phonetic context. The *ch* of Spanish corresponds to *it* of old French, frequently with total loss of the *t* in modern pronunciation when it occurs at the end of a word, not only in the case of *hecho = fait*, fact, but also in *noche = nuit*, night; *trucha = truit*, sow; *leche = lait*, milk; *techo = toit*, roof; *estrecho = étroit*, narrow; *pecho = poitrine*, chest; *conducto = conduit*, conduct; *producto = produit*, product; *bizcocho = biscuit*, biscuit; *dicho = dit*, said; *lecho = lit*, bed. Similarly, French initial *f* corresponds to silent *h* in Spanish orthography: *harina = farine*, flour; *hilo = fil*, thread; *hoja = feuille*, leaf; *haz = face*, face; *halcón = faucon*, falcon; *huir = fuir*, flee, *hembra = femme*, female; *hendir = fendre*, split; *hoyar = foyer*, hearth; *ahumar = fumer*, to smoke. (Spanish retains *f* in contact with certain sounds and it is also found in words borrowed directly from written Latin or from other languages.) The phonetic correspondence is established in certain words without difficulty—for example, *hendir = fendre*— and once established helps in the discovery of more concealed cognates, like *hecho = fait*. By use of this principle it is possible to prove the common origin of languages as divergent as Spanish, Hindi, Russian, and German; languages that separated at least forty-five centuries ago; and languages even more distantly related. In all of these cases, the discovery of the common origin of the languages indicates that the people who use them today once constituted a single community or at least had very intimate contact in prehistoric times.

Phonological regularity serves other purposes, equally important in the reconstruction of prehistory. For one thing, it distinguishes languages that actually had a common origin from those that only seem to be descended from a common ancestor because of the many casual similarities that are often discovered when languages are compared. For another, it enables us to recognize lexical borrowings—that is, words found in two languages whose similarity is not based on common origin, but rather on the fact that one language has taken them from the other. For example, we infer that *capitán* in Spanish is a borrowing of Italian *capitano* and not an ancient word inherited from Latin, since intervocalic *p* and *t* were in early times changed to *b* and *d*, with the loss, furthermore, of *i* in unaccented position, as in *caudillo*, chief (*cabdillo* in old Spanish), derived from *capitellu*; both words are formed from the same Latin root, *caput*, head. From this and other Italian loan words we have an indication of the superiority and influence that Italy once had over Spain in the area of military organization, among other things.

These examples should provide a general idea of what is involved in the science of comparative linguistics. The complete gamut of techniques, carefully applied, permits us to establish relationships among languages separated by thousands of years, to discover details of ancient culture, and to trace prehistoric contacts of various kinds.

Like all sciences, comparative linguistics continues to increase its knowledge and to refine its techniques. A decade ago, linguists lacked a simple method for estimating the time depth of relationships. They could determine only that related languages differed among themselves either a little or a lot, and that therefore they must have diverged a short or a long time ago. Some scholars dared to suggest, as a possible time of separation, an approximate number of centuries or millennia. Not only were these estimates only approximate; frequently different investigators gave very different dates for the same division, each evidently having his own preconceived criterion. But since 1949 we have had a technique that eliminates the personal factor almost completely.

The new method is based on the relatively constant rhythm of substitution in basic vocabulary, which I shall explain below. This principle, which seems as surprising as the law of phonetic change, has had the same fate as that "law" did in the last century: it has been greeted with considerable skepticism. A number of specialists have even presented arguments designed to show that it is impossible for the method to have any validity. But many others have become convinced by the results of studies already undertaken that it is effective and that it can be employed to produce important data in the fields of linguistic and cultural history.

I do not claim that lexicostatistic glottochronology is an instrument of great precision; I shall attempt only to show that it gives approximations that are useful in the difficult area of prehistory, a field that needs all the light we can shed upon it if we are ever to see it clearly. If competent investigators have noticed difficulties in the application of the method, it is because it does indeed present problems. If, on the other hand, others, equally capable, see real possibilities in it, it is because the method is based on real tendencies in language and because they believe the obstacles can be overcome, at least in part. Both the criticism and the approval of this technique derive from solid knowledge in linguistics. And now its application is lighting new paths and increasing scientific knowledge of the evolution of the primordial instrument of social communication, language.

The Lexical Chronometer

Lexicostatistic glottochronology resulted from an effort to find some index of time, however approximate; the degree of exactitude that it was going to achieve was not known. The initiators of the method knew, like all scientific linguists, that to a great degree the development of language is directed by social factors, including the adaptation of vocabulary to the level of culture and the tendency to assimilate the vocabularies, structures, and phonetics of neighboring languages; but they were also aware that certain aspects of language appear to be impermeable to cultural changes. They did not look for the desired index in phonological and structural changes, since these sometimes occur at a relatively rapid rate under the stimulus of neighboring languages, but at other times appear to come to a complete stop. Neither could they use the part of vocabulary that is called cultural—that is, words that signify products of human work, arts, customs, and other concepts intimately tied to the particular life of each human group—because such words can change with relative rapidity or resist modification almost indefinitely, according to the transformation or immobility that the culture is experiencing. Names of specific plants and animals also had to be avoided, because some are cultivated by man, and others, occurring in the natural environment, are subject to sudden change if the people move to a new region. Thus there remained only the vocabulary that is called "basic," or that of universal and simple things, qualities, and activities, which depend to the least degree possible on the particular environment and cultural state of the group. After all these things were taken into consideration, a "diagnostic" list was drawn up, consisting principally of pronouns, some quantitative concepts, parts and simple activities of the body, movements, and some general qualities of size, color, and so on. In addition to words of a cultural nature, words that in many languages are sound-imitative (onomatopoetic) were avoided, since this characteristic can impart to them an abnormal persistence; also avoided were terms with very specific meanings, because it would be difficult to identify their equivalents in other languages. The first research making use of the diagnostic list led to changes, the elimination of some elements and the substitution of others, and finally the selection of the hundred words that are listed on page 283.

Once the words for the diagnostic list were selected, it was still necessary to determine the maximum and minimum limits of the rhythm of lexical change in any language. In order to measure this rhythmical pattern, languages were sought which could be separated into two historically known periods many centuries apart, as for example the Latin of Plautus and the popular Spanish of today, the English of King Alfred and modern English, the classic Chinese of one thousand years ago and that spoken today.

Common and current equivalents of the elements on the diagnostic list were chosen for both the early and the late periods. Then a comparison of the two periods was made, the percentage of cognates was determined, and the relationship was established between this figure and the interval of time between the two epochs. Neither phonological changes nor modifications in the use of affixes were considered (for example, Latin *caput* or *capitem* and Spanish *cabeza* are treated as identical in spite of the change from *p* to *b* and the addition of the suffix).

At first it was expected that only a maximum rhythm of substitution would be found, but it was discovered that the percentage of retained cognates was almost proportional to the period of time involved. The historical cases that have been studied by means of the modified list have a maximum retention of 90 percent after a thousand years, a minimum of 81 percent, and an average of 86 percent. This final figure serves as the index of retention in the calculation of glottochronological dates.

Though the fluctuation in the percentage of retention cannot be disregarded, we have to attach great importance to the limits of the variation. If no rule were involved in the changes, we would have found languages that had totally replaced their vocabularies and others that had not changed a single element. The existence of a limited range of variation provides a basis for measuring time, at least approximately. In order to take advantage of this knowledge in making glottochronological measurements, we have to consider the relationship between lineal change and parallel differentiation among dialects that are separated. In the latter case the actual difference is the product of the changes undergone by each since their separation. The changes that have occurred in one will not have been extended to the other; that is, each will have had a separate and divergent development. The effect of lexical changes in the two lines is equal to that which would be produced by twice as much time in one. The common residue can be calculated by multiplying the two individual residues. For example, if each language has retained 80 percent of the original vocabulary, then, if they have developed entirely without mutual contact, 80 percent of 80 percent of their words will be cognates, or 64 percent. If they have had partial contact, this will have caused some additional agreements, including the retention of some of the same original elements and the introduction of some of the same new words. Partial contact can thus cause, in the example of 80 percent retention in each line, a correspondence of more than 64 percent, with the possibility of 100 percent if the separation has been very small.

This lexical chronometer is applied to languages whose common origin has been proved. The percentage of cognates in the diagnostic list is determined, and this figure is translated into minimum centuries of divergence, by means of a mathematical equation or by using a table of conversion. Here is part of the table (the full table appears at the end of the article):

Percentage of cognates

	70%	69%	68%	67%	66%	65%	64%	63%	62%	61%	60%
Minimum centuries of divergence	11·8	12·3	12·8	13·3	13·8	14·3	14·9	15·3	15·8	16·4	16·9

In order to give a concrete example of the application of the technique, I shall take two of the most divergent dialects of Nahuatl: the Nahuatl of Pochutla, on the Pacific coast, and that of Milpa Alta, near Mexico City. Cognates in these two dialects represent 69 percent of their basic vocabularies, thus indicating a minimum separation of 12.3 centuries.

The Order of Relationship

It is customary to speak of linguistic relationship and even of mother, daughter, and sister languages; but we must remember that these expressions are figurative and that the descent of languages has no similarity to kinship among persons. Latin did not give birth to French, Spanish, Italian, and Romanian; rather, the latter are modern forms of the former which have undergone gradual changes from generation to generation. No abrupt transformation has ever intervened between the Latin of antiquity and the Spanish spoken today; rather, grandparents and grandchildren have continued to understand one another without realizing the slow and constant transition of their language. Similarly, languages called sisters are merely parallel developments of the same original language which have diverged from one another because of a lack of mutual contact. And as I have pointed out, a partial contact diminishes the rate of differentiation among dialects. This circumstance gives rise to the phenomena of stepwise divergences, of great importance for the reconstruction of prehistory in all cases in which there are three or more languages belonging to a single genetic group.

If three dialects or languages are equally diverged from one another, we infer that they have developed under the same conditions of contact or separation. If two of them are more closely linked than either of them is with the third, we conclude that they have had more intimate contact or that they formed a single dialect at the moment of separation from the third. If one of the variants represents a type intermediate between the other two, this indicates to us that the three developed in a chain, the first dialect touching the second and the second the third, wihout any direct relations between the first and the third. These distinct types of relationship that I have explained with reference to three dialects become even more complicated when we are dealing with four, five, or more linguistic variants. Often the divergence picture is related to the geographic positioning of the languages. In cases in which the information provided by geography and lexicostatistics seems contradictory, we conclude that the original distribution must have been different from the present one. Furthermore, according to the gradual or abrupt nature of the interdialectal gradations, we can judge if the separations came early or late in the history of the group. And finally, if there are many well-differentiated divisions of a linguistic group in a geographic area and a few others spread through other regions, it is almost certain that the area of greater differentiation is the oldest.

In part this kind of reconstruction of prehistory can be carried out on the basis of phonological and structural traits; we search for greater or fewer similarities and draw the corresponding conclusions. But there is not always a sufficient number and variety of conveniently differentiated traits to permit the completion of the analysis of the order of relationship. Lexicostatistics, on the other hand, can be applied in all cases. Whenever it is possible, both types of analysis ought to be used, so that their results can be compared and it can be seen to what degree they are in agreement.

The study of a group of linguistic divergences has an additional validity. As I have already indicated, the divergence between two languages provides a time of minimal separation, but it says nothing about the total time. On the other hand, in a total network of divergences, we know that the greatest has to be closest to reality. There is a situation in which we have an index of the total time. Suppose that we have a series of languages in a chain in which A is separated from B by five minimum centuries, from C by six, from D by seven, and from E, F, G, and so on, by eight; that is, the stepwise divergence reaches a maximum that it does not exceed even with an increase in geographic distance. In this case, we can conclude that eight centuries represents the complete period from the time of the first separation.

The Dating of Cultural Reconstruction

I have spoken of the possibility of learning about the prehistoric culture of a group of people by means of cognates that are found in two or more languages derived from a common source. Data that are reconstructed in this manner are worth much more if we can date the common period. In the case of a chain of divergences, agreements are more significant if they come from languages that are not adjacent in the chain, since this tends to indicate that the agreements occur because of an ancient common trait and not because of a trait that might have passed from one group of people to a neighboring one in recent times. Phonology, as I have already indicated, also aids in distinguishing loan words from ancient retentions.

A special advantage of the dating of cultural reconstruction is that it permits us to compare linguistic findings with those of archeology. That is, if we have knowledge of a cultural complex dated glottochronologically together with its details based on actual cognates, we can look for an archeological site that has been calculated by archeological methods to belong to the same period and culture, and compare the artifacts found there with what we have learned from the language. Thus linguistics and archeology can mutually confirm and complete one another.

TOWARD GREATER ACCURACY IN DATING

One important result of the introduction of the lexicostatistical technique has been the radical growth in the number of dates that linguists have calculated. Before this technique was devised, scholars only rarely dared to estimate the time depth of linguistic relationships. In the main they were satisfied to qualify relationships as close or distant. The difficulty of judging the degree of divergence frequently discouraged them from attempting to do so. The new technique, on the other hand, so greatly facilitates calculation that it is possible to perform many calculations of this sort quite easily. This provides many opportunities for finding parallels between linguistic and archeological dates and for testing each one. The effect cannot fail to be beneficial for both comparative linguistics and the study of prehistory.

Before the appearance of lexicostatistical glottochronology, linguistic relationships were fairly ambiguous. Anthropologists knew, for example, that Huastec was related to Yucatec, and Chocho to Popoloca; but only a rare expert knew that the relationship is very close in the latter case and somewhat distant in the former. Now it is easy to measure the distance and establish a divergence of thirty-one minimum centuries between Huastec and Yucatec, while Chocho and Popoloca can be shown to be only eight centuries apart.

Another mistake that lexicostatistics helps to eliminate is the genealogical or family tree. According to the principles of comparative linguistics, linguistic relationships are presented in the form of successive separations from the protolanguage, with divisions, subdivisions, and even minor fractions. More recently linguists realized that normal development is in the form of stepwise dialects, with resulting chains and nets of relationship. But they lacked adequate techniques to establish the gradation, and therefore linguists continued to use the concepts of the family tree. Lexicostatistics now offers a means of measuring degrees of divergence and of establishing chains of relationship.

Remote Relationships

The technique of the diagnostic vocabulary, which was developed as an instrument of glottochronological measurement, has come to have other uses, above all some related to problems of remote relationship.

The possibility of establishing relationships among groups geographically or linguistically distant has always and quite correctly been a goal pursued by linguists. Some of the theories that have been offered in this connection are without doubt inspired and some worthless, but it is difficult to judge them. It has therefore become the fashion among scholars to make light of any hypothesis that is not presented complete with superabundant proof of cognates, inflective agreements, and so on. This attitude is unfortunate because it is not possible for languages remotely related to show a great many agreements, since the differences between them resulted from a long period of separation; nevertheless, comparisons of such languages are not beyond the scope of science. Furthermore, data from remote periods often illuminate more recent ones.

The lexicostatistic solution is to determine mathematically the greatest percentage of lexical similarities that can be produced by pure chance, given the number of consonants and vowels and the complexity of roots in the languages that are being studied. If the agreements found exceed by a sufficiently large margin the maximum figure attributable to chance, we can accept the probability that a relationship exists.

It is also possible to use lexicostatistics as an instrument of exploration. A diagnostic list is obtained for a series of languages whose linguistic classification is unknown. Provisional calculations of possible cognates are quickly made for each pair of these languages in order to learn where a more detailed study is likely to be fruitful. In such explorations chains of relationship are often discovered which facilitate enormously the establishment of remote relationships.

Limitations of Lexicostatistic Glottochronology

Up to now I have been discussing the possibilities of lexicostatistic glottochronology. Its limitations remain to be considered, as well as precautions that must be taken in its use.

1. Often the data necessary for the correct completion of the diagnostic list of a language are lacking. If possible, the words ought to be obtained from a linguist who is a specialist in the language. When only a mediocre dictionary is available, the investigator should study the words with much care and recognize that he may make some mistakes in selecting terms. If a fairly large portion of the hundred words cannot be supplied, the validity of the results will of course be diminished.

2. Even an expert in a language at times finds it difficult to determine the equivalents of the needed words because of the differences in meaning that exist from language to language. Such problems are resolved by adopting uniform criteria for all languages that are being compared. Some critics claim that semantic difficulties destroy the utility of the method; others feel that this criticism is exaggerated. Investigations in this area are needed to determine to what degree such problems limit the accuracy of glottochronological measurement.

3. In identifying cognates, we do not always have adequate knowledge of the phonology and structural characteristics of the languages with which we are dealing. The degree to which this affects the count fluctuates according to the obvious or complex nature of the facts in each pair of languages. Generally the comparison of very divergent languages is difficult, because of the accumulation of phonological and structural changes. All calculations made with insufficient data must be considered provisional.

4. When glottochronological measurement is applied to great divergences, it encounters such problems as low percentages of cognates and the subtle differences that mark long periods of time. For example, after seventy centuries of divergence only 12 percent of cognates remain, and the re-

duction of one cognate in the list is equivalent to about three centuries. In such circumstances a slight error in the identification of cognates has a very serious effect on the accuracy of the calculations.

5. The index of retention that is currently employed was determined on the basis of very few historical cases. Much additional research is needed in order to improve the statistical basis of the calculations. When this has been done, it will be possible to refine the technique. Some critics of glottochronology point to the possibility that more extensive inquiry will perhaps show still greater variation between the maximum and minimum limits of retention, which could destroy confidence in the method. But defenders and critics alike agree that more research is needed. As more and more experts in various languages have become interested in glottochronology, more and more research has been undertaken. So far, additional studies have confirmed the basis of glottochronology; but there are certain rare extraordinary cases in which exceptionally intimate contact between two groups can produce a radical change within a few generations. A great number of cases in which a radical transformation might be expected follow the normal rhythm; true exceptions occur only in very rare situations, such as the transformation of the aboriginal language of Santo Domingo when invading Caribs exterminated the Arawak men and remained with the wives of their victims.

6. Lexicostatistic glottochronology has been criticized for the disparity between the maximum and minimum limits of the range of retention, with the claim that after many centuries the error can reach enormous proportions. This danger seems exaggerated, since the periods of accelerated and retarded change probably cancel one another.

7. It has been objected that a diagnostic list of one hundred elements is very short for a statistical method, and that it ought to be much longer in order to avoid the effect of chance. This criticism has certain merit, above all when we are dealing with large divergences; but there is no point in extending the list if one cannot be sure of the quality of the elements. It is not easy to find words that are completely satisfactory, and this is the factor that up to now has impeded amplification of the list. If the list is changed, it will be necessary to investigate again the persistence of elements and to establish a new index of retention.

8. The diagnostic vocabulary is as noncultural as possible. The criticism has been put forth that completely noncultural words do not exist, and that there is variation in the implications or connotations of a term. For example, one can observe that such elements as *sun*, *moon*, and *fire* are not always only natural objects; at times they bear a relationship to deities. *Heart*, *eye*, and *hand* are not always merely parts of the body; they can at the same time signify such concepts as soul, understanding, and strength. These facts, however, do not destroy the usefulness of the method. Its usefulness is preserved by the employment of a hundred words rather than only a few.

If special influences affect one part of the list during some centuries, they do not completely alter the rhythm of change.

9. It has been established that not all the elements that form the diagnostic list have equal persistence. Certain elements tend to be lost sooner than others. After the disappearance of the less persistent words, there will remain a list of words with greater overall persistence than those that made up the original list, with the consequence that our estimate of the time periods involved in distant relationships may be too low. More research is needed before the influence of this factor can be determined.

Some of these deficiencies in the glottochronological technique may be overcome by future research and modifications; but others may remain. While efforts are under way to improve it in every way possible, the glotto-chronological method can continue to be used in order to obtain approximate measurements. These will have provisional utility in the study of prehistory and at the same time will contribute to the perfecting of the method.

Why?

We cannot discuss such phenomena as phonological regularity and constant rhythm in lexical change without asking ourselves what the cause might be. It is even more urgent for the scholar to understand the why of facts in order to guide his research. In the case under discussion, I believe I can provide a general explanation, but I shall not attempt to do so in strictly scientific form; such a task is better left to the experts in psychological and cultural theory.

The regularity of phonological changes seems to be related principally to the manner in which the mind and the senses work. The words of a language are composed of a limited number of basic sounds or phonemes, and each one is unconsciously perceived and formed as a unit by those who use the language. If there is modification, it has to be regular in all the words in which the phoneme appears. This phenomenon is both individual and social. In addition to being a human tendency, the consistent treatment of phonemes is demanded by the necessity of being understood by other members of the society.

The rhythm of change in vocabulary is related to the nature of language and its social function. Since words are only symbols, they do not need to have a particular phonetic form in order to perform their function: we can as well call a certain substance *water* or *agua* (as in Spanish) or *pani* (as in Hindi), as long as the entire community does the same. The symbols are therefore free to change and to replace one another as long as the modification is not sudden. Thus English *water* uses the same root as Spanish *sudor* (sweat), and Hindi *pani* has the same root as *potion* (that which is drunk). At the same time, Spanish *agua* is cognate to German *Aue*, which means "brook" or "rivulet." These differences reflect the possibilities of lexical substitution in language, the process we measure in glottochronology.

By limiting ourselves to "basic" vocabulary, we remain in the area of vocabulary that normally does not feel any pressure to change or to resist change. Nevertheless, it seems that if one of the elements is replaced, this prevents the same thing from happening to others at the same time. The necessity of maintaining communication between generations is probably the factor that prevents the rapid accumulation of changes in the basic vocabulary.

It is interesting to observe certain analogies between lexical substitution and the phenomenon of radioactivity: physicists can calculate the average time for the loss of an electron, but cannot predict when an electron will be lost from any particular atom. Of the millions of atoms that constitute a tiny piece of a substance, some will lose an electron immediately and others will wait an eternity. Of the hundred words on the lexicostatistic diagnostic list, we can say that one of them, without knowing which, will be replaced by another root within approximately seventy years, while others will remain for thousands of years. What is constant in radioactivity and determines its average rhythm is the balance of forces that tend to keep the electron within its atom and those that tend to remove it. What is constant in lexical substitution is the balance between the forces that maintain uniformity and those that encourage fluctuation.

Table A.1.   Basic Vocabulary List

1.	I	26.	root	51.	breasts	76.	rain
2.	you	27.	bark	52.	heart	77.	stone
3.	We	28.	skin	53.	liver	78.	sand
4.	this	29.	flesh	54.	drink	79.	earth
5.	that	30.	blood	55.	eat	80.	cloud
6.	who	31.	bone	56.	bite	81.	smoke
7.	what	32.	grease	57.	see	82.	fire
8.	not	33.	egg	58.	hear	83.	ash
9.	all	34.	horn	59.	know	84.	burn
10.	many	35.	tail	60.	sleep	85.	path
11.	one	36.	feather	61.	die	86.	mountain
12.	two	37.	hair	62.	kill	87.	red
13.	big	38.	head	63.	swim	88.	green
14.	long	39.	ear	64.	fly	89.	yellow
15.	small	40.	eye	65.	walk	90.	white
16.	woman	41.	nose	66.	come	91.	black
17.	man	42.	mouth	67.	lie	92.	night
18.	person	43.	tooth	68.	sit	93.	hot
19.	fish	44.	tongue	69.	stand	94.	cold
20.	bird	45.	claw	70.	give	95.	full
21.	dog	46.	foot	71.	say	96.	new
22.	louse	47.	knee	72.	sun	97.	good
23.	tree	48.	hand	73.	moon	98.	round
24.	seed	49.	belly	74.	star	99.	dry
25.	leaf	50.	neck	75.	water	100.	name

Table A.2.   The Conversion of Percentages of Cognates on Two Diagnostic Lists into Minimum Centuries

C	MC	C	MC	C	MC	C	MC	C	MC
100	0.0	80	7.4	60	16.9	40	30.3	20	56.6[b]
99	0.3	79	7.8	59	17.5	39	31.2	19	60.0[b]
98	0.7	78	8.2	58	18.0	38	32.1	18	63.6[b]
97	1.0	77	8.6	57	18.6	37	33.0	17	67.4[b]
96	1.4	76	9.1	56	19.2	36	33.8	16	71.4[b]
95	1.7	75	9.5	55	19.8	35	34.8	15	75.6[b]
94	2.1	74	10.0	54	20.4	34	35.7	14	80.2[b]
93	2.4	73	10.4	53	21.0	33	36.7	13	85.2[b]
92	2.7	72	10.9	52	21.7	32	37.7	12	90.4[b]
91	3.1	71	11.3	51	22.3	31	38.8	11	96.2[b]
90	3.5	70	11.8	50	22.9	30	39.9	10	102.6[b]
89	3.9	69	12.3	49	23.6	29	41.0	9	109.4[b]
88	4.2	68	12.8	48	24.3	28	42.2	8	117.2[b]
87	4.6	67	13.3	47	25.0	27	43.3	7	126.2[b]
86	5.0	66	13.8	46	25.7	26	44.6	6	136.4[b]
85	5.4	65	14.3	45	26.5	25	45.9	5	148.4[b]
84	5.8	64	14.9	44	27.2	24	47.3	4	163.2[b]
83	6.1	63	15.3	43	27.9	23	48.7	3	182.2[b]
82	6.6	62	15.8	42	28.7	22	50.2[b]	2	209.2[b]
81	7.0	61	16.4	41	29.5	21	53.4[b]	1	255.0[b]

C = Percentages of cognates.
MC = Minimum centuries.

[a] According to the formula $10MC = \dfrac{2 \log r}{\log C}$.

[b] This table has been calculated on the basis of the index of retention $r = 0.86$, which corresponds to that of the diagnostic list of one hundred words proposed by Morris Swadesh in "Towards Greater Accuracy in Lexicostatistic Dating," *International Journal of American Linguistics*, 21 (1955). A correction (2t–50) has been applied to the figures from 50.2 to 255 in order to avoid as far as possible a distortion that is implicit in the method when dealing with very large time periods. The very low percentages have been included in order to complete the table; if there is any possibility of working with quantities less than, say, 8 per cent, it will be only when the phonological and etymological analysis of the body of material being investigated is very precise.

The Mesh Principle in Comparative Linguistics

The phenomena of dialect intergradation and their reflection in varying degrees of similarity among the languages of a genetic group were pointed out by Schuchardt and Schmidt almost ninety years ago.[1] Since then the idea of a chain or mesh of relationships has frequently been mentioned in discussions of general linguistic theory and has occasionally been used to elucidate the nature of specific genetic relationships. Sapir frequently observed, like Schuchardt and Schmidt on the basis of an estimate of the sum total of likenesses and differences, that a given language was intermediate between two others, for example Eyak with reference to Tlingit and Athapaskan. In several studies of California languages by Kroeber and others in the early years of this century, we find the practice of counting the number of cognates found between pairs of languages or dialects in order to establish the order of relationship among the members of a group, and of representing the degrees of affinity in two-dimensional diagrams.[2] Later, statistics of phonologic, structural, and lexical items combined were used to obtain an index of degrees of affinities,[3] and in recent years lexicostatistics has taken us back to cognate counting. However, unquestionably the bulk of comparative studies up to the present make no mention of stepwise relationships, or even at times include remarks which suggest that the

Reprinted from *Anthropological Linguistics*, 1, no. 2 (1959): 7–14.

1. Hugo Schuchardt, *Über die Klassifikation der romanischen Mundarten* (Graz, 1900, but first presented orally in 1870); Johannes Schmidt, *Die Verwandschaftsverhältnisse der indo-germanischen Sprachen* (Weimar, 1872). Hermann Paul (*Prinzipien der Sprachgeschichte*, 4th ed. [Halle, 1920], p. 43) comments, "The figure of a stem chart [*Stammtafel*], with which they used to try to show the relationships, is always inaccurate. . . . If the outstanding criteria are really chosen, then perhaps one cannot deny all practical value to such a chart as a visualization, but one must not imagine that a really exhaustive and exact presentation of the relationships is thereby given."

2. For example, Alfred L. Kroeber, "The Yokuts Language of South Central California," *University of California Publications in American Archaeology and Ethnology*, 2 (1907) 169–377, and Samuel A. Barrett, "The Ethno-Geography of the Pomo Indians," *ibid.*, 6 (1908): 1–332.

3. See, for example, Alfred L. Kroeber and C. Douglas Chrétien, "Quantitative Classification of Indo-European Languages," *Language*, 13 (1937): 83–103; also references cited therein.

failure to apply the mesh principle seems to stem from the notion that it is a author considers the differences to have resulted from a series of relatively sharp splits. Only in the case of one or another self-made comparativist can one suspect ignorance of the theory of dialect gradation. In general the failure to apply the mesh principle seems to stem from the notion that it is a theoretic nicety that can be dispensed with in practice and from the belief that the results of reconstruction are pretty much the same either way. It is my purpose here to consider respects in which the explicit recognition of the mesh principle may modify and perhaps notably improve comparative linguistics.

The Use of Intermediate Links

From time to time scholars find themselves confronted with evidence which seems to point in two contradictory directions. A notable case is that of Yuki,[4] which Kroeber showed to have similarities with both Hokan and Penutian. Since then discussion has turned on whether it belonged to one or the other. A few years ago I took sides in the controversy when I found a number of concrete cognates linking Yukian particularly with certain languages of the Hokan complex. Just lately, William Shipley has published a number of good comparisons on the Penutian side, and now the case becomes even more complicated as we note such agreements as the following of Yukian with Ritwan and Algonkian: Wappo and Yuki *naw*-, Yurok and reconstructed Proto-Algonkian **new*, to see (incidentally, note also Arawakan *énawi*, Quechua *ñawi*, Mixtecan *énuu*, Zapotecan *élawa*, Esmeralda -*lo*, eye); Wappo *pol* and Yurok *pontet*, dust, ashes; Yuki *liy*- and Wiyot -*riiy*-, kill; Yuki *na-mlat* (from *énan-pla-t*, mouth-leaf) and Yurok -*hipl*, tongue; Yuki *noon* (Wappo *nano*) and Wiyot -*lul*, mouth; Yuki *k'i*, this, Wappo *k'ewi* and Wiyot *gowi?*, man. If it should develop that Yuki is simply an intermediate language, rising out of an in-between dialect of long ago, the mystery will be resolved with the recognition that Penutian and Hokan and even Ritwan and Algonkian are all related to each other. Instead of being a bone of contention, Yuki may prove to be a link serving to reveal a relationship that even Sapir did not suspect.

Similarly, Shafer observes[5] that there are points of contact between Nadene and Sino-Tibetan, and others but usually different ones between the latter and the Thai languages. He therefore wonders if Sino-Tibetan might not have arisen as a mixed language with elements taken from the other two entities. In attempting to solve this question, the possibility should also be considered of an old dialect chain in which the earlier forms of Thai and Nadene stood on opposite sides of Sino-Tibetan, possibly with

    4. See William Shipley, "Some Yukian Penutian Lexical Resemblances," *International Journal of American Linguistics*, 23 (1957): 269–74.
    5. Robert Shafer, "Classification of the Sino-Tibetan Languages," *Word*, 11 (1955): 110–11.

still other intermediate links in each case. Possibly it is only remoteness in time and the intervening linguistic differentiation which obscure the similarity which once existed between earlier stages of Thai and Nadene.

Another striking failure to recognize the mesh principle in the face of concrete evidence of its effect is expressed by Hale in his lexicostatistic study of Uto-Aztecan: "A . . . disturbing problem occurs . . . when a group of languages exhibits dates [he is actually dealing not with dates as such but with minimum centuries of divergence] which are consistently out of line. A basic assumption dictates that two closely related languages . . . must be equidistant in time from a language . . . which is more distant in time from each . . . than the latter are from each other."[6]

It is interesting to recall that Goddard[7] doubted Sapir's evidence for the relatedness of Tlingit and Athapaskan. Now, with the publication of Eyak material,[8] it becomes fairly self-evident that this language is closely related to Athapaskan, and one also notes more frequent similarities with Tlingit than for any ordinary language. Thus we see that intermediate links can serve to clarify broad relationships, opening the possibility of establishing with certainty what would otherwise go unnoticed or be left in doubt.

Needless to say, word borrowing and structural diffusion may be the cause of some of the cases of similarities found in more than one direction, and it depends on the discovery of certain kinds and quantities of evidence, in keeping with the usual criteria of proof in comparative linguistics, to determine whether genetic unity is involved.

Finding and Proving Affinity

The explicit recognition of the mesh principle in linguistic relationships can be of tremendous help in determining and demonstrating the placement of isolated languages and linguistic groups. Without it, this problem can be approached only if one starts with a definite theory of possible connections, perhaps arising out of knowledge of archeology or geographic probabilities, or the accidental discovery of one or more striking similarities in structure or vocabulary. Once one has a hypothesis, one can study a pair of languages or language groups in relation to each other to find if there are indeed enough systematic similarities to justify the supposition of common origin, but a thorough search for linguistic congeners is virtually impossible because there are hundreds of languages in each hemisphere and thousands in the

6. Kenneth Hale, "Internal Diversity in Uto-Aztecan," *International Journal of American Linguistics*, 24 (1958): 101–7.

7. Pliny E. Goddard, "Has Tlingit a Genetic Relation to Athapascan?", *ibid.*, 1 (1920): 266–79.

8. Fang-kuei Li, "A Type of Noun Formation in Athabaskan and Eyak," *ibid.*, 22 (1956): 45–48.

world as a whole. However, once we have established extensive networks of related languages connected with each other in a definite order of relative affinities, expressible, for example, in a two-dimensional diagram, it is possible to test each new language, as yet unplaced, at scattered points in the constellation to find where it comes the nearest to fitting. In that section or sections of the complex, one searches an increased sample of points to narrow the placement, until finally he can either establish a good fit within the complex or, if the evidence is weak, tentatively reject the possibility.

In my recent experience with South American languages, it has been possible to place, with what appears to be quite strong evidence of accuracy, a number of hitherto isolated languages and language groupings. Even if only a part of the apparent relationships should eventually work out in the light of intensive study, the procedure will have been very fruitful. Moreover, the proof no longer depends merely on the similarities found between two linguistic entities, but now can be based on multilateral connections with a cluster of languages found in a portion of the total constellation. That is to say, it becomes a requirement of proof that the language under study has apparent cognates not with just one language or linguistic group in the network but also with other languages known to be related to the first. This multiplies many times the guarantees against the false illusion of similarity based on chance convergence. For example, using a test vocabulary and the lexicostatistic technique, suppose the unplaced language is found to have seventeen cognates out of a hundred with one language; we expect to find a similar percentage relative to other languages of the same family, if it is a relatively narrow grouping, or no less than about 12 percent if the group is considerably divergent within itself. Likewise, we expect at least about 8 or 10 percent of agreement with languages of the groups next in line in each direction. If these conditions are not met, we suspect the apparent relationship; if they are, we tend to rely on our results.

In the first approximation of placement by this method, we sometimes use what has been called the inspection method; that is, we count apparent cognates despite relative ignorance of phonetic laws and the specific etymology of the elements on each side of the equation. As we continue our research, however, we concentrate more and more on the scientific testing of each relationship by the established criteria of phonologic consistency and on agreement with the internal evidence for the etymology of each element.

The great possibilities of this method of work are suggested by the fact that we have, in about four years of systematic study, succeeded in placing in one scheme almost all the language groups and isolated languages of America and several belonging to Eurasia. Certainly some parts of the scheme, based on insufficient material, will not hold up, but there have already been instances of independent corroboration by other scholars bearing out our findings. For example, a lexicostatistic inspection of Muskogi and Shawnee made in 1955 showed positive results, giving in a preliminary way the same conclusion as that arrived at separately by Haas.[9]

Rounding Out Comparisons

The proof of common origin and the phonologic, structural, and lexical reconstruction of the older periods of language are operations which depend on an adequate body of comparative material. To prove the systematic correspondence of a given phoneme of one language with a given phoneme of another language, it is necessary to have enough sets of convincing cognates showing the equivalence to eliminate the possibility of chance coincidence. When there are complicated matters of sound correspondence and differences of meaning, the validity of a pair of cognates may remain in doubt until collateral proof is found in other related languages, bringing out with more clarity the earlier form and meaning of the presumable common element or showing the steps of phonetic and semantic transformation. Not infrequently the comparativist finds himself with indications of cognancy without sufficient evidence to prove it beyond reasonable doubt. Because of this, other things being equal, it is easier to work with a stock made up of several languages than with one consisting of only two or three. Every comparativist knows this, but not all are fully alert to the value of parallel evidence from outside the immediate linguistic grouping. And yet, in such fields as Germanic or Romance or Slavic, it is commonplace that the internal comparison is aided by knowledge of Indo-European as a whole. In other words, a Slavicist will not hesitate to clear up doubtful points in Slavic comparative linguistics by evidence partly based on Germanic or Tocharian or Indic.

The methodologic lesson to be drawn from these considerations is that one should never confine himself entirely to the internal evidence of the linguistic grouping under study if there is any possibility of obtaining additional light from other, somewhat more distantly related languages. The more limited the number of languages in the complex being studied and the greater its internal divergence, the more important is the external evidence for filling out the picture. For this purpose, the mesh principle gives the lead. For each linguistic grouping, there is likely to be one or various others which represent the next links in the network of relationship. The mesh principle both tells us that we can expect to find such outside evidence and tells us where to look for it.

Dialectal Fluidity

In the process of the development of two or more mutually unintelligible languages out of what was in an earlier period a more or less homogeneous

9. Mary R. Haas, "A New Linguistic Relationship in North America: Algonkian and the Gulf Languages," *Southwestern Journal of Anthropology*, 14 (1958): 231–64.

speech form, it is normal for a period of local differentiation to have intervened. In this stage each locality had its peculiarities but neighboring
dialects were relatively similar. In an extensive area of local differentiation,
there may be marked differences between nonneighboring types of speech,
even to the point of nonintelligibility among very distant ones, but the area
up to some points maintains a unity through intermediate, mutually intelligible dialects. During this period linguistic innovations which arise at
one point may diffuse easily to the neighboring dialects, so that the common
features of contiguous dialects are partly due to common retentions and
partly to common innovations.

When the comparativist goes to work with already differentiated languages, he has to bear in mind that common features found between any two
of them need not necessarily go back to the period of maximum homogeneity
which may have preceded the dialectal differentiation, that they may have
had their origin later in an already differentiated situation. The developments of that time, then, have a blurring effect on the evidence. If one hopes
to penetrate past that period it may be necessary to use the collateral
evidence of more distantly related languages; that is, to use the device
recommended in general for obtaining more light on the language stage
being reconstructed. The procedure thus has more than one value.

Of course, the earlier common period reached by the broader comparison
probably brings with it an earlier period of dialectal blur, with its own
problems, but this does not impede the use of this evidence for clarifying, in
a relative degree, the later prehistoric period. For example, in the reconstruction of Proto–Uto-Aztecan, we find evidence in scattered divisions of
the stock for a verb root *nimi*, to live, to move; a nominal derivative means
"human being" among the northern divisions only, while two or three
other roots are found for this concept in the southern ones. One wonders
if the northern word is the original meaning of "human being" or whether
it is a regionalism that developed in the dialectal period. We look to other
stocks in the Amerindian mesh and find our root in two forms, *new* and
nem, widespread in the meaning of "live, dwell," and closely related concepts
(e.g., Atakapa *nul*, dwell; Chitimacha *namu*, village), but occasionally also
in the meaning of "person." The most common element for "person" and
"man" in America reconstructs to *weni* (e.g., Wintun *win-tun*, Sahaptin
ʔwinc, Mayan *winik*). At least tentatively, we can conclude that the use of
"to live" as the basis for a figurative expression of "human being" may be
very old, and contemporaneous with the use of *weni* for "person." The
figurative use must have been widespread and lasted for a long period of
time, but it is not too likely that it had become set in the earliest general
Uto-Aztecan, only to be replaced by other roots in the south. In fact, the
presence of different roots suggests that several figurative expressions may
have been in vogue. Solid conclusions in these matters cannot always be
drawn, but we can avoid falling into too ready acceptance of whatever

theory appeals subjectively to the comparativist.

One must be particularly cautious about dialect blur in drawing in-ferences about cultural prehistory from the evidence of common cultural terms. Cultural prehistorians in the Indo-European field have faced this problem, manifest to them because there are widespread terms which are nevertheless restricted to definite fractions of the total Indo-European area. Krahe[10] has responded to this situation by formulating the concept of Indo-European "fluidity," holding that there must have been a period of con-siderable relative heterogeneity, in which various regionalisms developed and attained different extensions of usage, before the crystallization of the later divisions, like Celtic, Romance, etc. This is simply a concrete instance of dialectal blue.

Krahe and those who follow him have not as yet discussed the possibility of periods of Celtic fluidity, Germanic fluidity, Baltic fluidity, and so forth, but linguistic theory leads us to suppose that such phenomena occurred, indeed that they flowed continuously and without pause out of Indo-European dialectal variation, and that the latter in its time must have been merely the continuation of whatever preceded it.

The Idea of Primitive Homogeneity

Such incisive theorists as Hermann Paul[11] hold that homogeneity of lan-guage may be a secondary product, resulting when a segment of a speech community becomes cut off from other related dialects and develops within itself a well-communicated situation in which all parts are in contact with all others. Under these circumstances old dialect differences will tend to be erased. Paul also shows with historically documented examples how old dialects may be regrouped within a total area by changes in the areas of maximum communication. These ideas, drawn from observation of dialect development on the European continent, doubtless have a general applica-tion. Movements toward and away from homogeneity may be going on at the same time. The presence of common features in a set of languages does not prove that they actually passed through a period of complete homo-geneity. Two related linguistic groups with a clear separation between them might once have been a single dialectal continuum or even a chain of fairly separate languages which broke into two by the elimination of some of the intermediate links. When we use an index capable of measuring degrees of divergence, we often find data which bear out such a conception. Linguistic stock A consists of languages a, b, c, d, stock B consists of m, n, o, p. Languages

10. Hans Krahe, "Indogermanisch und Alteuropäisch," *Saeculum,* 8 (1957): 1–16. On pp. 14–15: " 'Old European' of the second millennium before Christ was still not anything 'finished'; it was rather in this early time still so to speak all in flux . . . mainly still without incisive differentiation, with fluid transitions."

11. *Prinzipien der Sprachgeschichte.*

d and *m* show closer affinities than *a* and *p*, and there is a gradation of divergences, different from a single chain only in the presence of a particularly large contrast between the last language of the first segment and the first of the second.

Homogeneity is, then, a possible but not a necessary prior stage of a linguistic stock. Its former existence in any given case can only be deduced from concrete evidence, but concrete evidence may in another case point to the existence of a mesh even before this group broke off from the next group.

Salish Phonologic Geography

Introduction

Salishan is a widely ramified stock of considerable time depth and extensive geographic spread in western North America, where it comes into contact with a number of other distinct stocks. Because of its internal ramifications and its diversified external contacts, Salishan offers an extremely fruitful field for studying the effect of language on language in geographic and historic contexts.

Today the Salishan languages are found in a series of linguistic islands in the general English-speaking environment. Before the influx of English, they occupied an all but continuous territory from the Pacific Ocean as far east as the Yellowstone and Missouri rivers, and from the region of Rivers Inlet in British Columbia to a point far south of the Columbia River on the Oregon coast. The total area covered was probably greater than that of France, for it included practically all of the present state of Washington, much of Idaho, and large portions of British Columbia, Oregon, and Montana. The population was sparse by modern standards, especially in the inland plateau and mountain area. But the coastal Salish lived in an area of relatively heavy population in terms of the general distribution of people in pre-Columbian American. The total number of people speaking Salishan languages has been estimated at about 59,000 in 1780, over half of them (33,500) in the coastal areas.[1]

Reprinted from *Language*, 28, no. 2 (1952): 232–48. Footnotes have been renumbered. The orthography of the original article has been retained here, although it differs from that used in this book.

1. Population figures are based on James Mooney, "The Aboriginal Population of America North of Mexico," Smithsonian miscellaneous collections, 80, no. 7 (1928). Geographical locations given in this article are based on Franz Boas and Herman Haeberlin, "Sound Shifts in Salish Dialects," *International Journal of American Linguistics*, 4 (1927): 117–36, with map on p. 119.

At least twenty-six distinct and mutually unintelligible languages make up the Salishan stock. Some of them consist of two or more distinctive local dialects. The languages fall into four clearly separate divisions, two of which are internally ramified.[2] Bella Coola of British Columbia and Tillamook of Oregon each constitute a separate main division. The Interior Division is made up of seven languages, falling into five groups. What we call the Coast Division, but excluding Bella Coola and Tillamook, is the most ramified of all, since it includes seventeen languages in five branches, some of which are themselves complicated by internal groupings. The following are the names of the languages referred to in this paper, given in an order that shows, as well as possible, their relationships to each other (semicolons separate the divisions and the main branches of Coast Salish; languages that are relatively close together are joined by "and"): Bella Coola; Lillooet, Thompson and Shuswap, Columbia, Okanagon and Kalispel, Coeur d'Alene; Tillamook; Comox, Seshelt, Pentlatch; Squamish, Fraser and Nanaimo, Lummi and Lkungen and Clallam, Nootsack; Snoqualmie and Nisqualli; Twana; Cowlitz and Chehalis, Lower Chehalis, Quinault.

The bulk of the Salish territory is occupied by the seven languages of the Interior Division. This is in keeping with the general pattern of North American linguistic geography. In general the tribes of the Pacific coastal regions are the most restricted in territory, and the areas get larger as one goes to the east. However, even the largest Salish language areas, for example the Shuswap, do not compare with those of the most far-flung American languages, such as the Dakota and the Cree.

As a measure of the difference between one language and the next, I calculated in a previous paper the percentage of common elements used for items of basic vocabulary, and found, in the extreme case, that Bella Coola had only 11 per cent of cognates in common with Kalispel. In terms of known rates of change such a percentage indicates at least five thousand years of separate development.[3] In other words, the Salishan stock has a time depth comparable to that of Indo-European.

A number of distinct linguistic stocks border the Salish areas. On the west are Chemakuan (Chemakum and Quileute) and Wakashan (Nootkan and Kwakiutl); on the north is Athapaskan (Chilcotin, Carrier, Sekani, Beaver, Sarcee), and this family, a branch of the Nadene stock,[4] is also found in several small enclaves within the main Salish territory; on the northeast are Algonkian (Cree and Blackfoot), Siouan (the Assiniboin dialect of Dakota),

2. See Swadesh, "Salish Internal Relationships," *ibid.,* 16 (1950): 157.

3. The time depth, as calculated in my article "Salish Internal Relationships," runs as high as seven thousand years. Subsequent research on the rate of change suggests that the constant used in that study may represent a minimum rate. The time depth of Salish is perhaps better given as between five thousand and seven thousand years.

4. Although Sapir's Nadene theory has met with reserved judgment by some scholars, I regard it as proved. See Swadesh, "Diffusional Cumulation and Archaic Residue as Historical Explanations", *Southwestern Journal of Anthropology,* 7 (1951): 14ff.

Figure A.1. **Map of the Salish Language Area** showing northwestern Washington, southwestern British Columbia, and the southern end of Vancouver Island. The more crowded area is shown at twice the scale of the less densely settled areas: the black and white divisions in the border of the map mark off approximately equal distances.

Shadings indicate areas showing the principal reflexes of Proto-Salish *k* and *w*, as follows:

horizontal, solid lines .... $k > ç$
horizontal, broken lines .... $k > c$
from upper right to lower left .... $k > s$
vertical .... $w > g^w$ or g
from upper left to lower right .... $w > k^w$ or k

Crosshatching of various types is to be interpreted as a combination of simple shadings.

For the abberviations used on this map, see footnote 11.

and Kutenai; on the southeast is Shoshonean (Shoshoni and Bannock), a branch of Uto-Aztecan; on the south are Sahaptian (Nez Percé, Sahaptin, Cayuse), Chinookan, and Kalapuya-Yakonan. Salishan is at most very remotely related to some of its neighbors. Indeed, since the internal time depth of Salish must be more than five thousand years, it follows that any genetic connection with another stock must be distinctly more remote than that. Salish probably has distant affinities with Wakashan and Chemakuan; an even more remote connection has been suggested by Sapir with Kutenai and Algonkian.[5] For the purposes of the present study, however, possible genetic relations on so distant a plane may be disregarded, and all the neighbors of the Salish may be regarded as distinct stocks.

The problem of the present paper has to do with phonologic similarities and differences primarily among the languages of the Salish stock and to a lesser extent also between these and their non-Salish neighbors. Each case of shared phonologic features has to be considered with reference to the genetic and geographic relations of the languages involved. A common feature may be due to common origin; that is, the two languages may be alike in some respect because they were originally one language and because in this detail neither has yet changed. Or it may be due to mutual influence; that is, the two languages may have been originally different in a given respect but one or the other may have changed in the direction of its neighbor. Both types of phenomena, often intertwined, are found among the Salishan languages.

Source Material

Salish phonetics, perhaps even more than that of other northwest coast languages, presents a number of difficulties for the untrained fieldworker: glottal stops in various positions, glottalized stops and affricates, up to three voiceless laterals (λ, λ', $ł$), differentiation of two back series of consonants (e.g., k versus q), complex consonant clusters, intermediate quality of vowels, and, in certain areas, consonants intermediate or alternating between sibilant and shibilant. Such difficulties account for the variable recording of words and the general unreliability of much of the early fieldwork. However, there is one subtlety of Salish (and Kwakiutl) that has proved a trap even for well-trained phoneticians. It is a phenomenon which may be called the false vowel: a vocalic murmur between consonants in clusters, whose timbre is much influenced by the neighboring consonants. Probably because of its brevity and frequently indeterminate quality, the murmur has been recorded in various and unpredictable ways. Boas, who referred to the interconsonantic murmur as "the pepet vowel," evidently knew to a considerable

---

5. Evidence tending to substantiate the genetic relation of Salish, Chemakuan, and Wakashan is presented in Swadesh, "The Linguistic Approach to Salish Prehistory," in *Indians of the Urban Northwest*, ed. Marian Smith (New York, 1949), pp. 167–71.

extent which words contained it, and was able to discount it in his comparative work. Nonetheless, the fact that the false vowel is actually recorded with the same symbols as the phonemic vowels caused errors even in Boas' work.

There are recent published treatments of a few of the Salish languages, but for most of them the best materials available are still the field notes in the Boas Collection of the American Philosophical Society. It is fortunate that there is material on all the languages. Its quality varies with the fieldworker and the period when the study was made.

The present paper is based on a preliminary manuscript of mine, "Salish Comparative Phonology," in the Boas Collection. For the location of the languages and for most of the phonologic correspondences, my source is Boas and Haeberlin, "Sound Shifts in Salishan Dialects," *International Journal of American Linguistics*, 4:117 ff.

Phonemic systems

Among the phonemic systems of Salish there are several marked differences of detail. Nevertheless, certain phonemic features characterize all the Salishan languages, along with at least four of the bordering stocks: Chemakuan and Wakashan in the northwest, Kalapuyan and Yakonan in the south, all four located in the Pacific coastal area. The common traits include glottalized stops (and affricates), voiceless laterals (at least the spirant *ł*), contrast of midpalatal and postpalatal (e.g., *k* and *q*), complex consonant clusters, and, except for the northern dialect of Tillamook, the contrast of labialized and nonlabialized back consonants (e.g. q^w and *q*).[6]

BELLA COOLA PHONEMES

Occlusives	*p*	*t*		*c*	*k*	k^w	*q*	q^w	ʔ
Glottalized	*p'*	*t'*	*ƛ'*	*c'*	*k'*	k'^w	*q'*	q'^w	
Spirants			*ł*	*s*	*x*	x^w	*χ*	$χ^w$	*(h)*
Nasals	*m*	*n*							
Glottalized	*(m')*	*(n')*							
Continuants	*w*		*l*	*y*					
Glottalized	*(w')*		*(l')*	*(y')*					
Vowels	*u*			*i*					*a*

6. Italic letters in this paper represent phonemes; most of them need no phonetic explanation. The less familiar symbols may be phonetically characterized as follows: *c*, sibilant affricate; *ƒ*, shibilant affricate; *G*, voiced velar stop; *J*, voiced shibilant affricate; *R*, voiced pharyngeal spirant; *ʒ*, voiced sibilant affricate; *λ*, voiced lateral affricate; *ƛ*, voiceless lateral affricate; *χ*, voiceless velar spirant. An apostrophe after a letter indicates glottalization. Double vowel letters in Nootka forms denote long vowels.

Bella Coola may be taken as illustrating the simplest common denominator of Salish phonemics.[7]

The glottal spirant *h* is rare, being restricted to exclamations and to one nonexclamatory word, *y'anahu*, carrot, which is untypical (possibly a recent borrowing). There is no Salish language, with the exception of Tillamook, in which *h* is a common phoneme. With reference to the glottalized sonorants (*m'*, *n'*, *w'*, *y'*, *l'*) of Bella Coola, Newman writes, "They are found so rarely that their phonemic status is somewhat doubtful. . . ."

Essentially the same phonemic system as Bella Coola's is found also in Cowlitz, belonging to the Olympic branch of the Coast Division; in the Clallam and Nanaimo groups within the South Georgia branch, that is in Clallam, Lummi, Lkungen, Fraser and Nanaimo;[8] and in five of the seven Interior Division languages, namely Lillooet, Thompson, Shuswap, Columbia, and Okanagon. Differences of detail include presence of *λ* contrasting with *ł* in Cowlitz and the Interior languages, absence of *c* as well as *λ* in Lummi and Lkungen, absence of *n* in Fraser, *ŋ* added to the nasal series in the Clallam group, contrast of *r* and *l* in Columbia and Okanagon, presence of *z* in Lillooet and Thompson. It is noteworthy that all these languages form a geographic continuum, which is, however, separated from Bella Coola by eighty miles of Athapaskan (Chilcotin) territory.

More sharply modified forms of the Bella Coola system are presented by the two remaining languages of the Interior Division and by the remaining languages of the coastal Olympic branch. All these languages have *ç*, *ç'*, *ʃ* in place of *k*, *k'*, *x*. Spokan, a sister dialect of Kalispel in the Kalispel–Spokan–Pend d'Oreilles–Sematuse–Plains–Flathead language, has an *r* phoneme, like its neighbors, Columbia, Okanagon, and Coeur d'Alene. Also, as has been mentioned, glottalized continuants have been reported for Kalispel and Coeur d'Alene but not for the Olympic languages. Otherwise, Kalispel agrees in phonemic structure with Chehalis, Lower Chehalis, and Quinault, despite the intervening 150 miles.

Lower Chehalis and Quinault show a positional phonetic variation which

---

7. See Stanley Newman, "Bella Coola I: Phonology," *International Journal of American Linguistics*, 13 (1947): 129–34. The following sources are used for some of the languages in this paper: Franz Boas, "A Chehalis Text, *ibid.*, 8 (1934): 103–10; Gladys A. Reichard, "Coeur d'Alene", in *Handbook of American Indian Languages* (Washington, D.C., 1938), vol. 3, pp. 515–707; Hans Vogt, "The Kalispel Language" (Oslo, 1940); Colin Ellidge Tweddell, *The Snoqualmie-Duwamish Dialects of Puget Sound Salish*, University of Washington Publications in Anthropology no. 12 (1950), pp. 1–78; Edward Sapir, *Noun Reduplication in Comox, a Salish Language of Vancouver Island*, Department of Mines Geological Survey, memoir 63; Anthropological Series no. 6 (Ottawa, 1915); May M. Edel, "The Tillamook Language," *International Journal of American Linguistics*, 10 (1939): 1–57. For other languages I have consulted various manuscripts in the Boas Collection of the American Philosophical Society, especially Boas' comparative Salishan vocabularies (*c.* 1925).

8. The material on Clallam and Nanaimo was gathered some forty years ago, and gives no clear picture of the phonemic structure. In particular, it is not easy to tell whether the recorded sounds *c* and *ç* represent variations within one series or two distinct series. Because of frequent inconsistencies, I assume tentatively that no phonemic contrast exists between *c* and *ç*.

is of interest because it is related to a phonemic difference elsewhere in the Salish world. If our preliminary analysis of the data is correct, these two Olympic languages have an affricate variant (like English j) for y in prevocalic position. Similarly the phoneme w in Quinault, but not in Lower Chehalis, has the character of a voiced labiopalatal (like gw) in prevocalic position.

The major distinction between the two variant phonemic systems discussed so far—that is, between the Bella Coola and Kalispel types—can be conveniently shown by aligning two sets of occlusives, as follows:

Bella Coola	t	c	k	k^w	q	q^w
Kalispel	t	c	ς	k^w	q	q^w

Note that the relationship of Kalispel ς to k^w is, roughly, as Bella Coola k is to k^w. Some structural phonemicists might insist that this relationship is alone important and that the phonetic difference between ς and k is of no consequence. However, it must be considered that in addition to its relation to k^w, Kalispel ς has a degree of phonetic similarity to c far greater than that of Bella Coola k to c. Relations of phonetic similarity are not unimportant, as is amply evident in the historic development of phonologic systems.

Coeur d'Alene agrees with the languages just discussed in having ς in place of k, but it also has important differences which set it off from those languages, and in fact make it fairly unique in the whole stock. It adds a voiced-stop series to its inventory, consisting of d, J, g^w, and, in recent foreign words, also b. Furthermore, it has two velar voiced continuants, R, and R^w, not found in any other Salish language, and its vowel system is unique in having five vowels, i, $æ$, a, o, u, in place of the usual three. On the negative side, it lacks affricate laterals, even the glottalized one found in every other Salish language. And it lacks h. These features add up to the following system:

COEUR D'ALENE PHONEMES

p	t	c		ς	k^w	q	q^w	$\overline{?}$
p'	t'	c'		ς'	k'^w	q'	q'^w	
(b)	d			J	g^w			
		s	$\dotplus$	$\int$	x^w	χ	χ^w	
w	r		l			R	R^w	
w'	r'		l'			R'	R'^w	
m	n							
m'	n'							
u				i				
o				$æ$			a	

Coeur d'Alene, though distant from the region of Puget Sound and the Strait of Georgia, shares the series of voiced occlusives with the southern languages of that area, including the Puget branch and Twana. On the other hand, most of the Puget-Georgia languages have a trait lacking in all the languages discussed so far, namely that they contrast ç and *k*; where the previously discussed languages have either ç or *k*, these languages have both. The same contrast is found in the Chemakuan stock and the Nootka branch of Wakashan. Kwakiutl lacks ç and in this respect agrees with its northern Salish neighbor, Bella Coola. In the southern coastal area the contrast is found among the non-Salish neighbors of Tillamook, including Chinookan, Kalapuyan, and Yakonan. In the interior areas, certain adjoining stocks (Athapaskan, Sahaptian, Siouan) have ç contrasting with *k* and *c*, at least in some languages, but in all this area there is no correlation between Salish and non-Salish with regard to this matter.

To illustrate a Salish system with the ç-*k* contrast, we take Snoqualmie of the Puget Sound branch of Coast Salish:

SNOQUALMIE PHONEMES

p	t	λ	c	$ç$	k	k^w	q	q^w	'
p'	t'	λ'	c'	$ç'$	k'	k'^w	q'	q'^w	
b	d		$ʒ$	J		g^w			
(m)									
			$ł$	s	$ʃ$	x	x^w	$χ$	$χ^w$
w		l		y					
u				i				a	

Twaddell lists also *g*, but his examples suggest that this is an error of analysis. Thus, *li͞gub*, young man, probably should be written *lig͞wb*. His other phonemes seem well demonstrated. Only one word occurs with *m*, but it is a common one: *mimu?d*, small; this may represent a diminutive symbolism. Otherwise *m* and *n* are replaced by *b* and *d*.

The occurrence of *b* and *d* to the exclusion (or nearly so) of *m* and *n* is found also in Twana and in two non-Salishan languages of the area, Quileute of the Chemakuan stock and Makah-Nitinat of the Nootkan branch of Wakashan. Salishan Comox has a partial resemblance in the fact that *m* and *n* tend to be pronounced as voiced stops in prevocalic position.

Comox is the only other Salish language that has voiced stops. It has *J* and *g*, occurring only in prevocalic position—not as positional variants of *y* and *w* as in Quinault, but in contrast with *y* and *w*, since the latter also occur prevocalically. Symbols like *b*, *d*, *g* recorded in Tillamook turn out to represent unaspirated voiceless stops, which are positional variants of *p*, *t*, *k*. But Kwakiutl, the non-Salish neighbor of Comox, has a full set of voiced stops (*b*, *d*, *λ*, ʒ, *g*, *g^w*, *G*, *G^w*).

If one omits the voiced ʒ, *J*, *g^w* from the Snoqualmie table, one gets the system found in Twana. Omitting all voiced stops and restoring *m* and *n* in place of *b* and *d*, one gets the system of Nootsack and Squamish of the South Georgia branch.

Seshelt and Pentlatch of the North Georgia branch are like Nootsack and Squamish but lack *c* and *λ*. The remaining North Georgian language is

Comox, which also lacks the affricates *c* and *ƛ* but differs in having the two voiced occlusives *J*, *g*, as already mentioned.

Tillamook is unique in having no other labials than *w* and in having *h* as a frequent phoneme, occurring even in consonant clusters. Northern Tillamook, in distinction to the southern dialect of Siletz, furthermore has no labialized back consonants.[9]

TILLAMOOK PHONEMES

	t	*ƛ*	*c*	*ç*	*k*	*q*	*ʔ*
	t'	*ƛ'*	*c'*	*ç'*	*k'*	*q'*	
	ɬ	*s*	*ʃ*	*x*	*χ*	*h*	
	n						
w		*l*		*y*			
u				*i*		*a*	

The lack of labials is reminiscent of Athapaskan, which is generally weak in labials, with some languages having only *w*. It would be interesting to know if the Athapaskan neighbors of Tillamook had this characteristic. The northern Tillamook lack of labialized stops agrees with its non-Salish neighbor, Lower Chinook. (In the relatively infrequent cases where the literature has spellings like *kwa* in Chinook, this evidently denotes a sequence of phonemes, perhaps *kua*.)

Proto-Salish

To reconstruct the phonemic system of Proto-Salish, one has to examine cognate words, noting the phonemic correspondences among the sister languages. One then seeks a theory of original sounds which can provide an adequate explanation of the actual forms and which fit together into a realistic phonemic pattern. The present paper is based on a study of about two hundred cognate sets,[10] mostly additions to those given by Boas and Haeberlin. A few selected examples are given here by way of illustrating the relationships found. The phonetics of the sources are corrected without comment, on the basis of any available evidence; it is to be expected that some errors still remain or have been introduced in the effort at correction.[11]

9. On the presence of labialized consonants in Siletz, see Boas and Haeberlin, "Sound Shifts in Salish Dialects," p. 135. The Siletz vocabulary of Leo J. Frachtenberg (*International Journal of American Linguistics*, 1: 45–46) may actually be Northern Tillamook, since it includes *ynkas*, heart (from Proto-Salish *ynwas*), with unrounded *k*.

10. Swadesh, "Salish Cognates" (1951), MS in the Boas Collection.

11. The names of languages are abbreviated as follows: Be, Bella Coola; Ch, Upper Chehalis; Cl, Clallam; Cm, Columbia; Cr, Coeur d'Alene; Cw, Cowlitz; Cx, Comox; Fr, Lower Fraser; Ka, Kalispel; Li, Lillooet; Lk, Lkungen; Lm, Lummi; Lo, Lower Chehalis; Ni, Nisqualli; Nn, Nanaimo; Nt, Nootsak; Ok, Okanagon; Pr, Proto-Salish; Pt, Pentlatch; Qu, Quinault; Sa, Satsop; Sh, Shuswap; Sn, Snoqualmie; Sq, Squamish; St, Seshelt; Th, Thompson River; Ti, Tillamook; Tw, Twana.

Ti *çalſ*, hand; Th *kiyx*, Sh Cm *kalx*, Ok *kilx*, Ka *çilſ*; Cx *çayſ*, St Pt *çalſ*; Nt *çalſ*; Nnˊ Fr *cals*, Cl *cays*, Lm Lk *sals;* Ni Sn *çalſ*; Tw *çalſ*; Cw *kalx*, Ch Lo Qu *çalſ* (Lo Qu "limb of tree"). Pr *kalx*.

Be *yca*, tooth; Cx *Jns*, St Pt *yns;* Nn *yns*, Fr *yls*, Sq Nt *yns*, Cl Lm *cns;* Sn *Jds;* Tw *yds;* Ch Cw Qu *yns*. Pr *yns*. (Be from *ynsn*.)

Ti *knaw*, antler; Th Sh Ok *wnaw*, chisel; Pt *wnaw;* Nt *wnaw;* Ni Sn *gᵂadagᵂ;* Tw *wdaw;* Ch *wnaw*. Pr *wnaw, wanaw*.

Be *mus*, four; Ti *wus;* Interior *mus;* Cx St *mus;* Cl Lm Lk *ŋus;* Ni Sn *bus;* Tw *bus;* Olympic *mus*. Pr *mus*.

Ti *nc'u*, one; Sh Ka *nk'ᵂu?*, Cr *nk'ᵂ?;* Nn *nc'a*. Fr *lc'a*, Nt Sq *nç'u?*, Cl Lm Lk *nç'?;* Ni Sn *dic'u*. Pr *nk'u?*.

Be *cuca*, mouth; Li Th *cucn;* Cx St Pt *susn;* Nn *sasn*. Fr *cacl*, Sq *cucn*, Cl *cucn*, Lm Lk *susn*. Pr *cucn*.

Ti *nhak'aw-qn*, flower (*-qn*, head); Li Th Sh *spaq'm;* Cx *paq'm*, leaf; Nn Fr *spaq'm;* Tw *spq'am;* Ch Qu *spaq'm*. Pr *paq'am* (*n-* and *s-* are prefixes; Ti *k'* for *q'* may be a diminutive change).

Be *kᵂli*, green, yellow; Ti *cqlq*, green; Li *kᵂli*, yellow, Th *kᵂlu*, Sh *kᵂlt*, Cm *kᵂrik*, Ok *kᵂri*, Ka *kᵂali?*, Cr *kᵂar*. Pr *kᵂari?*.

La *ƛ'za*, Sh Cm *ƛ'ya*, Ok Ka *ƛ'yi?*, Cr *t'dœ?*. Proto-Interior *ƛ'ya?*.

In addition to the correspondence of sounds to each other, we see in the examples also the effect of functional phoneme alternation. Various Salish languages show interchange of consonants, along with reduplication and the insertion of a glottal stop, to express the diminutive. This process evidently goes back to Proto-Salish times. The dropping out of vowels, seen in related forms like *kᵂar* and *kᵂri* in the contemporary languages, is usually associated with affixation.

The net effect of the reconstructions of individual morphemes, considered in their combined relationships, gives us the following reconstructed system:

PROTO-SALISH PHONEMES

p	t	ƛ	c	k	kᵂ	q	qᵂ	ʔ
p'	t'	ƛ'	c'	k'	k'ᵂ	q'	q'ᵂ	
	ł	s,	x	xᵂ	χ	χᵂ	(h)	
m	n							
w	r	l		y		R	Rᵂ	
u			i				a	

Glottalized continuants (*m'*, etc.) have been omitted for want of data to prove or disprove their archaic character. The reconstruction of *R*, *Rᵂ* depends largely on Coeur d'Alene, with some additional evidence from Kalispel. Vogt has shown[12] that Kalispel has zero for Coeur d'Alene *R*, and has *w* for Cr *Rᵂ*. Where Coeur d'Alene has *a* or *æ* before *R* and *Rᵂ*, Kalispel always

---

12. Hans Vogt, *Salishan Studies: Comparative Notes on Kalispel, Spokan, Colville, and Coeur d'Alene* (Oslo, 1940).

has *a*, as in Cr *yaR*: Ka *ya*, assemble. Now, an original *a* develops in Kalispel to *i* unless there is a velar or *r* following. Therefore, the fact that we have Ka *ya* (and not *yi*) indicates that there must have been a velar following the vowel in an earlier stage of Kalispel. Reflexes in other languages have not yet been discovered.

Phoneme Shifts

The sound changes which produced the modern Salish phonemes out of their Proto-Salish originals must be specified geographically and chronologically as well as phonetically; it is important to know where and when each change took place, and to distinguish local from widespread changes. It is a matter of general linguistic experience that widespread changes commonly begin as local changes and then spread out farther and farther to languages touching on those that already have gone through the change. Probably the movement tends to be most rapid through a territory speaking a single language or closely related languages, and slowest in passing to unrelated languages with widely different phonemic systems. While the spread is still going on, new changes may affect the transformed sound, and these will appear in roughly concentric areas within the larger territory of the earlier shift. All these phenomena can be illustrated in Salish.

As an example of a local shift, restricted to a single language, we have the change of original *λ̓* to *t̓* in Coeur d'Alene or the development of original *p*, *m* to *h*, *w* in Tillamook. Even more restricted is the North Tillamook delabialization of rounded consonants—that is, *kʷ* to *k*, etc.—for Southern Tillamook (Siletz) had not yet gone through this change in the period when the language became extinct. Likewise, original *n* became *l* in Fraser, but there are still local dialects which remain in the *n* stage.[13]

Tillamook *kʷ* to *k* and Fraser *n* to *l* are obviously relatively recent shifts, for they have not had time to spread through the whole area of each language. In the case of Fraser, we have a means of determining approximately how recent the mutation is, based on the close relationship of Fraser to Nanaimo. These two languages were found to have 73 per cent of common elements in their basic vocabularies, from which we calculate that something like a thousand years ago they were either one homogeneous language or at most local dialects hardly different from one another. While today Fraser and Nanaimo are located on opposite sides of the Strait of Georgia, they could not have been so far apart for over a thousand years and still retain so high a degree of sameness. If the change of *n* to *l* had taken place in the common period of Proto–Nanaimo–Fraser, it would be found today in both languages. Since it is not, we know that it occurred after Fraser parted company with Nanaimo.

13. See Boas and Haeberlin, "Sound Shifts in Salish Dialects," p. 134.

Original *m* is found changed to *ŋ* only in Clallam, Lkungen, and Lummi. These three form a closely related group whose time depth is calculated at about a thousand years. They are now located in three distinct areas, separated by arms of the sea. Since no other languages with *ŋ* are in close contact with any member of the Clallam group, and since they could not each have acquired this sound separately, the shift must have taken place at a time when the present three languages were a single tongue occupying a small continuous territory. In other words, we have here a local, one-language change belonging to an earlier time level, with the modern spread resulting from the breakup of the old speech community. The change may be dated between one and three thousand years ago, the earlier date being indicated by the fact that no reflex of such a mutation is found in any of the other languages of the South Georgia branch or elsewhere.

A similar case is the shift of *u* to *o* in the two languages of the Nanaimo group. This must have happened in their common period, more recently than two thousand years ago, when the prototype of this group was one with that of Squamish.

Clear evidence of a mutational wave that spread beyond local limits is found in the shift of original *c* to *s* in the North Georgia branch and in four languages of the South Georgia branch, namely Nanaimo, Fraser, Lummi, and Lkungen. The beginning of the wave may have been in the common period of the North Georgia branch, about two thousand or so years ago. It could have spread to Proto-Nanaimo during the common Nanaimo–Fraser period, but did not reach the Clallam group until it was already divided into its present three components.

Another example of the diffusion of a change across a language boundary is shown by the substitution of *z* for original *y* in Lillooet and Thompson. This shift is not shared by Shuswap, which is linguistically close to Thompson. The change evidently passed from Lillooet to Thompson in a recent period, subsequent to the split-up of Thompson and Shuswap.

A very old diffusion which shows signs of having continued into modern times is that of the change of *r* to *l*. The original stage is maintained only in Okanagon, Columbia, Coeur d'Alene, and the Spokan dialect of Kalispel, forming a continuous geographic area surrounded on all sides by *r*-less speech. The dialects of Kalispel other than Spokan must have switched from *r* to *l* in very recent times. This is shown not only by the persistence of an *r*-dialect, but also by indirect reflexes in the *r*-less dialects. Kalispel *a* normally develops to *i* except before a velar consonant or an original *r*. In a word like *kʷali?*, yellow, the quality of the first vowel (*a* and not *i*) indicates that the following liquid was *r*. There is also proof of the relatively recent adoption of the mutation *r* to *l* in Thompson, where original *r* changed to *l*, original *l* to *y*, and original *y* to *z*. Since, despite these changes, there is no confusion in the reflexes of the three original sounds, it follows that *l* could have changed to *y* only after *y* had shifted, and *r* could have moved on to *l* only after *l* had changed. Since Thompson does not share the first two changes with Shuswap, they must belong to a period subsequent to the divergence of these languages—that is, to a period within the last thousand years. The *r* to *l* shift in Thompson is therefore the most recent of a series of three successive phonologic events, all of which fall within the last thousand years.

Another instance of a simple wave that has carried even farther than the one just discussed is the loss of original *R* and the corresponding change of *R^w* to *w*. If *R* and *R^w* were Proto-Salish phonemes, as I tentatively assume, then *R* was lost during the period of Salish divergence (that is, subsequent to the common period of Proto-Salish) in every part of the stock except Coeur d'Alene. Evidence has been given of the relatively recent disappearance of *R* and *R^w* in Kalispel. The evidence for *R* and *R^w* in languages of the Interior Division indicates that these phonemes were still present in the common period of the division. At that time, it might have been already lost in the prototypes of the three other divisions, at least so far as our present evidence goes.

Original *k* went through a series of changes, from *k* to *ç* to *c* to *s*, which successively spread over a series of languages. Exactly parallel changes affect *k'* and *x*, except for the last step; that is, *k'* and *x* changed to *ç'* and *ʃ*, which changed to *c'* and *s*. The greatest change, that of *k* to *s*, is found in the smallest area, being restricted to Lummi and Lkungen of the Clallam group. The prior change of *ç* to *c* affected two groups in the South Georgia branch, the Clallam and the Nanaimo. The first change, from *k* to *ç*, has achieved so wide a spread that only seven languages still retain the original *k* sound. Moreover, Nootka, a non-Salish language, has shared the change of *k* to *ç* with its Salish neighbors. The time of the Nootka change, during the period of its separate development and before the period when Nitinat-Makah and Nootka proper diverged into separate languages, places it approximately in the time span when the change was going on among the Salish neighbors of Nootka. Likewise, Chemakum of the Chemakuan stock has changed *k* to *ç* since its separation from Quileute.

It is clear that Salish had already split into the languages which eventually gave rise to its present divisions before the change of *k* to *ç* began. This follows from the fact that Bella Coola still has the original *k* and that the Interior Division has *ç* in only two of its component languages, Coeur d'Alene and Kalispel. In the Coast Division, there is still one language, Cowlitz, with original *k*. Since the Olympic branch, to which Cowlitz belongs, shows no special ramifications of *ç*, it seems reasonable to surmise that the change reached this area only in relatively recent times. In fact, the dialect which Boas calls Upper Chehalis 2 is actually a dialect of Cowlitz that has adopted the change of *k* to *ç* within the period of linguistic separation of Cowlitz and Chehalis. Boas' suggestion that Cowlitz may have taken over *k* for Olympic *ç* (a reversal of the change) from its Interior Salish neighbors is not convincing,[14] although it is likely enough that the presence of k languages on its borders retarded the adoption of the ς pronunciation by Cowlitz. If the shift of k to ς reached the Olympic branch only recently, then the ς mutation cannot have appeared until after the prototype of the Coast Division had already split up into separate languages.

The area of the ς languages in the Coast Division, if one includes those which still have ς and those which have a further reflex of ς, is continuous. But ς is also found in two cut-off areas, namely in Coeur d'Alene and Kalispel of the Interior Division and in Tillamook. We must ask whether these are languages which took part in the general shift of the Georgia coastal area and which have since migrated to their present location, or whether the same change took place independently in the three areas.

We can eliminate Kalispel from consideration because the closely related Okanagon is a k language. In other words, Kalispel has acquired the ς pronunciation only in relatively recent times; there can be no doubt that the shift spread from Coeur d'Alene to Kalispel.

With regard to Tillamook and Coeur d'Alene, the mutation might be regarded as a sheer coincidence were it not for another and even more striking agreement among Tillamook, Coeur d'Alene, and certain Coast Division languages. That is the treatment of original w.

The main sequence of change for w was first to g^w and then to k^w. In some languages it affected only non-final w, in others w in all positions. The languages showing the mutation of w are Tillamook, Coeur d'Alene, the Puget Sound branch, the Clallam group of South Georgian, and Comox of the North Georgia branch. Besides, Quinault of the Olympic branch has a g^w sound as the prevocalic variant of the w phoneme. The original mutation of w to g^w is found in the Puget languages and in Coeur d'Alene. The k^w stage is found in the Clallam group and in Tillamook, except that in the northern dialect of Tillamook a further change to k has taken place. In Comox there was delabialization of the voiced stage, g^w to g. The changes affect all positions in Puget and Coeur d'Alene; in Comox, the Clallam group, and Tillamook they are limited to prevocalic position. Chemakuan, a non-Salish neighbor of Clallam, has k^w for Proto-Chemakuan w in prevocalic position.

We must not attach too much importance to the coincidence of the unvoicing of g^w in Clallam and Tillamook, since any voiced stops must be expected to have only a precarious existence in an area that mainly lacks them. The two events may therefore have happened independently. But the basic change of w to g^w is very important, precisely because it produced something unusual in the region.

In view of this, and of the agreement in the ς mutation, we conclude with considerable confidence that Tillamook and Coeur d'Alene were once

14. See *ibid.*, pp. 126–27.

neighbors of the languages which have since developed into Nisquali, Snoqualmie, Clallam, Lkungen, and Lummi. The time of this proximity may be placed within the last two thousand years. It need not have been as long as a thousand years ago, but there is so far little basis for a narrower estimate. The detailed study of common vocabulary, with particular reference to borrowings, may eventually allow us to be more precise.

Supporting the evidence of *w* but not entirely parallel to it is the history of original *y*, which changed to *J* and subsequently to *ç* and *c* or to *d*. Tillamook does not share this change. Coeur d'Alene has the reflex *d* in all positions. Comox has *J*, but only prevocalically. And a *J*-sound as a positional variant of *y* is found in Quinault and Lower Chehalis. In the Clallam group the voiceless affricate *c* is found before vowels; the sequence of change must have been from *J* to *ç* to *c*, or from *J* to *ʒ* to *c*. In some way, the product of original *y* was kept apart from that of original *k*, since in Lkungen and Lummi the former is *c* but the latter is *s*. A possible explanation is that voiced obstruents (*g^w* and *ʒ*) were maintained until after the dialects had developed into distinct entities, though still in contact with each other. The unvoicing of *g^w* and *ʒ* to *k^w* and *c* respectively would then have taken place after Lkungen and Lummi had changed earlier *c* to *s*.

Proto-Salish *l* is replaced by *y* in Lillooet and Thompson[15] of the Interior Division, and in Clallam and Squamish of the South Georgia branch of Coast Salish. In North Georgian Comox, a similar change takes place, except that before or after *u* the result is *w* instead of *y*. Because of the geographic contact of Comox with Lillooet, it seems reasonable to suppose that the Comox represents a further development of the same mutation. In other words, the steps are *l* to *y*, then *y* in given surroundings to *w*.

Thompson, Lilloet, Squamish, and Comox make up a geographic continuum, but Clallam is separated from the others by water and by intervening languages. However, there can be no doubt that there has been some shifting around of the languages, and it is not improbable that Clallam was formerly in contact with at least one of the other languages. In particular, it should be noted that the three languages of the Clallam group are separated by sizeable water barriers, with Lkungen on Vancouver Island, Lummi on the eastern side of the Strait of Georgia, and Clallam to the south of Juan de Fuca Strait. We must suppose that the three languages, having developed out of a single earlier language, must have been all together at one time in the fairly recent past. This could have been either on Vancouver Island or on the mainland, and it is likely enough that an earlier form of Clallam was in contact with either Squamish or Comox or both.

Our final example of a sequence of changes is that of original *a* to *æ* to *i*

15. Boas and Haeberlin (*ibid.*, p. 128) say that of the Interior languages, only Thompson has *y* for *l*. But a number of Lillooet examples appear in Boas' comparative Salishan vocabularies (*c.* 1925). Since there are also Lillooet forms with *l* for *l*, it would seem that local dialects differ on this point.

in three contiguous Interior languages. The first change is found in Coeur d'Alene. The second step, merging the vowel with original *i*, is found in Kalispel and Okanagon. Presumably the first step of the change was taken in the common period of Kalispel and Okanagon. Because these languages have carried it furthest, it is likely that it was originated here and was subsequently adopted by Coeur d'Alene. The influence would then have been earlier and in the opposite direction to that of the *ç* mutation, which went from Coeur d'Alene to Kalispel in more recent times. It should be noted that interchange between back and front vowels is still a live process in the three languages: in Coeur d'Alene normal *æ* changes to *a* when a suffix with a velar consonant is added, in Kalispel and Okanagon certain stems with *i* change the vowel to *a* under the same conditions. However, the interchange is not entirely mechanical, since in both languages there are instances of unchanging *a*.

The foregoing is not a complete account of phoneme changes in Salish, but it is about as far as present research permits us to go. Two remaining problems may be mentioned in passing. Certain languages show rounded *kʷ* sounds where the reflexes in other languages suggest original *k* sounds. The explanation is connected with a following *u* vowel—that is, *ku* becomes *kʷu*; but the area of change and the full details of the conditioning factors are not yet clear. Another problem is raised by Boas and Haeberlin,[16] who give several examples of Li Th Sh *ƛ* for *t* in other languages. The assumption of a change from *ƛ* to *t* seems to be contradicted by other evidence and by inconsistencies even in the examples cited by Boas and Haeberlin. The explanation probably lies either in phonetic errors or in the use of different prefixes, or in a combination of the two factors.

Borrowing and Convergence

The transformation of original sounds is not the only process which affects the phonemic system. Innovations just as profound may come about through borrowing foreign words, whether from related or from unrelated forms of speech, provided that the divergent new sounds are kept intact during the process. If the foreign sounds are replaced by the nearest native equivalents, as often happens, the native system remains the same (except possibly for significant revisions of relative frequencies). At times, however, particularly when there are many bilinguals in the population, the foreign sounds are brought in with the new words.

Still another source of phoneme variation would seem to be very important among the northwest coast languages, namely symbolic phonetic change. For example, fronting, delabialization, and insertion of glottal stop are used in Bella Coola, in connection with reduplication, to denote

16. *Ibid.*, p. 136.

smallness.[17] Similar processes are found in various Salish and other north-west languages, often unconnected with reduplication; sometimes there are only scattered traces rather than a regularly functioning process. Such a symbolism may operate to restore midpalatals in a language which has shifted its original *k* to *ç*, and may thereby contribute to developing the typical *c–ç–k* configuration found in the Coast Division.

A third basis for introducing new phonemes is the use of special sounds in imitative words and in ejaculations, a phenomenon that can be illustrated in almost any language. If such elements come to be used in ordinary speech as normal word types, they may contribute new sounds to the system

In the present state of our knowledge of Salish, it is not possible to prove which of various possible causes it was that gave rise to a particular new configuration. I suspect that the reintroduction of *k* into the Coast Division languages was due to a combination of sound imitation, symbolism, and borrowing. In the material published by Sapir on Comox, there are very few examples of the *k* series, as is to be expected in view of the general change of original *k* sounds to *ç* sounds. The examples are *kaʃkaʃ*, bluejay; *k'ik'ak'*, crow; *k'kayu*, oar; *kit*, little finger. The first two of these are definitely imitative. The third is a Kwakiutl loan (*k'g-ayu*, pullback instrument). The last may be diminutive in origin, even though sound changes for small-ness are no longer active in Comox.

For "bluejay" and "crow" there are similar words in Nootka and Kwakiutl of the Wakashan stock. These suggest that the influence of neighboring languages may have played a role. The Nootka words are respectively *xʷaaʃxʷiip* and *k'ee?in*; the Kwakiutl words are *kʷaskʷas* and *k'an'a*. The words used to imitate the sound of these two birds in Nootka are *kaak* and *k'aak*. The words for "raven" are connected: Nootka *qu?iʃin* (probably from *qʷi?iʃin* or *qʷe?iʃin*), Kwakiutl *Gʷaw'ina*; the Nootka imitative word is *qaaq*. The relation of "crow" to "raven" is seen to show diminutive-augmen-tative symbolism.

Cases of prevocalic *y* and *w* in Sapir's Comox material are similarly much fewer than cases of *J* and *g*. They are *yipixʷ*, hole; *yaχay?*, pack basket; *waχac'i*, pipe; *wi?walus*, young man; *?awakʷ*, tobacco. Of these, "pipe" has been identified as Kwakiutl "smoke-receptacle." The others have not been traced, but are clearly words of a type that is readily borrowed. (A possible exception is "hole"; but this may have come over in some special sense, or may be based on an imitative verb for "bore.")

Our material amply demonstrates the tendency for phonemic systems in neighboring languages to approach each other. At the same time it is clear that this approach does not take place suddenly upon first contact, or in any mechanical way. Many centuries may pass without noticeable effect; at the fastest rate, it probably takes a few generations. In all cases, bilinguals

---

17. See Newman, "Bella Coola I: Phonology," p. 134.

undoubtedly play a principal if unconscious role. In considering the way in which contact convergence comes about and particularly in trying to understand how it may be resisted for long periods of time, one must bear in mind that a language frequently has more than one phonological system on its borders. This means that there may be influences pulling it in different directions. The monolingual populations, along with all neighbors having the same phonemic system, will tend to keep the language in the old pattern. Sometimes the influence of a contiguous language may have no profound effect until the speech community has broken into a series of subareas with distinctive dialects. The presence of the neighbor language may be a factor in hastening the split-up of the area.

The simplest kind of contact convergence is that affecting not the number of phonemes but their phonetic norms. Comox and Bella Coola share with Kwakiutl, their common neighbor, a fronted pronunciation of k sounds, giving a y-like timbre to k and g, and speaking x like German front *ch* in *ich*. This is evidently an ancient trait of the northwest coast, which was doubtless a factor in opening the way to the mutation of k to $ç$ in Nootka and in the Coast Salish languages. Comox must have copied this timbre from the Kwakiutl, since it had no k-series after common North Georgian had shifted original k to $ç$. An interesting feature of the whole series of events is the probability that the fronted type of k recently borrowed by Comox from Kwakiutl duplicates the norm of pronunciation that prevailed in the time of ancient Salish k. On the other hand, Comox fronted g, so similar to the Kwakiutl, normally has a very different origin as the delabialized form of earlier g^w.

The borrowing of phonetic norms probably plays an important role in the diffusion of phonetic changes, when neighboring languages one after the other go through the same sound shift. Let us suppose a geographic sequence of languages or dialects, A, B, C, D, E. Suppose that in C there occurs a shift in the phonetic norm of k, so that it sounds like ky. This style of speaking after a time infects B and D at those points where they are in contact with C. Before the ky norm has diffused all the way through B and D, C may have advanced to a pronunciation like English *ch*. Eventually A and E may start pronouncing ky, but by that time B and D may have begun to copy the *ch*. Finally, by the time A and E have begun to adopt the second new norm, a third may develop in C; for example, a kind of *ts*. This example is only a simplified version of what must have taken place in Salishan, centering more or less around the southern area of the Strait of Georgia. In real life, however, diffusion does not move evenly through an inert homogeneous mass, but accelerates and decelerates in response to changes in the social relationships of the communities.

Let us turn now to changes that not only affect the phonetic norms but involve additions and reductions in the phoneme inventory. New phonemes may be acquired from a neighbor language in borrowed words; or, under the influence of another form of speech, native imitative words with special sounds may be incorporated unchanged into the normal vocabulary. Often the foreign pattern serves to crystallize an existing positional variation into a phonemic split. This is presumably what happened to Proto-Salish *w* in languages like Coeur d'Alene and Comox. We may suppose an early phonetic pattern in which a trace of palatal friction accompanied *w* in syllabic initial position only; at the end of a syllable *w* may have been like a vowel, except that it did not carry syllabic emphasis. A language with such a positional variation comes into contact with a foreign tongue, for example Kwakiutl, which has a series of voiced stops including g^w. Since this sound and the syllable-initial variant of *w* are fairly close to each other, bilinguals of the g^w language are likely to use their g^w in place of the special variant of *w*. If this pronunciation is generalized in the population, the initial variant of *w* comes to be a stop. This may have happened in Quinault, where evidently g^w is still only a positional variant of *w*. When, however, new words come into the language, by borrowing or otherwise, with initial *w* contrasting with g^w, the g^w variant is effectively separated from the syllable-final *w*. The old relationship may be preserved on the morphophonemic level. This is precisely the case of Comox, which has both *g* and *w* for original *w*, alternating according to syllabic position; e.g., *qiʔwχ*, steelhead salmon, reduplicated diminutive *qiqgiχ* or *t'igim*, sun, moon, diminutive reduplication *t'it'gim* but plural reduplication *t'wt'igim*. Where *w* occurs in borrowed words or where it is derived from earlier *l*, it does not interchange with *g*.

Finally we come to phoneme reduction under foreign influence. This takes the form of merging two original phonemes into one, for example *k* and k^w into *k* in North Tillamook, presumably under the influence of Chinookan, or *c* and *ç* into *c* in the Nanaimo group, presumably under the influence of Interior Division languages. If it is correct to assume Chinook influence in Tillamook, it would seem that Tillamook syllables like $k^w a$ sounded to bilinguals more like Chinook *ka* than like *kua*. (In syllable-final position the labialization sounded like nothing at all in Chinook.) The merging of *ç* and *c* in the Nanaimo group could have resulted very easily from the tendency in the northern Interior languages to pronounce *c* with a *ç*-like quality.

Through the loss of *ç* as an independent phoneme, the affected Coastal languages took the last step in a roundabout convergence with the Interior phonemic pattern. Thus, Lillooet and Thompson have the set $c–k–k^w$ by virtue of preserving the original system. Nanaimo and Fraser, on the contrary, went through a gamut of changes: first *k* was changed to *ç*, giving the set $c–ç–k^w$; then new instances of *k* were presumably added by processes like borrowing and sound symbolism, giving $c–ç–k–k^w$; finally the merging of *c* and *ç* brought the configuration back to $c–k–k^w$. Though Fraser and Lillooet have the same phonemes in their inventories, they do not necessarily have them in the same words.

Independent Shifts

In theory it may be assumed that phonetic and phonemic changes can arise spontaneously—that is, without the influence of neighboring languages and dialects. Such a case, however, is hardly to be discovered through the methods of comparative phonology. Since our reconstruction of the past can never be complete, there is always the possibility that some language may once have existed in exactly the right place and time to provide the impulse for sound shifts that now appear to be independent. Be that as it may, it is impressive to discover how many of the prehistoric Salish developments can be associated with definite neighboring languages, whose modern forms still exist in or near the same area. I conclude that the interplay of interdialectal and interlinguistic influences in a complex linguistic situation accounts for very nearly all phonological developments.

The Culture Historic Implications of Sapir's Linguistic Classification

Time Perspective

Culture prehistorians using Sapir's synthesis of North American language classification (1929) need to exercise one essential precaution: to bear in mind the approximate scale and implicit time depth of each connection. Lackner and Rowe (1955) seem to think that the problem is one of fact versus fancy—that is, whether the languages are actually related or merely asserted to be so without foundation—but this can be shown to be a misapprehension.

While it was not customary in his day for scholars to commit themselves on the actual time depth of linguistic groupings, Sapir gave this matter more than passing attention. The following remarks (1916, pp. 77–78, and 1929) are particularly interesting:

> There can be no doubt that a very great lapse of time (probably several millennia) must be assumed to account for the geographical distribution and dialectic differentiation of the Algonkin languages proper. . . . The morphological and lexical differences that obtain between even the most divergent Algonkin languages, say Cheyenne and Micmac, while by no means inconsiderable, are of comparatively little moment when set by the side of analogical differences obtaining between two such Penutian languages as Yokuts and Miwok. There can be no doubt, then, that the distribution of Penutian-speaking tribes antedates, as a whole, the scattering of Algonkin peoples from a comparatively restricted center. If under the term "Algonkin" we include the remotely related Yurok and Wiyot of California, a comparison with the California Penutian group as to relative age of linguistic differentiation might well favor the former.
>
> . . . One corollary of great historical interest follows from our argument

Reprinted from *To William Cameron Townsend on the Twenty-fifth Anniversary of the Summer Institute of Linguistics,* Cuernavaca, Mexico: Tipográfica Indígena, 1961, pp. 663–71.

as to the chronological significance of linguistic differentiation. . . . We must allow a tremendous lapse of time for the development of such divergences, a lapse of time undoubtedly several times as great as the period that the more conservative archaeologists and palaeontologists are willing to allow as necessary for the interpretation of the earliest remains of man in America. . . . While it is absurd to juggle with specific figures, it may be interesting to note that at a recent scientific meeting a well-known palaeontologist, who is at the same time conversant with the problem of early man in America, expressed himself as believing ten thousand years an ample, indeed a maximum, period for the human occupation of this continent. . . . This would make it practically imperative to assume that the peopling of America was not a single historical process but a series of movements of linguistically unrelated peoples, possibly from different directions and certainly at very different times. This view strikes me as intrinsically highly probable. As the latest linguistic arrivals in North America would probably have to be considered the Eskimo-Aleut and the Nadene (Haida, Tlingit, and Athapaskan).

. . . The more deep-lying resemblances, such as can be demonstrated, for instance, for Shoshonean, Piman, and Nahuatl (Mexico) or for Athapaskan and Tlingit, must be due to a common origin now greatly obscured by the operation of phonetic laws, grammatical developments and losses, analogical disturbances, and borrowing of elements from alien sources.

While the last citation does not speak of time periods as such, it helps to round out the other remarks. From all of them together and from the arrangement of groupings by headings and subheadings, we find the following time judgments to be stated or implied by Sapir: *(a)* Algonkin proper, several thousand years; *(b)* California Penutian, more than several thousand years; *(c)* Algonkin-Ritwan, more than *b*; *(d)* Penutian as a whole, more than *b* and probably more than *c*; *(e)* Uto Aztecan, enough to account for considerable differences and possibly similar to *a*; *(f)* Aztec-Tanoan, more than *e*; *(g)* Athapaskan-Tlingit, approximately like *e*; *(h)* Nadene, more than *g* but definitely less than the maximum; *(i)* Eskimo-Aleut, definitely less than the maximum. On the basis of the older estimates of the antiquity of man in America, Sapir considered the maximum time depth of any phylum developed in America to be ten thousand years, but this figure has been extended in recent years.

To the extent that the above-listed groupings have been tested by the recently developed lexicostatistic method (Swadesh, 1954a), Sapir's judgment has proved to be consistently sound.

Sapir did not achieve correct estimates of time depth by magic, but by a definite method, the basis of which is simply: "The greater the degree of linguistic differentiation within a stock, the greater is the period of time that must be assumed for the development of such differentiation" (1916, p. 76). He made time estimates by comparing the differentiation within a given language group with that found in some other family or stock of more or less known history, such as English-German or Indo-European. The successful practice of the method called for the ability to see complicated linguistic details in the perspective of their relative historical importance, and to heed objective facts rather than preconceptions. It was a kind of mental arithmetic, based on external facts, even when the weighting procedure was not written out.

The new lexicostatistic method represents an externalization of one part of Sapir's procedure, in that the data are always written out in the form of a standard vocabulary of noncultural words, constituting the diagnostic word list. It furthermore involves a simplification, in that Sapir's multiple lexical-morphological criteria are reduced to one, which has been found to be a reliable and easily determined index of the passage of time. The calculation (Swadesh, 1955) is based on the percentage of cognates (C) found in the diagnostic vocabularies of two related languages, considered in the light of a standard retention rate (r) or, in other words, the normal percentage of elements retained after a given unit of time as determined in a series of control languages. Divergence is determined in separation-time units (st), which is equal to minimum time (min t) of nonunity. Actual time (t) can be known once one establishes which cases within a language grouping involve complete separation (max s = 1 by definition). Time (t) is usually given in centuries. Once one has found t, one can then obtain a numerical index of the average degree of separation (s) for every pair of languages during the entire period since complete unity was first broken. Thus we learn not only the time depth but the degree of contact between two languages during their period of separate development. The equation and its derivatives are:

$$st = \log C \div \log r^2$$
$$\min t = \log C \div \log r^2$$
$$t = \log C \div s \log r^2$$
$$s = \log C \div t \log r^2$$

Sapir's indications of time depth for American linguistic groupings are not complete, as one may well understand in view of the difficulty of estimating them by his procedure. By the aid of lexicostatistic techniques the problem has become much simpler. What is needed is a collection of diagnostic word lists at least for all the key languages. I now have about three hundred from different parts of the New World,[1] about a third of these being from North America, which have made possible the evaluation of Sapir's estimates as already indicated.

1. A large fraction of these were supplied by linguists of the Summer Institute of Linguistics, particularly because of the cooperation of its founder, William C. Townsend. This is one of many ways in which we see fulfilled the scientific promise of Townsend's dream, applauded and encouraged by Sapir at its inception, of an institution to train linguistic workers and place them among the many tribes of America.

Proof of Common Origin

Lackner and Rowe (1955) have the impression that Sapir "proposed to classify languages primarily by similarities of morphology." They term this "Sapir's classificatory principle" and argue that it "remains a shaky basis on which to erect a genetic classification of languages." They are no doubt correct in suggesting that Sapir made use of morphological criteria "in setting up his famous classification of all North American languages into only six superstocks," but they are surely wrong in believing that this was his primary criterion of relationship. The best proof of their misconception is to be found precisely in the only article Sapir ever wrote dealing primarily with a purely structural feature of one of his linguistic phyla, the paper entitled "A Characteristic Penutian Form of Stem" (1921). While the bulk of this article is devoted to a structural matter, it also contains a full explanation of why he recognized a Penutian phylum at all. Morphological traits are found to be secondary.

Sapir starts by citing and quoting from Frachtenberg's *Comparative Studies in Takelman, Kalapuyan, and Chinookan Lexicography,* and goes on to say (emphasis added):

. . . All this is very interesting to me, as it chimes with conclusions or hypotheses I had arrived at independently. On the appearance of Frachtenberg's Coos grammar, it soon became clear to me that the morphological and *lexical resemblances* between Takelma and Coos were too numerous and fundamental to be explained away by accident or plausibly accounted for by borrowing. This *in spite of the very great differences of phonetics and structure* that separate the two languages. . . . Meanwhile comparison of Takelma, Coos, and Siuslaw with Dixon and Kroeber's Penutian of California (Costanoan, Miwok, Yokuts, Wintun, and Maidu) disclosed an astonishing number of *both lexical and morphological* correspondences, correspondences which were first dimly brought to my consciousness years ago by certain morphological resemblances between Takelma and Yokuts, later and more vividly by the decided Penutian "feel" of Coos grammar. After hesitating for a long while to take up seriously the possibility of affiliating Chinook, one of the most isolated and morphologically specialized languages in America, with the Penutian languages of Oregon, I now find myself forced by the evidence to admit such an affiliation as not only possible but decidedly probable. In view of the clear points of *lexical contacts* and of the phonetic shifts that Frachtenberg has established . . . between Takelma and Kalapuyan, his further hypothesis of a fundamental connection between Kalapuya and Chinook was, for me, to be looked for *a priori.* I believe it only fair to add that the manuscript evidence that I possess of the relation between Chinook and various languages to the south is much stronger than the comparatively scanty *lexical data* presented by Frachtenberg. . . .

The greatest surprise was still awaiting me: Tsimshian. . . . A tentative comparison with the Penutian . . . languages of Oregon revealed a considerable number of correspondences both *in the lexical material* and in some of the more intimate and fundamental features of morphology. . . .

The data for the various assertions I have made in this paper I expect to present *in extenso* in the future. . . .

It is seen here that morphological resemblances led Sapir to *look for* lexical correspondences, but are nowhere considered in themselves sufficient to prove relationship. In fact, Sapir at times finds reason to infer common origin "in spite of great differences of structure." While recognizing great stability in certain fundamental areas of morphology, he is equally aware that any of it is subject to change, given sufficient time and the continued exposure to diffusional and other influences. There is, then, no contradiction when he observes (1929) that "Chinook seems to have developed a secondary 'polysynthetic' form on the basis of a broken-down form of Penutian; while Tsimshian and Maidu have probably been considerably influenced by contact with Mosan and with Shoshonean and Hokan respectively."

That Sapir was not alone in attaching considerable importance to morphology may be seen from the following remark by Truman Michelson (1921):"When there are far-reaching structural resemblances between two or more supposedly distinct (and especially contiguous) stocks, we may legitimately infer an ancient connection which perhaps can no longer be proved owing to very early differentiation."

Evidence

When Lackner and Rowe speak of Sapir's groupings as made "on an impressionistic basis," they seem to be repeating Voegelin's use of the same adjective (1941, pp. 27–29). However, Voegelin explains (p. 27) that "a distinction is made between impressionistic classifications and classifications based on published evidence." In other words, "impressionistic" is here a special shorthand for "based on evidence not yet published." and Voegelin's usage is completely consistent throughout his paper, even though it may be confusing for any hasty reader. He has occasion to speak of undocumented connections at only four points: (*a*) the combining of Kutenai, Wakashan, and Salishan with Algonkin-Ritwan; (*b*) the inclusion of Zuñi in Aztec-Tanoan; (*c*) the inclusion of Klamath-Modoc, Molale, Sahaptin, Alsea, and Tsimshian in the Penutian phylum; (*d)* the inclusion of Yuki, Caddoan, Keresan, and Yuchi in Hokan-Siouan, and "special sub-relationships, such as Caddoan to Iroquoian." Hoijer (1946, pp. 13–23) notes the same instances, plus (*e*) the connection of Timuqua and Natchez-Muskogian.

The roster of relationships supported by published evidence is, of course, expanded from time to time. If one takes into account new works published since the Voegelin and Hoijer papers, plus unpublished manuscripts, plus research material now being assembled (see references under Sapir, Sapir and Swadesh, Haas, Jacobs, Greenberg and Swadesh, and Granberry), very few of the relationships in Sapir's synthesis remain undocumented.

Were any of Sapir's groupings literally impressionistic or purely speculative? Apparently not. The indications are that Sapir had actually examined material for every language or language family in his scheme, and made no groupings without having found specific evidence to support them. He frequently penciled comparisons in the margins of works in his library (see e.g. Sapir 1952) or wrote out lists of cognates, and his students know that he could cite cognates in support of many relationships from memory. Of course, he was also thoroughly familiar with the published literature on comparative linguistics. The Sapir classification is a synthesis of his own findings and those of his predecessors and contemporaries, but in no case did he cite published findings without having verified the evidence on which they were based.

Standard of Proof

In Voegelin's review of Sapir's synthesis, the only point at which he suggests possibly inadequate standards of proof is in connection with the Hokan-Siouan grouping. Thus (1941, p. 29):

> Paul Radin announced that Yuki belonged with Penutian . . . but credited the insight to Kroeber. Kroeber refused the honor. Sapir finally classified Yuki with Hokan-Siouan . . . possibly because Yuki would not fit in any other group. That is to say, this final group is loosely enough characterized to admit languages otherwise unclassifiable.

The fact that Yuki resisted the first efforts to classify it does not in itself prove that Sapir had no evidence for his placement of it. Our recent studies show that Penutian and Hokan are only different portions of a single network of linguistic groups, and that Yuki belongs with those Hokan languages which come the closest to Penutian.

Hoijer is very specific in acknowledging the rigor of Sapir's work, saying (1941, p. 8), "He achieved his revisions of the Powell classification by the strict application of the comparative method to American Indian materials." However, it happens that Hoijer sets an extraordinarily high standard of what constitutes indisputable proof of linguistic relationship, and by this yardstick Sapir's evidence of Hokan, along with that of Dixon and Kroeber, remains "far from conclusive."

Hoijer accepts modifications of Powell in only two cases, Uto-Aztecan, based on Sapir's work (1946, pp. 21–22), and Shasta-Achomawi, based on Dixon's (p. 16). He is less rigorously critical of Powell's work, saying this (p. 10):

> Though a number of far-reaching modifications of this classification have been suggested since, the groups set up by Powell still retain their validity.

In no case has a stock established by Powell been discredited by later work; the modifications that have been suggested are all concerned with the establishment of larger stocks to include two or more of the Powell groupings. . . . Most of these modifications have not as yet been indisputably established. . . .

Hoijer disregards the fact that the Powell classification was published without any documentary proof, even though he otherwise refuses to accept "unsupported" claims of relationship, e.g., Sapir's broad Penutian, the documentation for which had not yet been published when Hoijer wrote his paper (Sapir and Swadesh, 1953; also Sapir, *c*. 1920).

It is not quite true that only fusions of Powell groups have been proposed. Hoijer himself reports the opposite case with respect to Yakonan (p. 15):

Powell included in this group the Yakona, Alsea, Siuslaw and Lower Umpqua tribes . . . Wissler, in 1938, lists Siuslaw and Lower Umpqua together and puts Yakona and Alsea in a separate group. He gives no authority for this division of the Powell stock.

If we seek out Wissler's authority, we find it must have been Frachtenberg, in the Handbook of American Indian Languages, who tells (1922, p. 437):

In 1884 J. Owen Dorsey spent a month at the Siletz reservation, Oregon, collecting short vocabularies of the Siuslaw and Lower Umpqua, as well as other languages. Prior to Dorsey's investigations the linguistic position of Siuslaw and Lower Umpqua was a debated question. Some investigators believed that these two dialects belonged to the Yakonan family; while others, notably Latham and Gatschet, held them to form a distinct stock, although they observed marked agreement with some features of the Yakonan. After a superficial investigation, lasting less than a month, Dorsey came to the conclusion that Siuslaw and Lower Umpqua were dialects belonging to the Yakonan stock. This assertion was repeated by J. W. Powell in his "Indian Linguistic Families." . . . It is not at all impossible that this stock, the Yakonan, and perhaps the Kalapuyan, may eventually prove to be genetically related. Their affinities are so remote, however, that I prefer to take a conservative position, and to treat them for the time being as independent stocks.

From examination of some of the comparative material, I feel that Frachtenberg's view may be the better founded, and that at any rate the Yakonan-Siuslawan relation is distant. This case serves as a reminder that standards of accuracy need to be applied to Powell just as much as to Dixon, Kroeber, Swanton, Harrington, or Sapir. The norm should provide a good margin of safety to clearly separate agreement based on common origin from chance similarity. Any excessive standard is a wasteful luxury, which has the effect of unduly foreshortening the time depth penetrable by comparative linguistics. To get away from arbitrary subjective conceptions of proof requirements, one may make a mathematical calculation of the maximum effect of pure chance in a lexicostatistic test (see Swadesh, 1954b, pp. 312–15). The indications are that Sapir's yardstick was fully adequate.

Diffusion

Powell and most of his successors have evidently felt that in linguistics, unlike some other aspects of culture, it is usually possible to differentiate clearly between genetic and diffusional agreements. Powell's only remark bearing on the subject is (p. 26): "Neither coincidences nor borrowed material . . . can be properly regarded as evidences of cognation," evidently assuming that the cases could be recognized. Boas felt that this was ordinarily true but that occasionally an ambiguous situation might arise. The only concrete example of such a case he ever suggested was that of Tlingit-Athapaskan, but evidently even this case finally yielded to accumulated evidence, for we learn from Jacobs (1954) of:

> Evidence that Tlingit constitutes a subdivision of Nadene. Such evidence was assembled by Mrs. Melville Jacobs in a manuscript prepared in 1936 following her field research on southwestern Oregon Athapaskan Nadene dialects. Her discovery of many regular sound shifts between Tlingit and Athapaskan impressed Boas and Sapir with the unexpectedly close relationship of these groups. Boas then agreed that he and P. E. Goddard had been unduly hesitant about accepting the claim of Sapir that Tlingit was affiliated genetically with Athapaskan languages.

Language is that part of culture which is, as a whole, the least subject to diffusional changes. As Sapir put it (1930, p. 220), "Language is probably the most self-contained, the most massively resistant of all social phenomena. It is easier to kill it off than to disintegrate its individual form." Moreover, insofar as language is subject to the influence of diffusion, certain aspects are much more resistant than others. Consequently it is possible to single out certain aspects of linguistic morphology, phonetics, and vocabulary which tend to change at a rate so low that many centuries will elapse before any considerable difference has occurred. In the realm of vocabulary, the hard core of resistance to change generally and to diffusional change specifically is the noncultural vocabulary. Since words from foreign sources are also often to be detected by phonetic form, it is possible to build up a very dependable linguistic methodology for separating the influences of diffusion from ancient heritage. Lexicostatistics strengthens that methodology by permitting the study of maximum rates of diffusional replacement in diagnostic lists (Swadesh, 1951). With or without this refinement, the danger that "any significant fraction of the case represents old borrowing or convergence" (Lackner and Rowe, 129) in any critically developed genetic classification is, to say the least, not great.

Limitations

In Sapir's *Britannica* article, he describes his scheme of classification as

"suggestive but not demonstrable in all its features at the present time."
What are the features that Sapir considered chiefly undemonstrable? A
general consideration of Sapir's thinking on the problem of classification,
as expressed in his writings and teaching, suggest that they have been
principally matters of time scale. Is language A closer to B than to C?
Should a group A-B be set up alongside of C, or should the three be set on
a par? And finally, how do "wave" influences modify the hierarchical
scheme of groups, subgroups, and further subdivisions?

Sapir's conception of the wave theory did not confine it to the operation
of diffusion, but recognized also the common retention of like features among
a series of neighboring dialects. The system of showing relationships in a
sequence of headings and subheadings is not subtle enough to show these
relationships. If A, B, and C are branches of the same linguistic grouping,
they may be parallel and equivalent branches, so that the order in which the
three are set down makes no difference. In other instances, B may be an
intermediate type, with A and C further removed from each other than either
from B. In this event B might be a little closer to one than to the other
without actually forming a subgroup with it. These subtleties, reflecting
details in the prehistory of language groupings, were important to Sapir.
Where he had made a sufficient study, he could express his observations
in detailed discussion, but the outline form was not adequate. To improve
on his bird's-eye view of American languages would require a parallel
commentary, worked out only after a great deal of study, or some new
devices in the technique of outlining which could reflect the same facts.

Voegelin's suggestion that Sapir sometimes had to put languages in a
given place because they would not fit anywhere else may not be literally
correct, but there were related problems of relative time scale which left
an area of uncertainty as to where a given linguistic entity should fall
within the main divisions. Thus Zuñi fits poorly with Aztec-Tanoan, as
is indeed reflected in Sapir's question mark. If Zuñi is related to this phylum,
it is not on a par with the other two stocks, and it is not necessarily more
closely related to them than to other phyla in Sapir's classification. I feel
it may be somewhat closer to Penutian.

Sapir tried to overcome the artificial geographic limitation of "north of
Mexico" which Powell had been forced by practical considerations to adopt.
However, lack of data still prevented him from embracing all the languages,
regardless of location, which might belong with his phyla. This limitation
is now gradually being overcome.

Suggestions for Further Reading

Frachtenberg, Leo J.
  1922. "Siuslawan (Lower Umpqua)." In *Handbook of American Indian Languages*,
    ed. Franz Boas, Bureau of American Ethnology bulletin no. 40, pt. 2,
    pp. 431–629. Washington, D.C.: Smithsonian Institution. P. 437.

Granberry, Julian
    1955. "Current Research Materials on Relationship of Timuqua and Mus-
        kogian." Gainesville: Department of Social Sciences, University of Florida.
Greenberg, J. H., and Swadesh, M.
    1953. "Jicaque as a Hokan Language." *International Journal of American Linguistics*
        19:216–22.

Haas, Mary R.
    1951. "The Proto-Gulf Word for *Water* (With Notes on Siouan-Yuchi)." *Inter-
        national Journal of American Linguistics* 17:71–79.
    1952. "The Proto-Gulf Word for *Land* (With a Note on Proto-Siouan)." *Inter-
        national Journal of American Linguistics* 18:238–40.
    1954. "The Proto-Hokan-Coahuiltecan Word for *Water*." In *Papers from the
        Symposium on American Indian Linguistics*, University of California Publica-
        tions in Linguistics 10:1–68; pp. 57–62.

Hoijer, Harry
    1941. "Methods in the Classification of American Indian Languages." In
        Language, Culture, and Personality: Essays in Memory of Edward Sapir, ed.
        Leslie Spier *et al.*, pp. 3–14. Menasha, Wisc.: Sapir Memorial Publication
        Fund.
    1946. *Introduction to Linguistic Structures of Native America*. Viking Fund Publications
        in Anthropology no. 6, pp. 9–29.

Jacobs, Melville
    c.1930. "Molale Grammar." MS in the University of Washington Library, Seattle.
    1954. "The Areal Spread of Sound Features in the Languages North of Cali-
        fornia." In *Papers from the Symposium on American Indian Linguistics*, University
        of California Publications in Linguistics 10:1–68; p. 47, fn. 2.

Lackner, Jerome A., and Rowe, John H.
    1955. "Morphological Similarity as a Criterion of Genetic Relationship Between
        Languages." *American Anthropologist* 57:126–29.

Michelson, Truman
    1921. "The Classification of American Languages." *International Journal of
        American Linguistics* 2:73.

Powell, John W.
    1891. *Indian Linguistic Families of America North of Mexico*, Bureau of American
        Ethnology seventh annual report, pp. 7–142. Washington, D.C.: Smith-
        sonian Institution.

Sapir, Edward
    1916. *Time Perspective in Aboriginal American Culture: A Study in Method*, Bureau of
        Mines Geological Survey, memoir 90. Ottawa: Canadian Government
        Printing Office.
    c.1920. "Comparative Penutian glosses," (compiled from marginal notes in books
        and offprints which had belonged to Sapir). In the Franz Boas Collection
        of the American Philosophical Society Library, Philadelphia.
    1921a. "A Characteristic Penutian Form of Stem." *International Journal of American
        Linguistics* 2:58–67.
    1921b. "A Bird's-Eye View of American Languages North of Mexico." *Science*
        54:408.
    1929. "Central and North American Languages." In *Encyclopaedia Britannica*,
        14th ed., 5:138–41.

Sapir, Edward, and Swadesh, Morris
    1953. "Coos-Takelma-Penutian Comparisons." *International Journal of American
        Linguistics* 19:132–37.

Swadesh, Morris
  1951.   "Diffusional Cumulation and Archaic Residue as Historic Explanations."
          Southwestern Journal of Anthropology 7:1–21.
  1954a. "Time Depths of American Linguistic Groupings." *American Anthropologist*
          56:361–64.
  1954b. "Perspectives and Problems of Amerindian Comparative Linguistics."
          Word 10:306–32.
  1955.   "Towards Greater Accuracy in Lexicostatistic Dating." *International
          Journal of American Linguistics* 21, no. 2.
Voegelin, C. F.
  1941.   "North American Indian Languages Still Spoken and Their Genetic
          Relationships." In *Language, Culture, and Personality: Essays in Memory of
          Edward Sapir*, ed. Leslie Spier *et al.*, pp. 15–40. Menasha, Wisc.: Sapir
          Memorial Publication Fund.

Bibliography of Morris Swadesh

This bibliography to a great extent reflects a collective effort. In 1967 I first prepared a bibliography in connection with my article on Morris Swadesh for *Anales de Antropologia* (5:213–225 [1968]), using that of Juan Jose Rendon (*America Indigena* 27[4]:740–746 [1967]), and being aided by Regna Darnell and Joel Sherzer. My 1967 bibliography was not published, but contributed to the biobibliography in the second edition of *La nueva filologia* (1968a: 311–332), prepared from the work of Evangelina Arana de Swadesh, Daniel Cazes, Jaime Espinosa, Juan Jose Rendon, Madalena Sancho, and myself. In June and July 1970 I have worked from the mimeographed 1967 bibliography, revising it in the light of Stanley Newman (*Language* 43 [4]:950–957 [1967]), *La nueva filologia*, additional information from Evangelina Arana de Swadesh as to more recent publications, further research. I am indebted to Murphy Smith for assistance with unpublished materials in the Library of the American Philosophical Society, and to Freeman and Smith 1966, as a guide to them.

It has been possible to add a few minor items for earlier years, as well as more recent publications; to add a few unpublished manuscripts of significance to the development of Swadesh's work; and to amplify the information for a good many items, as well as to correct errors of date and pagination. With but one exception (1939i), it has been possible to verify all respects in which the information given here differs from previously published bibliographies. It is the hope of all of us who have contributed to this work that the results will be seen, not only as testimony to a varied and productive career, but also as an aid to the further study and understanding of that career, and of the many activities, significant to the present and future of linguistics and the human sciences, of which that career has been part.   Dell Hymes

Abbreviations

AA	American Anthropologist
A de A	Anales de Antropología (México, D. F., UNAM, IIH, Sección de Antropología)
ACLS	American Council of Learned Societies
AL	Anthropological Linguistics
Am Sp	American Speech
APS	American Philosophical Society
	APSY, PAPS, TAPS: Yearbook, Proceedings, Transactions
CA	Current Anthropology
ENAH	Escuela Nacional de Antropología e Historia
IIH	Instituto de Investigaciones Históricas
IJAL	International Journal of American Linguistics
INAH	Instituto Nacional de Antropología e Historia

INI	Instituto Nacional Indigenista
Lg	Language
PAPS	See APS
RMEA	Revista Mexicana de Estudios Antropológicos
SWJA	Southwestern Journal of Anthropology
TAPS	See APS
UNAM	Universidad Nacional Autónoma de México

1931   *Nootka Aspect.* Unpublished M.A. thesis. Chicago, Illinois, University of Chicago. [Revised as "The Nootka Aspect System," 1931–32 (Freeman 2421).]

1932   Sapir, Edward, and Swadesh, Morris. *The expression of the ending-point relation in English, French and German.* Edited by Alice V. Morris. (Language Monographs 10.) Baltimore, Linguistic Society of America. Pp. 125.

1933a   *The Internal Economy of the Nootka Word: A semantic study of word structure in a polysynthetic language.* Unpublished Ph.D. dissertation. New Haven, Connecticut, Yale University. [Freeman 2420] [See also 1939a, c.]

1933b   "Chitimacha Verbs of Derogatory or Abusive Connotation, with Parallels from European Languages." *Language* 9:192–201.

1933c   Swadesh, Mary Haas, and Swadesh, Morris. A Visit to the other World. A Nitinat text (with translation and grammatical analysis). *International Journal of American Linguistics* 7:195–208.

1934a   "The Phonemic Principle." *Language* 10:117–129. [Reprint in Joos 1957:32–37.]

1934b   "The Phonetics of Chitimacha." *Language* 10:345–362.

1934c   Herzog, G., Newman, S., Sapir, E., Swadesh, M. H., Swadesh, Morris, and Voegelin, C. Some Orthographic Recommendations Arising out of Discussions by a Group of Six Americanist Linguists. *American Anthropologist* 36:629–631.

1935a   "The Vowels of Chicago English." *Language* 11:148–151.

1935b   "Twaddell on Defining the Phoneme." *Language* 11:245–250.

1935c   Review of Manuel T. Andrade, Quileute. *International Journal of American Linguistics* 8(3–4):219–220.

1936a   "Phonemic Contrasts." *American Speech* 11:298–301.

1936b   Review of S. C. Boyanus. "A Manual of Russian Pronunciation." *Language* 12:147–149.

1936c   Review of Melville Jacobs. "Northwest Sahaptin Texts, Part 1". *The Pacific Northwest Quarterly* 27:179–180.

1936d   Review of G. K. Zipf. "The Psycho-Biology of Language." *American Anthropologist* 38:505–506.

1937a   Swadesh, Morris (ed. and author). *Bulletin of information on the scientific study of American Indian languages.* [Typed ms. Pp. 57 with appendices by E. Sapir, L. Bloomfield, et al. (Freeman 1977 and Boas Papers Miscellaneous B/B61).]

1937b   "The Phonemic Interpretation of Long Consonants." *Language* 13:1–10.

1937c   "Some Minimally Different Word Pairs." *American Speech* 12:127.

1937d   Newman, Stanley, and Trager, George L. "Comments and Suggestions For an American Phonemic Dictionary." *American Speech* 12:138–139.

1937e   "A Method for Phonetic Accuracy and Speed." *American Anthropologist* 39:728–732.

1937f   Review of Ruth Bunzel, Zuni. *Language* 13:253–255.

1937g   Swadesh, Morris, Boas, Franz. "Report by Investigators, (3) Report of Progress, 1936," Annex 8, Research on American Native Languages. *American Council of Learned Societies Bulletin* 26 (June): 74–77.

1938   "Bibliography of American Indian Linguistics," 1936–1937. *Language* 14:318–323.

1939a   Sapir, Edward, and Swadesh, Morris. *Nootka texts. Tales and ethnological narratives, with grammatical notes and lexical materials.* William Dwight Whitney Linguistic Series. Philadelphia, Linguistic Society of America, University of Pennsylvania.

1939b   *Chitimacha Grammar, Texts, and Vocabulary.* Typed ms. Pp. 606. [Freeman 732]

1939c   Swadesh, Morris, and Voegelin, Charles F. "A Problem in Phonological Alternation." *Language* 15:1–10. [Reprinted in Joos 1957:88–92]

1939d   "Nootka Internal Syntax." *International Journal of American Linguistics* 9:77–192

1939e   A Condensed Account of Mandarin Phonetics. Etudes phonologiques dedié à la memoire de M. le prince N. S. Trubetzkoy, 213–216. (Travaux du Cercle Linguistique de Prague 8.) Prague, Jednuta českých matematiků a fysiků.

1939f   El congreso lingüístico y la educacíon rurál. *Tesis* 1:5–7.

1939g   Sobre el alfabeto quechua-aymara. *Boletín Bibliográfico de Antropología Americana* 3:14–15.

1939h   Edward Sapir (Bibliography) *Boletín Bibliográfico de Antropología Americana* 3:80–86. México, D. F.

1939i   Proyecto de plan de educación indígena en lenguà nativa tarasca. *Boletín Bibliográfico de Antropología Americana* 3 (3):222–227. México, D. F.

1939j   La incorporación.. Dos caminos. Memoria de la Conferencia Nacional de Educación, México, 81–83.

1939k   El proyecto Tarasco. Memoria de la Conferencia Nacional de Educación, México, 83–88.

1939l   Sapir, Edward. *Language* 15:132–135.

1939m   Review of Investigaciones Lingüísticas (Organo del Instituto Mexicano de Investigaciones Lingüísticas) and Cuadernos Lingüísticas (Suplemento escolar de Investigaciones Lingüísticas). *International Journal of American Linguistics* 9:120–122.

1940a   *Orientaciones lingüísticas para maestros en zonas indigenas.* México, D. F., Departamento de Asuntos Indígenas de la República Mexicana. Pp. 77.

1940b   El proyecto tarasco. La enseñanza en lengua nativa. *Tesis* 2:13–18.

1941a   *La nueva filología.* (Biblioteca del maestro, 4.) México, D. F., El Nacional. 2nd ed., 1968. Pp. 288.

1941b   Swadesh, Morris, Lounsbury, Floyd, and Archiquette, Oscar, eds. *OnΛ yeda?a·ga· Deyeliwahgwa·ta* [Oneida Hymn Book]. Oneida, Wisconsin, F. Lounsbury ["né· detolisdohlala·kᵘ"' = "he printed/typed it"]. Mimeographed and bound. Pp. 100.

1941c   Spier, Leslie, Hallowell, A. Irving, and Newman, Stanley S., eds., *Language, Culture and Personality: Essays in Memory of Edward Sapir.* Menasha, Wisconsin, Banta. 59–65. Observation of pattern impact on the phonetics of bilinguals. [Reprinted Swadesh 1960a, 37–45. Book republished, Salt Lake City, University of Utah Press, 1960.]

1943   [Abstract.] The Future of Basic English. *Bulletin.* Linguistic Circle of New York. Mimeographed. [Inferred from *Word* 1:95 (1945).]

1944a   Office of Strategic Services. *How to Pick Up a Foreign Language.* Washington, D. C., Pamphlet. Pp. 16.

1944b   "Scientific Linguistics and Basic English." Basic English, The Reference Shelf 17 (1):194–206.

1945a   *Talking Russian Before You Know It.* New York, Holt. Pp. 134.

1945b   Office of Strategic Services. *The Words You Need in Burmese.* Washington, D. C., Pamphlet. Pp. 35.

1946a Hoijer, Harry, et al., "South Greenlandic Eskimo." *Linguistic Structures of Native America.* (Viking Fund Publications in Anthropology 6) 30–54. New York, Wenner-Gren Foundation for Anthropological Research [then, Viking Fund].

1946b Hoijer, Harry, et al., "Chitimacha." *Linguistic Structures of Native America* (Viking Fund Publications in Anthropology 6), 312–336. New York, Wenner-Gren Foundation for Anthropological Research [then, Viking Fund].

1946c Phonologic Formulas for Atakapa-Chitimacha. *International Journal of American Linguistics* 12:113–132.

1946d Sapir, Edward, and Swadesh, Morris. "American Indian Grammatical Categories." *Word* 2:103–112. [Reprinted in Hymes 1964:100–107.]

1946e "Talk Russian." *Review and Digest* (June, July, August, September). Pp. 20 total.

1947a "Atakapa-Chitimacha *kʷ." *International Journal of American Linguistics* 13:120–121.

1947b La planeación científica de la educación indígena en México. Actas de la primera sesion del XXVII Congreso Internacional de Americanistas (Mexico City, 1939). 2:261–268. México, D. F., *Instituto Nacional de Antropología e Historia,* Secretaria de Educacion Publica.

1947c "On the Analysis of English Syllabics." *Language* 23:137–150.

1947d "The Phonemic Structure of Proto–Zapotec." *International Journal of American Linguistics* 13:220–230.

1948a *Chinese in Your Pocket.* (Foreword by Yuen Ren Chao.) New York, Holt. Pp. xvi, 185, illus., maps. 2nd ed., 1964.

1948b "South Greenlandic Paradigms." *International Journal of American Linguistics* 14:29–36.

1948c "Motivations in Nootka Warfare." *Southwestern Journal of Anthropology* 4:76–93. (Also Swadesh 1960a, 13–35.)

1948d "A Structural Trend in Nootka." *Word* 4:106–119.

1948e "Sociologic Notes on Obsolescent Languages." *International Journal of American Linguistics* 14:226–235. [Also Swadesh 1960a, 65–79.] [First given as a lecture, 1938.]

1948f "On Linguistic Mechanism." *Science and Society* 12:254–259.

1948g "The Time Value of Linguistic Diversity." Paper presented at the Viking Fund Supper Conference, March 12, New York City. [Abstract in part, 1952a:454.]

1948h Review of Franz Boas. "Kwakiutl Grammar With a Glossary of The Suffixes." *Word* 4:58–63.

1948i Review of Benvenute Terracini. "Que es la lingüística?" *Language* 24:182–183.

1949a El idioma de los Zapotecos. L. Mendieta y Núñez (ed.), Los Zapotecos. Monografía Histórica, Etnográfica y Económica, 415–448. México, D. F., *Universidad Nacional Autonoma de Mexico,* Instituto de Investigaciones Sociales.

1949b Smith, Marian W., ed., "The Linguistic Approach to Salish Prehistory." *Indians of The Urban Northwest.* New York, Columbia University Press, 161–173.

1949c Swadesh, Morris, and Léon, Frances. "Two Views of Otomi Prosody." *International Journal of American Linguistics* 15:100–105.

1950a "Salish Internal Relationships." *International Journal of American Linguistics* 16:157–167.

1950b Review of Rafael Girard. "Los Chortís ante el problema maya." *Word* 6:201–203.

328 *The Origin and Diversification of Language*

1950c   [On magnetic recording of texts in Makah and Nootka.] C. F. Voegelin, Magnetic recording of American Indian languages and the relationship of this to other kinds of memory. *Proceedings, American Philosophical Society* 94(3):295–300, pp. 299–300. [Reply to circular letter summarized by Voegelin.]

1951a   "Basic Vocabulary of Glottochronology." Mimeographed. Denver.

1951b   "Diffusional Cumulation and Archaic Residue as Historical Explanations." *Southwestern Journal of Anthropology* 7:1–21. [Revised as "Glottochronology" in Fried 1959:199–218; 2nd ed., 1968. A revised version in Hymes 1964: 624–635. Bobbs-Merrill reprint A–220.]

1951c   "Kleinschmidt Centennial III: Unaaliq and Proto-Eskimo." *International Journal of American Linguistics* 17:66–70.

1951d   Swadesh, Morris, and Marsh, Gordon. "Eskimo–Aleut Correspondences." *International Journal of American Linguistics* 17:209–216.

1951e-j   [Articles in Collier's Encyclopedia, New York, P. F. Collier and Son. Pagination as of 1953 ed. Page i = "First published in complete form in 1952." Morris Swadesh cited (p. xlix) as of his 1948–49 position.]
     1951e   American Indian Languages. 1:477.
     1951f   Basic English. 3:220.
     1951g   English language. 7:332–333.
     1951h   Eskimo-Aleut. 7:414.
     1951i   Edward Sapir. 17:344.
     1951j   Slang. 17:631–632.

1951k   "Chitimacha." *Encyclopedia Britannica* 5:602. Chicago, Encyclopedia Brittanica. [Unsigned; cited from 1953 ed.]

1951l   La glotocronología del nahuatl. Trabajo presentado en las Mesas Redondas de Antropología e Historia, celebrados en Jalapa, Veracruz, el mes de julio de 1951.

1951m   La glotocronología del Uto-Aztecan. Conferencia de Mesa Redonda de Jalapa.

1951n   Review of Lorenzo Dow Turner. "Africanisms in the Gullah Dialect." *Word* 7:82–84.

1951o   Review of Nils N. Holmer. "Lexical and Morphological Contacts Between Siouan and Algonquian." *Word* 7:85.

1952a   "Lexico–Statistic Dating of Prehistoric Ethnic Contacts (With Special Reference to North American Indians and Eskimos)." *Proceedings, American Philosophical Society* 96:452–563.

1952b   "Salish Phonologic Geography." *Language* 28:237–48.

1952c   "Unaaliq and Proto–Eskimo II: Phonemes and Morphophonemes." *International Journal of American Linguistics* 18:25–34.

1952d   "Unaaliq and Proto–Eskimo III: Synchronic Notes." *International Journal of American Linguistics* 18:69–76.

1952e   "Unaaliq and Proto–Eskimo IV: Diachronic Notes." *International Journal of American Linguistics* 18:166–171.

1952f   "Unaaliq and Proto–Eskimo V: Comparative Vocabulary." *International Journal of American Linguistics* 18:241–256.

1952g   "Communication: Nationalism and Language Reform in China." *Science and Society* 16:273–280.

1952h   "Comment on Robert Shafer, Athabaskan and Sino–Tibetan." *International Journal of American Linguistics* 18:178–181.

1953a   "Mosan I: A Problem of Remote Common Origin." *International Journal of American Linguistics* 19:26–44.

1953b Sapir, Edward, and Swadesh, Morris. "Coos–Takelma–Penutian Comparisons." *International Journal of American Linguistics* 19:132–137.

1953c Andrade, Manuel J., ed. "Relations between Nootka and Quileute." *International Journal of American Linguistics* 19:138–140. [Editorial note, 138; analytic notes, passim.]

1953d "Comment on Hockett's critique." *International Journal of American Linguistics* 19:152–153.

1953e Greenberg, Joseph, and Swadesh, Morris. "Jicaque as a Hokan Language." *International Journal of American Linguistics* 19:216–222.

1953f "Mosan II: Comparative Vocabulary." *International Journal of American Linguistics* 19:223–236.

1953g "Salish–Wakashan Lexical Comparisons noted by Boas." *International Journal of American Linguistics* 19:290–291.

1953h "Archaeological and Linguistic Chronology of Indo-European Groups." *American Anthropologist* 55:349–352.

1953i Carnegie Institute of Washington, "The Language of The Archaeologic Huastecs." *Notes on Middle American Archaeology and Ethnology* 114, 223–227. Washington, D.C.

1953j Cuestionario para el cálculo léxico-estadístico de la cronología prehistórica. *Boletín Indigenista Venezolano* 1:517–519.

1954a *Amerindian non-cultural vocabularies*. First ed. Denver.

1954b "On the Penutian Vocabulary Survey." *International Journal of American Linguistics* 20:123–133. [Section 4, Report on audition of the tapes, by Florence M. Voegelin, 129–133.]

1954c Algunas fechas glotocronológicas importantes para la prehistoria nahua. (Sociedad Mexicana de Antropología, VI Mesa Redonda (Chapultepec). *Revista Mexicana de Estudios Antropológicos* 14(1):173–192.

1954d "Perspectives and Problems of Amerindian Comparative Linguistics." *Word* 10:306–332.

1954e "Time Depths of Amerindian Linguistics Groupings." *American Anthropologist* 56:361–364. [With comments by G. I. Quimby, H. B. Collins, E. W. Haury, G. F. Ekholm, F. Eggan, 364–377.] *AA* 56:361–377.

1954f Newman, Stanley. "American Indian Linguistics in the Southwest." Comments *American Anthropologist* 56:639–642.

1954g Review of Eugene A. Nida. "Learning a Foreign Language." *Word* 10:83–85.

1954h Review of J. A. Mason. "The Language of The Papago Indians." *Word* 10:110–114.

1954i Review of Marcel Cohen. "Le langage, structure et evolution." *International Journal of American Linguistics* 20:342–345.

1955a *Amerindian cultural vocabularies*. Revised ed. Denver.

1955b Sapir, Edward, and Swadesh, Morris. *Native Accounts of Nootka Ethnography*. Indiana University Research Center in Anthropology, Folklore and Linguistics, Publication 1. Bloomington. Pp. 457. [Appreciation, p. 5, dated 1950.]

1955c Roberts, Helen H., and Swadesh, Morris. "Songs of the Nootka Indians of Western Vancouver Island." [Based on phonographic records, linguistic and other field notes made by Edward Sapir.] *Transactions, American Philosophical Society* 45(3):199–327.

1955d "Linguistic and Ethnological Aspects of Nootka Songs." Part II, 310–327, of 1955c.

1955e "La variacion *a-e* en los dialectos nahuas." *Archive Nahuas* 1:3–15.

1955f "The Culture–Historical Meaning of Sapir's Linguistic Classification." *The Journal of the Colorado–Wyoming Academy of Sciences* 4:23–24.

1955g   "Papago Stop Series." *Notice* 11:191–193.
1955h   "Chemakum Lexicon Compared with Quileute." *International Journal of American Linguistics* 21:60–72.
1955i   "Towards Greater Accuracy in Lexico–Statistic Dating." *International Journal of American Linguistics* 21:121–137.
1955j   Baldus, Herbert, ed. "Towards a Satisfactory Genetic Classification of Amerindian Languages. *Anais de XXXI Congresso Internacional de Americanistas* (São Paulo, 1954), 1001–1012. São Paulo, Editora Anhembi.
1955k   "Linguistic Time Depths of Prehistoric America: Penutian." [Report on grant.] *American Philosophical Society Yearbook* (1954), 375–377.
1955l   Review of Arthur Thibert, "English–Eskimo, Eskimo–English Dictionary," and of Mary R. Haas, "Tunica Dictionary." *Word* 11:350–352.
1955m   "Review of Papers From the Symposium on American Indian Linguistics Held at Berkeley, July 7, 1951." *Word* 11:353–358.
1956a   "La capacidad expresiva de las lenguas nativas." *Accion Indigenista* 32:2–4.
1956b   "Problems of Long–Range Comparison in Penutian." *Language* 32:17–41.
1956c   Conceptos geográfico-cronológicos de cultura y lengua. Estudios antropólogicos publicados en homenaje al Doctor Manuel Gamio, 673–683. México, D. F., Dirección General de Publicaciones. [Reprinted, 1960a 81–92.]
1956d   Swadesh, Morris, Castro, A., Pedraza, J., and Wallis, E. *Los Otomies hablamos en Castellano. Juegos para aprender castellano.* México, D. F., Instituto Indigenista Interamericano.
1956e   Patronato Indigena del Valle del Mezquital e Instituto Linguistico de Verano. Mimeographed 1921.
1956f   "Some Limitations of Diffusional Change in Vocabulary." *American Anthropologist* 58:301–306.
1956g   "American Aboriginal Languages." *Encyclopedia Brittanica* 1:751–752D. Chicago, William Benton. [Cited from 1958 edition.]
1956h   The present state of research into the interrelation of language families. Contribution, Section B, Comparative Linguistics 5, F. Norman, ed., Proceedings of the Seventh International Congress of Linguists (London 1952), 134. London, [distributed by] International University Booksellers for the Seventh International Congress of Linguists.
1956i   [On quantitative criteria for proving linguistic relationships. Response to organizer's question:] What special problems arise in the comparative study of languages without a history? What special methods are applicable in such fields. General Discussion. Section B, Comparative Linguistics 1. F. Norman, ed., Proceedings of the Seventh International Congress of Linguists (London 1952), 380–389. London [distributed by] International University Booksellers for the Seventh International Congress of Linguists.
1956j   Review of Johannes Friedrich. "Kurze Grammatik der alten Quiché–Sprache im Popul Vuh." *Language* 32:819–822.
1957a   *Términos de parentesco comunes entre Tarasco y Zuni.* (Cuadernos del IIH de la UNAM Serie Antropológica 3). México, D. F., *Universidad Nacional Autónoma de México* Pp. 39.
1957b   *Materiales para un diccionario del filum penutióide.* (Cuadernos del Instituto de Historia, Serie Antropológica 6.) México, D. F., *Universidad Nacional Autónoma de México.* [Cited to Cuadernos by Swadesh 1960l:157. Carbon of ms. so identified on title page (received by Hymes, Dec. 1957).]
1957c   "Quiénes eran los proto penutióides." Cited to Gloto-cronología y las lenguas oto-mangues (Cuadernos del Instituto de Historia) by Swadesh 1960l:157.

1957d Review of Manfred Sandmann. "Subject and Predicate." *Language* 33: 190–193.

1957e Joos, Martin, ed., *Readings in Linguistics*, 32–37, 88–92. (Reprinting of 1934a, 1939e.) Washington D. C., American Council of Learned Societies.

1958a–1960 *Materiales para un diccionario comparativo de las lenguas Amerindias*. Manuscript.

1958b Hanke, Wanda, Swadesh, Morris, and Rodriguez, Arion D. Notas de fonología Mekens. Miscellanea Paul Rivet, octogenario dicata 2:187–217. [Printed 1959.] [Tribute from.] (El XXXI Congreso Internacional de Americanistas.) (Publicaciones del Instituto de Historia, serie 1, no. 50.) México, D. F., *Universidad Nacional Autónoma de México*.

1958c "Some New Glottochronologic Dates for Amerindian Linguistic Groups." *Proceedings of the 32nd International Congress of Americanists* (Copenhagen 1956), 671–674. Copenhagen, Munksgaard.

1958d Canonge, Elliott. Introduction to "Comanche Texts." *Linguistic Series 1*. Norman, Oklahoma, Summer Institute of Linguistics.

1959a *Indian Linguistic Groups of Mexico*. (Tlatoani, Boletín de la Sociedad de Alumnos de la Escuela Nacional de Antropología e Historia.) México, D. F., *Escuela Nacional de Antropología e Historia, Instituto Nacional de Antrología e Historia*. Pp. 14; 2 maps. [Published in commemoration of the fifty-eighth annual meeting of the American Anthropological Association, held in Mexico City in December 1959.]

1959b *Mapas de clasificación lingüística de México y las Américas*. (Cuadernos del Instituto de Investigaciones Históricas de la Universidad Nacional Autónoma de México, Publicaciones 5, serie 1, Serie Antropológica 8.) México, D. F. Pp. 37, 3 maps.

1959c "Linguistics as an Instrument of Prehistory." *Southwestern Journal of Anthropology* 15:20–33. [Reprinted in Hymes 1964:575–583. Bobbs-Merrill Reprint A–221. Revised, 1960b; see 1960a, 93–128.]

1959d "The Mesh Principle in Comparative Linguistics." *Anthropological Linguistics* 1(2);7–14.

1959e Fernandez, Maria Th. de Miranda, Swadesh, Morris, and Weitlaner, R. J. "Some Findings on Oaxaca Language Classification and Cultural Terms." *International Journal of American Linguistics* 25:54–58.

1959f Cook de Leonard, Carmen, ed., Ochenta lenguas autóctonas. El esplendor del México Antiguo 1:85–96. México, D. F., Centro de Investigaciones Antropológicas de México. [Reprinted with some modifications as "Las lenguas indígenas de México," Swadesh 1960a: 153–159.]

1959g (Miguel Othón de Mendizàbal, Wigbert Jiménez Moreno, Morris Swadesh, and Evangelina Arana Osnaya.) Mapa de las lenguas indígenas de México, Distribución antigua. Carmen Cook de Leonard, ed., Esplendor del México Antiguo 1:96 (unpaginated insert). México, D. F., Centro de Investigaciones Antropológicas de México.

1959h La lingüística de las regiones entre las civilizaciones mesoamericanas y andinas. Actas del XXXIII Congreso Internacional de Américanistas (San Jose, Costa Rica, 1958), 1:123–136. San Jose, Costa Rica, Editorial Antonio Lehmann. [Vol. 1, 15 August 1959; vol. 2, 30 April 1960.]

1959i Don Gumesindo Mendoza y el origen del Náhuatl. México en la Cultura Novedades (April 12).

1959j El origen de 2000 lenguas indígenas en América. México en la Cultura, Novedades (October 18). [Reprinted, Swadesh 1960a, 145–151, as "El origen de las 2,000 lenguas en América."]

1959k   Review of Martha Hildebrandt. "Sistema Fonémico del Maoíta." *Language*
         35:105–108.

19591   "Glottochronology." Fried, Morton H., ed., *Readings in Anthropology*, 199–218.
         New York, Thomas Crowell. 2nd ed., 1968. (Revised reprinting of 1951b.).

1960a   *Estudios sobre lengua y cultura.* Prefacio, Guillermo Benfil B. (Acta Antro-
         pólogica, 2a Epoca, II-2). México, D. F., *Escuela Nacional de Antropología e
         Historia*, Sociedad de Alumnos, Moneda 16. Pp. 190; 1 map. Containing:
             Observaciones del conflicto fonético en personas bilingües, 37–45 [1941]
             Algunas técnicas fáciles de lingüística para el etnólogo, 47–64.
             Notas sociológicas sobre la extinción de lenguas, 65–79 [1948]
             Conceptos geográficos-cronológicos de cultura y lengua, 81–92 [1956]
             La lingüística como instrumento de la prehistoria, 93–128 [1959, 1960]
             ¿Que es la gloto-cronología? 129–143.
             El origen de las 2,000 lenguas en América, 145–151 [1959]
             Las lenguas indígenas de México, 153–169 [1959]
             Las lenguas aborígenes de América, 171–190.

1960b   *La lingüística como instrumento de la prehistoria.* Con traducción y material
         ilustrative de Leonardo Manrique. (Dirección de Prehistoria, Publicación
         9.) México, D. F., *Instituto Nacional de Antropología e Historia*. Pp. 36. [Revised
         from 1959b; reprinted in 1960a.]

1960c   *Tras la huella lingüística de la prehistoria.* (Suplementos del Seminario de
         Problemas Científicos y Filosóficas, 2a Serie, 26:97–145), México, D. F.,
         Universidad Nacional Autónoma de México.

1960d   Sapir, Edward, and Swadesh, Morris. *Yana dictionary.* Edited by Mary R.
         Haas. (University of California Publications in Linguistics 22.) Berkeley and
         Los Angeles, University of California Press, Pp. 267.

1960e   Hymes, Dell. "Lexicostatistics So Far." (Comments) *Current Anthropology*
         1:3–44. [Passim]

1960f   "On the Unit of Translation." *Anthropological Linguistics* 2(2):39–42.

1960g   "The Oto–Manguean Hypothesis and Macro–Mixtecan." *International
         Journal of American Linguistics* 26:79–111.

1960h   Problems in language salvage for prehistory. International Committee on
         Urgent Anthropological and Ethnological Research, Bulletin 3:13–19.
         Vienna, International Union of Anthropological and Ethnological Sciences.

1960i   "On Interhemispheric Linguistic Connections." *Culture in History: Essays in
         Honor of Paul Radin.* Stanley Diamond, ed., New York, Columbia University
         Press 894–924. [(Abridged) Owen, Roger, Deetz, James, and Fisher,
         Anthony, eds., *The North American Indians.* A sourcebook, 91–95. New York
         Macmillan.]

1960j   Unas correlaciones de arqueología y lingüística. Pedro Bosch-Gimpera, El
         problema indoeuropa, Apéndice, 343–352 (with maps). (Publicaciones del
         Instituto de Historia, 1 ser., no. 45.) México, D. F., *Universidad Nacional
         Autónoma de México, Instituto de Investigaciones Históricas.*

1960k   Discussion of Norman A. McQuown, Middle American Linguistics 1955.
         Gordon Willey, et al. (eds.), Middle American anthropology 2:32–34.
         (Social Science Monographs 10.) Washington, D.C., Pan American Union.

19601   Swadesh, Morris, Fernandez, Maria Th. de Miranda, and Weitlaner, R. J.
         El panorama etnolingüístico de Oaxaca y el Istmo. (Sociedad Mexicana de
         Antropología, VII Mesa Redonda (Oaxaca).) *Revista Mexicana de Estudios
         Antropológicos* 16:137–157.

1961a   The Culture Historic Implications of Sapir's Linguistic Classification. A
         William Cameron Townsend en el vigésimo quinto aniversario del Instituto
         Linguístico de Verano, 663–671. México, D. F.

1961b   Interrelaciones de las lenguas Mayas. Anales del *Instituto Nacional de Antropología e Historia* (1960) 13:231–267.

1961c   Los Supuestos Australianos en América. Homenaje a Pablo Martínez del Río en el XXV Aniversario de la edición de los Orígenes Americanos, 147–161. México, D. F. *Instituto Nacional de Antropología e Historia.*

1961d   Algunos reflejos lingüísticos de la prehistoria de Chiapas. Los mayas del sur y sus relaciones con los nahuas meridionales, 145–159. (Sociedad Mexicana de Antropología, VIII Mesa Redonda (San Cristobal las Casas, Chiapas).) México, D. F.

1961e   Problemas en el salvamiento del lenguaje para la prehistoria. *Revista del Museo Nacional* (Lima) 30:60–64.

1961f   Swadesh, Morris, and Escalante, Roberto. Resumen. (Una aportación lingüística a la prehistoria indoeuropa.) Gerhard Besu (ed.) with Wolfgang Dehn. Bericht über den V. Internationalen Kongress fur Ver- und Frühgeschichte (Hamburg 1958); 799. Berlin, Verlag Gebr. Mann.

1961g   Notas a "El método lexicostatística y su aplicacion a las relaciones del Vascuence" (por Antiono Tovar). *Boletín de la Real Sociedad Vascongado de los Amigos del País* 17 (3):18–21.

1962a   McQuown, Norman A., and Swadesh, Morris. Bericht der vom. 33. Internationalen Amerikanistenkongress eigesetzen linguistischen Kommission. Akten des 34. Internationalen Amerikanistenkongresses (Wien 1960). 727–728. Horn-Wien, Verlag Ferdinand Berger.

1962b   Afinidades de las lenguas Amerindias. Akten des 34. Internationalen Amerikanistenkongresses (Wien 1960), 729–738. Horn-Wien, Verlag Ferdinand Berger.

1962c   Poppe, Nicholas, ed. "Archaic Doublets in Altaic." *American Studies in Altaic Linguistics*, 293–330. (Ural and Altaic Studies 13) Bloomington, Indiana University.

1962d   "Lingustic Relations Across Bering Strait." *American Anthropologist* 64: 1262–1291.

1962e, f [Resumen.] El idioma como estructura lingüística. Guía para el Maestro. La Ensenanza de lengua en Puerto Rico, 9. Educación. San Juan, Puerto Rico. Departmento de Instrucción Pública. [The full article was published in 1962 in the Puerto Rican journal *Educación*, not available to me now.]

1962g   Bergsland, Knut, and Vogt, Hans. "On the Validity of Glottochronology." Comments. *Current Anthropology* 3:143–145.

1962h   Prólogo. Carlos Robles Uribe, Manual del Tzeltal. Ensayo de Gramática del Tzeltal de Bachajon, 9–11. (Universidad Iberamericana, Publicaciones en Antropología.) México, D. F. [Presentado como Tesis de Maestría en la ENAH.]

1962i   Review of Knut Bergsland. "Aleut Dialects of Atka and Attu." *Language* 38:101–103.

1963a   El Tamaulipeco. *Revista Mexicana de Estudios Antropológicos* 19:93–104.

1963b   "A Punchcard System of Cognate Hunting." *International Journal of American Linguistics* 29:283–288.

1963c   "Nuevo ensayo de glotocropología yutonahua." Anales del *Instituto Nacional de Antropología e Historia* 15:263–302.

1963d   Tax, Sol. "Aboriginal Languages of Latin America." Comment. *Current Anthropology* 4(3):317–318.

1963e   Review of Viola G. Waterhouse. "The Grammatical Structure of Oaxaca Chontal." *American Anthropologist* 65:1197–1198.

1963f   Swadesh, Morris, et al. Projecto de *Libro de Lectura*. Presentado a la Comisión Nacional del Libro de Tento Gratuito. México. Pp. 150.

334   *The Origin and Diversification of Language*

1963g   Proyecto de *Cuaderno de Trabajo de Lengua Nacional para 6° Ano*. Presentado a
         la Comisión Nacional del Libro de Tento Gratuito. México. Pp. 200.
1964a   *Conversational Chinese for Beginners*. New York, Dover. [Revised ed., 1948b.]
1964b   Algunos problemas de la lingüística oto-mangue. *Anales de Antropología*
         (México, D. F., UNAM, IIH, Sección de Antropología) 1:91-123. (IIH,
         Publicación 82.)
1964c   "Comparative Penutian Glosses of Sapir." Bright, William, ed., *Studies in
         Californian Linguistics*, 182–191. (University of California Publications in
         Linguistics 34.) Berkeley and Los Angeles, University of California Press.
         [Festschrift for Muray Emeneau.]
1964d   "Interim Notes on Oaxacan Phonology." *Southwestern Journal of Anthropology*
         20:168–189.
1964e   "Linguistic Overview." Norbeck, Edward, and Jennings, Jesse, eds., *Pre-
         historic Man in the New World*, 527–556. Chicago, University of Chicago Press.
1964f   Primitivismo en. las lenguas de américa y eurasia. Acta y Memorias del
         XXXV Congreso Internacional de Americanistas (Mexico 1962), 2:465–
         469. México, D. F., *Instituto Nacional de Antropología e Historia*.
1964g   Problemas del estudio lingüístico de la transculturación religiosa. Acta y
         Memorias del XXXV Congreso Internacional de Americanistas (Mexico,
         1962), 2:609–615. México, D. F., *Instituto Nacional de Antropología e Historia*.
1964h   "Glottochronology," *A Dictionary of the Social Sciences*, 289–290. Paris,
         UNESCO.
1964j   "Semantics." *A Dictionary of the Social Sciences*, 632–634.ˑParis, UNESCO.
1964j   "Chibchan." *Encyclopedia Britannica* 5:480. Chicago, Wm. Benton. [Exact
         date uncertain, but after 1958.]
1964k   "Eskimo–Aleut." *Encyclopedia Britannica* 8:706–707. Chicago, Wm. Benton.
         [Exact date uncertain, but after 1958.]
1964l   Hymes, Dell, ed., *Language in Culture and Society*, 100–107, 624–635, 575–583.
         New York, Harper and Row. (Reprinting of·1946d, 1951b, 1959c.)
1965a   Arana, Evangelina, and Swadesh, Morris. *Los elementos de Mixteco Antiguo*.
         México, D. F., Instituto Nacional Indigenista. Pp 200.
1965b   Origen y evolución del lenguaje humano. A de A2:61–88. (Instituto de
         Investigaciones Históricas, Publicación 97).
1965c   "Kalapuya and Takehna." *International Journal of American Linguistics*,
         31:237–240.
1965d   "Language Universals and Research Efficiency in Descriptive Linguistics."
         Canadian Journal of Linguistics 10 (2–3):147–155.
1965e   "Ways of writing sounds." Syracuse University, Department of Anthro-
         pology. Mimeographed, pp.3.
1965f   Swadesh, Morris, and Velásquez, Pablo. Apéndice. D.E. López Sarrelangue,
         La nobleza indígena de Patzcuaro en la época virreinal. México, D. F.,
         Instituto de Investigaciones Históricas.
1965g   Hymes, Dell, ed. "Machine-aided Linguistic Research in National University
         of Mexico". *The Use of Computers in Anthropology*, 523–525. The Hague,
         Mouton.
1966a   *El lenguaje y la vida humana*. Prólogo para Arguelos Vela. México, D. F.,
         Fondo de Cultura Económica. Pp. 396.
1966b   Swadesh, Morris, and Sancho, Madalena. Prólogo de Miguel Léon-Portillo.
         Los mil elementos del mexicano clásico. Base analítica de la lengua nahua. (Serie de
         Cultura Náhuatl, Monografías, 9.) México, D. F., IIH, *Universidad Nacional
         Autónoma de México*. Pp. ix, 89.
1966c   Swadesh, Morris, Chuairy, Maria, and Gómez, Guido. *El árabe literario*.
         México, D. F., Edición del Colegio de México. Pp. 321.

1966d Algunos sistemas para la comparación lingüística. Ciencias de la Información y la Computación 1:5–28. México, D. F., *Universidad Nacional Autónoma de México.*

1966e Swadesh, Morris, and Arana, Evangelina, with Bendor-Samuel, John T., and Wilson, W. A. A. "A Preliminary Glottochronology of Gur Languages." *Journal of West African Languages* 3 (2):27–66.

1966f Van der Merwe, Nicholas J. "New Mathematics for Glottochronology." Comments. *Current Anthropology* 7:497.

1966g La huelga estudiantil a través de unas ventanas. Historia y Sociedad 5, Suplemento 1:10–11.

1966h Porhé y Maya. *Anales de Antropología (México, D. F., UNAM, IIH, Sección de Antropología)* 3:173–204.

1966i Swadesh, Morris, and Arana, Evangelina. Algunos conceptos de la prehistoria yutonahua. Suma Antropológica en homenaje a R. J. Weitlaner, 573–578. México, D. F., *Instituto Nacional de Antropología e Historia.*

1967a Swadesh, Morris, and Arana, Evangelina. *Diccionario analítico de la lengua Mampruli.* Con una introducción etnográfica por Susan Drucker Brown. México, D. F., Museo de las culturas, *Instituto Nacional de Antropología e Historia.* Pp. 95.

1967b Cuatro siglos de transculturación lingüística en el Porhé. *Anales de Antropología (México, D. F., UNAM, IIH, Sección de Antropología)* 4:161–185.

1967c Hymes, Dell, ed. "Linguistic Classification in the Southwest." *Studies in Southwestern Ethnolinguistics,* 281–309. The Hague, Mouton. [Festschrift for Harry Hoijer.]

1967d McQuown, Norman A., ed. "Middle American Languages." *Lexicostatistic Classification,* Vol. 5, Linguistics, 79–116. (Robert Wauchope, ed., Handbook of Middle American Indians.) New Orleans, Tulane University Press.

1967e El impacto sociológico de la ensenanza en lengua vernácula. El simposio de Bloomington (Agosto de 1964), Actas, informes, y comunicaciones, 212–220. Bogotá, Instituto Caro y Cuervo.

1967f Swadesh, Morris, Grimes, Joseph, and Manrique, Leonardo. Proyecto para desarrollar la investigación de las lenguas autóctonas de México. El simposio de Bloomington (Agosto de 1964), Actes informes y comunicaciones, 250–253. Bogotá, Instituto Caro y Cuervo.

1967g Las lenguas de Oaxaca. Serie: Culturas de Oaxaca. (Conferencias dictadas en el Museo Nacional de Antropología.) Edición Mimeográfica.

1967h Review of István Fodor. "The Rate of Linguistic Change." *American Anthropologist* 69:255.

1968a *La nueva filología.* 2nd edition. (Colección de obras de Mauricio Swadesh editadas por sus alumnos, 1.) Pp. 334. México, 20, D. F., Evangelina Arana Swadesh, Arquitectura 45.

1968b Algunas orientaciones generales sobre la escritura maya. Estudios de Cultura Maya 7:33–47. México, D. F., *Universidad Nacional Autónoma de México.*

1968c Las lenguas indígenas del noreste de México. Anales del *Instituto Nacional de Antropología e Historia* 5:75–86.

1968d Biloxi words. Included in Mary R. Haas, "The Last Words of Biloxi." *International Journal of American Linguistics* 34:77–84. Freeman 463.

1969a *Elementos del tarasco antiguo.* México, D. F., *Instituto de Investigaciones Históricas, Universidad Nacional Autónoma de México.* Pp. 190.

1969b Un nexo prehistórico entre quechua y tarasco. Anales del *Instituto Nacional de Antropología e Historia,* Epoca 7, 1:127–138.

1971 Swadesh, Morris. *The Origin and Diversification of Language.* Edited by Joel Sherzer. Chicago, Aldine · Atherton.

UNPUBLISHED:

Ms.   Sapir, Edward, and Swadesh, Morris. "Nootka Legends and Stories." Cited
        as in preparation, 1955b:1.

1965   Swadesh, Morris, Alvarez, María Cristiana, Arzápalo, Ramón, and
        Bastarraches, Juan R. Diccionario de elementos de la lengua Maya.
        Seminario de Estudios de la escritura Maya. *Universidad Nacional Autónoma
        de México.* In revision.

Language Index

General Index

Absorption, 23–26
   See also Divergence and convergence
Accent alternation, 55
Acronyms, 51
Affixes:
   in Chinese, 70
   in Fula-Bantuan, 102, 103
   in Indo-European, 90, 110, 122, 123
   and loss of consonants, 132
   in Semitic, 123
   substitution of relational particles and
      auxiliary words for, 76
Alexander the Great, 23, 61, 62
Alphabets:
   Amheric, 65
   Armenian, 63
   Cyrillic, 59
   Germanic, 54
   Greek, 60–61
   hand, 165
   Indic, 62
   Iranian, 63
   Slavic, 59
   Tibeto-Burman, 73
   Turkish, 73
   See also Writing systems
Alternation. *See* Accent alternation;
   Articulation points, alternation in;
   Consonant alternation; Phonemic
   alternation; Symbolic sounds and
   alternation; Vowel alternation
American Anthropological Association,
   238, 248–50
American Philosophical Society, 250–51,
   254, 255, 297
Amerindian Non-Cultural Vocabularies
   (Swadesh), 256

Andrews, James, 240–41
Animal phonetics, 171–76
   vs. human, 174–76
Animal sounds, 3, 5–6, 132, 157–62, 173
   See also Communication, animal
Arana, Evangelina, 257
Archeological data, 40–41, 79–80, 87
Articulation points, 110–11
   alternation in, 150–54
   imitative value of, 200–201
Articulation strength, 132–34
Articulation types, 126–30
Aspirate continuants, 129–30
Aspirates:
   relation of, to fricatives, 127–28
   voiced vs. unvoiced, 84, 127
Aspiration, 108, 110, 177
   and reduplication, 149
   symbolism of, 200
   tendency to loss of, 84
Australopithecus, 158
Auxiliary languages, 74
Auxiliary verbs:
   in Hindi, 63
   in Indo-European, 90–93
   in Romance, 58

Benedict, Ruth, 241
Bilingualism. *See* Multilingualism
Bloch, Bernard, 232–34, 246, 247
Bloomfield, Leonard, 229–33, 237–39,
   241, 242, 246
Boas, Franz, 231, 235–40, 245, 246, 253,
   296–97, 305, 308, 320
Bopp, Franz, 116
Borrowings, 36–37, 49–50, 113, 119, 287
   in Arabic, 64–65